SCIENCE IN
ARCHAEOLOGY

SCIENCE IN ARCHAEOLOGY

an agenda for the future

edited by Justine Bayley

ENGLISH HERITAGE

1998

First published 1998 by
English Heritage, 23 Savile Row,
London W1X 1AB

Printed by BAS Printers Ltd, Over Wallop, Hants

ISBN 1 85074 693 1
Product Code XB20001

A CIP catalogue record for this book is available from the British Library

Design and layout by Mind's Eye Design, Lewes

Edited and brought to press by David M Jones, Publications, English Heritage

Contents

Contributors vi
Figures vii
Tables ix
Acknowledgements x
Summary x

1 Introduction 1

The Palaeolithic

2 Questions for Palaeolithic science and science
for Palaeolithic questions
by Clive Gamble 3

3 The return of the natives: AMS radiocarbon dating
of Magdalenian artefacts and recolonisation of
northern Europe after the last ice age
by Rupert A Housley 9

4 Genetics and the Palaeolithic
by Bryan Sykes 21

5 The 'expensive tissue hypothesis' and the evolution
of the human adaptive niche: a study in
comparative anatomy
by Leslie C Aiello .25

6 Priority and opportunity: reconstructing the
European Middle Palaeolithic climate and landscape
by Tjeerd H van Andel and P C Tzedakis 37

7 Large mammal hunting strategies in the Palaeolithic
of Europe: a taphonomic approach
by Sabine Gaudzinski 47

Mesolithic to early Iron Age

8 What do we want to know? Questions for archaeological science from the Mesolithic to the Iron Age
by Richard Bradley 63

9 Detection of human impact on the natural
environment: palynological views
by Kevin J Edwards 69

10 The study of food remains from prehistoric Britain
*by Tony Legge, Sebastian Payne,
and Peter Rowley-Conwy* 89

11 Some thoughts on using scientific dating in English
archaeology and buildings analysis for the next decade
by Alex Bayliss 95

12 Approaches to the study of metal in the insular
Bronze Age
by William O'Brien 109

Late Iron Age and Roman

13 Archaeological science and proto-historic societies
by Martin Millett .123

14 The expansion of agricultural production in late
Iron Age and Roman Britain
by Marijke van der Veen and Terry O'Connor 127

15 Changing the Roman landscape: the role of
geophysics and remote sensing
*by Vincent L Gaffney, Christopher F Gaffney,
and Mark Corney* .145

16 Ceramics and lithics: into the future
by David Peacock .157

17 Metals and metalworking in the first millennium AD
by Justine Bayley .161

Medieval and later

18 Medieval and later: composing an agenda
by Grenville Astill .169

19 Continuity and change: environmental
archaeology in historic periods
by Martin Bell and Petra Dark 179

20 The archaeological study of medieval English
human populations, AD 1066–1540
by Simon Mays 195

21 On science, buildings archaeology, and new agendas
by Matthew H Johnson 211

22 The archaeologist and evidence from field sampling
for medieval and post-medieval technological
innovation
by David Crossley .219

23 Organic artefacts and their preservation
by Jacqui Watson .225

24 An agenda for archaeological science:
concluding remarks
by Martin Jones 237

Contributors

Leslie Aiello
Department of Anthropology, University College
London, Gower Street, London WC1E 6BT

Grenville Astill
Department of Archaeology, University of Reading,
Whiteknights, PO Box 218, Reading RG6 6AA

Justine Bayley
Ancient Monuments Laboratory, English Heritage,
23 Savile Row, London W1X 1AB

Alex Bayliss
Ancient Monuments Laboratory, English Heritage,
23 Savile Row, London W1X 1AB

Martin Bell
Department of Archaeology, University of Reading,
Whiteknights, PO Box 218, Reading RG6 6AA

Richard Bradley
Department of Archaeology, University of Reading,
Whiteknights, PO Box 218, Reading RG6 6AA

Mark Corney
Department of Archaeology, University of Bristol,
Bristol BS8 1TB

David Crossley
Division of Continuing Education,
University of Sheffield, Sheffield S10 2TN

Petra Dark
Department of Archaeology, University of Reading,
Whiteknights, PO Box 218, Reading RG6 6AA

Kevin Edwards
Department of Archaeology and Prehistory,
University of Sheffield, Sheffield S10 2TN

Christopher Gaffney
GSB Prospection, The Old Sunday School,
Kipping Lane, Thornton, Bradford

Vincent Gaffney
BUFAU, University of Birmingham, Edgbaston,
Birmingham B15 2TT

Clive Gamble
Department of Archaeology, University of
Southampton, Southampton SO17 1BJ

Sabine Gaudzinski
RGZM Forschungsbereich Altsteinzeit,
Schloss Monrepos, 56567 Neuwied, Germany

Rupert A Housley
Department of Archaeology, 10 The Square,
University of Glasgow, Glasgow G12 8QQ

Matthew Johnson
Department of Archaeology, University of Durham,
South Road, Durham DH1 3LE

Martin Jones
Department of Archaeology, University of Cambridge,
Downing Street, Cambridge CB2 3DZ

Tony Legge
Centre for Extramural Studies, Birkbeck College,
University of London, 26 Russell Square, London,
WC1B 5DQ

Simon Mays
Ancient Monuments Laboratory, English Heritage,
23 Savile Row, London W1X 1AB

Martin Millett
Department of Archaeology, University of Durham,
South Road, Durham DH1 3LE

William O'Brien
Department of Archaeology, National University of
Ireland, Galway, Republic of Ireland

Terry O'Connor
Department of Archaeological Sciences,
University of Bradford, Bradford BD7 1DP

Sebastian Payne
Ancient Monuments Laboratory, English Heritage,
23 Savile Row, London W1X 1AB

David Peacock
Department of Archaeology, University of
Southampton, Southampton SO17 1BJ

Peter Rowley-Conwy
Department of Archaeology, University of Durham,
South Road, Durham DH1 3LE

Bryan Sykes
University of Oxford, Institute of Molecular Medicine,
Oxford OX3 9DS

P C Tzedakis
Godwin Institute for Quaternary Research and
Department of Geography, Downing Street,
Cambridge CB2 3EQ

Tjeerd H van Andel
Godwin Institute for Quaternary Research and
Department of Earth Sciences, Downing Street,
Cambridge CB2 3EQ

Marijke van der Veen
School of Archaeological Studies, University of
Leicester, University Road, Leicester LE1 7RH

Jacqui Watson
Ancient Monuments Laboratory, English Heritage,
23 Savile Row, London W1X 1AB

Figures

The return of the natives *by Rupert A Housley*
Fig 3.1 Regions of late glacial northern Europe
Fig 3.2 AMS determinations on humanly modified bone and antler from Kesslerloch and Schweizersbild
Fig 3.3 AMS and radiometric determinations on charcoal from Monruz and Champréveyres
Fig 3.4 AMS determinations on unmodified bone and antler from the Höhlefels
Fig 3.5 AMS determinations on mostly unmodified bone and antler from Geissenklösterle
Fig 3.6 AMS and radiometric dates from Andernach-Martinsberg, Gonnersdorf, and Oberkassel
Fig 3.7 AMS dates on cutmarked bone and antler from a selection of Magdalenian cave sites in the Ardennes region, Belgium
Fig 3.8 AMS dates on unmodified bone and charcoal from Magdalenian sites of Pincevent and Etiolles
Fig 3.9 Selected AMS dates on human remains or modified bone and antler from Britain for the period after the LGM and before 12,000 years
Fig 3.10 The moving sum distribution of AMS radiocarbon determinations by region
Fig 3.11 Map showing the start of the pioneer phase
Fig 3.12 Map showing the start of the residential phase

Genetics and the Palaeolithic *by Bryan Sykes*
Fig 4.1 A network of the commoner European mitochondrial haplotypes

The 'expensive tissue hypothesis' *by Leslie C Aiello*
Fig 5.1 The increase in absolute hominoid cranial capacity over time
Fig 5.2 Percentage body mass and total body basal metabolic rate for each of the expensive tissues
Fig 5.3 The observed and expected organ mass

Priority and opportunity *by Tjeerd H van Andel and P C Tzedakis*
Fig 6.1 Oxygen isotope-based calendrical chronology of the last 80 ka
Fig 6.2 Frequency distribution of calendrical dates from late Middle and early Upper Palaeolithic sites
Fig 6.3 Data points for the reconstruction of European OIS 3 landscapes

Fig 6.4 Precipitation and temperature history for OIS 3
Fig 6.5 OIS 3 climate oscillations
Fig 6.6 Europe during OIS 3

Large mammal hunting strategies in the Palaeolithic of Europe *by Sabine Gaudzinski*
Fig 7.1 Skeletal element representation for bovids
Fig 7.2 Bone mineral density versus %-MNI for Mauran, Wallertheim, Il'skaja, and La Borde
Fig 7.3 Map of Europe showing the location of sites mentioned in the text with monospecific or species dominated bone assemblages
Fig 7.4 Age profile for *Rangifer tarandus* from Salzgitter-Lebenstedt
Fig 7.5 Age-profile for *Rangifer tarandus* from Lommersum
Fig 7.6 Bone tool from Salzgitter Lebenstedt

Detection of human impact on the natural environment *by Kevin J Edwards*
Fig 9.1 Selected pollen and spore taxa from Loch an t-Sil, South Uist
Fig 9.2 Cumulative summary curve of microscopic charcoal records from northernmost Scotland compared with 'effective' precipitation curve for north-west Europe
Fig 9.3 Elm pollen, cereal-type pollen and microscopic charcoal records from Rhoin Farm, Kintyre
Fig 9.4 Some of the computer routines accessible from data produced in TILIA
Fig 9.5 Ordination plot of pollen taxa from within zone KQ1-3n at Kilconquhar Loch, Fife
Fig 9.6 Map of interpolated grass pollen percentages in north-eastern England
Fig 9.7 Triangular ordination plots showing the relationship between number of archaeological sites and averaged arboreal, herb, and heath pollen values

Some thoughts on using scientific dating in English archaeology *by Alex Bayliss*
Fig 11.1 Taking a core for tree-ring analysis at Stokesay Castle
Fig 11.2 Axonometric projection showing the surviving elements of the seventeenth-century roof construction of the Stable Building at Forty Hall Farm, Enfield, Middlesex

Fig 11.3 Location of dated (●), and sampled but undated (□) buildings in Devon and Cornwall up to August 1997

Fig 11.4 Histogram showing the number of dated prehistoric oak samples from England and Wales per calendar year BC

Fig 11.5 Measuring the tree-ring widths on a sample of waterlogged wood

Fig 11.6 Tree-ring sample from a conifer timber

Fig 11.7 The House Mill, Bromley-by-Bow, a complex industrial building largely constructed from conifers that have recently been sampled for dendrochronology

Fig 11.8 Probability distributions of dates from Phase 1 at Stonehenge

Fig 11.9 Graph showing the median error term quoted on AMS measurements funded by English Heritage 1986–1997

Changing the Roman landscape *by Vincent L Gaffney, Christopher F Gaffney, and Mark Corney*

Fig 15.1 Villa and bathhouse at Charlton, Wiltshire

Fig 15.2 General results from magnetometry survey at Wroxeter, Shropshire

Fig 15.3 Magnetometer data illustrating a large stone building at Wroxeter

Fig 15.4 Magnetometry data for the north-western area of Wroxeter

Fig 15.5 Magnetic data showing a structure interpreted as a church at Wroxeter

Fig 15.6 Stone buildings at Wroxeter associated with enhanced magnetic values

Fig 15.7 Enclosure at Norse Road, Bedfordshire

Fig 15.8 Detail of stone building with portico produced from automated resistivity survey

Fig 15.9 Time-sliced ground-probing radar data showing stone structure at Wroxeter

Metals and metalworking in the first millennium AD *by Justine Bayley*

Fig 17.1 Reconstuction of a metal workshop

Fig 17.2 Distribution map of Roman tin and pewter working finds in England

Fig 17.3 Distribution map of Roman copper alloy working finds in England

Fig 17.4 Histogram showing that many early Roman brooch types have a preferred alloy composition

Fig 17.5 Ternary diagram showing the tight compositional cluster for British Aucissa brooches

Continuity and change *by Martin Bell and Petra Dark*

Fig 19.1 The relationship between time and different sources of environmental knowledge

Fig 19.2 Locations of pollen sequences with evidence for environmental continuity and change in the period AD 400–800

Fig 19.3 Summary pollen percentage diagram from Sidlings Copse

Fig 19.4 A lynchet at Bishopstone, Sussex

Fig 19.5 Colluvial valley sediments at Chalton village, Hampshire

The archaeological study of medieval English human populations *by Simon Mays*

Fig 20.1 Carbon stable isotope data from the burials from the York Fishergate site

Fig 20.2 Three mandibular measurements, showing trends in British material from the Neolithic to the ninteenth century AD

Fig 20.3 Stature plotted against age for the Wharram Percy children

Organic artefacts and their preservation *by Jacqui Watson*

Fig 23.1 Roman wooden bowls from Carlisle, Cumbria

Fig 23.2 Roman leather saddlery from Carlisle, Cumbria

Fig 23.3 Clench nails from York Minster

Fig 23.4 Iron Age sword hilt from Burton Fleming, Yorkshire

Fig 23.5 Reconstruction of Bronze Age dagger hilt from Gravelly Guy, Oxfordshire

Fig 23.6 Reconstruction of an Anglo-Saxon casket from Harford Farm, Norfolk

Fig 23.7 Possible reconstruction of Anglo-Saxon bed from Barrington, Cambridgeshire

Fig 23.8 Reconstruction of Roman dagger scabbard from Chester

Tables

The return of the natives *by Rupert A Housley*

3.1 Rates of expansion in the recolonisation of northern Europe

Large mammal hunting strategies in the Palaeolithic of Europe *by Sabine Gaudzinski*

7.1 Mammals identified from sites where bovids predominate

7.2 Mammals identified from sites where reindeer predominate

Detection of human impact on the natural environment *by Kevin J Edwards*

9.1 Plants of potential economic importance in the Mesolithic of north-west Europe and levels of pollen taxonomic precision

Some thoughts on using scientific dating in English archaeology *by Alex Bayliss*

11.1 Medieval and post-medieval buildings sampled for dendrochronology in Devon and Cornwall before 1994

Changing the Roman landscape *by Vincent L Gaffney, Christopher F Gaffney, and Mark Corney*

15.1 Primary technical problems at Wroxeter

The archaeological study of medieval English human populations *by Simon Mays*

20.1 Some large medieval English assemblages with bone reports

20.2 Arm position in adult burials from Ipswich Blackfriars

20.3 Age structure of burials to the immediate north of the church compared with those from other areas at Wharram Percy

20.4 Porotic hyperostosis at Wharram Percy and St Helen-on-the-Walls, York

20.5 Periostitis at Wharram Percy and St Helen-on-the-Walls, York

20.6 Proportions of infants at various sites

20.7 Age distribution of Wharram Percy adult burials

20.8 Age distribution in Russell's and Thrupp's demographic studies

Acknowledgements

The help of past and present colleagues within English Heritage who assisted with both organising and running the conference is gratefully acknowledged: Stephanie Allen, Mike Corfield, Andrew David, Graham Fairclough, Kate Foley, Tim Horsley, Louise Hyde, Adrian Olivier, Sebastian Payne, Steve Trow, and Geoffrey Wainwright. English Heritage's Science and Conservation Advisory Panel provided support from the beginning. One of its former chairman, Colin Renfrew, introduced the conference, neatly paraphrasing its theme as 'questions for archaeological science and science for archaeological questions', and its present chairman, Martin Jones, provided a masterly summing up, reproduced here.

The four session coordinators, Clive Gamble, Richard Bradley, Martin Millett, and Grenville Astill, proved invaluable in helping to assemble a rich and varied progamme of speakers, and for setting the tone in their sessions.

The contributors all rose to the challenge of looking at their work from an unusual viewpoint and must be thanked for producing texts to a tight schedule, allowing the rapid publication of their papers. Those who helped with refereeing the papers in this volume are also thanked for their assistance, as is David M Jones, who oversaw its design and production.

Summary

These papers were originally presented at a conference held in London on 7–9 February 1997. Their theme is the contribution of the sciences to archaeology, in retrospect and prospect. Each paper therefore has an element of reporting and review but, more importantly, identifies archaeological questions that existing scientific techniques have the potential to answer in the short to medium term.

The papers are grouped by broad chronological period, from the Palaeolithic to medieval and later, though, as the concluding remarks show, many recurring themes cut across these conventional divisions. A collection of this size cannot be all-inclusive, but most areas of current activity in archaeological science are discussed in the context of at least one of the periods.

1 Introduction

There is a common but limited vision of archaeological science as a collection of scientific disciplines investigating aspects of the past. Much better, and far more constructive, is the alternative view that sees it as an integral part of archaeology, addressing the same sorts of questions, differing only in the techniques used to answer them. This collection of papers, originally presented at a conference in February 1997, reflects the latter approach and takes a strategic view of the contribution of the sciences to archaeology, filling a gap that had been identified by those working in archaeological science in Britain.

The need for this conference and the reason for its success have twin origins. The first of these is the need to bring all parts of our profession together and to demonstrate how our goals are held in common. The background to this is the growth of archaeological science in all its forms and the essential contribution that it makes to our understanding of the past. For over 40 years, I have observed the development of this contribution and participated in it from time to time. As one whose first published papers were on palaeopedology and who later came to the directing of archaeological projects, I have occasionally despaired at the gulf in understanding and willingness to integrate different but closely related skills into the success of the same project. The second reason for the conference was the need to define worthwhile directions for future investigation: an agenda for the future. Some regard an agenda as undermining their right to freedom of investigation. On the contrary, an agenda to which all have contributed provides focus and strength to joint endeavours – particularly in a multi-disciplinary profession such as our own – and maximizes the most effective use of scarce resources.

In both areas, the conference was a brilliant success. The delegates demonstrated that multi-disciplinary mix for which the organisers had planned, and the papers and debate showed an understanding of each other's aspirations and potential far in excess of any similar gathering that I have attended. The need to produce a joint agenda was accepted by all who were present and the publication of the proceedings of the conference sets out aspects of that agenda for our profession as a whole. English Heritage will continue to have a part to play in realising these aims. We are revising our consultation document, *Archaeology Division research agenda*, to include a prioritised selection of topics where science will contribute to advances in archaeological knowledge and understanding. It was a refreshing experience to participate in the conference and I look forward to the next occasion when progress towards the implementation of that agenda can be reviewed and new routes charted into the future.

Geoffrey Wainwright
Chief Archaeologist, English Heritage

2 Questions for Palaeolithic science and science for Palaeolithic questions

by Clive Gamble

Abstract

Scientific advances have transformed the Palaeolithic. The advent of absolute dating methods beyond conventional ^{14}C (eg TL, ESR, OSL, and U series) and the opportunity to date objects directly by AMS are having a tremendous impact. Most importantly they are beginning to free us from the overriding concern of constructing relative chronologies, thereby allowing us to explore other questions concerning the abilities of early hominids. At the same time, Quaternary science now provides more detail concerning the environment that surrounded these hominids and that applied important selection pressures for behavioural and anatomical change. These studies also raise the issue of the timescales over which evolutionary change operates. The biological aspects of adaptation and hominid variability can now be traced through genetic markers in modern populations as well as through comparative anatomy from a larger sample of fossil hominids. This new wealth of data and techniques can be brought to bear on questions of population movement and variability, environmental change, adaptation, and survival. The aim must be to finally dispel, if they still exist, any lingering doubts that questions about the Palaeolithic are limited by the poor survival of meagre evidence for past hominid activity.

Introduction

It is almost 30 years since the second edition of *Science in archaeology: a survey of progress and research* (1969) appeared, edited by Don Brothwell and Eric Higgs. In the intervening period science-based archaeology has changed out of all recognition. In 1969 the agenda set by the papers was very much directed towards developing techniques of analysis to garner new information from artefacts and landscapes. It was a celebration that we could now date, measure, probe, and characterise what previously we could only guess at and describe.

It was not always clear, however, what questions about past human behaviour some of this information might address. These were being discussed elsewhere by the 'New Archaeology' (Binford and Binford 1968). *Science in archaeology* was dismissively superior about this debate (Brothwell and Higgs 1969, 30) trusting instead to the integrating power of the ecosystem alone to bring order to the 'horrid porridge' (ibid, 31) of uncoordinated scientific endeavour. As a result their volume was organised under seven topics; dating, environment (the largest section with 28 papers), man, microscopy and radiography, artefacts, statistics, and prospecting.

This volume has the same main title but a different subtext: *an agenda for the future*. It has been organised by period, with an emphasis on the relevance of science-based archaeology to major research questions within each of the four time zones being covered. We have now moved well beyond the exploratory phase of scientific techniques and procedures and into a mature research culture where archaeology without science is inconceivable at a professional and public level. Such a position is particularly keenly felt by those of us studying the Old Stone Age.

In this introductory paper I want to present the case for a Palaeolithic science, akin to Quaternary science but with humans as the focus, which has evolved in the last 30 years. The papers that follow will demonstrate through their case studies some of its range and potential. Palaeolithic science is based on two key words: integration and interdisciplinarity. The latter is exemplified by the range of disciplines from which the speakers in even this small session are drawn and the former by the nature of archaeological research projects in general.

I want to concentrate on just one research theme – the investigation of humans/hominids as colonising animals – to justify my selection of papers and to illustrate a future agenda for Palaeolithic science. This theme is particularly relevant to north-west Europe and the British Isles but obviously applies much more widely to the Palaeolithic world. In order to address this question I need to be able to examine hominid behaviour at the scale of continents and landscapes. I also need to examine selection pressure on anatomy and behaviour at a much more local level and immediate timescale. I must have chronological control that ranges from blocks of time of about 70,000 years to seasonal and even daily data on individual activity. I require independent means to test what I suspect were very different colonising capabilities during the 500,000 or more years during which this northern continent was settled.

Interdisciplinarity

Research questions about the Palaeolithic and the early hominids are now framed within an interdisciplinary context. It is not uncommon to find site reports such as Boxgrove and La Cotte in this country, the Abri Vaufrey in France or Klithi in Greece with up to 50 specialist contributors covering all seven topics and more in Brothwell and Higgs' (1969) framework. Indeed, the value of a site is sometimes crudely measured by the number of research opportunities it presents, particularly within the highly specialised branches of environmental analysis. The result of such activity has been the ever closer definition of early Palaeolithic landscapes and the surfaces upon which hominids walked, sat, dropped stone tools, and butchered animals. This precision is commendable and is matched by the archaeologists' refitting of flint artefact scatters so that precise moments of time can be reconstructed.

The results have been dramatic. We now see that for much of the Palaeolithic the concept of a site, so familiar to other periods in archaeology, is misleading. Rather we are investigating episodes of activity across landscapes. A locale such as Boxgrove is not, as the late Mary Leakey proposed for Olduvai Gorge (1971), a series of living floors with the implication of continuity and permanence, but rather the remarkably well preserved traces of brief, repetitive activities involving stone, food, and other hominids.

This punctuated rhythm to the archaeological record of such early behaviour is matched at a regional scale by the evidence for geographical shifts in population. This might be expected in northern latitudes subject to glacial cycles but until recently has not been possible to document in detail. A recent paper by Holdaway and Porch (1995) reports on work in the Pleistocene caves of south-west Tasmania where radiocarbon dates, when treated as data using a moving sum method (Rick 1987) reveal a pattern of occupational intensity that is strongly correlated to rainfall, a key variable in this region. I suspect that in many parts of the Palaeolithic world a similar constant redistribution of population was also the norm. Rupert Housley's paper on the late glacial recolonisation of northern Europe and Britain examines one aspect of the ebb and flow of regional population after 14,000 years ago (see Housley *et al* 1997). Besides providing detailed information from AMS dating on the timing and speed we can now characterise the process as *directed* rather than *random* a conclusion reached previously for farmers by van Andel and Runnels (1995).

The present challenge of this aspect of hominids as colonising animals is to determine the amplitude and frequency of such changes within the Palaeolithic record and to determine change, if any, through time in hominid capabilities. Such shifting demography will have had undoubted effects upon the genetic mixing and isolation of populations as well as on the cultural transmission of social and survival behaviour.

Such close definition of the Palaeolithic record would not have taken place without a specifically scientific approach. Advances in absolute dating have made it possible to replace informed guesswork with standard chronologies both within and between sites of all ages. In particular these new chronologies, now referenced to

the continuous chronology of the Pleistocene obtained from the marine isotopic record contained in foraminifera and more recently from Greenland ice cores, provided a spur to the study of faunal evolution. The turnover rates of species, including hominids, can now be studied and the resulting biostratigraphical patterns are proving very important in the debate over the age of the earliest Europeans. The so-called vole clock proposed by von Koenigswald and van Kolfschoten (1996) is, in essence, a means of calibrating widely dispersed Pleistocene sections only a few of which are fixed into the marine isotope chronology and even fewer of which are dated by absolute techniques. Similar faunal materials were available to pioneers such as Zeuner and Oakley with their magisterial syntheses, respectively *The Pleistocene period* (1959) and *Frameworks for dating fossil man* (1964); but what has changed is the use to which these cross-dating results are put. No longer is it just a claim for great antiquity but rather a series of questions about the timing of early hominid colonisation and the selection pressures placed upon them.

For example, there are currently three chronologies for the earliest Europeans: the short, the long, and the very long (Carbonell *et al* 1995; Gamble 1995; Roebroeks and van Kolfschoten 1994). The chronology that eventually wins the day will determine how we view the adaptive patterns of these early humans faced with barriers to colonisation and range expansion. Those barriers, it appears, are not so much physical and anatomical as social and behavioural (Gamble 1993).

Of course what is required in the study of colonisation as a process rather than as an event is some form of independent check on the significance of such behaviour in human evolution. Perhaps the most dramatic advance since *Science in archaeology* appeared in 1969 has been the advent of genetic-based studies, which can now address issues of population movement and the origins of human diversity. One of the classic icons of Palaeolithic archaeology is now the mtDNA 'horseshoe' of 148 individuals determined from five of the worlds populations (Cann *et al* 1987), which strongly supports an African origin and subsequent dispersals for all modern populations (Lahr and Foley 1994). It is good to know that disciplines other than archaeology can, and are, prepared to extrapolate from very small samples to large-scale patterns. The power of the technique is, however, best demonstrated, as Sykes' paper (this volume) shows, when considering population movements within continents and where greater control over genetic markers can be exercised. His findings redefine the role of Palaeolithic populations in the events of later European prehistory – an arena from which they have been traditionally excluded.

Integration

Interdisciplinarity is a fact of Palaeolithic research. My other keyword – integration – is equally important when investigating a question such as the colonising abilities of hominids. The essence of successful integration is to combine results from different disciplines in order to build models about the past. Human palaeontology has been particularly successful in building such a synthesis from a wide array of comparative studies involving primates and humans, as well as aligning themselves firmly within evolutionary ecology. As a result there have been advances in the study of early cognition and language which now command respect rather than reservations (Aiello and Dunbar 1993; Dunbar 1996). There are even claims from evolutionary psychologists for an environment of evolutionary adaptedness within which the basic modules of the mind were genetically fixed before we left Africa sometime between one and two million years ago (Barkow et al 1992).

On inspection this claim is weakened by the lack of integration of the various strands of evidence that such a synthesis requires. As an example of why such integration is a necessity Aiello's paper (this volume) presents a model to explain the direction that human evolution took. The immediate environment of selection, which comes down to energy, food quality, and accessibility, obviously has implications for the expansion of hominids. Hominids had to be physically as well as behaviourally adapted to the environments through which they had to pass to reach northern Europe from the tropics. Integrating these aspects builds stronger models and explanations about the past.

In the same way there has been considerable debate over the environmental tolerances of early hominids. Could they live in forests or did they require open, steppe environments with large herds of prey species? Following from this discussion is a further interest in the means by which northern foods were obtained. Was this primarily through scavenging or seeking out and killing animals? Depending on the outcome of the debate what role did different technologies and systems of landscape management play in distinguishing between different hominid species?

Recently there has been a re-examination of the habitat tolerances of the earliest hominids (Roebroeks et al 1992). This has centred upon the ability, or not, of hominids to exploit climax deciduous forests (Gamble 1984). The ecological argument is that such forests contain abundant but inaccessible food resources (Kelly 1983), so that we should not be unduly surprised to find populations abandoning such areas during those interglacials that were comparable in magnitude to our present one.

The alternative viewpoint, based on a critical examination of the local environmental evidence, suggests a wide variety of conditions for these locales (Roebroeks et al 1992). Moreover these authors prefer Guthrie's model of mosaic rather than zonal habitats for Pleistocene environments (Guthrie 1984). Nonetheless they persist in representing the disputed habitat as an undifferentiated vegetation zone (Roebroeks et al 1992, fig 3), which suggests that we are still wrestling with ways of transforming the proxy data on habitat structure into archaeologically usable models. At such times we seem to have advanced little beyond reconstructing the zonal deciduous forest from a few pollen grains or the mammoth steppe from the presence of lemmings. The challenge to do better in the future is obvious. For example, we now have, thanks to the English Heritage-funded English Rivers Palaeolithic Survey, full and detailed coverage of the earliest occupation of this country (Wymer 1996). Any agenda for the future must seek to combine with these data the reconstructions now becoming available from Quaternary science. We must do more than provide simple environmental backdrops and instead deal with the measures of structure, productivity, and accessibility that impinged on hominid decisions and adaptations.

Such issues are clearly important for evolutionary questions. Did, for example, the Neandertals in the last interglacial of northern Europe 130–120,000 years ago maintain permanent population across the region; firstly within the deciduous forest zone and secondly against a background of dramatic climatic changes? For example the Greenland ice core (Dansgaard et al 1993; GRIP 1993) covering the 10,000 interglacial years of marine isotope sub-stage 5e produced one event, at the end of MIS 5e1, which lasted only an estimated 70 years, but during which the oxygen isotope values plunged in this brief time to mid-glacial levels (GRIP 1993, 206). These data demonstrate that changes within interglacials of up to 10°C are possible in 20 years, or even within a decade (White 1993), and certainly within the lifetime of individual hominids. While the impact of such sudden changes in the polar ice caps still has to be assessed in the latitudes where hominids were living, it is nonetheless against this background of rapid change that we need, as van Andel and Tzedakis argue (this volume), to standardise and integrate the varied lines of evidence (van Andel and Tzedakis 1996).

It is good that a debate now exists about habitat tolerance among hominids. But it is equally necessary to recognise that such a debate will only be resolved once we have sorted out the taphonomy of Quaternary data as it relates to measures of ecological productivity at both a local and regional scale for human adaptation.

An example of where a systematic re-appraisal of biological evidence can get us is shown by the study of animal bones. In the 1969 *Science in archaeology* volume there was no mention of taphonomy. Since then it sometimes feels as though we have heard of little else. But studying the laws of burial and applying a comparative approach to the reconstruction of hominid diet as reconstructed from animal bones has been very productive. As Sabine Gaudzinski has shown (Gaudzinski 1992; 1996), hunting prime age prey has a much longer ancestry than the Upper Palaeolithic and modern humans. The recent discovery of thrusting and throwing spears from Schöningen (Thieme 1997), possibly 400,000 years old, is finally proof of what we suspected all along: that to live in northern latitudes hominids had to kill animals (Gamble 1987). The possible integration here with Aiello's diet hypothesis is obvious, as is the importance of being able to place all this within a well understood, dynamic, and measured landscape, as Tjeerd van Andel proposes (this volume). With such approaches the quest for evidence of undoubtedly important behaviour, such as the earliest traces of fire-making and its importance for cooking and changing the value of food, assumes a significance for our understanding of how hominid evolution has been an interplay between genes and culture.

Conclusion

Interdisciplinarity and integration will ensure a bright future for Palaeolithic science applied to such Palaeolithic questions as humans/hominids as colonising animals. This fusion of science and archaeology has transformed our knowledge of the period, making it seem now as complex and complicated as the Neolithic or the Iron Age, where only a few years ago it was seen as simple and as unvarying as a medieval peasant (although later papers in this volume show that this stereotype is also grossly unfair).

Neither is this a one-sided relation, with science making all the running. The need for independent tests based on archaeological evidence is making us look for new patterns in the data. A final example is the characterisation of lithic raw material. This has become a major topic in Palaeolithic studies using nothing more complicated that basic petrology (Féblot-Augustins 1990; 1993; Floss 1994; Geneste 1988; Svoboda 1994; White 1995). The distances over which tools and raw materials were transferred can be compared to the foraging ranges of the great apes and carnivores (Steele 1996). What Steele has found is that the African data prior to the first dispersal into other parts of the Old World sometime between 1.8 and 1 million years ago

indicates a primate range size. The earliest European data, from 500,000 years ago, points on the other hand towards a scale of raw material transfers more comparable to the ranges of carnivores such as wolves.

Now, if archaeology can begin to supply estimates of the size of hominid ranges from the ubiquitous stone tools, then we might find ourselves in a position to use our distribution maps, such as those I mentioned above from the English Rivers Palaeolithic Survey, as a means to establish whether or not we can see the wood for the trees when it comes to being precise about the colonising abilities of early hominids. This certainly poses some questions for Palaeolithic science and will ensure a rich future for our investigations.

References

Aiello, L, and Dunbar, R, 1993 Neocortex size, group size, and the evolution of language, *Curr Anthropol*, **34**, 184–193

Barkow, J H, Cosmides, L, and Tooby, J, eds, 1992 *The adapted mind: evolutionary psychology and the generation of culture*, New York

Binford, S R, and Binford, L R, eds, 1968 *New perspectives in archaeology*, Chicago

Brothwell, D, and Higgs, E S, 1969 Scientific studies in archaeology, in *Science in archaeology* (eds D Brothwell and E S Higgs), 23–34, London

Cann, R, Stoneking, M, and Wilson, A, 1987 Mitochondrial DNA and human evolution, *Nature*, **325**, 31–6

Carbonell, E, Mosquera, M, Rodriguez, X P, and Sala, R, 1995 The first human settlement of Europe, *J Anthropol Res*, **51**, 107–14

Dansgaard, W, Johnsen, S J, Clausen, H B, Dahl-Jensen, D, Gundestrup, N S, Hammer, C U, Hvidberg, C S, Steffensen, J P, Sveinbjörnsdottir, A E, Jouzel, J, and Bond, G, 1993 Evidence for general instability of past climate from a 250-kyr ice-core record, *Nature*, **364**, 218–20

Dunbar, R, 1996 *Grooming, gossip, and the evolution of language*, London

Féblot-Augustins, J, 1990 Exploitation des matieres premieres dans l'Acheuléen a'Afrique: perspectives comportementales, *Paléo*, **2**, 27–42

—, 1993 Mobility strategies in the late middle palaeolithic of central Europe and western Europe: elements of stability and variability, *J Anthropol Archaeol*, **12**, 211–65

Floss, H, 1994 *Rohmaterialversorgung im Paläolithikum des Mittelrheingebietes*, Römisch-Germanishches Zentralmuseum, Forschungsinstitut für Vor- und Frühgeschichte **21**, Bonn

Gamble, C S, 1984 Regional variation in hunter-gatherer strategy in the upper Pleistocene of Europe, in *Hominid evolution and community ecology* (ed R Foley), 237–60, London

—, 1987 Man the shoveller: alternative models for middle Pleistocene colonization and occupation in northern latitudes, in *The Pleistocene Old World: regional perspectives* (ed O Soffer), 81–98, New York

—, 1993 *Timewalkers: the prehistory of global colonization*, Stroud

—, 1995 The earliest occupation of Europe: the environmental background, in *The earliest occupation of Europe* (eds W Roebroeks and T van Kolfschoten), 279–95, Leiden

Gaudzinski, S, 1992 Wisentjäger in Wallertheim: zur taphonomie einer mittelpaläolithischen Freilandfundstelle in Rheinhessen. *Jahrbuch des Römisch-Germanischen Zentralmuseums Mainz*, **39**, 245–423

—, 1996 On bovid assemblages and their consequences for the knowledge of subsistence patterns in the Middle Palaeolithic, *Proc Prehist Soc*, **62**, 19–39

Geneste, J-M, 1988 Systemes d'approvisionnement en matières premières au paléolithique moyen et au paléolithique supérieur en Aquitaine, *L'Homme de Néandertal*, **8**, 61–70

GRIP (Greenland Ice-core Project Members), 1993 Climate instability during the last interglacal period recorded in the GRIP ice core, *Nature*, **364**, 203–7

Guthrie, R D, 1984 Mosaics, allelochemics, and nutrients: an ecological theory of Late Pleistocene megafaunal extinctions, in *Quaternary extinctions: a prehistoric revolution* (eds P Martin and R Klein), 259–98, Tucson

Holdaway, S, and Porch, N, 1995 Cyclical patterns in the pleistocene human occupation of south-west Tasmania, *Archaeology in Oceania*, **30**, 74–82

Housley, R A, Gamble, C S, Street, M, and Pettitt, P, 1997 Radiocarbon evidence for the Late glacial human recolonisation of northern Europe, *Proc Prehist Soc*, **63**, 25–54

Kelly, R, 1983 Hunter-gatherer mobility strategies, *J Anthropol Res*, **39**, 277–306

Lahr, M M, and Foley, R, 1994 Multiple dispersals and modern human origins, *Evol Anthropol*, **3**, 48–60

Leakey, M D, 1971 *Olduvai Gorge: excavations in Beds I and II 1960–1963*, Cambridge

Oakley, K P, 1964 *Frameworks for dating fossil man*, London

Rick, J, 1987 Dates as data: an examination of the Peruvian preceramic radiocarbon record, *Amer Antiq*, **52**, 55–73

Roebroeks, W, Conard, N J, and van Kolfschoten, T, 1992 Dense forests, cold steppes, and the Palaeolithic settlement of northern Europe, *Curr Anthropol*, **33**, 551–86

Roebroeks, W, and van Kolfschoten, T, 1994 The earliest occupation of Europe: a short chronology, *Antiquity*, **68**, 489–503

Steele, J, 1996 On predicting hominid group sizes, in *The archaeology of human ancestry* (eds J Steele and S Shennan), 230–52, London

Svoboda, J, 1994 *Paleolit Moravy a Slezska*, Dolnovesonické studies 1, Brno

Thieme, H, 1997 Lower palaeolithic hunting spears from Germany, *Nature*, **385**, 807–10

van Andel, T H, and Runnels, C N, 1995 The earliest farmers in Europe, *Antiquity* **69**, 481–500

van Andel, T H, and Tzedakis, P C, 1996 Palaeolithic landscapes of Europe and environs, 150,000–25,000 years ago: an overview, *Quat Sci Rev*, **15**, 481–500

von Koenigswald, W, and van Kolfschoten, T, 1996 The *Mimomys-Arvicola* boundary and the enamel thickness quotient (SDQ) of *Arvicola* as stratigraphic markers in the Middle Pleistocene, in *The early Middle Pleistocene in Europe* (ed C Turner), 211–26, Rotterdam

White, J W C, 1993 Don't touch that dial, *Nature*, **364**, 186

White, M J, 1995 Raw materials and biface variability in southern Britain: a preliminary examination, *Lithics*, **15**, 1–20

Wymer, J J, 1996 The English rivers Palaeolithic survey, in *The English Palaeolithic reviewed* (eds C S Gamble and A J Lawson), 7–22, Salisbury

Zeuner, F E, 1959 *The Pleistocene Period*, London

3 The return of the natives: AMS radiocarbon dating of Magdalenian artefacts and the recolonisation of northern Europe after the last ice age

by Rupert A Housley

Abstract

Archaeologically the direct movement of past peoples cannot always be distinguished from the transmission of ideas. Change in material culture may be seen to occur but the mechanism responsible is not always identifiable. In situations where humans are acting as colonists into formerly uninhabited regions, however, the picture is often more straightforward and discernible. The retreat of the last ice sheets after the last glacial maximum presented just such a situation to Magdalenian human communities of western Europe in that it opened a vast 'new frontier' to the north. The expansion of such groups out of areas of refuge and into the 'lands of opportunity' can be chronicled by the application of AMS radiocarbon dating, which enables us to determine questions of timing and routes of colonisation. Such an approach also has the potential to reveal the mode of settlement that these people adopted in their expansion, as well as something of the processes they used to exploit the new situations they encountered.

Introduction

In his introduction, Clive Gamble (this volume) emphasized the point that the concept of the site, meaning a focus of continuity of occupation over a measurable period of time, is almost certainly misleading when dealing with human settlement during the Palaeolithic. Instead he advanced the view that we should rather be thinking in terms of identifying episodes of activity within landscapes. If we accept this change of perception then it behoves us to consider what a date from such an archaeological locality is really telling us.

Suppose most of Palaeolithic artefacts simply represent individual actions that took place over short moments of time before a locality was abandoned, for example a few hours activity spent butchering a horse or reindeer carcass. Then the purpose of dating a site changes, and gone is the issue of duration of occupation. None of our present methods of dating can hope to measure time that lasted no more than weeks, days, or sometimes only hours. Instead determinations begin to represent point markers that flag the presence of humans at a particular place in time and space. As such they almost become proxy markers for human activity (Rick 1987). There is one proviso though. The association

between the object being dated and the human action being commemorated has to the valid. Spurious associations simply lead to bad data and erroneous conclusions.

If single dates become point markers for hominid activity, then what do suites of dates on discrete samples tell us? The problem is one of knowing whether successive determinations are merely repeatedly measuring the same episode of activity, or whether different dates on separate items represent repeated separate phases of activity – perhaps different visitations at unknown intervals. The pertinent issue here is whether discrete actions in the archaeological record can be discerned from compound ones that resulted in multiple by-products. Sometimes lithic refitting studies can help in such circumstances, often showing that what may at first seem like separate phases are all part of a single event. Scheer's (1993) paper is a good example of this: conjoins from three Gravettian sites in the same valley demonstrate the contemporaneity of some of the assemblages, implying simultaneous, or at least closely related, phases of occupation. Also pertinent is the question whether measurement precision is sufficiently good to discriminate between events that occurred at different moments of time. This, in part, depends on the length of time between activity episodes and the degree of precision that is technically achievable. Such issues need to be considered on a case-by-case basis.

Viewing archaeological dates in such a way has advantages: it can chart patterns of chronological windows of exploitation where humans were successful in using appropriate adaptive strategies that ensured a presence in a region. Once we have a clear chronology of human presence within particular regions during the Palaeolithic, it is feasible to look for explanations as to why at other times there is no presence. Absence is a more intractable problem but of equal concern to us. It is harder to demonstrate because lack of evidence is never conclusive, it may simply represent an inadequate knowledge base. Periods of hominid absence, however, particularly in regions where we know they were present in earlier periods, should be of interest to us since they provide insights into the limits of hominid adaptive ability.

By modifying our concept of what is a Palaeolithic site and thinking in terms of short-lived activity events within landscapes, what effect has this on our perceptions of the period? One effect is to make the whole Palaeolithic settlement system more dynamic. Continuity is only to be seen on a regional scale.

Mobility is the overriding feature, and individual localities were sometimes seeing repeated use by the same group, while other sites may have been visited only intermittently over thousands of years. The normal pattern of Palaeolithic settlement thus becomes a series of punctuated waves of demographic movement within changing environmental regions – a long term rhythmic process of colonisation and abandonment.

The driving force for demographic change may, at times, be climate, although cultural or evolutionary change may well have been consequential. If environmental change was an important criterion (the data presented by van Andel and Tzerdakis [this volume] for Oxygen Isotope Stage 3 suggests that it was), then the scale, rapidity, and form in which change was manifested would also have been important. Time is as relevant to cultural change as it is to environmental adaptation to different climate parameters. Cultural transformation, be it a new tool kit or a changed social structure, may have been just as necessary for exploitation of a new environment. We may thus encounter periods of hesitancy in advance of the process of recolonisation; an immediate advance in the wake of the retreating icecaps may not have been the rule.

It is unlikely that changing cultural factors resulted in the abandonment of already exploited regions, and so we are probably safe in assuming that fluctuating environmental conditions were responsible for the closing down of regions to successful human exploitation. But how exactly did our ancestors respond to deteriorating environmental conditions? We take for granted the peripatetic nature of Palaeolithic hunter and gatherer populations commensurate with the exploitation of niches with different resources, but how would deteriorating conditions have affected such groups? Would we expect to see a shift in group territories – perhaps reflected archaeologically by a gradual decline in the number of sites? Should we be looking for evidence of increased marginality – perhaps reflected in changes to the food base or a switch to the hunting of alternative prey? Were mass migrations ever a feasible reaction? While long-term regional shifts may be identifiable, is abandonment due to short-term deteriorations discernible (the Younger Dryas would be a case in point)? How quickly would groups have reacted? Can we say anything about the societal changes that such a process may have caused, be it enhanced cultural transformation, the mixing of populations, or changes in the structure of settlement? These are all issues that may be relevant when attempting to examine Palaeolithic demographic movements.

Two specific considerations are particularly relevant to the British Palaeolithic. The first is the fact that for most, if not all, of this period Britain would have been marginal to many of the developments that were happening in the rest of the Old World. This peripheral position on the margins of Europe probably exacerbated the already intermittent nature of Palaeolithic settlement in this region. One may almost argue that absence or 'just visiting' was more the norm for Palaeolithic peoples in Britain than a consistent 'in residence' state of affairs. But there is a second factor, which tended, at times, to exacerbate this marginality, but which at other times tended to mitigate its effects, namely Britain's physical links to the continental mainland. Funnell (1995) has argued that for much of the later Pliocene and Pleistocene the mainland of Britain was connected to the continent by a land bridge. The only exception seems to have been the periods of the Middle Tiglian, the Ipswichian–Eemian, and the Holocene, when the existence of a channel linking the Atlantic Ocean to the southern North Sea can be demonstrated.

Thus for much of the lower Palaeolithic, a dryland passage existed linking north France to lowland England and free migration was possible. The position may have been partly reversed during the middle Palaeolithic: during the Ipswichian–Eemian there is clear evidence of a well established marine connection through the Dover Strait, linking the southern North Sea and the English Channel (Funnell 1995, 11), and this could possibly be responsible for the paucity of middle Palaeolithic archaeological remains. These arguments bring home the need not to be too insular in our view of the British Palaeolithic. If we accept that large-scale movements are a feature of settlement in this period, then ignoring the wider European context makes little sense. It is for this reason that I make no apology for focusing on Europe even though this collection of papers primarily concerns an agenda for English archaeology.

Palaeolithic demographies: charting recolonisation

Colonisation of new lands by past peoples is a topic that has attracted considerable recent attention (Fagan 1990; Lahr and Foley 1994; Stringer and Gamble 1993). Within the Palaeolithic Period the spread of anatomically modern humans on a global scale to areas not previously inhabited by hominids, such as the Americas and Australia, has justifiably attracted much attention; however, subcontinental colonisation of new resource zones is an equally fruitful topic of research.

A major difficulty with fine-grained Palaeolithic settlement studies is the paucity of find localities over much of Europe (find localities are very abundant in some places but these are the exception). Such paucity may be a consequence of the many taphonomic factors that have buried or destroyed evidence of human activity. A low density of sites makes statements based on paucity of evidence dangerous, but this is an inherent problem in attempting to address the Palaeolithic.

This problem is evident if past models of demographic expansion are examined (eg Birdsell 1958; Martin 1973): they have tended to defy close testing with prehistoric hunter and gatherer data. In contrast, the wave-of-advance model proposed for early agriculturalists by Ammerman and Cavalli-Sforza 1973; 1979) has been more amenable to analysis (van Andel and Runnels 1995; Zvelebil 1986). Although far from ideal, there now exist sufficient late glacial archaeological data for northern Europe to overcome some of these taphonomic problems and to enable an examination of the process of recolonisation after the height of the Last Glacial Maximum (LGM) or pleniglacial of the Würm/Weichselian.

Recolonisation after 18,000 BP: a case study

The LGM is ideal for such a study for three further reasons:

- There is good circumstantial evidence that, at its height, the LGM was of sufficient severity to force the abandonment of much of northern Europe for, at least, part of the period between 21,000–13,000 years BP (Gamble 1991). Thus one is looking for settlement against the backdrop of a 'clean slate'.
- The period after 18,000 years BP is well within the age range of ^{14}C dating and thus the technology exists on which to found a reasonable chronology.
- Over recent years a number of important ^{14}C dating studies pertinent to this period have been made (Evin *et al* 1994; Gowlett 1986; Housley 1991; Street *et al* 1994; Tolan-Smith forthcoming).

Hereafter, all cited dates were determined by the radiocarbon technique.

When testing rates of demographic recolonisation certain methodological criteria need addressing. Reliable dating is essential, but there are two aspects to consider. One is the technical aspect that the laboratory should manage (the application of an appropriate chemical pre-treatment, rigorous quality control in the dating procedure, etc), the other is the reliability of the association, and this should be the primary concern of the archaeologist. A clear link must be demonstrable between the event being dated and the selected samples. The archaeologist has to be clear that, in the case of radiocarbon, the time when the sample stops exchanging carbon with the atmosphere coincides with the archaeological moment in question.

In the case of recolonisation the issue is human presence and so the sample should either have a form that derives from human modification (eg organic artefact, butchery marks on bone, etc), or can be directly linked to human presence (eg a bone from a human skeleton). This removes any ambiguity that otherwise can creep in. In the past problems have occurred when dates have been obtained from bones that were the result of carnivore predation – in such cases the date almost certainly charts a time when humans were *absent*; or when fragmented material has been combined to produce a single date where the layer is a palimpsest, ie the material is of more than one age. Clearly such situations are potentially very misleading. Conservation practices after excavation may also have introduced a chemical contaminant into the sample, which has biased the age. Practical concerns do not always allow such a rigorous approach, but where less suitable samples are used the potential for bias should always be borne in mind.

The lack of suitable AMS determinations on worked or cutmarked items from some areas of Europe further hinders discussion. Radiometric ^{14}C measurements do give a good indication of the age of faunal accumulations provided the samples consist of a single large bone rather than a collection of bone fragments of differing age. The problem of potential use of conservation chemicals needs to be taken into account. Provided attention is paid to potential biases, however, such determinations can be helpful.

All recolonisation studies need a point of origin from which to chart routes and rates of expansion. In terms of the LGM in western Europe, the best locality for the existence of a human refugium is in southern and southwestern France at sites characterised by Solutrean or Proto-Magdalenian artefact assemblages. Farther north the evidence is patchy and an uncritical consideration could suggest continued occupation. For example, in southern Germany, Weniger's (1990) study of conventional radiocarbon determinations on unmodified bone from localities with Magdalenian assemblages identified potential human occupation before 15,000 years BP on at least four sites – Hohlefels, Schussenquelle, Munzingen, and Spitzbubenhöhle – even though the majority of faunal accumulations only began after 13,500/13,000 years BP, coinciding with the start of the Bølling late glacial interstadial. But closer examination (Housley *et al* 1997) of the measurements from these four sites indicates problems both of a technical nature and in linking them to human actions, leaving a general impression that Germany was probably depopulated before 13,500–14,000 years BP.

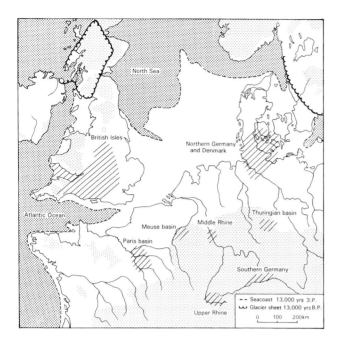

Fig 3.1 Regions of late glacial northern Europe

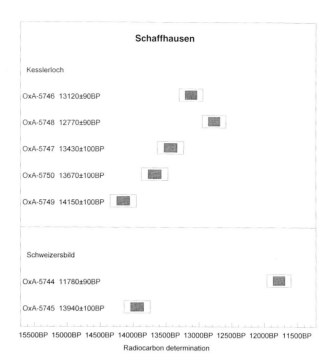

Fig 3.2 AMS determinations on humanly modified bone and antler from the cave sites of Kesslerloch and Schweizersbild, Schaffhausen, Switzerland

The recolonisation process

Tolan-Smith (forthcoming), drawing on observations made by Campbell (1977, 32–3, 159–60), refers to the possibility that Britain was resettled from two directions, from the North Sea Lowlands, and from the English Channel Plain. For this reason it is necessary to look at the Continental situation both in France and in the Low Countries and Germany if we are to understand the process by which Britain was resettled (Fig 3.1).

Southern and eastern France: According to Evin (*et al* 1994) most pre 15,000 year-old terminal Würm sites are located west of the Saône and Rhône rivers, Solutré being the prime example. East of these rivers there is little sign of human presence before 14,800 years BP, except at Arlay, which lies on the fringes of the Jura near Bescançon in north-east France (Allain *et al* 1985, 110; David and Richard 1989, 117). With its distinctive industry, including antler *navettes* (Allain *et al* 1985) and two early determinations (15,320 ± 370 [Ly-497] and 15,770 ± 390 BP [Ly-559]), Arlay is perhaps best seen as the first staging post north of the main southern French refugium on the way to the Upper Rhine. Admittedly much earlier than the majority of non-refugium sites, the location and date does not detract from the main pattern, in which recolonisation occured in a north-eastwards direction through the Belfort Gap to the Upper Rhine by 14,800–14,200 years BP.

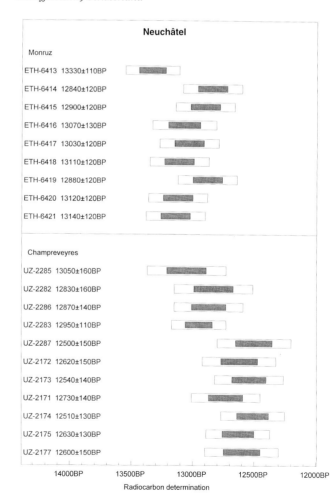

Fig 3.3 AMS and radiometric determinations on charcoal from Monruz (Neuchâtel) and Champréveyres (Hauterive), Switzerland (data taken from SPM I 1993, 201)

Schaffhausen/Engen (Upper Rhine): The cave of Kesslerloch has a rich and diverse Magdalenian mobiliary art assemblage from which good AMS samples were available. The resulting ages (Fig 3.2) suggests that occupation began by *c* 14,150 years BP with continued visits over the next millennium until *c* 12,800 years BP. The nearby cave of Schweizersbild may also have first been visited by Magdalenian groups about the same time as Kesslerloch, but the unavailability of further samples has prevented more investigation of the pattern of use once people had returned to the area. There is an 'older' and a 'younger' Magdalenian horizon from the site, but the two dated samples cannot be tied directly to the two respective layers. Two other Swiss sites near Neuchâtel, Monruz and Champreveyres, have extensive groups of ^{14}C determinations (SPM I 1993, 201) (Fig 3.3). In general these are later than the Kesslerloch and Schweizersbild dates, but they reinforce the idea that once Magdalenian groups moved into a region they aimed to stay. The large Magdalenian site of Petersfels in south-west Germany has similar conventional ^{14}C ages.

The Swabian Alb: East of the Rhine, between the Köln basin and the Schaffhausen/Engen region, is the limestone escarpment of the Swabian Alb and its many cave systems. In the Ach valley near Ulm are two caves, Geissenklösterle and Höhlefels (Blumentritt and Hahn 1978) that, although better known for their Aurignacian and Gravettian levels, have Magdalenian material from their upper strata, although heavily mixed with residual, pre-LGM material. With the exception of an unmodified ibex rib from Geissenklösterle (OxA-5156: 16,940 ± 180 BP), the general pattern (Figs 3.4–3.5) is one of no faunal accumulation after *c* 25,000–24,000 and before *c* 13,350 years BP. If one postulates a link between faunal accumulation and human activity, although admittedly not yet demonstrable, then the absence of fauna *may* be charting absence of people. Supporting evidence in the form of ages of similar magnitude on worked artefacts comes from the Altmühl Valley in Bavaria (Housley *et al* 1997).

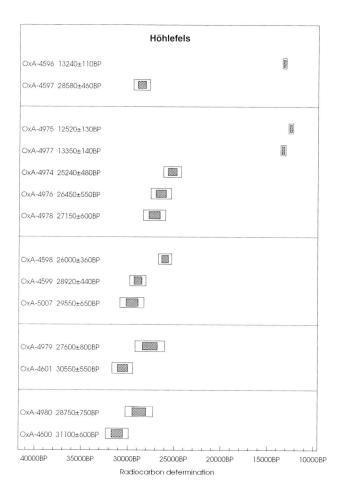

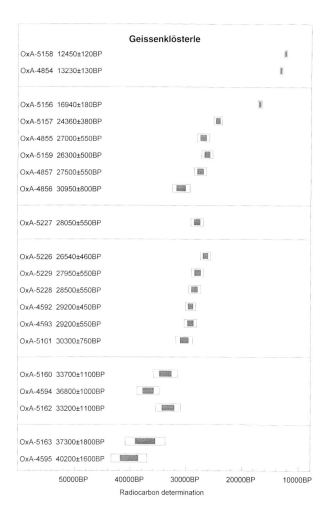

Fig 3.4 AMS determinations on unmodified bone and antler from the Höhlefels, Schelkingen, Alb-Donau-Kreis, Baden-Württemberg

Fig 3.5 AMS determinations on mostly unmodified bone and antler from Geissenklösterle, Gem Blaubeuren-Weiler, Alb-Donau-Kreis, Baden-Württemberg (only OxA-4857 has possible cutmarks)

Fig 3.6 *AMS and radiometric dates from Andernach-Martinsberg, Gonnersdorf, and Oberkassel; the AMS measurements from Andernach-Martinsberg and Gonnersdorf are on bones from sealed pits; * = possible bias by a chemical preservative*

Fig 3.7 *AMS dates on cutmarked bone and antler from a selection of Magdalenian cave sites in the Ardennes region, Belgium (after Charles 1996)*

The Middle Rhine: The late glacial archaeology of the central Rhineland Basin (Street *et al* 1994) is important because of its particular wealth of material culture, including art, boneworking, and evidence of dwellings from the site of Gönnersdorf (Bosinski 1979). Before AMS dating, the ¹⁴C chronology of Gönnersdorf had been problematic (Fig 3.6) but the new determinations suggest a tighter chronology that is particularly informative when compared to Andernach-Martinsberg (Street 1995a). Together they show the central Rhineland must have been repopulated by *c* 13,200–12,900 years BP. The double burial at Oberkassel near Bonn (Street 1995b), previously thought to be early owing to a contour *découpé* with Magdalenian IV affinities, is now thought to be later, although problems of conservation shroud the issue of its precise age.

The Meuse Basin: Charles (1996) has comprehensively presented the dating evidence for Magdalenian settlement in the Ardennes (Fig 3.7). She makes a good case for believing that the Meuse Basin had definitely been resettled by hunter and gatherer groups by *c* 12,900–12,800 years BP. The early conventional determinations from the lower and middle layer III at the Trou de Blaireaux have not, so far, been incontrovertibly linked to human, as against carnivore, activity. The pre-13,000 years AMS measurement (OxA-4201) is suspect in that the modification may not be the result of humans.

The Paris Basin: The two sites of Pincevent and Etiolles (Rensink 1993; Taborin 1994) suggest expansion into the northern Plains. Etiolles has produced determinations very much in line with the Belgian evidence, ie 13,000–12,800 years BP (Fig 3.8), which coincides with

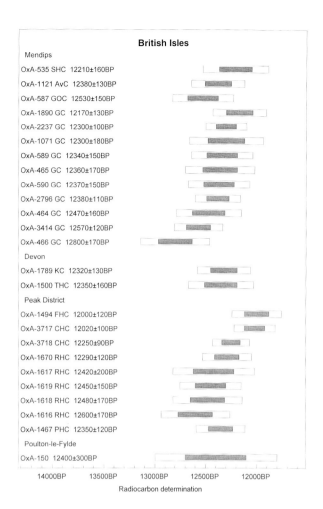

Fig 3.8 AMS dates on unmodified bone and charcoal from Magdalenian sites of Pincevent and Etiolles, Paris Basin, France (after Gowlett 1986); non-Pleistocene determinations have been omitted

Fig 3.9 Selected AMS dates on human remains or modified bone and antler from Britain for the period after the LGM and before 12,000 years BP (after Housley (1991) and Jacobi (1991), with additions): AvC = Aveline's Hole Cave, SHC = Sun Hole Cave, GC = Gough's Cave, GOC = Gough's Old Cave, KC = Kent's Cavern, THC = Three Holes Cave, CHC = Church Hole Cave, FHC = Fox Hole Cave, RHC = Robin Hood's Cave, PHC = Pin Hole Cave

the end of Dryas I and the start of the Bølling interstadial. The one anomalous site of Hallines (Fagnart 1988) in the north of the Paris Basin, with its Badegouliantype transverse burins on notches, large Hamburgiantype becs, and very early ¹⁴C date (16,000 ± 300 BP, Gif-1712), could very well represent a brief human visitation during the pleniglacial, and provides a warning that stadial conditions may not have precluded occasional northward forays. In terms of resettlement of the region by groups using Late Magdalenian tool assemblages, however, its relevance is probably minimal.

North Germany: The earliest post-18,000 years BP settlement on the north European Plain of Germany begins with the Hamburgian shouldered-point industries (Burdukiewicz 1986; Grønnow 1987). These include the well preserved open sites of Meiendorf,

Poggenwisch, and Stellmoor, which begin from c 12,500 years BP, ie the middle of the Bølling interstadial. This implies an appreciable hesitancy between reaching the edge of the uplands and venturing onto the North European Plain.

The British Isles: Ireland and Scotland have, so far, failed to produce good evidence for settlement before the onset of the Holocene (Morrison and Bonsall 1989; Woodman 1985; Woodman et al 1997). England and Wales, in contrast, have produced late Upper Palaeolithic material from both open and cave sites (Campbell 1977; Green and Walker 1991). Over the last ten or more years AMS dating has transformed our knowledge of the British late glacial archaeology (Gowlett 1986; Housley 1991). The result is the picture (Fig 3.9) from which it is clear that the majority of the cut and worked bone from the thirteenth millennium BP begins after *c* 12,600 years BP, although there are isolated determinations as early as 12,800 ± 170 BP (OxA-466, from a cut red deer metapodial from Gough's New Cave). It seems likely therefore that warmer conditions associated with the first half of the Windermere interstadial, ie synonymous with the Bølling, facilitated the resettlement of lowland Britain.

Attempts to determine whether Britain was colonised from the North Sea Lowlands or from the English Channel Plain (Smith 1992, 165–7) have generally centred on typological comparisons with adjoining areas of the Continent (the latter representing peripheral manifestations of regions no longer available for study today (Tolan-Smith forthcoming)). Given that the British Creswellian manifests both Hamburgian and Magdalenian artefactual affinities (Jacobi 1991, 138), it may be supposed that the North Sea Lowlands were a key area from which hunter and gatherer groups first moved back into Britain.

How rapid was the process and which regions were recolonised first?

It is possible to get some idea of the speed of recolonisation by treating the ^{14}C measurements as data points to determine intensity of occupation, as was first done by Rick (1987), using a moving sum to explore the pattern of human occupation on a regional scale. By taking the approach of Holdaway and Porch (1995) and modifying it to take account of the shorter age range involved in this study (ie a 400 year moving sum and a 200 year span)

the result is the data summarised in Figure 3.10, three conclusions can be derived, from which:

- The order (and, by inference, the route) in which regions were recolonised seems to have been the Upper Rhine first, then the Middle Rhine, the Meuse Basin, southern German uplands, the Paris Basin, northern Germany/Denmark, and lastly Britain (southern Germany appears anomalously late in this list because the ^{14}C samples have failed to pick up the earlier stages of the recolonisation process in preference to more established Magdalenian settlement).

- The nature of the process, ie that recolonisation was a two-stage affair beginning with a *pioneer phase*, when only a few small hunting parties moved to explore and exploit a previously unpopulated region (Fig 3.11), followed 400–600 years later by a *residential phase*, when larger camps were established (Fig 3.12).

- An indication of the rate or speed with which recolonisation was achieved (Table 3.1). To put this into context it is necessary to look at the figures proposed for the spread of the earliest agriculturalists. Ammerman and Cavalli-Sforza (1973) proposed a rate of about one kilometre a year based on random dispersal. At first glance the rates obtained here are slightly less, and are more in keeping with those of van Andel and Runnels (1995), who modelled directional rather than random movement. The actual rate of dispersal, however, is probably twice as high since one must measure the residential phase in the Upper Rhine compared to the first pioneers in other regions. If this

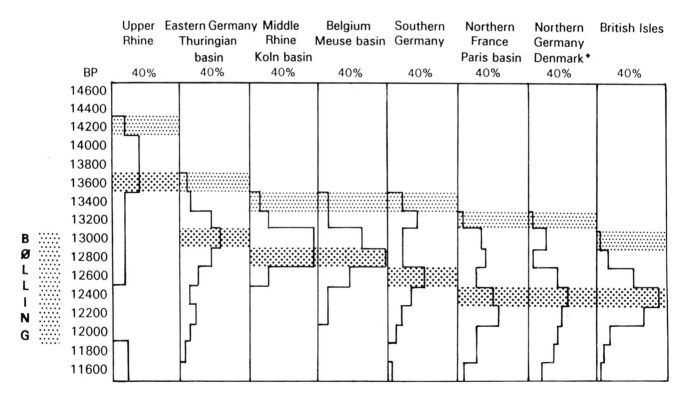

Fig 3.10 The moving sum distribution of AMS radiocarbon determinations by region; conventional dates are indicated by ✱

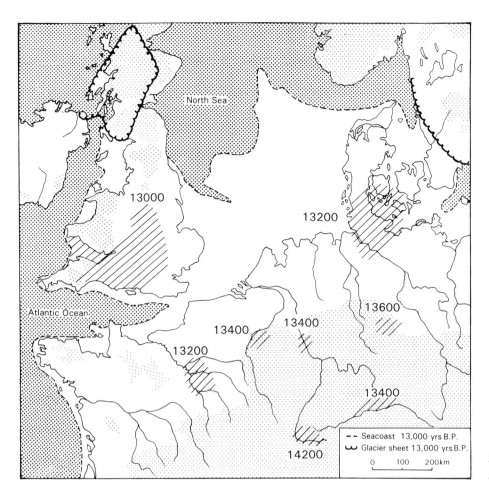

Fig 3.11 Map showing the start of the pioneer phase

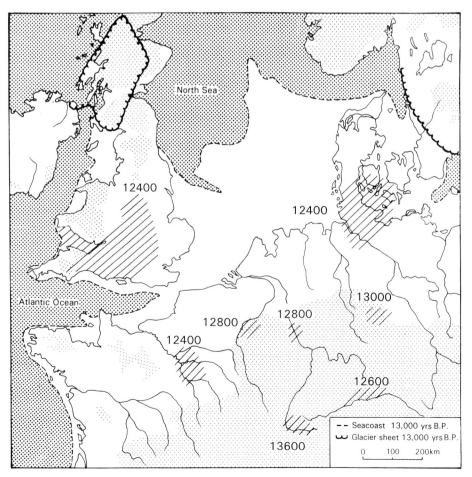

Fig 3.12 Map showing the start of the residential phase

Table 3.1 Rates of expansion in the recolonisation of northern Europe: the agricultural rates are calculated from van Andel and Runnels 1995

				km	*yr*	*rate (km/yr)*
pioneer to pioneer						
upper Rhine	to	British Isles		925	1200	0.77
upper Rhine	to	north Germany/Denmark		814	1000	0.81
upper Rhine	to	Meuse/middle Rhine		407	800	0.51
upper Rhine	to	Thuringia		407	600	0.68
residential to residential						
upper Rhine	to	Paris/British Isles		925	1200	0.77
upper Rhine	to	north Germany/Denmark		814	1200	0.68
upper Rhine	to	Meuse/middle Rhine		407	800	0.51
upper Rhine	to	Thuringia		407	600	0.68
residential to pioneer						
upper Rhine	to	British Isles		925	600	1.54
upper Rhine	to	north Germany/Denmark		814	400	2.04
upper Rhine	to	Meuse/middle Rhine		407	200	2.04
upper Rhine	to	Thuringia		407	1	407.00
agricultural wave of advance						
Jericho	to	Tavoliere		2000	2300	0.87
Jericho	to	Sava valley		1800	2800	0.64
Çayönü	to	Tavoliere		1900	2300	0.83
Çayönü	to	Sava valley		1600	2800	0.57

is correct then why should Magdalenian hunter-gatherers have been able to achieve a rate double that of agriculturalists? Perhaps, as Zvelebil (1986) has argued, it is that the existence of successful mesolithic foragers slowed the expansion of early agriculturalists whereas the Magdalenian groups were unfettered by the presence of existing groups in having an open frontier across which to move.

Implications for British Palaeolithic archaeology: an agenda for the future?

So far the discussion has centred on continental Europe but what of the implications for British Palaeolithic archaeology? As Tolan-Smith (forthcoming) has recently emphasized, the North Sea Lowlands were probably the key entry point for Palaeolithic colonisers into England and although now mostly submerged, there may well be some potential for the discovery of offshore Palaeolithic archaeology (G N Bailey personal communication). Although many areas will have been lost through erosion and scouring, there are almost certainly others that have survived under acceptable depths of Holocene sediment. The logistical problems in doing such investigations are

admittedly great, but opportunities should be sought to undertake exploratory studies. Bryony Coles, in a forthcoming paper on the lost land of Dogger (the seabed around Dogger Bank [Coles forthcoming]), has pointed to the potential for studying Britain's cultural connections with the continent in the late Pleistocene and early Holocene shown by the few individual lithic and antler finds recovered in fishing nets (eg the uniserial antler point from Leman and Ower, dated 11,740 ± 150 [OxA-1950], is an example from the North Sea [Smith and Bonsall 1991]). Closer cooperation with researchers in other disciplines would be necessary in such undertakings, but the input to archaeological questions may lead to interesting opportunities.

The second issue is the reverse of that described above, ie the abandonment process by which humans vacated a region in advance of deteriorating conditions. We should try to examine whether demographic decline happened slowly over time – a gradual abandonment in the face of increased marginality – or whether it took the form of a rapid exodus. The early Upper Palaeolithic (EUP) may be the best timeframe in which to investigate such a question because of the possibility of using ^{14}C dating, although the present level of precision for ^{14}C dates in the 35,000 and 20,000 years BP period and the problems in overcoming contamination from younger carbon at all stages of the dating process makes it far less amenable than the 18,000 to 13,000 years BP period (P A Mellars personal communication).

In Britain, a start has already been made by trying to date the early Upper Palaeolithic from Pin Hole and Hyena Den Caves (R Jacobi personal communication) and Paviland Cave (S Aldhouse-Green personal communication), but since spatial as well as temporal issues are concerned in this debate, more known EUP material from other localities needs comprehensive dating.

Finally, what chances do we have to construct an Upper Palaeolithic chronology based on a calendrical timeframe rather than having to use the present uncalibrated ^{14}C timescale? The establishment of a high-precision, bi-decadal calibration curve has undoubtedly greatly benefitted post-Pleistocene prehistoric archaeology, but what of earlier periods? Extensions to the tree-ring master curve now cover the Holocene and are beginning to extend into the very end of the Late Glacial (Stuiver *et al* 1993). Between 10,000 years BP (*c* 11,400 cal BP) and 18,000 years BP the lack of dendrochronological evidence forces a reliance on ^{230}Th-^{234}U and ^{14}C measurements from corals (Bard *et al* 1993), which, although promising, still lack the level of precision provided by dendrochronology.

Van Andel and Tzedakis (this volume) draw attention to the valuable role that examination of the intensity of the Earth's magnetic field has in determining the magnitude of these offsets. Most of the Holocene variation between ^{14}C age and calendrical time can be ascribed to fluctuations in the ^{14}C production rate, with the long-term peak-to-trough change being attributed to planetary magnetic field strength variations, which in turn affect the cosmic-ray flux. We can therefore use the intensity of the Earth's magnetic field to partially correct for changes in upper atmosphere ^{14}C production (Mazaud *et al* 1991), but, because solar modulation of the cosmic-ray flux causes shorter-term wiggles of 100–200 year magnitudes, not all of the variation can be corrected for. This is unfortunate because it is these shorter-term wiggles that affect discussion of detailed Palaeolithic chronologies.

An example of this is whether the clustering of ^{14}C ages for findspots with trapezoidal blades in Britain to about 12,300 to 12,400 years BP (Jacobi 1991, 133) actually reflects a discreet short-lived cultural episode as against merely being an artefact of the ^{14}C calibration curve where long periods of calendrical time coincide with little change in atmospheric ^{14}C levels.

Still, there have been attempts to interpret Palaeolithic archaeology in a calibrated framework (Street *et al* 1994). Developments along such lines would certainly put the Upper Palaeolithic more in line with the situation prevailing in later periods of prehistory and is an aim that should be on our agenda.

Acknowledgements

I wish to thank Clive Gamble, Martin Street, and Paul Pettitt for their assistance in the original research. Thanks also to Geoff Bailey, Bryony Coles, Roger Jacobi, and Christopher Tolan-Smith for advice, discussions, and permission to refer to unpublished work and, finally, to the anonymous referee whose valuable comments improved the text.

References

Allain, J, Desbrosse, R, Kozlowski, J K, and Rigaud, A, 1985 Le Magdalénien à Navettes, *Gallia Préhist*, **28**, 37–124

Ammerman, A J, and Cavalli-Sforza, L L, 1973 A population model for the diffusion of early farming in Europe, in *The explanation of culture change* (ed A C Renfrew), 343–58, London

—, 1979 The wave of advance model for the spread of agriculture in Europe, in *Transformations: mathematical approaches to culture change* (eds A C Renfrew and K Cooke), 274–94, London

Bard, E, Arnold, M, Fairbanks, R G, and Hamelin, B, 1993 ^{230}Th-^{234}U and ^{14}C ages obtained by mass spectrometry on corals, in Stuiver *et al* 1993, 191–9

Barton, N, Roberts, A J, and Roe, D A, eds, 1991 *The Late Glacial in North-west Europe: human adaptation and environmental change at the end of the Pleistocene*, CBA Res Rep, **77**, London

Birdsell, J B, 1958 On population structure in generalized hunting and collecting populations, *Evolution*, **12**, 189–205

Blumentritt, R, and Hahn, J, 1978 *Der Hohlefels bei Schelklingen, Alb-Donau-Kreis. Eine urgeschichtliche Fundstelle im Achtal*, Kulturdenkmale in Baden-Württemberg, Kleiner Führer, **46**, 4S

Bosinski, G, 1979 *Die Ausgrabungen in Gönnersdorf 1968–1976 und die Siedlungsbefunde der Grabung 1968: der Magdalénien-Fundplatz Gönnersdorf 3*, Wiesbaden

Bosinski, G, Street, M, and Baales, M, eds, 1995 *The Palaeolithic and Mesolithic of the Rhineland*, Quaternary Field Trips in Central Europe 15, **2** (ed W Schirmer), 14th INQUA Congress Berlin, Munich

Burdukiewicz, J M, 1986 *The Late Pleistocene shouldered point assemblages in western Europe*, Leiden

Campbell, J B, 1977 *The Upper Palaeolithic of Britain*, Oxford

Charles, R, 1996 Back into the north: the radiocarbon evidence for the human recolonisation of the north-west Ardennes after the Last Glacial Maximum, *Proc Prehist Soc*, **62**, 1–19

Coles, B, forthcoming Doggerland: a speculative survey, *Proc Prehist Soc*, **64**

David, S, and Richard, H, 1989 Les cultures du tardiglaciaire dans le nord-est de la France, in *Le Magdalénien en Europe* (ed J Ph Rigaud), 101–58, Liège

Evin, J, Bintz, P, and Monjuvent, G, 1994 Human settlements and the last deglaciation in the French Alps, *Radiocarbon*, **36**(3), 345–57

Fagan, B, 1990 *The journey from Eden: the peopling of our world*, London

Fagnart, J P, 1988 Les Industries lithiques du Paléolithique supérieur dans le nord de la France, *Revue Archéologique de Picardie*, special number

Funnell, B M, 1995 Global sea-level and the (pen-) insularity of late Cenozoic Britain, in *Island Britain: a Quaternary perspective* (ed R C Preece), Geology Society Special Publication, **96**, 3–13, London

Gamble, C S, 1991 The social context for European Palaeolithic art, *Proc Prehist Soc*, **57**, 3–15

Gowlett, J A J, 1986 Radiocarbon accelerator dating of the Upper Palaeolithic in north-west Europe: a provision-al view, in *The Palaeolithic of Britain and its nearest neigh-bours: recent trends* (ed S N Colcutt), 98–102, Sheffield

Green, H S, and Walker, E, 1991 *Ice Age hunters: Neanderthals and early modern hunters in Wales*, Cardiff

Grønnow, B, 1987 Meiendorf and Stellmoor revisited. An analysis of Late Palaeolithic reindeer exploitation, *Acta Archaeol*, **56**, 131–66

Holdaway, S, and Porch, N, 1995 Cyclical patterns in the Pleistocene human occupation of south-west Tasmania, *Archaeol Oceania*, **30**, 74–82

Housley, R A, 1991 AMS dates from the Late Glacial and early Postglacial in north-west Europe: a review, in Barton *et al* 1991, 25–39

Housley, R A, Gamble, C S, Street, M, and Pettitt, P, 1997 Radiocarbon evidence for the Lateglacial human recolonisation of northern Europe, *Proc Prehist Soc*, **63**, 25–54

Jacobi, R A, 1991 The Creswellian, Creswell and Cheddar, in Barton *et al* 1991, 128–140

Lahr, M M, and Foley, R, 1994 Multiple dispersals and modern human origins, *Evol Anthropol*, **3**, 48–60

Martin, P S, 1973 The discovery of America, *Science*, **179**, 969–74

Mazaud, A, Laj, C, Bard, E, Arnold, M, and Tric, E, 1991, Geomagnetic field control of ^{14}C production over the last 80 ky: implications for the radiocarbon time scale, *Geophys Res Lett*, **18**, 1885–8

Morrison, A, and Bonsall, C, 1989 The early post-glacial settlement of Scotland: a review, in *The Mesolithic in Europe* (ed C Bonsall), Edinburgh, 134–42

Rensink, E, 1993 Moving into the north: Magdalenian occupation and exploitation of the loess landscapes of north-western Europe, unpubl PhD thesis, Univ Leiden

Rick, J, 1987 Dates as data: an examination of the Peruvian preceramic radiocarbon record, *Amer Antiq*, **52**, 55–73

Scheer, A, 1993 The organisation of lithic resource use during the Gravettian in Germany, in *Before Lascaux: the complex record of the early Upper Palaeolithic* (eds H Knecht, A Pike-Tay, and R White), 193–210, Boca Raton

Smith, C, 1992 *Late Stone Age hunters of the British Isles*, London

Smith, C, and Bonsall, C, 1991 Late Upper Palaeolithic and Mesolithic chronology: points of interest from recent research, in Barton *et al* 1991, 208–12

SPM I, 1993 *Die Schweiz vom Paläolithikum bis zum frühen Mittelalter. Paläolithikum und Mesolithikum*, Basel

Street, M, 1995a Andernach-Martinsberg, in Bosinski *et al* 1995, 910–18

Street, M, 1995b, Bonn-Oberkassel, in Bosinski *et al* 1995, 940-941

Street, M, Baales, M, and Weninger, B, 1994 Absolute Chronologie des späten Paläolithikums und des Frühmesolithikums im nördlichen Rhineland, *Archäologisches Korrespondenzblatt*, **24**, 1–28

Stringer, C B, and Gamble, C S, 1993 *In search of the Neanderthals: solving the puzzle of human origins*, New York

Stuiver, M, Long, A, and Kra, R S, eds, 1993 Calibration 1993, *Radiocarbon*, **35**(1), 1–244

Taborin, Y, 1994 *Environnements et habitats magdaleniens dans le centre du Bassin Parisien*, Documents d'Archéologie Française, **43**, Paris

Tolan-Smith, C, forthcoming, Radiocarbon chronology and the Lateglacial and early Postglacial resettlement of the British Isles, in *As the world warmed* (eds B Eriksen and L Straus), London

van Andel, T H, and Runnels, C N, 1995 The earliest farmers in Europe, *Antiquity*, **69**, 481 500

Weniger, G-C, 1990 Germany at 18,000 BP, in *The world at 18,000 BP: high latitudes, vol 1* (eds O Soffer and C Gamble), 171–92, London

Woodman, P C, 1985 Prehistoric settlement and environment, in *The Quaternary history of Ireland* (eds K J Edwards and W P Warren), 251–78, London

Woodman, P C, McCarthy, M, and Monaghan, N, 1997 The Irish Quaternary fauna project, *Quat Sci Rev*, **16**, 129–59

Zvelebil, M, 1986 Mesolithic societies and the transition to farming: problems of time, scale, and organisation in *Hunters in transition* (ed M Zvelebil), 167–88, Cambridge

4 Genetics and the Palaeolithic

by Bryan Sykes

Abstract

Genetic interpretations of European prehistory over the past decade have suggested three models. The first is that a wave of expansion of Neolithic agriculturalists from the Middle East absorbed Mesolithic hunter-gatherer populations. Its opposing model, indigenous development, proposes that there was minimal diffusion of peoples but that some European hunter-gatherer groups adopted Neolithic agriculture, either independently or as a result of the diffusion of ideas and the trade of crops. A third model, pioneer colonisation, assumes some role for migrations but sees this in terms of selective colonisation by fairly small groups.

We have analysed the pattern of maternally inherited mitochondrial DNA (mtDNA) variation in Europe and asked which of these models best explains the data. Using a sample of 871 individuals from 12 locations we were able to draw a network connecting their maternal genealogies and divided this into five clusters. By counting the number of mutations that had arisen in each cluster we could estimate the length of elapsed time since they last shared a common ancestor. The dates for all but one cluster were Upper Palaeolithic. Our interpretation is that the large majority of European maternal lineages date back well before the arrival of agriculture and are signatures of the indigenous Palaeolithic population rather than of an advancing wave of Neolithic farmers.

I was recently telephoned by a member of a County Archaeological Unit who was preparing a budget for an excavation during which the unit expected to retrieve a number of human skeletons. I was asked if my laboratory could perform DNA tests on these skeletons and how much it would cost. I asked what DNA tests they were thinking about and what they were trying to find out from them. It soon transpired that they really had no idea what DNA tests might reveal or, to be frank, why they were doing them at all. If you need an example of the perceived omnipotence of genetics in the late twentieth century, whether it be in medicine, forensic science, or archaeology, then this was it. Though this is undeniably the golden age of molecular genetics let me reassure you that DNA is not that powerful. Archaeologists rightly turn to geneticists for an independent contribution to their reconstruction of prehistory. Equally geneticists, such as myself, are primarily concerned with trying to explain the genetic diversity we observe with reference to, among other things, population events inferred from the archaeological records.

Although we are now quite sure that DNA survives in archaeological specimens, it is still the case, and likely to remain so, that interpretations of past events are largely inferences from the study of modern gene distributions. In the case of the Palaeolithic in Europe a lot can happen in 40,000 years to distort or blur the reconstruction of the genetics of the earliest Europeans. Since we rely so much on the modern survivors of the Palaeolithic gene pool it might be worth asking whether there are many left.

The dominant work on European genetic prehistory has been done by Luca Cavalli-Sforza and his colleagues (Ammerman and Cavalli-Sforza 1984; Cavalli-Sforza *et al* 1993). Their main, qualitative, conclusion is that the indigenous Palaeolithic/Mesolithic hunter-gatherers were overwhelmed by a 'demic diffusion' of Neolithic agriculturalists. That being the case, one might imagine that the remnants of the Palaeolithic gene pool would be few and far between among modern Europeans.

This is not a view we share with Cavalli-Sforza, at least for the gene that we know most about: mitochondrial DNA (mtDNA). As I shall endeavour to explain, our interpretation of the variation observed among modern Europeans leads us to believe that the major patterns of modern mtDNA diversity were well established in Europe well before the introduction of agriculture (Richards *et al* 1996). This is not the place to explain how two such discordant conclusions can both come from genetics. Let me just say that the idea of the overwhelming nature of the Neolithic genetic intrusion has so influenced the collective consciousness that its true magnitude may, by some process perhaps not unlike a cultural diffusion, have been exaggerated. What I mean by this is that a fresh look at the data may discover that the conclusions of Cavalli-Sforza and ourselves are not as discordant as they now appear to be.

We began to look at the mtDNA diversity in Europe after finding it invaluable in our first study area: the Polynesian Islands (Sykes *et al* 1995). There, mtDNA was able to give a crystal-clear answer to a question that has puzzled scholars for more than 200 years: the origin of the Polynesians. We could say with absolute certainty that, as far as mtDNA is concerned, the bulk of the modern Polynesian gene pool had its origin in South East Asia, quite possibly Taiwan, with a minority (about 5%) coming from Melanesia, most probably Papua, New Guinea. Since this agreed with the majority view constructed by linguists and archaeologists, with the notable exception of Thor Heyerdahl who favoured an origin in the Americas, our conclusions, though very clear, were uncontroversial. Perhaps just as important, it gave us the confidence that the way we were analysing DNA was solid and capable of producing both geographical connections between genes and reasonable estimates of time depths.

It is time to explain exactly what we do with mtDNA. Unlike nuclear DNA, which comes equally from both parents, an individual inherits mtDNA only from his or her mother. The prosaic explanation for this is that mitochondria are to be found in the cell cytoplasm and human eggs have abundant cytoplasm while sperm have virtually none. Thus, in a fertilised egg all the mitochondria have come from the mother. This pattern persists through the embryo, foetus, and into adult life and, if that adult is a woman, she will pass her mtDNA to all her children.

Consider now what happens when you look backwards in time. You, the reader, inherited your mtDNA from your mother. She inherited it from her mother who inherited it from her mother who inherited it from her mother and so on back in time. At any one time in the past, whether it be 100, 1000, 10,000 or even 100,000 years ago only one woman alive at that time was your mitochondrial ancestor. It is also a logical inevitability that any two individuals can trace their maternal ancestry

back to a single female – the only question being how long ago did that woman live? That date, the coalescent time, can be estimated by the number of mutations that have accumulated in the interim. We sequence about 400 base pairs of the most variable segment of mtDNA to look for these mutations, which appear as changes from one base to another. A useful analogy is that of a long 400-letter word in which we are checking for spelling differences between individuals. The more there are, the longer time has elapsed since the common maternal ancestor was alive.

Just as we can estimate the time since the maternal ancestry of two individuals coalesced, so we can do the same thing for an entire population. We display this as what we call a phylogenetic network. The network in Figure 4.1 is constructed from the most frequent mitochondrial 'spellings' or, more correctly, sequence haplotypes from a sample of 871 Europeans. Each circle is a single haplotype and its area is proportional to the number of people in the population who share it. Thus big circles are common haplotypes and small circles are rare ones. The lines that connect haplotypes represent mutations somewhere in the 400-base pair region.

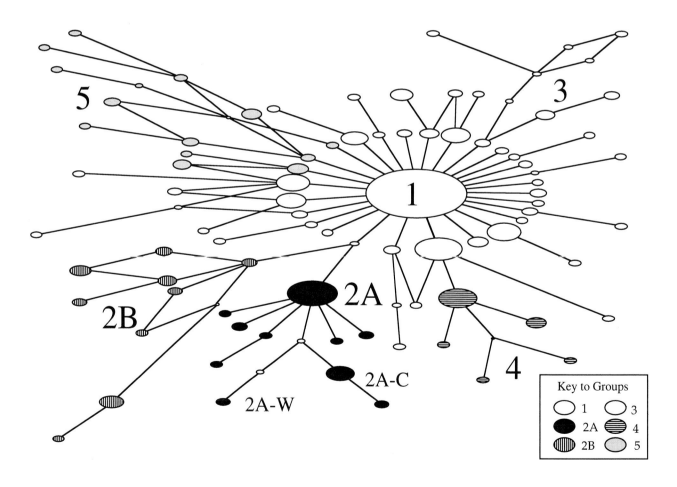

Fig 4.1 A network of the commoner European mitochondrial haplotypes: ovals are different sequence haplotypes with areas proportional to their frequencies in the sample; their most likely evolutionary relationships are denoted by connecting lines and when there is uncertainty two or more routes may be given. The lineage groups have different shadings denoted by the key

What are the features of this network and how can we explain them? The first is that there is a very common central haplotype with radiating satellites at one or two mutations away. We know from studying other positions in mtDNA that are not shown here that this is the pattern you would expect from an expansion of individuals from the central haplotype occurring about 20–25,000 years ago. As well as this group of sequences, which we unimaginatively call Group 1, there are other longer branches which cannot be reasonably explained by divergence from the central ancestral type over the same period.

From other sites in mtDNA we believe that these shared a common ancestor with Group 1 many tens of thousands of years earlier. In an attempt to introduce at least some order we have divided the other groups into five clusters and calculated the divergence time of each of them separately. With the exception of Group 2A all of them coalesce between 18,000 and 40,000 years ago, ie well into the Palaeolithic. We next looked for recent ancestors of these sequences in the Middle East and were surprised to find that only Group 2A ancestors were present in any numbers.

While we have used three independent estimates of the mutation rate, we were nevertheless concerned that our dates might be out by a factor of two or more and that the commonest group, Group 1, was Neolithic after all. That is when we got involved with the Basques.

The Basques speak an ancient, non-European language and have been considered by many to be a relic of pre-Neolithic Europeans. Were that the case, and if we had badly underestimated the mutation rate so that Group 1 was Neolithic in Europe, we would have expected the Basques to belong to one of the fringe lineage groups that are now uncommon elsewhere.

To our astonishment we found the opposite to be the case. The Basques have a higher frequency of Group 1 lineages than any other European population. Not only that, it was the only population in which there were virtually no Group 2A sequences present. So our interpretation of the network topology is that Group 2A, with its clear Middle Eastern origins and relatively recent divergence date, combined with its virtual absence in Iberia, might be explained by its association with agricultural intrusion in the Neolithic. On the other hand, the bulk of the other haplotypes, which do not have clear Middle Eastern connections and have accumulated much more diversity than Group 2, would need to have their origins in an older, Palaeolithic population.

It is always worth reminding ourselves at junctures such as this that mtDNA is only showing us information about the female population. The study of mtDNA has absolutely nothing to say about the behaviour of men and is utterly silent on possibilities such as a demic diffusion of primarily male agriculturalists. Remember too that the demic diffusion model looks at nuclear genes, which comprise an average of male and female contributions. So while we would not see a massive influx of Middle Eastern males, the nuclear gene frequency data would register it as somewhere between the two extremes of Neolithic males and Palaeolithic females. Speculation is idle because the question can be answered fairly soon by the study of the Y-chromosome, which, as it is paternally inherited, gives the equivalent male history.

The point has been well made that the composition of the Middle East reference population is important since the lack of ancestral sequences for all groups other than 2A is an important element of our interpretation. What if the demic diffusion came not from the Middle East but from Anatolia? It's clear from the sequences that we, and others, have studied from modern Turkey that they are more like the rest of Europe than the Middle East and contain representatives of most of the lineage groups we see in the rest of Europe. The question boils down to whether the diversity in modern Europeans, which we have used to date the coalescences of the various groups, was already present in Anatolia and then migrated *en bloc* to Europe.

This is technically a much more difficult question to resolve and we have begun to tackle it by looking at haplotype matches between Anatolia and Europe but have not yet done enough to come to any solid conclusions. Suffice it to say though that it still does not explain the unusual position of the Basques. So for the purposes of argument, let us move on and suppose that, other than Group 2A, the other mitochondrial lineage groups are of largely Palaeolithic origin in Europe.

Perhaps the most astonishing feature of the network is Group 1. There is little doubt that an expansion has occurred in this group some time after the end of the last Ice Age. Could this be a signature of the re-emergence of hunter-gatherers from glacial refuges who colonised northern Europe as the ice retreated? Its high concentration among the present-day Basques would suggest that this might have been the focal point of an expansion. But why is it restricted to this group and, to a lesser degree, to Group 4? (In a network of all haplotypes, not just the commonest as in Figure 4.1, Group 4 is also a 'star-like' cluster, which is the signature of an expansion.)

Unlike the connection between Group 1 and the Pyrenees, Group 4 is not particularly concentrated in the Alps as far as we can see. Other Alpine valleys such as the Val Gardena in northern Italy, do have an extraordinarily high concentration of group 2B lineages, a group that is otherwise widespread throughout Europe. Again we have no good explanation for this intriguing observation. Group 3, which is largely confined to the margins such as western Britain, has, of all the European mitochondrial groups, the closest connection with our African ancestors. From the internal diversity we can estimate this is the oldest group in Europe, coalescing about 50,000 years ago.

There is also some geographical specificity in the distribution of Group 5. It is found more commonly in Scandinavia and northern Europe than in the south. It, too, has a long history in Europe, coalescing about 35–40,000 years ago. The estimation and interpretation of each group's coalescence times is far from certain and would only be near the mark with particular demographic histories. Thus we cannot say with any certainty that each group represents separate migrations into Europe during the Palaeolithic – but they might.

Finally, let me mention the value of ancient DNA in all of this. It is my firm view that the best use of ancient DNA is to test hypotheses formulated by looking at modern gene distributions. Thus, if our hypothesis that the largely Palaeolithic origin of most extant mitochondrial haplotypes were correct, we would expect to find them in Palaeolithic remains. If, on the other hand, there are relatively few Palaeolithic mitochondrial haplotypes around nowadays, we would expect any sequences recovered from earlier Europeans to be comparatively rare in the modern population.

Well-preserved human Palaeolithic remains are few and far between and curators are naturally wary of allowing the destructive testing that ancient DNA recovery necessitates. We therefore developed a method of drilling into the dentine and pulp cavity of molar teeth from beneath the enamel cap while the tooth is still in the jaw. Filling the small entry hole with colour-matching cement minimised the visual impact of the extraction. We, in collaboration with Chris Stringer at the Natural History Museum, have done most work on the remarkably well-preserved 13,000-year-old mandible excavated from Gough's Cave in Somerset. Although contamination is always a problem there is enough DNA in the molar teeth in this young man to be fairly certain that the recovered sequences are genuine.

I cannot pretend we were not delighted when this sequence fell squarely into the centre of Group 1. This is direct proof that Group 1 was already present in Britain some 7000 years before agriculture arrived. Though this is, of course, only a single sample, it is completely at home among the majority of modern European mitochondrial haplotypes. Though there are elaborate scenarios that might yet make this consistent with demic diffusion, the simplest explanation is that the commonest European mitochondrial group, accounting for over 40% of the modern distribution, was well established in the Palaeolithic.

To summarise, we have good reasons to believe that the bulk of modern European mtDNA is of Palaeolithic origin. By extension its current distribution, though blurred by time and reinforced by relevant ancient DNA recoveries, does have something useful to say about the Palaeolithic. Perhaps its greatest strength is that the evidence is entirely independent and can be used legitimately to confirm or refute hypothetical models arrived at by other data, such as archaeological evidence.

As the field matures, however, I am optimistic that genetics will not only be used to test the ideas of others but also to discover new patterns and models of its own, which might stimulate a re-examination of existing archaeological models. As for the omnipotence of genetics and DNA I hope I have persuaded you, and the County Archaeological Unit who requested 'DNA tests' that genetics is not about to solve everything at a stroke and its application to the reconstruction of prehistory needs just as much imaginative interpretation as archaeology itself.

References

Ammerman, A J, and Cavalli-Sforza, L L, 1984 *The Neolithic transition and the genetics of populations in Europe*, Princeton

Cavalli-Sforza, L L, Menozzi, P, and Piazza, A, 1993 Demic expansions and human evolution, *Science* **259**, 639–46

Richards, M R, Corte-Real, H, Forster, P, Macaula, V, Wilkinson-Herbots, H, Demaine, A, Papiha, S, Hedges, R, Bandelt, H-J, and Sykes, B, 1996 Paleolithic and Neolithic lineages in the European mitochondrial gene pool, *Amer J Human Genet* **59**, 185–203

Sykes, B C, Leiboff, A, Low-Beer, J, Tetzner, S, and Richards, M, 1995 The origins of the Polynesians: an interpretation from mitochondrial lineage analysis, *Amer J Human Genet* **57**, 1463–75

5 The 'expensive tissue hypothesis' and the evolution of the human adaptive niche: a study in comparative anatomy

by Leslie C Aiello

Abstract

The reconstruction of human evolutionary history involves more than just the excavation of fossils, and of artefactual and contextual information preserved in the archaeological and palaeontological record. This information needs to be interpreted and tested against models that put it in a broader evolutionary framework. The 'expensive tissue hypothesis' is such a model. It argues that a high quality diet, based on animal products obtained either through hunting or scavenging, is a necessary concomitant of the relatively large human brain. Such a diet permits the digestive system to be relatively small and energetically cheap. This in turn releases the energetic constraints on the evolution of relatively large and energetically expensive brains. The 'expensive tissue hypothesis' also posits that such a high quality diet was fundamental in constraining many aspects of human biology and culture throughout prehistory. Arguments are presented which suggest that a high quality diet underlies the evolution of human life-history characteristics such as extended longevity, the menopause, and extended childhood. A high quality diet would also be at the root of the evolution of cultural features such as habitual food-sharing between mothers and offspring and between kin. It would also form the basis of inter-gender relationships, which include economic division of labour. On the basis of the arguments presented, a hypothetical reconstruction is offered for human lifestyle during the Early and Middle Pleistocene. Suggestions are also made for testing the hypotheses.

Introduction

When we think about advances in scientific archaeology that have been of particular relevance to the field of human evolution, we tend to think primarily of those methodological advances that have allowed us to glean more information from the sites, artefacts, and skeletal material that we excavate. Such advances include sophisticated methods of dating, and of palaeoenvironmental and dietary determination.

There is no doubt that this type of information has given us a much better and more detailed picture of who our early ancestors were, the environments they lived in, and what they ate. This information is not sufficient in itself, however, to build convincing models about human evolutionary history. For this goal it is desirable to adopt a broader interdisciplinary perspective designed to understand constraints that may have operated throughout human evolutionary history. Understanding constraints is important because it also allows us to begin to understand the anatomical and behavioural trade-offs that were possible for our early ancestors in various environments and at various periods throughout our evolutionary history. This in turn provides an insight into the evolutionary pressures that may have been important in our past.

This type of approach can be subsumed under the general heading of behavioural, or evolutionary, ecology. To date the majority of work in human behavioural ecology has focused on modern humans, and particularly on foraging societies, and has emphasised issues such as life history, subsistence strategies, mating ecology, spatial organisation, and patterns of cooperation and competition (Smith 1992a; 1992b). One point that has been repeatedly stressed in this work is the wide network of interrelated constraints and dependencies that is involved with any one of these particular issues. With a few notable exceptions (eg Foley 1988), human palaeontologists have been relatively slow to realise that the network of interdependencies allows us to construct hypotheses about those aspects of the lifestyles of our early ancestors that are not directly preserved in the fossil or archaeological records. It is also possible through this approach to construct models relevant to the broader adaptive niches of our early ancestors and the selective pressures that would have been important during the course of human evolutionary history.

It is the purpose of this paper to illustrate the potential of this type of approach for the interpretation of human evolutionary history. By so doing, I also wish to argue that human behavioural ecology, together with related fields such as comparative anatomy, physiology, and animal behaviour upon which it draws, are as important a part of scientific archaeology as the more traditional disciplines. Development of models based on these lines of evidence should be a central part of the agenda for the future development of scientific archaeology.

Where to begin?

I will begin with what is arguably the most characteristic human anatomical feature, our unusually large brains. In absolute terms average modern human brains are three times the average size of the brains of our closest living relatives, the chimpanzees (Fig 5.1). In relative terms, the average human brain is about five times the size that would be expected for an average mammal of our body size (encephalization quotient = 5.02, Ruff *et al* 1997). For comparison, the average chimpanzee brain is between 1.9 (*Pan troglodytes schweinfurthii* ♂) and 1.6 (*Pan troglodytes troglodytes* ♀) the size that would be expected for an average mammal of similar body size (Kappelman 1996).

The human adaptive niche is dependent on this large relative brain size, but not in the way one might think. Although the advantages of a large brain and associated cognitive abilities are generally emphasised in the literature, we can learn much more about the evolution of our adaptive niche by looking at the disadvantages, or costs, of our large brains. The brain is a metabolically very expensive organ. Brain tissue has over 22 times the mass-specific metabolic rate of skeletal muscle (brain = 11.2w kg^{-1}, skeletal muscle = 0.5w kg^{-1}; Aschoff *et al* 1971). The average human brain is about 1kg larger than would be expected for an average mammal of our body size (65kg) and the metabolic cost of this brain would be just under five times that of the brain of the average mammal (humans = 14.6 watts, average mammal of human body size = 3.0 watts; Aiello and Wheeler 1995). The 'expensive tissue hypothesis' posits that the necessity of providing for this high energetic cost has constrained and guided hominin[1] lifestyle throughout prehistory.

The relationship between relatively large brains and their high energetic costs has been frequently discussed in the literature (Armstrong 1982; 1983; 1985a; 1985b;

1990; Hofman 1983; Leonard and Robertson 1992; 1994; 1996; Martin 1981; 1983; 1996). The general interpretation has been that large brains require high quality food to provide sufficient energy to fuel them (Leonard and Robertson 1992; 1994; 1996). In the course of human evolution we might then expect to see major changes in diet accompanying the major increases in relative brain size.

Some authors have also hypothesised that high quality food, and particularly the act of obtaining high quality food, would also select for large brains. This might either be through the relatively complicated strategies needed for extracting or obtaining high-quality foodstuffs (Gibson 1986; Parker and Gibson 1979), or through the need for a more sophisticated mental map for the location and exploitation of widely spread high quality food resources (Clutton-Brock and Harvey 1980; Milton 1979; 1981).

Diet could therefore be interpreted as both a factor selecting for increase in relative brain size and a necessary requirement for the maintenance of relatively large and energetically expensive brains (Aiello 1997). This line of reasoning would fit comfortably with the transition to a diet based on more animal products in *Homo erectus* in relation to the earlier australopithecines (Aiello 1996a; 1996b) and may also be relevant to the introduction of cooked food more recently in the evolutionary record (Aiello and Wheeler 1995). The increased energy requirement of the relatively large brain would thereby be fundamental in constraining the type of diet and general lifestyle that could have been adopted by our early ancestors.

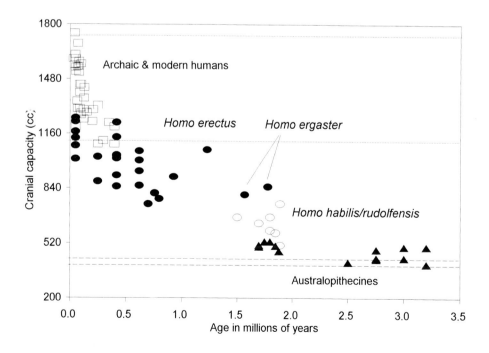

Fig 5.1 The increase in absolute hominoid cranial capacity over time. Brain sizes from Aiello and Dean (1990) and ages (except for the Ngandong Homo erectus*) from Aiello and Dunbar (1993): dashed lines represent ± 2 standard deviations from the mean chimpanzee cranial capacity (400cc); dotted lines represent 2 standard deviations above the average human male cranial capacity (1467cc) and 2 standard deviations below the average human female cranial capacity (1299cc); data for chimpanzee cranial capacities from Ashton and Spence (1958) and for modern human cranial capacities from Martin (1986)*

The 'expensive tissue hypothesis'

There is, however, one serious problem with this argument. In humans, even though our brains are over a kilogram larger than would be expected for an average mammal of our body mass, we have the basal metabolic rate (BMR) that would be expected for that average mammal (Aiello and Wheeler 1995; Leonard and Robertson 1994; Martin 1996). There is, therefore, no evidence in humans for the increased energy that is needed to support our relatively very large brains.

This discrepancy is also true in other mammals. Various analyses of the relationship of relative brain size to relative BMR in placental mammals have shown either no significant correlation (McNab and Eisenberg 1989) or an extremely weak correlation (Martin, personal communication 1997) between these factors. Furthermore, Martin (1996) has also pointed out that the variance in relative brain size in placental mammals is much greater than that in relative BMR. The lack of apparent association between relative brain size and relative BMR brings into doubt whether our relatively large brain, and its metabolic requirements, are really fundamental constraining factors on the human adaptive niche.

The 'expensive tissue hypothesis' (Aiello 1997; Aiello and Wheeler 1995; Wheeler and Aiello 1996) offers an answer to the apparent paradox of how adult humans can have relatively large brains without also having the relatively high BMR that this would seem to require. The basic point is that the brain cannot be studied in isolation. It is not the only energetically expensive tissue in the body. As a result, the relationship between diet and energy requirements of the brain cannot be explained without also taking into consideration the total energy requirements of the body and specifically the energy requirements of the other energetically expensive tissues.

In addition to the brain, there are four other expensive tissues in the body: the heart, the kidneys, the liver, and the gastrointestinal tract (Aiello and Wheeler 1995). Together, the metabolic requirements of these five organs in humans make up just under 70% of the total BMR of the human body even though they account for just under 7% of total body mass (Fig 5.2). The expensive tissue hypothesis posits that the way in which humans can maintain relatively large brains without also having relatively high BMRs is simply by reducing the size (and thereby the metabolic cost) of one or more of these other expensive tissues.

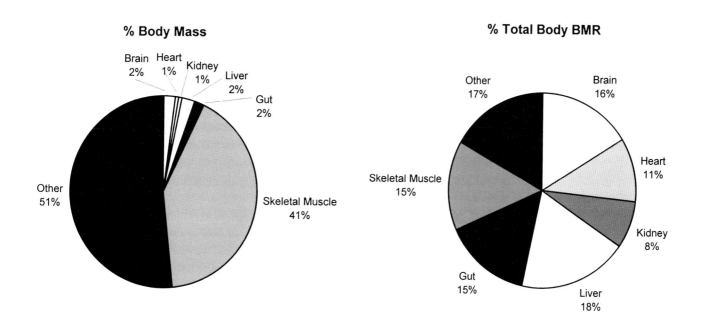

Fig 5.2 Percentage body mass and percentage of total body basal metabolic rate (BMR) for each of the expensive tissues in a reference modern human male (65kg); data from Aiello and Wheeler (1995)

When the observed mass of each of the five 'expensive tissues' in an average human (65kg) is compared with the expected mass for each of these organs in an average primate of human body mass the results are quite startling (Aiello and Wheeler 1995) (Fig 5.3). The combined mass of the metabolically expensive tissues for the reference adult human is very close to that expected for the average primate of human body size. For the individual organs, human hearts, kidneys, and livers are just about as heavy as would be expected in an average primate of our body mass. The mass of the splanchnic organs (the liver and the gastro-intestinal tract) is approximately 900g less than expected. Almost all of this shortfall is due to a reduction in the gastrointestinal tract (780g), the total mass of which is only about 60% of that expected for a similar-sized primate. The increase in mass of the relatively large human brain (850g larger than would be expected) is more than compensated for by the reduction in the size of the splanchnic organs and, particularly, the gastrointestinal tract. Because the mass specific metabolic rates of the brain and the splanchnic organs are virtually the same, the metabolic costs of the relatively large human brain are balanced by the reduced metabolic costs of the relatively smaller splanchnic organs, and particularly the gastrointestinal tract.

The answer to the question of how humans can energetically afford to have relatively large brains lies with the identification of the factors that allow us to have relatively small gastrointestinal tracts. Although the size of the gastrointestinal tract is related to body size, both the size and proportions of the tract are also strongly influenced by diet (Chivers and Haldik 1980; 1984; MacLarnon *et al* 1986a; 1986b; Martin 1990; Martin *et al* 1985). Gut size is associated with both the bulk and the digestibility of food (Milton 1986; 1993; Milton and Demment 1988). In primates and other mammals, diets that are characterised by smaller amounts of food of high digestibility, such as animal products, require relatively smaller guts than do diets characterised by larger quantities of food of low digestibility. This suggests that the association between diet quality and relative brain size is really a relationship between relative brain size and relative gut size, the latter being determined by dietary quality (Aiello and Wheeler 1995).

On this basis, a high quality diet would release the constraints on encephalisation. It would relax the metabolic constraints on a relatively large brain by permitting a relatively smaller gut and thereby balance the considerable metabolic cost of brain (Aiello and Wheeler 1995). In this sense a high quality diet would be a 'prime releaser' for the evolution of the human brain and would be a fundamental feature of the human adaptive niche.

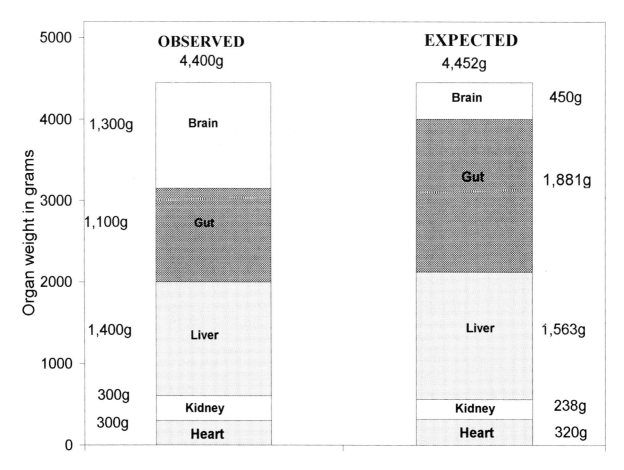

Fig 5.3 The observed and expected organ mass for a reference 65kg human (after Aiello and Wheeler 1995)

Ontogeny, diet, and the evolution of the human adaptive niche

In what ways does a high quality diet put constraints on human adaptation and on the human adaptive niche? One way to approach this question is by focusing not only on adult humans but also on the young. The metabolic requirements of a relatively large brain are not confined to the adult. They are also highly important during growth and development. Martin (1981; 1983; 1996) has repeatedly stressed that the energetic costs of brain growth must be borne by the mother both *in utero* and during the post-natal period before weaning. For example, Foley and Lee (1991) calculate that up to the age of 18 months, human infants are just under 9% more energetically costly than chimpanzee infants. This is due entirely to the increased level of encephalization in human infants over chimpanzee infants. A higher quality diet along with increased foraging efficiency in the hominins would be consistent with these increased energy requirements (Foley and Lee 1991; Leonard and Robertson 1992). Foley and Lee (ibid) stress that changes in life-history parameters could also be effective. In particular, slowing growth and extending the period of lactation would spread the increased energy requirement over a longer period of time, thereby reducing the daily energy requirements of the mother.

The relationship between the energy requirements for the growth of the encephalized human brain and a high quality diet is likely also to have had additional profound implications for hominin life-history and social behaviour and, therefore, for the human niche. These would include biological features as fundamental to humans as the menopause and extended longevity, a relatively late age at maturity, the small size of the human infant at weaning and the documented relatively high level of human fertility in relation to the apes (Hawkes *et al* 1997). They also would be expected to encompass changes in gender relationships that would include an economic division of labour (Key and Aiello forthcoming; Power and Aiello 1997).

The basic point underlying these implications is that the high quality diet presupposed by the expensive tissue hypothesis is not immediately and directly accessible to weanlings (Hawkes *et al* 1997a; 1997b; forthcoming). In non-human primates, weanlings and juveniles tend to forage for themselves and therefore both they and their mothers are limited to resources that can be obtained without undue skill or learning. A high quality diet that included significant amounts of animal products would require regular provisioning of the weanling. This situation would imply a significant amount of mother–infant food sharing, as well as increased maternal investment to train the infant to obtain the food resource.

In essence this practice would amount to an extra-somatic form of nursing as it would extend maternal investment in the offspring significantly past the weaning period.

This implication would also herald a major change in human lifestyle in relation to earlier hominins and to our non-human primate relatives. It would open up the opportunity for kin other than the mother to also provision the weanling as well and thereby enhance their own reproductive fitness by contributing to the weanling's chances of survival.

In the Hadza, who are modern-day hunters and gatherers from Tanzania, it has been demonstrated that senior post-menopausal women can significantly affect the nutritional status of their grandchildren by helping their daughters provision these children (Hawkes *et al* forthcoming). This has led Hawkes and her co-workers (Hawkes *et al* 1997a; 1997b; forthcoming) to argue that if senior females could increase the fecundity of junior female kin enough to more than offset their own age-related reduced fecundity there would be a clear fitness benefit to menopause and an extended, post-reproductive lifespan. Genes for longevity would be selected because those females with surviving mothers who helped to provision them and their offspring would be under less energetic stress than females without surviving kin. The offspring would be expected to have a better chance of survival and could be weaned at a younger age, allowing mothers to have a shorter inter-birth interval and consequently an increased reproductive output. Furthermore, an increase in lifespan is associated with a reduction in growth rates across primates and this would result in a longer actual time to maturity (Hawkes *et al* forthcoming), thereby setting the stage for an increase in learned (cultural) behaviour.

This 'grandmothering' hypothesis is consistent with the results of computer simulations based on the prisoners' dilemma model (Key and Aiello forthcoming), which suggests that high energetic costs of reproduction are crucial in determining patterns of cooperation within groups. In particular, when female reproductive costs are high in relation to those of the male, greater cooperation between co-resident females in a group would be expected. This model, however, also predicts increased cooperation between the sexes (Key and Aiello forthcoming). This situation would imply that the evolution of paternal investment in the young through provisioning of both mother and offspring (and by extension the evolution of human family structure and an economic division of labour) would also appear as a necessary correlate of the energetic requirements of increased encephalization in hominin evolution.

Hawkes and her co-workers argue that large animal hunting by males is an unreliable strategy for feeding

dependent offspring, particularly in the type of savannah environment suggested for early humans (Hawkes
1993; Hawkes *et al* 1991). They stress that hunting cannot cover the day-to-day nutritional requirements of
weaned offspring and conclude that 'the assumption
that nuclear families are fundamental *economic* units
among modern human foragers, let alone ancestral
hominins, is due for revision' (Hawkes *et al* 1997b). The
implication would be that modern human males hunt
primarily for prestige value in the context of mating
effort (ensuring mating opportunities) or alliance formation.

This interpretation appears to be highly context specific, however. For example, evidence from another
modern human foraging group, the Ache of eastern
Paraguay, indicate that men contribute greater that 85%
of the total caloric intake of the group (Hill *et al* 1987).
Among the Ache there was also no significant relationship between survivorship of juveniles or fertility of
females and surviving post-menopausal grandmothers
or mothers (Hawkes *et al* 1997b).

In the context of the expensive tissue hypothesis and
its relation to the evolution of the hominin niche, the
important point is that a high quality diet would put the
mother under increased reproductive stress. It not only
would give female kin the opportunity to enhance their
own reproductive fitness by provisioning their daughter's offspring, but it would also provide the mother with
a strong incentive to encourage provisioning from others
in the group who would not necessarily have a strong
incentive to do so.

It has been frequently pointed out that male and
female reproductive strategies are fundamentally different and potentially conflicting (Trivers 1972). Whereas
females are limited in the number of children they can
conceive, bear and raise to maturity, males are only limited by the number of available females they can insem-
inate. With increasing reproductive stress brought on by
the necessity for a high quality diet, female reproductive
fitness would be considerably reduced by the increased
investment in time and resources that each infant would
imply. There is no doubt that grandmothering would be
an important mechanism by which this stress could be
reduced. One problem, however, is that in the early
stages of hominin evolution few females would have
grandmothers to help to provision their offspring.

One major reason for the absence of older females
would be an inferred high level of adult, and particularly
young adult, mortality. Although there is insufficient
evidence from the earlier periods of human evolution to
directly document mortality levels, we do know that in
the Neandertal and pre-Neandertal periods the level of
mortality was such that few individuals lived past 40 or
50 years of age (Bermúdez de Castro and Nicolás 1997;

Trinkaus 1995; Wolpoff 1979). Mortality evidence from
chimpanzees in the wild also suggests that this high level
of adult mortality may have been characteristic of the
ancestral pattern (Goodall 1986; Nishida *et al* 1990). A
second factor related to the absence of older females
could have been an ancestral tendency toward female
natal dispersal, a pattern that is primitive in the African
ape and human clade (Rodseth *et al* 1991; Wrangham
1987). If in early hominins mature females left the social
unit of their birth for another, there would be little
opportunity for senior female kin to provision younger
females and juveniles.

Under both of these conditions – high adult mortality and female natal dispersal – hominin mothers may
well have had a strong incentive to encourage provisioning from other members of the group and particularly
from males. It is interesting to note that one aspect of
human female physiology may serve just this purpose.
Human females do not have an oestrus period but rather
are characterised by concealed ovulation and continuous
sexual receptivity. Because there is no obvious clue to
particular fertile periods, there would be considerable
male uncertainty over fertilization success (Alexander
and Noonan 1979; Power and Aiello 1997). This would
be expected to lead to longer courtships thereby reducing the time a male would have to mate with others.
Reproductive seasonality would further constrain the
male (Power *et al* 1997). If all of the females were fertile
during the same season of the year, there would be
severely reduced philandering opportunities. The reason
for this is that once a male's partner is impregnated, no
other cycling females would be available until the following season. Seasonality and concealed ovulation would
together also encourage larger numbers of males in the
group. This is because high-ranking males could not
monopolise multiple females during the extended
'courtships' implied by these factors.

In primate societies, birth seasonality has been
demonstrated to undermine both the correlation
between male dominance and mating success
(Cowlishaw and Dunbar 1991) and to improve levels of
investment and attentiveness by males (Dunbar 1988;
Ridley 1986). Seasonality of birth has also been
reported in many human populations (see Bronson
1995 and Lam and Miron 1991 for reviews). In these
human populations there is a marked correlation
between rainfall and food supply and seasonal variation
in conception rate (Bailey *et al* 1992; Ellison *et al* 1993;
Leslie and Fry 1989). On the basis that nutritional status has a direct effect on ovarian function and fecundity
we might expect that during the course of human evolution there would be an increase in seasonality of birth
that correlated with the increase in energetic stress experienced by the female (Power *et al* 1997). This increased

energetic stress would result not only from the increasingly seasonal environment in eastern Africa during the Pliocene–Pleistocene (Foley 1993) but also from the energetic challenge experienced by the female resulting from the necessity to maintain a high quality diet for herself and her dependent offspring.

The male investment implied by concealed ovulation and reproductive seasonality would be in the context of mating effort – assuring successful fertilization of a female – rather than direct paternal investment in the young. It would be analogous to the mating effort observed in male bonobos, where males will give food to females immediately after, or even during intercourse (de Waal 1987; Kuroda 1984, 301–24). However, there is also evidence from non-human primates that the categories of mating effort and paternal investment in offspring sometimes blur. For example, subordinate males in baboon harem groups often form special friendships with females, helping them in the care and protection of offspring in the expectation of future matings (Smuts 1985).

Social and evolutionary implications of the expensive tissue hypothesis

The basic arguments for increased co-operation and food sharing, both through grandmothering and male investment, are unavoidable implications of the expensive tissue hypothesis and the high- quality diet it implies. They are based on the specific fact that a high quality diet imposes an increased energetic load on early hominin mothers. Long-term male investment in a single female and her offspring beyond the period of mating effort, however, is not necessarily implied by the arguments given so far. Such long-term investment would be directly dependent on both a very high level of infant mortality and a correspondingly high level of paternity certainty. If an infant had a high probability of dying without the protection or provisioning of its father, then it would not pay the male to seek new mating opportunities after fertilisation was assured. His best strategy would be to remain with the mother and infant and assure the survival of that infant.

One possible source of increased infant mortality would be a heightened risk of infanticide by the female's consort during her next fertile period. This would be expected to be an increased danger in hominins because the weaning (the previous infant) would still require resources from the females in the form of provisioning and training. This would theoretically take away from investment in the current infant. More important might be the increased infant mortality directly associated with the high-quality diet. If the mother was carrying out

hunting and/or scavenging for animal products she would be covering larger geographical areas than if she confined herself to gathering vegetable foods (Leonard and Robertson 1994; 1996; 1997). Her field metabolic rate would be increased, which would jeopardise the energy she could provide to a nursing infant. Furthermore, she would be exposing either a nursing infant or a weanling to greater danger from accidental death, especially from non-human competition for any carcasses. Even with grandmothering or other female involvement in shared infant care, there would still be an increased mortality danger.

Whether these increased dangers in relation to infant mortality would tip the balance towards male long-term fidelity would be dependent on whether the mother and any other female help available to her could successfully provision young in the absence of male help. Being able to do so would be dependent on the nature of the food supply and on the prevailing ecological conditions. One thing would be clear, however. Until there was significant incentive for male fidelity and paternal care, there could not be any significant economic division of labour between the sexes. There would be simply no incentive to the male in terms of his own reproductive fitness to remain with a female and enter into a specialised food-sharing relationship with her. Furthermore, the transmission of technical skill, involving both tool-making and hunting expertise, would necessarily pass down the generations through the females rather than the males (Shennan and Steele forthcoming). In much the same way, as it is the female house cat that teaches her litter how to hunt when the tom is long gone on his search for other females, it would be the hominin female who had the incentive to ensure that her offspring were well tutored in the required subsistence skills necessary for survival.

The question is when in human evolution did the social organisation of our ancestors assume a form that involved significant male fidelity, paternal investment, and economic division of labour? Returning to the pattern of increase in human brain size through human evolution (Fig 5.1), the first major increase in brain size occurs with the appearance of early *Homo* sometime around two million years ago. It has been previously argued that this is the period when a high-quality diet involving significant quantities of animal-based food would have been adopted by early hominins (Aiello 1997; Aiello and Wheeler 1995; see also Foley and Lee 1991; Leonard and Robertson 1992; 1994). At this stage, the necessity to provision the weanling would have provided the incentive for older female kin to provision younger female kin and their offspring, ultimately resulting in the fundamental human life-history features of increased longevity, the menopause, and slower growth rates. Furthermore, if the ancestral social pattern had been one of female natal dispersal, there would also have been a strong incentive at this stage to reverse this pattern to one where female kin became the stable core of the society. This would be driven simply by the increased fitness benefits to the older female of curtailing her own reproduction in order to increase the successful reproductive output of her daughters.

There is some evidence from the fossil record that hominin growth and development during this period were more similar to modern humans than to the inferred, more ape-like condition of the early australopithecines (Aiello 1996a; 1996b; Power and Aiello 1997; Smith 1993; Shipman and Walker 1989). This may imply that grandmothering behaviour was already in place at this stage (Hawkes *et al* 1997b). There would also be a clear fitness benefit to those females who succeeded in attracting sustained mating effort from males. Increasing environmental seasonality together with the occupation of more open savannah environments during this period of hominin evolution would have placed the hominin female under an increasing energetic challenge, which would have affected her fecundity. These conditions would have provided a strong impetus for the evolution of concealed ovulation.

How much long-term male fidelity and paternal investment in the offspring was present at this stage is unknown. It is clear, however, that pressures in this direction would have already been in existence. Not only would there have been the previously mentioned increased probability of infant mortality but also the infant would have been born at a more altricial (helpless) stage of development (Shipman and Walker 1989) and be dependent and vulnerable for a longer period of time. It is possible, however, that the incentives driving sustained male investment at this stage of hominin evolution would not yet be overriding. In addition to the benefits of grandmothering, Power and Aiello (1997) have argued that the marked increase in female body size that occurred with the appearance of *Homo ergaster* could have helped to offset, at least in part, the increased energetic costs of the first phase of brain expansion.

Another feature that may also have been important was the development of the considerable fat stores that are characteristic of human females. One function of these fat stores would be to subsidise the energetic costs of lactation, particularly during periods of relative food shortage (Prentice and Whitehead 1987). Furthermore, concealed ovulation itself may have offered some insurance against heightened infant mortality by reducing the level of paternal certainty (Hrdy 1981).

Diet and the evolution of cooperation in during the Early and Middle Pleistocene

Based on this line of reasoning, one hypothesis would view hominin lifestyle during the Early and Middle Pleistocene periods as primarily matrifocal. It would imply that there was little direct investment by males in either the nutritional well-being or technical 'education' of his offspring. Because the male would have little incentive, in terms of his reproductive fitness, to engage in long-term fidelity and/or paternal investment in the offspring, tool-making and hunting skills would necessarily pass through the female line. Much as bonobo mothers patiently develop nut-cracking skills in their offspring over an extended period of time (Boesch 1993), hominin mothers in the Middle Pleistocene Period may well have been responsible for the transference of hunting and scavenging skills as well as the Acheulian tool technology. Furthermore, if this were the case it would imply that during the Early and Middle Pleistocene there would be little or no division of labour between the sexes in food acquisition techniques. If the female was the primary tutor, it is logical to assume that the same suite of techniques would be passed to both male and female offspring.

In the fossil record for hominin evolution there is no direct evidence that might be attributed to division of labour until relatively recently in time. For example, differences in cortical thickness and robusticity in Neandertal arm bones dating from the Late Pleistocene (Ben-Itzhak *et al* 1988) might suggest a difference in arm usage between male and female Neandertals. This difference would be consistent with increased male strength in the right arm and its implications for spear throwing and hence hunting behaviour. There is no doubt that a better fossil and archaeological record is needed to directly inform us about gender differences in subsistence behaviour. One clue that we do have, however, may be important in this context. From the first appearance of *Homo ergaster* approximately 1.8 million years ago, there is no significant increase in hominin brain size until the second half of the Middle Pleistocene Period (Fig 5.1). Absolute and relative brain size during this period were both approximately two-thirds of that found in modern humans. The marked increase in brain size occurring after 500,000 years ago would have put both females and juveniles under increased energetic stress. The implications for increased infant mortality could have provided increased incentive for fidelity in the males.

It is interesting that at this stage we see the first definite evidence of large game hunting in the archaeological record. Both Boxgrove and Schöningen (Thieme 1997) suggest that by 500,000 to 400,000 years ago, hominins were engaging in specialised hunting that would have been as unpredictable, and most probably considerably more dangerous to the hunter, than hunting observed in the Hadza. This may be our first sign of specialised division of labour between the sexes. If, as in the Hadza, hunting was a prestigious but unreliable source of calories, the male hunter would be in need of provisioning himself to sustain a hunting speciality. The incentive to the female of food-sharing with a successful male hunter would be to ensure continued mating effort as well as paternal investment from him in the form of both meat and 'training' in hunting skills for the offspring. It is not hard to envision that under these circumstances success in hunting would become an important component in success in reproduction, and that the transference of these skills to male offspring would greatly enhance the reproductive fitness of the hunter.

Conclusions

The arguments presented here suggest that the expansion of the human brain is fundamental to the definition of the human adaptive niche. Many of the biological and social features found in humans can be directly connected to the high quality diet that is presupposed by the expensive tissue hypothesis. These features include life-history characteristics such as extended longevity, the menopause, and extended childhood. They also include cultural attributes such as habitual food-sharing between mothers and offspring and between kin as well as gender relationships based on an economic division of labour. The key to this network of dependencies is the fact that the energetic requirements of a relatively large brain are not confined to the adult. The costs of brain growth must be borne by the mother *in utero*, during lactation, and during the post weaning juvenile period. These increased costs and their effect on both female and male reproductive fitness provide the basis for a model of human lifestyle during the Early and Middle Pleistocene that suggests a fundamental matrifocal society characterised by limited economic division of labour between the sexes. A further implication is that the Acheulian and other stone tool traditions of this period, along with their inherent hunting and/or scavenging strategies, were transmitted down the generations through the female line.

This hypothesis is based on the principles of evolutionary ecology and draws on inferences from comparative anatomy, physiology, and animal behaviour. Although it is consistent with what is currently known about the fossil record for human evolution, it needs to be tested against data which for the most part do not currently exist. An agenda for the future in scientific archaeology would be to develop the methodologies to provide such data. This might involve the development and refinement of techniques for accurately ageing and sexing fossil hominins, for determining developmental rates, for inferring functional capabilities at a level that would differentiate between sexes and age categories, and for directly inferring diet and energy requirements of the hominins. It would also include support for continued excavation of Pleistocene archaeological sites and for the development of new methodologies for the analysis of the activity patterns preserved at sites in the variety of habitats occupied by the hominins as they spread out of Africa.

Models such as the 'expensive tissue hypothesis' provide a means of contextualising the material remains left by our ancestors and suggesting answers to questions of 'how' and 'why' in human evolution. If they are to become anything more than interesting intellectual exercises, however, they need to be tested against the material evidence preserved in archaeological sites. The challenge for scientific archaeology in the future is to provide the quality of evidence needed to test hypotheses derived from models such as these.

Acknowledgements

I would like to thank Peter Wheeler of the Liverpool John Moores University who has collaborated with me over the past few years on the development of many of the ideas presented in this paper. I would also like to thank the following for discussion, criticism, and collaboration: Robin Dunbar, Rob Foley, Kathleen Gibson, Catherine Key, Dan Nettle, Camilla Power, Stephen Shennan, Alan Walker (who coined the phrase 'the expensive tissue hypothesis'), and Bernard Wood. Finally, I would like to thank Clive Gamble for inviting me to present this paper at the 'Science in Archaeology' conference and Justine Bayley for being an understanding editor.

Note

1 According to recent taxonomic practice, 'hominin' is used here in preference to 'hominid' to refer to all members of the human line since it separation from that leading to the African apes.

References

Aiello, L C, 1996a Hominine preadaptations for language and cognition, in *Modelling the early human mind* (eds P Mellars and K Gibson), McDonald Institute Monogr, 89–99, Cambridge

—, 1996b Terrestriality, bipedalism and the origin of language, *Pro Brit Acad*, **88**, 269–89

—, 1997 Brains and guts in human evolution: the expensive tissue hypothesis, *Braz J Genet*, **20**, 141–8

Aiello, L C, and Dean, M C, 1990 *An introduction to human evolutionary anatomy*, London

Aiello, L C, and Dunbar, R I M, 1993 Neocortex size, group size, and the evolution of language, *Curr Anthropol*, **34**, 184–93

Aiello, L C, and Wheeler, P, 1995 The Expensive Tissue Hypothesis: the brain and the digestive system in human and primate evolution, *Curr Anthropol*, **36**, 199–221

Alexander, R D, and Noonan, K M, 1979 Concealment of ovulation, parental care, and human social evolution, in *Evolutionary biology and human social behaviour* (eds N Changon and W Irons), 436–53

Armstrong, E, 1982 A look at relative brain sizes in mammals, *Neurosci Lett*, **34**, 101–4

—, 1983 Brain size and metabolism in mammals, *Science*, **220**, 1302–4

—, 1985a Relative brain size in monkeys and prosimians, *Amer J Phys Anthropol*, **66**, 263–73

—, 1985b Allometric considerations of the adult mammalian brain, with special emphasis on primates, in *Size and scaling in primate biology* (ed W L Jungers), 115–46, New York

—, 1990 Brains, bodies, and metabolism, *Brain, Behaviour, and Evolution*, **36**, 166–76

Aschoff, J, Günther, B, and Kramer, K, 1971 *Energiehaushalt und Temperaturregulation*, Munich

Ashton, E H, and Spence, T F, 1958 Age changes in the cranial capacity and foramen magnum of hominoids, *Proc Zool Soc London*, **130**, 169–81

Bailey, R C, Jenike, M R, Ellison, P T, Bentley, G R, Harrigan, A M, and Peacock, N R, 1992 The ecology of birth seasonality among agriculturalists in Central Africa, *J Biosocial Sci*, **24**, 393–412

Ben-Itzhak, S, Smith, P, and Bloom, R, 1988, Radiographic study of the humerus in Neanderthals and *Homo sapiens sapiens*, *Amer J Phys Anthropol*, **77**, 231–42

Bermúdez de Castro, J M, and Nicolás, M E, 1997 Palaeodemography of the Atapuerca-SH hominid Middle Pleistocene sample, *J Human Evol*, **33**, 333–55

Boesch, C, 1993 Aspects of transmission of tool-use in wild chimpanzees, in *Tools, language, and cognition in human evolution* (eds K R Gibson and T Ingold), 171–83, Cambridge

Bronson, F H, 1995 Seasonal variation in human reproduction: environmental factors, *Quart Rev Biol*, **70**, 141–64

Chivers, D J, and Haldik, C M, 1980 Morphology of the gastrointestinal tract in primates: comparisons with other mammals in relation to diet, *J Morphol*, **166**, 337–86

—, 1984, Diet and gut morphology in primates, in *Food acquisition and processing in primates* (eds D J Chivers, B A Wood, and A Bilsborough), 213–30, New York

Clutton-Brock, T H, and Harvey, P H, 1980 Primates, brains, and ecology, *J Zool, London*, **190**, 309–23

Cowlishaw, G, and Dunbar, R I M, 1991 Dominance rank and mating success in male primates, *Animal Behaviour*, **41**, 1045–56

de Waal, F M B, 1987 Tension regulation and nonreproductive functions of sex among captive bonobos, *Nat Geogr Res*, **3**, 318–35

Dunbar, R I M, 1988 *Primate social systems*, London

Ellison, P T, Panter-Brick, C, Lipson, S, and O'Rourke, M T, 1993 The ecological context of human ovarian function, *Human Reproduction*, **8**, 2248–58

Foley, R A, 1988 *Another unique species: patterns in human evolutionary ecology*, Harlow

Foley, R A, 1993 The influence of seasonality on hominid evolution, in *Seasonality and human ecology* (eds S J Ulijaszek and S S Strickland), 15–64, Cambridge

Foley, R A, and Lee, P C, 1991 Ecology and energetics of encephalization in hominid evolution, *Phil Trans Roy Soc, London*, ser B, **334**, 223–32

Gibson, K R, 1986 Cognition, brain size and the extraction of embedded food resources, in *Primate ontogeny, cognition, and social behaviour* (eds J G Else and P C Lee), 93–105, Cambridge

Goodall, J, 1986 *The chimpanzees of Gombe*, Cambridge, MA

Hawkes, K, 1993 Why hunter-gatherers work; an ancient version of the problem of public goods, *Curr Anthropol*, **34**, 341–61

Hawkes, K, O'Connell, J F, and Blurton Jones, N G, 1991 Hunting income patterns among the Hadza: big game, common goods, foraging goals, and the evolution of the human diet. *Phil Trans Roy Soc*, ser B, **334**, 243–51

Hawkes, K, O'Connell, J F, and Rogers, L, 1997a The behavioural ecology of modern hunter-gatherers, and human evolution, *Trends in Ecol and Evol*, **12**, 29–32

Hawkes, K, O'Connell, J F, and Blurton Jones, N G, 1997b Hadza women's time allocation, offspring provisioning, and the evolution of long post-menopausal lifespans, *Curr Anthropol*, **38**, 551–77

Hawkes, K, O'Connell, J F, Blurton Jones, N G, Alvarez, H, and Charnov, E L, forthcoming Grandmothering and the evolution of human life histories

Hill, K, Hawkes, K, Kaplan, H, and Hurtado, A M, 1987 Foraging decisions among Ache hunter-gatherers: new data and implicatons for optimal foraging models, *Ethol and Sociobiol*, **8**, 1–36

Hofman, M A, 1983 Energy metabolism, brain size and longevity in mammals, *Quart Rev Biol*, **58**, 495–512

Hrdy, S B, 1981 *The woman that never evolved*, Cambridge, MA

Kappelman, J, 1996 The evolution of body mass and relative brain size in fossil hominids *J Human Evol*, **30**, 243–76

Key, C, and Aiello, L C, forthcoming A prisoner's dilemma model of the evolution of paternal care, *Folia Primatologia*

Kuroda, S, 1984 Interactions over food among pygmy chimpanzees, in *The pygmy chimpanzee* (ed R Susman), New York, 301–24

Lam, D A, and Miron, J A, 1991 Seasonality of births in human populations, *Social Biol*, **38**, 51–78

Leslie, P W, and Fry, P H, 1989 Extreme seasonality of births among Turkana pastoralists, *Amer J Phys Anthropol*, **79**, 103–15

Leonard, W R, and Robertson, M L, 1992 Nutritional requirements and human evolution: a bioenergetics model, *Amer J Human Biol*, **4**, 179–95

—, 1994 Evolutionary perspectives on human nutrition: the influence of brain and body size on diet and metabolism, *Amer J Human Biol*, **6**, 77–88

—, 1996 On diet, energy metabolism, and brain size in human evolution, *Curr Anthropol*, **37**, 125–8

—, 1997 Comparative primte energetics and hominid evolution, *Amer J Phys Anthropol*, **102**, 265–81

MacLarnon, A M, Chivers, D J, and Martin, R D, 1986a Gastro-intestinal allometry in primates including new species, in *Primate ecology and conservation* (eds J G Else and P C Lee), 75–85, Cambridge

MacLarnon, A M, Martin, R D, Chivers, D J, and Haldik, C M, 1986b Some aspects of gastro-intestinal allometry in primates and other mammals, in Sakka 1986, 293–302

MacNab, B K, and Eisenberg, J E, 1989 Brain size and its relation to the rate of metabolism in mammals, *Amer Naturalist*, **133**, 157–67

Martin, R D, 1981 Relative brain size and metabolic rate in terrestrial vertebrates, *Nature*, **393**, 57–60

—, 1983 *Human brain evolution in an ecological context*, 52nd James Arthur lecture on the evolution of the human brain, New York

—, 1986, Ontogenetic and phylogenetic aspects of human brain size, in Sakka 1986, 325–41

—, 1990 *Primate origins and evolution*, London

—, 1996 Scaling of the mammalian brain: the maternal energy hypothesis, *News Physiol Sci*, **11**, 149–56

Martin, R D, Chivers, D J, MacLarnon, A M, and Haldik, C M, 1985 Gastrointestinal allometry in primates and other mammals, in *Size and scaling in primate biology* (ed W L Jungers), 61–89, New York

Milton, K, 1979 Spatial and temporal patterns of plant foods in tropical forests as a stimulus to intellectual development in primates, *Amer J Phys Anthropol*, **50**, 464–5 abstract

—, 1981 Diversity of plant foods in tropical forests as a stimulus to mental development in primates, *Amer Anthropol*, **83**, 534–48

—, 1986 Digestive physiology in primates, *News Physiol Sci*, **1**, 76–9

—, 1993 Diet and primate evolution, *Sci Amer*, **269**, 86–93

Milton, K, and Demment, M W, 1988 Digestion and passage kinetics of chimpanzees fed high and low fibre diets and comparison with human data, *J Nutrition*, **118**, 1082–8

Nishida, T, Takasaki, H, and Takahata, Y, 1990 Demography and reproductive profiles, in *The chimpanzees of the Mahale Mountains* (ed T Nishida), 63–97, Toyko

Parker, S T, and Gibson, K R, 1979 A developmental model for the evolution of language and intelligence in early hominids, *Behaviour and Brain Sci*, **2**, 367–407

Power, C, and Aiello, L C, 1997 Female proto-symbolic strategies, in *Women in paleoanthropology* (ed L Hager), 153–71, London

Power, C, Arthur, C, and Aiello, L C, 1997 Seasonal reproductive synchrony as an evolutionary stable strategy in human evolution, *Curr Anthropol*, **38**, 88–91

Prentice, A M, and Whitehead, R G, 1987 The energetics of human reproduction, *Symposia of the Zoological Society of London*, **57**, 275–304

Ridley, M, 1986 The number of males in a primate troop, *Animal Behaviour*, **34**, 1848-58

Rodseth, L, Wrangham, R W, Harrigan, A M, and Smuts, B B 1991 The human community as primate society, *Curr Anthropol*, **32**, 221–54

Ruff, C B, Trinkaus, E, and Holliday, T W, 1997 Body mass and encephalization in Pleistocene *Homo*, *Nature*, **387**, 173–6

Sakka, M, ed, 1986 *Définition et origines de l'homme*, Paris

Shennan, S J, and Steele, J, forthcoming Cultural learning in hominids: a behavioural ecological approach, in *Social learning in mammals* (eds K R Gibson and H O Box), Symposia of the Zoological Society, London

Shipman, P and Walker A, 1989 The costs of being a predator, *J Human Evol*, **18**, 373–92

Smith, B H, 1993 The physiological age of KNM-WT 15000, in *The Nariokotome* Homo erectus *skeleton* (eds A Walker and R E Leakey), 196–220, Cambridge, MA

Smith, E A, 1992a Human behavioural ecology: I, *Evolutionary Anthropol*, **1**, 20–25

—, 1992b Human behavioural ecology: II, *Evolutionary Anthropol*, **1**, 50–55

Smuts, B B, 1985 *Sex and friendship in baboons*, New York

Thieme, H, 1997 Lower palaeolithic hunting spears from Germany, *Nature*, **385**, 807–10

Trinkaus, E, 1995, Neandertal mortality patterns, *J Archaeol Sci*, **22**, 121–42

Trivers, R L, 1972 Parental investment and sexual selection, in *Sexual selection and the descent of man* (ed B J Cambell), 136–79, Chicago

Wheeler, P E, and Aiello, L C, 1996 On diet, energy metabolism, and brain size in human evolution – reply, *Curr Anthropol*, **37**, 128–9

Wolpoff, M H, 1979, The Krapina denal remains, *Amer J Phys Anthropol*, **50**, 67–114

Wrangham, R W, 1987 The significnce of Africa apes for reconstructing human social evolution, in *The evolution of human behaviour: primate models* (ed W G Kinzey), 51–71, Albany, NY

6 Priority and opportunity: reconstructing the European Middle Palaeolithic climate and landscape

by Tjeerd H van Andel
and P C Tzedakis

Abstract

Key events in human history, including the entry and dispersal of modern humans into Europe and the subsequent demise of their predecessors, the Neandertals, took place between 50,000 and 25,000 years ago during a mild interval in the middle of the last glacial period. Our understanding of these events depends critically on answers to this question: did environmental conditions and their changes play a significant role in early human history or did they not? The evidence, summarised below in the form of a provisional correlation between two mild climatic events of the later midglacial and high values of a proxy for population density, suggests that indeed they do. An initial attempt to reconstruct palaeoenvironments for this interval points to an environmental backdrop far more varied in space and time than is usually envisaged. Thus, a concerted interdisciplinary effort to examine the role of climate and environments in the European late Middle and early Upper Palaeolithic is required.

Science-based archaeology for a major Palaeolithic problem

Among the great Palaeolithic issues the migration of ancient and modern human beings from Africa eastward into Asia and northward into Europe is today one of the most widely discussed. At present, the earlier, almost circumglobal phases of this migration lack the data needed for a rigorous science-based investigation, but for the entry of modern human beings into Europe and subsequent demise of the Neandertals a respectable, although still narrow, evidential base exists. These late events are often placed against the harsh, bleak background of a fully glacial landscape, but those conditions apply to only a small fraction (*c* 10%) of Late Pleistocene time. Especially during the middle pleniglacial (Fig 6.1: 60–25 ka Cal BP, oxygen isotope stage 3 [OIS 3] of Martinson *et al* 1987), the landscape was much less barren and the climate far milder than is generally assumed. Recent studies (Broglio 1996; Gamble 1993; Kozlowski 1996; Mellars 1996a; 1996b; Miskovsky 1992; Stiner 1994) display a growing awareness of the moderate climate of OIS 3, but the true nature of the environments and of their temporal variations remains nebulous, as does

their meaning in terms of human resources. Even during a glacial maximum, for example, summers were as long and winters as short between 40° and 50° N lat as they are today and not comparable to the conditions of the present Canadian Arctic or northern Siberia.

Thus far the dialogue about Palaeolithic landscape and climate on one side and human history on the other has mostly involved archaeologists, and the effort devoted to assembling and evaluating the existing climatic and landscape data has been small. Yet whether or not environments and environmental changes played a significant role in the human history of the last glacial cycle is a crucial question and the time has come to deal with it on the solid foundation of an integrated, interdisciplinary study planned and executed jointly by palaeoclimatologists, archaeologists, and geologists.

Such an enterprise might address many important questions, but the following four alone justify the entire effort. The first two are in the domain of Palaeolithic prehistory:

- Do late Middle and early Upper Palaeolithic events reflect the OIS 3 climatic and environmental history?
- How do the palaeoenvironmental units commonly used to define glacial landscapes relate to the resources required and exploited by late Middle and early Upper Palaeolithic human beings?

These questions cannot be addressed without simultaneous significant advances in our understanding of environments and environmental history of the mid-pleniglacial interval:

- What were the climatic conditions and environments of the middle pleniglacial and how did they vary in space and time?
- What was the impact in Europe of the large and rapid climate oscillations observed recently in Greenland ice cores?

Middle pleniglacial chronology and climate

Diverse studies contemplating possible connections between human events and environments have arrived at diverse conclusions (eg Gamble 1986; 1987; Roebroeks *et al* 1992). The various opinions can be truly tested only by rigorously comparing well defined human and palaeoclimatic event sequences. That this requires a well supported common chronology has been emphasised by the recent discovery in Greenland ice and North Atlantic sediment cores that the glacial climate contains 15–20 events[1] that were up to 7°C warmer than the intervening cold spells and at times only 2°C below the local Holocene average (Bond *et al* 1993; Dansgaard *et al* 1993; GRIP 1993; McManus *et al* 1994). The unstable, bipolar climatic sequence contrasts sharply with the usual view of a long and stable mid-glacial pause implied by the OIS 3 oxygen isotope record (Fig 6.1).

The impact of the often brief but sharp climate fluctuations on the landscape may have been dramatic, possibly affecting early human affairs to a similar degree. How can we test this possibility?

As Rick (1987) has shown, the frequency distribution of a large set of archaeological dates may, with proper cautions, be used as a proxy for population density variations. A comparison with the OIS 3 ice-core palaeoclimatic history might therefore help us decide whether further study of the postulated relation between Palaeolithic climate and human history would be worthwhile.

Even if we ignore the briefest climatic events, the correlation of climatic and human events on a time-scale of a few millennia is difficult and needs a coherent calendrical chronology. [14]C dates, by far the most common

kind of date for the late OIS 3 interval, deviate from calendrical dates by several millennia and cannot be merged with U/Th, ESR and TL dates and the calendrical SPECMAP and ice core time-scales without calibration (Mercier and Valladas 1993). The calibration, until recently impossible beyond *c* 20 ka Cal BP, can now be derived from variations in the intensity of the Earth's magnetic field (Mazaud *et al* 1991), the main control of upper atmospheric ^{14}C production; for details and confidence limits see Laj *et al* (1996).

From a large set of European archaeological site dates provided by Clive Gamble, Paul Pettitt, and William Davies we eliminated all those that were marked by the original publications or by the compilers as questionable. From closely spaced sets of dates at single sites we adopted only those that were spaced at least 0.5 ka apart. The remaining 306 U-series, TL, ESR and ^{14}C dates, the latter calibrated after Laj *et al* (1996, fig 3) show clear maxima at *c* 40–44 and *c* 31–6 ka Cal BP, coincident with the warm Hengelo and Denekamp events of OIS 3 (Fig 6.2). Notwithstanding the wide error margins and other problems associated with dates used as proxies for population density (Rick 1987), the exercise clearly encourages a more thorough pursuit of the potential relations between the human history of the mid-glacial interval and its environments.

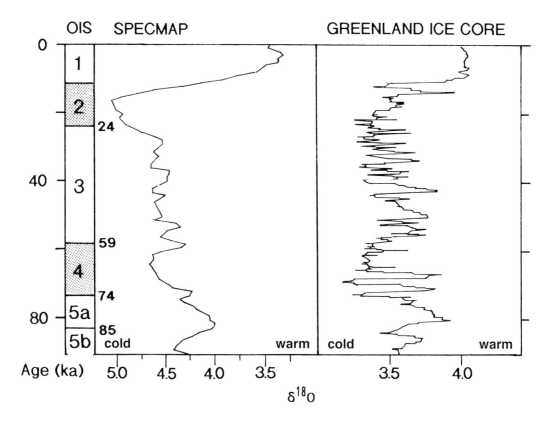

Fig 6.1 Oxygen isotope-based (δ^{18}O) calendrical chronology of the last 80 ka: OIS = oxygen isotope stages; small numbers are stage boundary ages (Martinson et al 1987); curve on left (SPECMAP: Imbrie et al 1984) reflects broad global climate changes that contrast sharply (right) with the many clusters of brief, major climate excursions recorded in Greenland ice cores (GRIP Members 1993, fig 1)

European mid-Palaeolithic palaeoenvironments

To explore the potential of an integrated archaeological and palaeoenvironmental study of the middle pleniglacial, a brief synthesis of the climate and land-scape of Europe between 60 and 25 ka Cal BP is useful. The images are speculative but bring into sharper focus the opportunities and difficulties associated with the task of setting Palaeolithic humans in the context of their landscapes. The synthesis rests on data from long sediment cores (Fig 6.3) supplemented by a few securely dated but short sediment records that have survived the ice erosion of OIS 2 (Fig 6.3). For methodology and bibliography see van Andel and Tzedakis (1996).

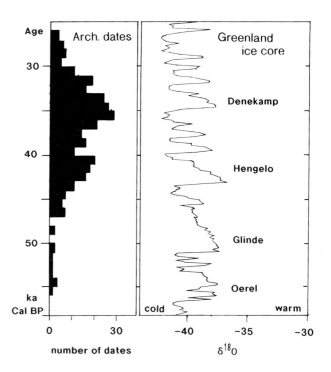

Fig 6.2 Frequency distribution of calendrical dates from late Middle and early Upper Palaeolithic sites compared with the Greenland ice core climatic record (GRIP Members 1993, fig 1)

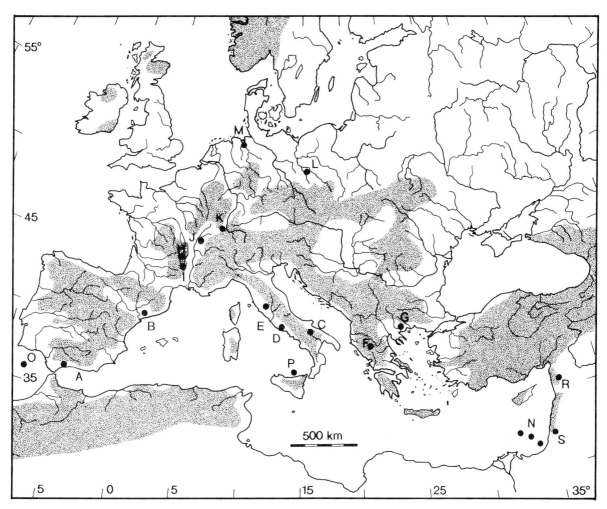

Fig 6.3 Data points for the reconstruction of European OIS 3 landscapes. A = Padul, B = Banyoles, C = Monticchio, D = Valle di Castiglione, E = Vico, F = Ioannina, G = Tenaghi Philippon, H = Bouchet, I = Ribains, J = Les Echets, K = Grande Pile, L = Samerberg, M = Oerel, N = S-E Mediterranean, O = N-W Africa, P = Tyrrhenian Sea, R = Ghab valley, Syria, S = Lake Huleh, Israel (see van Andel and Tzedakis (1996) for references); mountainous regions are shaded

The first major ice advance of the last glacial began in OIS 4. The ice may have crossed the western Baltic, but withdrew soon and the global ice volume stabilised for more than 30 ka Cal BP at about two thirds of its value during the subsequent OIS 2 glacial maximum. During OIS 3 a rather small icecap (Porter 1989), which did not quite reach the west coast of Norway, covered the Scandinavian mountains, but Denmark, probably most of lowland Sweden and southern Finland were ice free, as non-glacial deposits dated between 32 and 42 ka Cal BP indicate (Andersen and Mangerud 1989; Donner 1995, fig 9.1). Elsewhere in Europe no major icecaps appear to have existed (Benda 1995, 268; de Beaulieu *et al* 1991; Frenzel 1991; Schlüchter 1991). With only small icecaps on the northern hemisphere, the level of the sea remained between -70 and -85 m, before plunging steeply to -120 m at the onset of the glacial maximum. With this level the Baltic must have been a freshwater lake, but its size, which is important because large inland water bodies have a major influence on climate and which depends on the combined effect of runoff, evaporation, and glacio-isostatic compensation, cannot yet be reliably estimated.

A few long cores have yielded quantitative temperature and precipitation estimates derived from pollen and beetle data (Guiot 1990; Ponel 1995). At Les Echets (Massif Central, France; Guiot *et al* 1989) warm, wet events lasting several millennia reached 7°C (the present annual mean is 11°C) and precipitation was 500–600 mm (Fig 6.4). The intervening brief cold events had annual mean temperatures of 0–2°C, fairly close to those of the late OIS 4 glacial advance, and were drier. At Grande Pile in the Vosges (north-eastern France), two warm events at *c* 31–5 and *c* 40–43 ka had July temperatures of 20–22°C based on pollen or 16–18°C on pollen and beetles combined (Guiot *et al* 1993, figs 9–10). The trends clearly show the existence of warm, moist intervals lasting several thousand years, long enough to affect both vegetation and wildlife significantly.

The Greenland OIS 3 ice record may be divided into two parts: from *c* 60–40 ka Cal BP low frequency climate oscillations lasting about 3 ka dominated, whereas between 40 and 25 ka Cal BP high-frequency changes lasting 1 ka or less were common. In contrast, European pollen records show a distinct geographical division in the response of the vegetation to climatic events. The main warm periods of northern Europe, the Oerel, Glinde, Hengelo, and Denekamp, are reflected by large arboreal pollen excursions both north and south of the

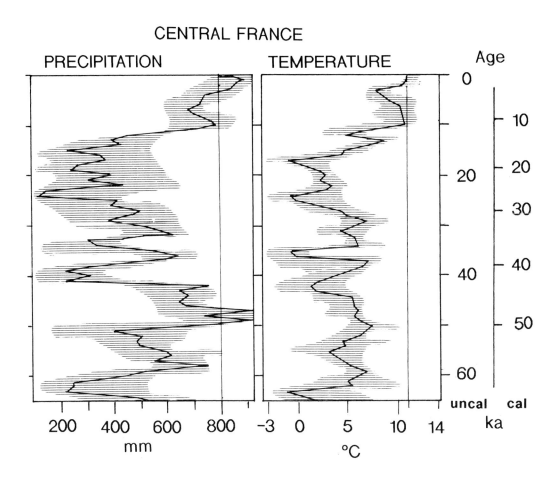

Fig 6.4 Precipitation and temperature history for OIS 3 from a long pollen core at Les Echets, eastern Massif Central, France (Guiot et al 1989): shading indicates confidence limits of estimates; calendrical timescale (non-linear) added

Alps, but the brief events are seen only in Mediterranean records. This difference between north and south is evident when comparing continuous pollen sequences (Fig 6.5) from France at Grande Pile (de Beaulieu and Reille 1992a; Woillard 1978; Woillard and Mook 1982), Les Echets and Lac du Bouchet (Reille and de Beaulieu 1990) with Valle di Castiglione (Follieri et al 1988), Lagaccione, Vico, and Straciacappa (Follieri et al 1997) and Monticchio (Watts et al 1996) in Italy.

The OIS 3 vegetation history north of the Alps differs from that south of the mountains in other ways. In France all warm, moist events display an increase in conifers (pine and spruce) and birch at the same time when a deciduous woodland of oak, hazel, elm, lime, and beech expanded in Italy. At Monticchio the longest warm/moist events, probably equivalents of the Glinde and Hengelo, contain a temporal sequence that began with birch and oak, was followed by elm, ash, and hornbeam and closed with beech and fir, a succession that, although compressed, resembles the full interglacial successions of southern Europe. Brief warm/moist events in the south, on the other hand, show a quasi-synchronous expansion of tree populations. There is no evidence for a temporal tree succession north of the Alps where all warm events are represented by conifers, while even

farther north, in the plains of Germany and the Low Countries, warm/moist event pollen records record a shrub tundra with dwarf birch, willow, and juniper.

Because warm/moist events are observed not only in Greenland but also in the North Atlantic, it is unlikely that they affected only Mediterranean Europe. This suggests that the north–south contrast was due to internal vegetation dynamics rather than to a northern continental climate regime free of high-frequency oscillations. Of course, it might simply have been too cold there for tree growth, but beetle records from warm OIS 3 events (Coope et al 1998) in London show that the temperature was close to that of today at the same time that pollen and plant macrofossils indicate a tundra with sporadic occurrences of dwarf birch and pine. More likely the lack of tree expansion during brief (<1 ka) climate oscillations north of the Alps was the result of the inability of trees to spread northwards fast enough, given poor soil development and slow tree migration rates. The dominance of coniferous over deciduous trees that marks longer warm/moist events north of the Alps probably reflects the close proximity to central Europe of coniferous tree refugia and the competitive advantages of those trees in rapidly colonising poor immature soils.

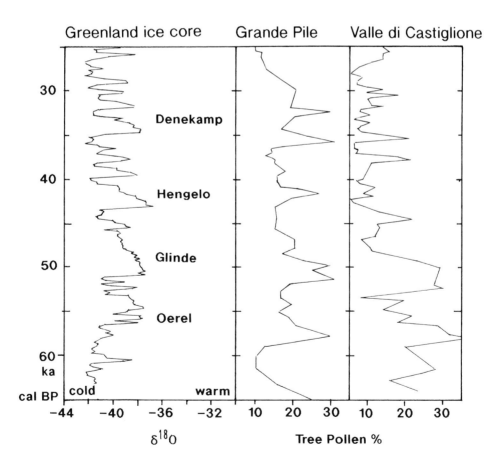

Fig 6.5 OIS 3 climate oscillations displayed by the δ¹⁸O record of the GRIP ice core (Greenland) and arboreal pollen percentages from Valle di Castiglione (Italy) and Grande Pile (Vosges, France); calendrical timescale

The north–south climatic gradient is clear (Fig 6.5), but a west–east gradient, as yet obscure, is to be expected because eastward the cold and warm events of the maritime climate of Greenland and the North Atlantic must have been modified progressively by continental conditions. To understand middle pleniglacial climate conditions and environments of central and eastern Europe, this gradient requires urgent attention, primarily by studies of loess deposits.

Reconstruction of OIS 3 warm/moist and cold/dry landscapes

The temporal and geographic variations described above are well enough established to permit a provisional reconstruction of European vegetation patterns during the warm and moist Hengelo and preceding cold and dry events, chosen because they are better dated than earlier events. During the Hengelo, arctic and subarctic vegetation covered Scandinavia (Donner 1995) and shrub tundra with juniper, dwarf birch and willow spread across northern Germany and the Low Countries (Behre 1989), sprinkled with spruce in the eastern Baltic (Liivrand 1991). France and the north Alpine foreland had an open pine, spruce and birch parkland without other deciduous trees (de Beaulieu and Reille 1984; 1992a; 1992b; Grüger 1989; Reille and de Beaulieu 1990).

South of the mountains a mixed pine woodland with deciduous oak was found in Catalunya (Perez-Obiol and Juliá 1994), and deciduous woodland with hazel, oak, beech, lime, and elm occurred in central Italy (Follieri *et al* 1988; 1997; Leroy *et al* 1996; Watts *et al* 1996) and northern Greece (Tzedakis 1994; Wijmstra 1969). Southern Spain had evergreen and deciduous oak woods with pine and juniper (Carrión 1992; Pons and Reille 1988) and in southern Greece a similar Mediterranean woodland of juniper, pine, and evergreen and deciduous oak expanded. The warm interstadial vegetation was open in aspect and higher tree densities were found only at specific places where enough moisture and optimal soil conditions existed.

Except for a much reduced Fenno-Scandinavian ice-cap, the cold, dry interval preceding the Hengelo resembled OIS 4 (van Andel and Tzedakis 1996, fig 13). In northern Europe south of the ice limit sandy deposits called 'polar desert' were found; whether they were wholly barren or had a low, patchy vegetation, as on Svalbard today, that left no trace in the permeable soil is not known. South of the mountains cold steppe and tundra/steppe dominated, and warmth-loving trees contracted even within such major refuge regions as northwest Greece. A large decrease in arboreal pollen percentages and concentrations implies a sparse, discontinuous tree cover.

The herbaceous vegetation of the cold period preceding the Hengelo event was qualitatively different from that of OIS 4, because sagebrush (*Artemisia*) and chenopods, prominent during OIS 4, were largely replaced by grasses. Chenopods tolerate a very arid, cold climate (rainfall <100 mm/yr) and sagebrush needs only a little more rain, but grasses flourish only at 300 mm/yr (Rossignol-Strick 1995). Evidently, the OIS 3 cold events, although similar in gross vegetation pattern, were less dry than during the arid OIS 4 stage (as indeed Figure 6.4 confirms) and formed vast grass steppes.

Sketch of a programme of study: from database to synthesis

The interval from *c* 45 to 25 ka Cal BP witnessed one of the most important events in the entire human history, the entry of modern humans into Europe and the disappearance of Neandertals. The role played in that history by climate and environment, and particularly by the numerous brief but large climate oscillations, is unclear, even controversial. Further consideration of that role demands international and truly interdisciplinary – as contrasted with multi-disciplinary – programmes.

The reconstructions of Figure 6.6 rest on limited data and a provisionally adjusted chronology; both are capable of considerable improvement. Even so, the images are useful because they define the state of our knowledge and identify the principal issues that next demand attention and investigation. A science-based archaeological programme designed to raise our understanding of relations between human history and the climatic and environmental changes of the later mid-pleniglacial might contain these elements:

- compilation of a high-quality set of dates of archaeological sites, followed by a programme of supplementary dating addressed to open-air as well as cave sites
- compilation of an archaeological database for the late Middle and early Upper Palaeolithic that includes open-air as well as cave sites and environmental as well as archaeological data
- using the database for the construction of space and time models to establish the relation between Neandertal and modern human distribution patterns and associated landscape and climate changes, and the entry and dispersal paths of modern human beings

The full interpretation of any models should be closely integrated with a parallel programme of studies of the climatic and landscape history of the late mid-pleniglacial, which would additionally require:

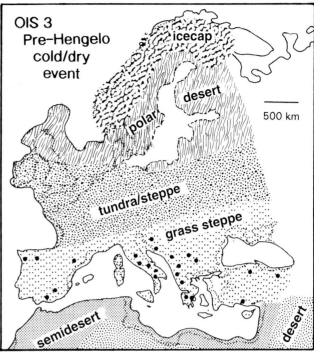

Fig 6.6 Europe during OIS 3: sketch maps of the Hengelo warm/moist event at approximately 43–40 ka and the preceding cold/dry event at c 45 ka Cal BP. Fennoscandian icecap modified from Andersen and Mangerud (1989). Coastline based on -70m isobath for warm/moist and - 85m for cold/dry events (based on modern isobaths from Lambeck 1995); shores of the Baltic Sea are speculative; the black dots on the earlier map indicate tree refugia

- Compilation from the archaeological and late Quaternary literature of a palaeobotanical and palaeozoological database designed to increase the information content of descriptive landscape units, especially with regard to their human resource potential (eg Miracle 1995, ch 4).

A related palaeoclimatic and palaeoenvironmental programme based on climate and environment modelling, the 'Stage Three Project'[2], will, in its early phase, rest similarly on databases compiled from existing icecap, sea-level, palaeobotanical and such geological data as permafrost patterns. The two sections above are provisional examples of what that programme will attempt to achieve in a rigorous manner. Global climate circulation models (GCMs) with their wide grid spacings are not capable of extracting from those databases the detail needed for the construction of climate, landscape, and ultimately human resource models, because critical variables such as precipitation vary on a regional or even local scale. Therefore, a recently developed 'nested' strategy is employed where GCMs provide global wind, pressure, moisture, and temperature patterns as lateral boundary conditions for a 'limited area model' (LAM) designed for high-resolution simulation on a fine grid. The key LAM conditions that must be specified are sea

surface temperature and sea ice, icecaps, land topography, and vegetation cover in terms of evergreen *v* deciduous forest or grassland *v* tundra. Other more detailed inputs are also possible. Sensitivity experiments can be used to evaluate the impact of a range of conditions or uncertainties in the data.

High-resolution simulations can furnish palaeoclimates, weather variability, soil moisture, and other variables for Europe and adjacent seas that provide important guidance for the interpretation of archaeological models, but a close collaboration *ab initio* between archaeologists and Quaternary scientists would not just be fruitful, it is essential.

Acknowledgements

We thank Clive Gamble, Paul Pettitt, and William Davies for the compilations of archaeological dates they have generously provided. To Eric Barron, Paul Mellars, Phil Gibbard, Clive Gamble, Nick Shackleton, and other members of the Stage Three Project from the Godwin Institute for Quaternary Research as well as from elsewhere we are indebted for advice, encouragement and assistance in formulating how the conditions of OIS 3, the longest, mildest segment of the last glacial, and its human population can be clarified.

Notes

1 In recent years the terms stadial and interstadial, originally well defined, have been used in various ways. Not wishing to take a stand on the proper use of the terms, we shall refer to the cold/dry and warm/moist intervals within OIS 3 as 'events'.

2 Further information regarding this project is available from the authors.

References

Andersen, B G, and Mangerud, J, 1989 The last interglacial-glacial cycle in Fennoscandia, *Quat Internat*, **3–4**, 21–29

Behre, K-E, 1989 Biostratigraphy of the last glacial period in Europe, *Quat Sci Rev*, **8**, 25–44

Benda, L (ed), 1995 *Das Quartär Deutschlands*, Berlin

Bond, G C, Broecker, W D, Johnsen, S, McManus, J, Labeyrie, L, Jouzel, J, and Bonani, G 1993 Correlations between climate records from North Atlantic sediments and Greenland ice, *Nature*, **365**, 143–7

Broglio, A, 1996 The appearance of modern humans in Europe: The archaeological evidence from the Mediterranean, *XIII International Congress of Prehistoric and Protohistoric Sciences, Forlì, Italy, Colloquia*, **5**, 237–49

Carrión, J S, 1992 A palaeoecological study in the western Mediterranean area: the Upper Pleistocene pollen record from Cova Benito (Alicante, Spain), *Palaeogeogr, Palaeoclimatol, Palaeoecol*, **92**, 1–14

Coope, G R, Gibbard, P L, Hall, A R, Preece, R C, Robinson, J E, and Sutcliffe, A J, 1998 Climatic and environmental reconstructions based on fossil assemblages from Middle Devensian (Weichselian) deposits of the River Thames at South Kensington, central London, *Quat Sci Rev*, **16**, 1163–96

Dansgaard, W, Johnsen, S J, Clausen, H B, Dahl-Jensen, D, Gundestrup, N S, Hammer, C U, Hvidberg, C S, Steffensen, J P, Sveinbjörnsdottir, H, Jouzel, J, and Bond, G, 1993 Evidence for general instability of past climate from a 250-kyr ice-core record, *Nature*, **364**, 218–20

de Beaulieu, J-L, Monjuvent, G, and Nicoud, G, 1991 Chronology of the Würmian glaciation in the French Alps: a survey and new hypotheses, in *Klimageschichtliche Probleme der letzten 130,000 Jahre* (ed B Frenzel), 435–49, Stuttgart

de Beaulieu, J L, and Reille M, 1984 A long Upper Pleistocene pollen record from Les Echets near Lyon, France, *Boreas*, **13**, 111–32

—, 1992a Long Pleistocene pollen sequences from the Velay Plateau (Massif Central, France), 1 Ribains Maar, *Vegetation History and Archaeobotany*, **1**, 223–42

—, 1992b The climatic cycle at Grande Pile (Vosges, France): A new pollen profile, *Quat Sci Rev*, **11**, 431–8

Donner, J, 1995 *The Quaternary of Scandinavia*, Cambridge

Follieri, M, Magri, D, and Sadori, L, 1988 250,000-year pollen record from Valle di Castiglione (Roma), *Pollen et Spores*, **30**, 329–56

Follieri, M, Giardini, M, Magri, D, and Sadori, L, 1997 Palynostratigraphy of the last glacial period in the volcanic region of Central Italy, *Quat Internat* (in press)

Frenzel, B, 1991 Über einem frühen letzteiszeitlichen Vorstosz des Rheingletschers in das deutsche Alpenvorland, in *Klimageschichtliche Probleme der letzten 130,000 Jahre* (ed B Frenzel), 377–99, Stuttgart

Gamble, C S, 1986 *The Palaeolithic settlement of Europe*, Cambridge

Gamble, C S, 1987 Man the shoveler: alternative models for Middle Pleistocene colonization and occupation in northern latitudes, in *The Pleistocene Old World, regional perspectives* (ed O Soffer), 98, New York

Gamble, C, 1993 People on the move: interpretations of regional variation in Palaeolithic Europe, in *Cultural transformations and interactions in eastern Europe* (eds J Chapman and P Dolukhanov), 36–55, Aldershot

GRIP (Greenland Ice-core Project) Members, 1993 Climate instability during the last interglacial period recorded in the GRIP ice core, *Nature*, **364**, 203–7

Grüger, E, 1989 Palynostratigraphy of the last interglacial-glacial cycle in Germany, *Quat Internat*, **3–4**, 69–79

Guiot, J, 1990 Methodology of the last climatic cycle reconstruction in France from pollen data, *Palaeogeogr, Palaeoclimatol, Palaeoecol*, **80**, 44–69

Guiot, J, Pons, A, de Beaulieu, J L, and Reille, M, 1989 A 140,000-year continental climate reconstruction from two European pollen records, *Nature*, **338**, 309–13

Guiot, J, de Beaulieu, J L, Cheddadi, R, David, F, Ponel, P, and Reille, M, 1993 The climate in western Europe during the last glacial/interglacial cycle derived from pollen and insect remains, *Palaeogeogr, Palaeoclimatol, Palaeoecol*, **103**, 73–94

Imbrie, J, Hays, J D, Martinson, D G, McIntyre, A C, Mix, A C, Morley, J J, Pisias, N G, Prell, W L, and Shackleton, N J, 1984 The orbital theory of Pleistocene climate: support from a revised chronology of the marine $\delta^{18}O$ record, in *Milankovitch and climate* (eds A L Berger, J Imbrie, J D Hays, G J Kukla, and B Saltzman), 269–306, Dordrecht

Kozlowski, J K, 1996 Cultural context of the last Neandertals and early modern humans in central-eastern Europe, *XIII International Congress of Prehistoric and Protohistoric Sciences, Forlì, Italy, Colloquia*, **5**, 205–18

Laj, C, Mazaud, A, and Duplessy, J C, 1996, Geomagnetic intensity and ^{14}C abundance in the atmosphere and ocean during the past 50 kyr, *Geophys Res Lett*, **23**, 2045–8

Lambeck, K, 1995 Late Devensian and Holocene shorelines of the British Isles and North Sea from models of glacio-hydro-isostatic rebound, *J Geol Soc London*, **152**, 437–48

Leroy, S A G, Giralt, S, Francus, P, and Seret, G, 1996 The high sensitivity of the palynological record in the Vico Maar lacustrine sequence (Latium, Italy) highlights the climatic gradient through Europe for the last 90 ka, *Quat Sci Rev* **15**, 189–202

Liivrand, E, 1991 *Biostratigraphy of the Pleistocene deposits in Estonia and correlations in the Baltic region*, University of Stockholm, Department of Quaternary Geology, Report **19**, Stockholm

Martinson, D, Pisias, N G, Hays, J D, Imbrie, J, Moore jr T C and Shackleton, N J, 1987 Age dating and the orbital theory of the Ice Ages: development of a high-resolution 0–300,000-year chronostratigraphy, *Quat Res*, **27**, 1–29

Mazaud, A, Laj, C, Bard, E, Arnold, M, and Tric, E, 1991 Geomagnetic field control of ^{14}C production over the last 80 ky: implication for the radiocarbon time scale, *Geophys Res Lett*, **18**, 1885–8

McManus, J F, Bond, G C, Broecker, W S, Johnsen, S, Labeyrie, L, and Higgins, S, 1994 High-resolution climate records from the North Atlantic during the last interglacial, *Nature*, **371**, 326–9

Mellars, P A, 1996a *The Neanderthal legacy: an archaeological perspective from western Europe*, Princeton, NJ

Mellars, P A, 1996b Models for the dispersion of anatomically modern populations across Europe: Theoretical and archaeological perspectives, *XIII International Congress of Prehistoric and Protohistoric Sciences, Forli, Italy, Colloquia*, **5**, 225–36

Mercier, N, and Valladas, H, 1993 Contribution des méthodes de datation par le carbone 14 et la thermoluminescence à la chronologie de la transition du Paléolithique moyen au Paléolithique supérieur, in *El origen del hombre moderno en el suroeste de Europa* (ed V Cabrera Valdés), 47–60, Madrid

Miracle, P T, 1995 Broad-spectrum adaptations re-examined: hunter-gatherer responses to late glacial environmental changes in the eastern Adriatic, unpubl PhD thesis, Univ Michigan, Ann Arbor, MI

Miskovsky, J-C, (ed), 1992 *Les applications de la géologie à la reconnaissance de l'environnement de l'homme fossile*, Mémoires de la Société Géologique de France, nouvelle serie, **160**, Paris

Pérez-Obiol, R, and Juliá, R, 1994 Climatic change on the Iberian Peninsula recorded in a 30,000-year pollen record from Lake Banyoles. *Quat Res*, **41**, 91–7

Ponel, P, 1995 Rissian, Eemian, and Würmian coleoptera assemblages from the Grande Pile (Vosges, France), *Palaeogeogr, Palaeoclimatol, Palaeoecol*, **114**, 1–41

Pons, A, and Reille, M, 1988 The Holocene and Upper Pleistocene pollen record from Padul (Granada, Spain): a new study, *Palaeogeogr, Palaeoclimatol, Palaeoecol*, **66**, 243–63

Porter, S C, 1989 Some geological applications of average Quaternary glacial conditions, *Quat Res*, **32**, 245–61

Reille, M, and de Beaulieu, J L, 1990 Pollen analysis of a long upper Pleistocene continental sequence in a Velay Maar (Massif Central, France), *Palaeogeogr, Palaeoclimatol, Palaeoecol*, **80**, 35–48

Rick, J W, 1987 Dates as data: an examination of the Peruvian preceramic radiocarbon record, *Amer Antiq*, **52**, 55–73

Roebroeks, W, Conard, N J, and van Kolfschoten, T, 1992 Dense forests, cold steppes, and the Palaeolithic settlement of northern Europe, *Curr Anthropol*, **33**, 551–86

Rossignol-Strick, M, 1995 Sea-land correlation of pollen records in the eastern Mediterranean for the glacial-interglacial transition: biostratigraphy versus radiometric time-scale, *Quat Sci Rev*, **14**, 893–915

Schlüchter, C, 1991 Fazies und Chronologie des Letzteiszeitlichen Eisaufbaus im Alpenvorland der Schweiz, in *Klimageschichtliche Probleme der letzten 130,000 Jahre* (ed B Frenzel), 401–8, Stuttgart

Stiner, M C, 1994 *Honor among thieves – a zooarchaeological study of Neandertal sociology*, Princeton, NJ

Tzedakis, P C, 1994 Vegetation change through glacial-interglacial cycles: a long pollen sequence perspective, *Phil Trans Roy Soc London*, **B 345**, 403–32

van Andel, T H, and Tzedakis, P C, 1996 Palaeolithic landscapes of Europe and environs, 150,000–25,000 years ago, *Quat Sci Rev*, **15**, 481–500

Watts, W A, Allen, J R M, and Huntley, B, 1996 Vegetation history and palaeoclimate of the last glacial period at Lago Grande di Monticchio, southern Italy, *Quat Sci Rev*, **15**, 133–53

Wijmstra, T A, 1969 Palynology of the first 30 metres of a 120m deep section in northern Greece (Macedonia), *Acta Botanica Neerlandica*, **25**, 297–312

Woillard, G M, 1978 Grande Pile peat bog: A continuous pollen record for the last 140,000 years, *Quat Res*, **9**, 1–21

Woillard, G M, and Mook, W G, 1982 Carbon-14 dates at Grande Pile: correlation of land and sea chronologies, *Science*, **215**, 159–61

7 Large mammal hunting strategies in the Palaeolithic of Europe: a taphonomic approach

by Sabine Gaudzinski

Abstract

This review considers big-game hunting from a taphonomic perspective, focusing on the Middle to Final Palaeolithic period. Current views on Middle and Upper Palaeolithic subsistence are discussed, and it is argued that at least for the Middle and early Upper Palaeolithic synthetic views obtained by analysing faunal assemblages with diverse species representation are heavily biased. Zooarchaeological studies from sites with monospecific or species-dominated faunal records provide a promising area for future research. In comparison with assemblages with diverse species representation, prey-species as well as the mode of meat procurement can be defined quite clearly. Analysis of these assemblages through time shows that big-game hunting of gregarious species was a commonly used mode of meat procurement at least from the Eemian Interglacial to the Late Glacial. Although studies of these assemblages are still in their infancy, the faunal evidence does not indicate changes in subsistence tactics. In contrast, changes in carcass processing can be observed during the Late Glacial.

Current views of 'archaic' subsistence

Big-game and big-game hunting has always played a major role in cultural-evolutionary models. Since early work on Pleistocene archaeology at the end of the last century (eg de Mortillet 1890) hunting has been considered to be the primary mode of meat acquisition. It was not until the mid-1960s with the 'Man the Hunter' symposium (Lee and Devore 1968) that the hunting way of life was put into an evolutionary perspective that initiated further discussion. Contributions such as Washburn and Lancaster's (1968) paper on 'The evolution of human hunting' underlined the key position of hunting within human evolution and explained the consequences for the social organisation of our ancestors. Big-game hunting can be considered as the basis for hunter-gatherer societies and the following hypotheses have been made: big-game hunting indicates food sharing and the transport of carcasses to base camps. It leads to a gender-specific division of labour that could be regarded as the basis for the emergence of family units as we know them. Evidence of big-game hunting within the archaeological context therefore documents one of the basic aspects of human behaviour.

Pleistocene archaeology was confronted with new questions in considering these basic assumptions, which finally led to the development of a new research approach, described here as 'faunal analysis'. The first bone assemblages studied in this way were from the Pliocene–Pleistocene boundary (eg Bunn *et al* 1980) and it was only during the mid 1980s that research on Middle Palaeolithic assemblages intensified.

It is remarkable that most of the 'new' methods and observations resulting from this new perspective had been around for quite a long time. In 1926 Wasmund outlined the differences between a biocoenosis and a thanatocoenosis (Wasmund 1926). At the same time Weigelt studied natural death of vertebrates to assess their relevance for fossil material (Weigelt 1927). In 1922 Soergel considered the age structure of a fossil thanatocoenosis as helpful in explaining how animals died and how their bones accumulated at a site, reflecting one of the first discussions about mortality patterns in a Pleistocene context. Modification of bone assemblages and bone surfaces by carnivores (Zapfe 1939; 1940), rodents (Feyfar 1958), through trampling (Korby 1941), breakage (Murray 1936) or diagenetic processes (Barber 1941; Kučera 1927; Rogers 1924) were also quite well known. With this background, it seems obvious that it was an interdisciplinary approach rather than new methods that resulted in the elimination of the strict barrier between palaeontology and archaeology; this was the strength of the first applications of faunal analysis at the beginning of the 1980s (eg Binford 1981; Brain 1981).

Faunal analysis applied to Middle Palaeolithic sites (Binford 1984; 1985) resulted almost immediately in the invalidation of the historical concept of our ancestors' ability to hunt, and scavenging and hunting of small to moderately sized mammals was postulated as the primary mode of meat acquisition (Binford 1984; 1985). That some hunter-gatherers obtain their meat not only by big-game hunting but also by scavenging was known from ethnographical sources, and at times when big-game hunting was considered as the primary way to obtain meat in an archaeological context, scavenging was supposed to be an additional source (eg Adam 1951; Bartholomew and Birdsell 1953; Clark 1959; Narr 1956; Soergel 1922). With a basic concept equating the emergence of big-game hunting to the emergence of 'modern kinds' of human behaviour, ideas about scavenging changed. But scavenging as a concept for the Middle Palaeolithic was based on a weak data set, and the evidence for this mode of meat acquisition has never been unambiguous. Studies of the bone assemblage from the African Middle Stone Age site of Klasies River Mouth (Binford 1984) pointed to certain modifications on bones as diagnostic for scavenging, but it could be shown that the same traces could be observed within a faunal accumulation obtained by hunting (Lupo 1994). Similarly, taphonomic studies on the Middle Palaeolithic faunal assemblage from Grotte Vaufrey in France suggested scavenging as the primary mode of meat acquisition (Binford 1988), but reconsideration of this material (Grayson and Delpech 1994) demonstrated that considerable reanalysis is needed before we will know whether the data support the postulated results.

Nevertheless, at least in the Anglo-Saxon world, the view of opportunistic subsistence in which big-game hunting played only a marginal role was adopted, as taphonomic case studies demonstrating big-game hunting during the Middle Palaeolithic were as rare as case studies for scavenging.

Another factor reinforcing this view were results obtained from several regional studies (eg Mellars 1989; Straus 1987) dealing with the Middle–Upper Palaeolithic transition. Because there were no taphonomic studies, faunal records were treated by analysing faunal lists, supposing that the excavated bone assemblages were representative of the human accumulations originally present. As a result, faunal assemblages showing a diverse species representation were generally regarded as characteristic for pre-Upper Palaeolithic sites and rather opportunistic and unsystematic subsistence strategies were implied for the Middle Palaeolithic as an explanation for diversity in faunal assemblages in comparison with the species-specialized faunas of the Upper Palaeolithic. In this scenario the early Upper Palaeolithic is considered to document gradual adaption to 'modern' forms of behaviour despite the lack of supporting data (eg Straus and Heller 1988).

Comparison of faunal lists cannot be considered an adequate method for obtaining relevant results, as is illustrated by a comparison of Middle Palaeolithic and Final Palaeolithic faunal assemblages from open-air sites from the Central Rhineland of Germany. Examples for the Middle Palaeolithic include Schweinskopf (Schäfer 1990), Wannen (Justus 1988; Justus and Urmersbach 1987), Tönchesberg (Conard 1992), and for the Late Glacial Urbar, Andernach, Niederbieber, and Kettig (Baales and Street 1996). Both groups of sites display highly diverse species representation, with faunal assemblages including many perissodactyls and artiodactyls and enriched by several species of carnivores. The Middle Palaeolithic sites show considerable differences in the individual site histories (expressed for example in the depth of their stratigraphical sequences that can be as much as several meters), and in ecological conditions (expressed in a different species representation). Since ecological conditions during the Late Glacial are far better understood than those of earlier periods, diverse bone accumulations are considered to be generated by highly adaptive hunters who had the choice of a variety of game animals.

Today, nearly 20 years after the first application of these important new approaches to the Middle Palaeolithic, there is only a single zooarchaeological regional study examining subsistence strategies. Stiner's study of West Central Italian cave faunas concludes that at about 55,000 years ago a change in subsistence patterns becomes visible. Prior to this date years human occupants of this region were engaged in non-confrontational scavenging, while after that time ambush hunting of prime-aged ungulates was the main mode of meat procurement (Stiner 1994). Subsequent comment has pointed out that although the study provides a very valuable conceptual framework, substantial reanalysis of these data is needed before we will know to what extent these conclusions are actually warranted (Gaudzinski 1996a; Grayson 1996; Klein 1995). The critics of this study raise methodological problems of faunal analysis, and in this context two points should be mentioned: the significance of ungulate skeletal part representation in vertebrate faunas and the interpretation of mortality patterns.

Ungulate skeletal part representation has long been considered a tool for recognising economic decisions by carnivores and/or Pleistocene humans (Binford 1981; Perkins and Daly 1968). We had to learn that skeletal part frequency is very often correlated with, and probably a result of, bone density (Lyman 1994). In most cases skeletal part data describe the constituents of a bone assemblage without providing a basis for further interpretation (Gaudzinski 1996b). This is illustrated by a comparison of bovid body profiles from four Early Weichselian Middle Palaeolithic sites. At all these sites bovid skeletal element representation is similar (Fig 7.1) although obvious differences can be seen in the relative quantities of bones. The finds from the La Borde sample were redeposited by colluvial processes and the quantitative representation results in a flat %MNI (minimum number of individuals) curve. In contrast, the Mauran record is characterised by deposition in situ and shows a steep %MNI curve. A plot of the %MNI against values for bison-bone mineral density (Fig 7.2, cf Gaudzinski 1996b, tab 6) shows that with increasing bone-mineral density, frequency of skeletal parts increases, and differential destruction of bones according to bone density influenced the composition and quantity of the bovid bone assemblages.

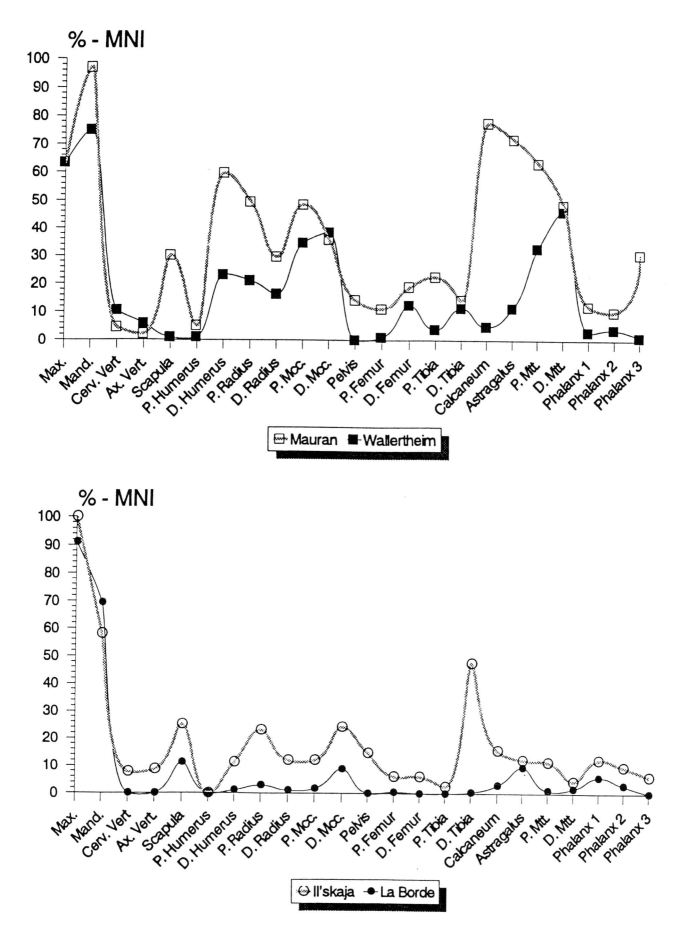

Fig 7.1 Skeletal element representation for bovids as % MNI (minimum number of individuals) (cf Gaudzinski 1996b, tab 5)

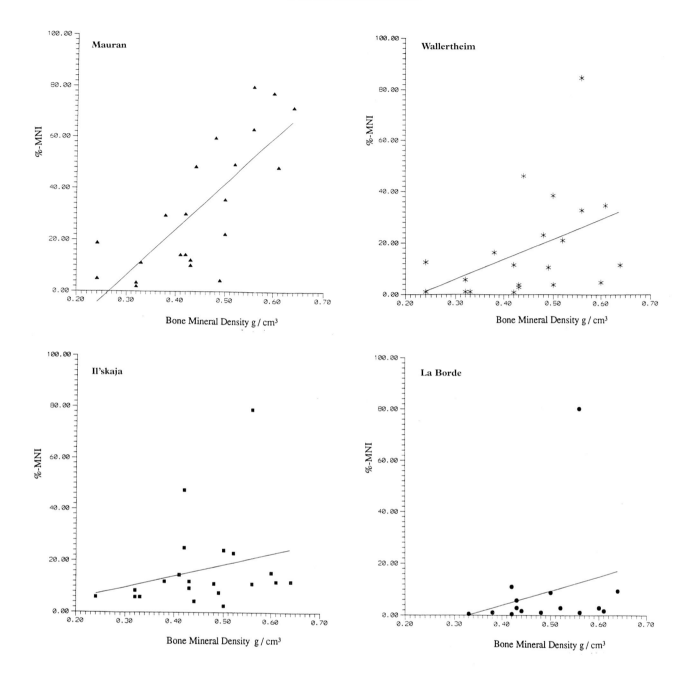

Fig 7.2 Bone mineral density versus % MNI for Mauran, Wallertheim, Il'skaja, and La Borde (cf Gaudzinski 1996b, tab 6)

The second point to be mentioned in this context is the significance of interpretation of mortality patterns. Analysis of age structure in an animal population allows recognition of catastrophic or attritional mortality. Both are independent theoretical representations of the age structure of a stable living population and its natural fall off (Klein *et al* 1983; Klein and Cruz-Uribe 1984; Stiner 1990). In an archaeological sample the age structure can indicate whether the death of the animals was due to mass kill or ambush hunting by hominid or non-hominid predators. In the archaeological context the number of mortality profile types has been expanded (eg Levine 1983; Stiner 1990); 'prime dominated' mortality was considered to indicate ambush hunting by humans

(Stiner 1990). Klein (1995) has pointed out that this mortality pattern could be explained as a statistical departure from the theoretically expected curve of a 'catastrophic' or 'attritional' mortality. Even in wildlife biology uncertainties in age-estimation, population instability, or census bias are factors that make most observed age-profiles depart significantly from the theoretically expected patterns (Klein 1995). Since interpretation of mortality structures in the archaeological record depends on data for the range of variation in modern mortality patterns, which is not well understood, our use of this population parameter is still in its infancy, making interpretation of mortality patterns in archaeological contexts very difficult.

Consideration of the two points above gives some idea of the problems that hamper faunal analysis. In most cases faunal analysis can show that man has contributed to the bone accumulation but it is not possible to more closely define the scale and form of this influence (eg Stopp 1993). Comparison of assemblages from different sites is a questionable approach when we are not dealing with *in situ* sites, when bone decomposition is significant, and when faunal assemblages can not exclusively be attributed to man.

Archaeozoological case studies have led to different results, especially for the Middle Palaeolithic, so an enormous variation in subsistence options can be postulated, ranging from the scavenging of large mammals with simultaneous hunting of small to moderately sized mammals (Binford 1984; 1985) through to subsistence strategies where both scavenging and hunting of large mammals played a role (Chase 1989; Stiner 1994). Common to all of these studies is that changes in the faunal records are interpreted as changes in hominid subsistence strategies.

Even if changes in subsistence tactics become visible these changes are not necessarily indicative of a different subsistence strategy. In this context it is interesting to note that regional studies of Late Pleistocene subsistence based on faunal material indicate high seasonal variability. Evidence from northern Europe shows that in late summer mainly birds and perhaps horse were obtained, while in autumn and spring reindeer were exploited in hunting camps by a combination of driving and stalking. Evidence from sites on the border of the North European plain belonging to the Magdalenian tradition suggest a shift from specialized reindeer hunting in autumn and spring to a more varied range of game dominated by horse in winter and summer (Bratlund 1996, 41). Evidence from south-west Germany and the Thuringian Basin (Eriksen 1996) as well as studies from the Paris Basin (Audouze and Enloe 1991) also suggest that changing season led to the use of different hunting strategies.

Taking the aspects outlined above into account, our view of Middle and early Upper Palaeolithic subsistence has to be considered as very preliminary, governed by studies of a handful of sites that could be separated in time and space by thousands of years and thousands of kilometres. At least for the Middle Palaeolithic and the pre-Magdalenian, analysis of the faunal record does not yet provide a convincing basis either for synthetic statements about general subsistence patterns, nor about general changes in the mode of meat procurement.

Monospecific or species-dominated faunal assemblages

A rather promising area of future research is the presence of a number of Middle and Upper to Final Palaeolithic open-air sites where monospecific or species-dominated faunal assemblages convincingly indicate big-game hunting (Fig 7.3). These accumulations are characterized by the presence of 20 to over 100 individuals of a gregarious species, associated with lithic tools. Human interaction with the bones is indicated by cut and fracture marks caused by meat and marrow processing.

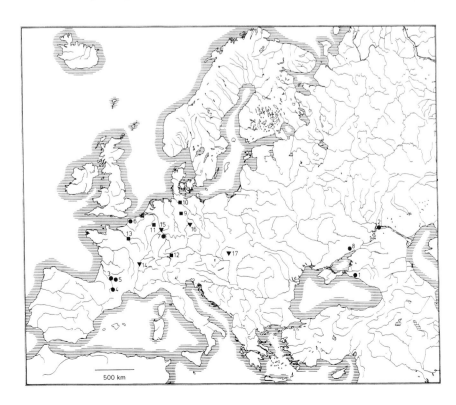

Fig 7.3 Map of Europe showing the location of sites mentioned in the text with monospecific or species dominated bone assemblages (● = bovids, ■ = reindeer, and ▼ = horse): 1 Il'skaja, 2 Sukhaja Mečetka, 3 La Borde, 4 Mauran, 5 Coudoulous, 6 Hénin-sur-Cojeul, 7 Wallertheim, 8 Amvrosievka, 9 Salzgitter-Lebenstedt, 10 Stellmoor and Meiendorf, 11 Lommersum, 12 Schussenquelle, 13 Pincevent, 14 Solutré, 15 Gönnersdorf and Andernach, 16 Oelknitz, 17 Zwoleń

Although monospecific carcass assemblages can occur as a result of disastrous effects without human interference as described by Berger (1983) and Lyman (1987), one can hardly imagine another natural cause for their regular presence other than big-game hunting by humans. Monospecific hunting demonstrates considerable understanding of animal behaviour and a level of social organization capable of conducting a communal hunt.

Analysis of these assemblages provides a welcome addition to our current incomplete understanding of subsistence strategies during the Middle and Upper Palaeolithic periods. It is remarkable that none of the assemblages mentioned below was discovered recently. All sites have been known for at least 20 years though some (such as the site of Coudoulous in France [Jaubert et al 1995]) have recently been re-opened or published. Until the beginning of the 1990s not one of these Middle Palaeolithic assemblages had been analysed taphonomically. Their presence was known but they were either considered to be ambiguous records (Straus 1983) or were treated as rare exceptions (Stringer and Gamble 1993).

Monospecific assemblages in the Pleistocene faunal record

Monospecific or species-dominated assemblages are very well documented after the Eemian Interglacial (OIS 5e). The appearance of these assemblages corresponds to changes in the Pleistocene faunal record before and after the later part of the Middle Pleistocene. It has been noted elsewhere (Gaudzinski and Turner 1996) that certain forms of human interference such as the use of bones for tool production, meat, marrow, or fur acquisition as well as evidence for intentional and focused hunting behaviour in the form of monospecific assemblages occur from the earliest occupation of Europe onwards. For earlier periods evidence for hunting activities can only rarely be seen in bone accumulations, although the wooden spears that have recently discovered at Schöningen (D) (Thieme 1997) indicate that this mode of meat acquisition was undertaken. Only anecdotal presence of assemblages showing meat and marrow procurement can be shown for faunal records from earlier periods.

Faunal assemblages providing evidence for monospecific exploitation of the biomass occur only anecdotally as at the early Middle Pleistocene Caune de L'Arago and Grotte du Lazaret in France. At the Caune de l'Arago, soil level L, reindeer (*Rangifer*) dominates the bone accumulation with over 75% of the total, representing a minimum of 40 individuals. At Grotte du Lazaret, dated by ESR to between 170,000 and 130,000 years, red deer (*Cervus elaphus*) represents 80% of the faunal assemblage with at least 105 individuals (Valensi 1996).

It should be mentioned that the dating for both sites is under discussion and Late Pleistocene dates have been proposed (Dubard 1995; Lister 1990).

From the later part of the Middle Pleistocene there is a change in the quality and quantity of the archaeological faunal record: human interference with bones, of the types outlined above, seem to be standard elements of archaeological faunal assemblages. This is underlined by a regular appearance of single carcass sites (eg Aridos I and II in Spain [Santonja and Villa 1990] or Gröbern [Mania et al 1990] and Lehringen [Thieme and Veil 1985] in Germany) providing evidence for the direct interaction of humans with a single animal carcass. Evidence for the use of fur (eg at Biache St Vaast in France [Auguste 1992] or at the Kudaro caves in Russia [Lioubin and Baryshnikov 1984]) or spatial arrangements of bones (Callow and Cornford 1986) occur from this period onwards.

Major ecological changes during OIS 7 (eg Kahlke 1994) resulting in changes in human economical conditions, changes in human economic practices, or a change in our information basis could be responsible for the outlined differences.

Monospecific or species-dominated bovid assemblages

For the Middle Palaeolithic period, a number of End-Eemian/Early Weichselian sites characterised by an overwhelming presence of bovids are now known. These include Mauran (Farizy et al 1994), La Borde (Jaubert et al 1990), Coudoulous (Jaubert et al 1994; 1995), and Hénin-sur-Cojeul (Marcy et al 1993) in France, Il'skaja (Hoffecker et al 1991) and Sukhaja Mečetka (Vereščagin and Kolbutov 1957; Zamjatnin 1929 and 1961) in Russia, and Wallertheim (Gaudzinski 1995) in Germany. The sites spread across Europe showing that bovid dominance in faunal assemblages is not regionally restricted (Fig 7.3). All these sites have been interpreted as kill sites and analysis suggests that the bovid accumulations result from selective and focused hunting activities by humans over a long period of time. Where data are available, evidence for a seasonal restriction of hunting is not obvious. At these sites a general preference for a particular topographic position cannot be shown. The lithic assemblages from all sites are characterized by unmodified flakes, denticulates and simple scrapers produced *ad hoc* from locally available raw material.

Four faunal assemblages coming from Il'skaja, La Borde, Mauran, and Wallertheim have been studied (Table 7.1). All are characterised by the dominant presence of *Bison priscus* or *Bos primigenius* (in the La Borde case) with a MNI ranging from 27 at La Borde to 83 at Mauran. Analysis of these assemblages was hampered by factors mentioned above as well as by those related to

Table 7.1 Mammals identified from sites where bovids predominate

species	Il'skaja[1] MNI	NISP	Il'skaja[2] MNI	NISP	La Borde[3] MNI	NISP	Mauran[4] MNI	NISP	Wallertheim[5] MNI	NISP
Canis lupus	3	15	4	19	2	10	–	–	1	1
Cuon alpinus caucasicus	1	1	–	–	–	–	–	–	–	–
Vulpes corsac	1	4	–	–	–	–	–	–	–	–
Ursus spelaeus	1	3	2	2	–	–	–	–	–	–
Ursus sp	–	–	–	–	–	–	1	1	–	–
Crocuta spelaea	3	12	7	24	–	–	–	–	–	–
Crocuta sp	–	–	–	–	–	–	–	–	1	1
Panthera leo cf spelaea	–	–	–	–	–	–	–	–	1	1
Elephas primigenius	–	–	5	210	–	–	–	–	–	–
Mammuthus cf chosaticus	2	7	–	–	–	–	–	–	–	–
Equus cf mosbachensis	2	21	–	–	–	–	–	–	–	–
Equus przewalskii	–	–	–	–	–	–	–	–	13	228
Equus germanicus	–	–	–	–	–	–	–	–	–	?
Equus caballus	–	–	5	13	2	15	–	–	–	–
Equus A. hydruntinus	2	6	2	23	1	2	–	–	–	–
Equus sp	–	–	–	–	–	–	3	37	–	–
Dicerorhinus cf hemitoechus	–	–	–	–	–	–	–	–	1	1
Sus scrofa	1	1	–	–	–	–	–	–	1	1
Cervus elaphus	2	16	–	–	1	3	1	5	1	21
Megaloceros giganteus	3	25	4	37	–	–	–	–	–	–
Bison priscus	51	1334	43	2401	–	–	83	4150	52	861
Bos primigenius	–	–	–	–	27	410	–	–	–	–
Saiga tatarica	1	2	2	38	–	–	–	–	–	–
Lepus aff europaeus	–	–	1	15	–	–	–	–	–	–
Sicista cf caucasica	–	–	2	2	–	–	–	–	–	–

notes:

MNI = minumum number of individuals
NISP = number of individual specimens

1 Data from Hoffecker *et al* 1991, tab; mammals from all horizons
2 Data from Vereščagin 1967, tab 7
3 Data from Jaubert *et al* 1990, 34–68; taking tooth wear stages into account,
  the MNI for *Bos primigenius* increases to 40 individuals
4 Data from Farizy *et al* 1994; the MNI for *Equus* sp is given as 3 or 4;
  the MNI for *Bison priscus* can be increased to 137 using tooth wear stages
5 Macrofauna from the main level; if the unstratified bones are included the MNI and
  NISP are 14 and 574 for *Equus przewalskii*, and 59 and 1557 for *Bison priscus*

recovery bias and post-excavation loss of material (Gaudzinski 1996b). Bovid body profiles, age structures, and sex determination, as well as meat and marrow procurement tactics for these faunal assemblages, are now briefly examined.

Body profiles illustrating the skeletal element representation were calculated for each bone and site and plotted (Fig 7.1, cf Gaudzinski 1996b, tab 5). As noted earlier, skeletal element representation for all sites is similar.

Differences can be seen for the ankle-joint with astragalus and calcaneum for Wallertheim and Mauran which most probably reflect post-excavation loss of material (cf Gaudzinski 1996b). Since positive correlation between the frequency of the skeletal elements can be observed, body profiles are helpful in documenting the quality and quantity of the bovid bone assemblage.

Age profiles were calculated for each site from crown height measurements on isolated teeth (Farizy *et al* 1994;

Gaudzinski 1995; Hoffecker *et al* 1991; Jaubert *et al* 1990). At all sites dominance of adult individuals within a certain age-class has been noted that could be interpreted as prime-dominated mortality (Gaudzinski 1996b, fig 6 and tab 2). Within an animal population a prime-dominated age structure reflects selective mortality over a long period of time (Haynes 1991). Such a mortality pattern only rarely occurs in nature and differs from those that are the result of prey-selection patterns of non-human predators and from that of a stable living population. It also differs from mortality patterns observed regularly in nature without human interference and such patterns have been interpreted (based on ethnoarchaeological and archaeological sources) as resulting from selective ambush hunting by humans (Stiner 1994). The same age pattern has also been interpreted as a catastrophic mortality pattern disturbed by taphonomic agents, resulting in the selective decomposition of juvenile teeth.

Only for the Mauran and La Borde assemblages are data on sex composition available, and this shows a dominance of cows. For both sites it has been suggested that this sex composition is specific for a living herd during rutting season.

Human interaction with the bones is shown by cut and fracture marks resulting from meat and marrow processing. A comparative consideration of these traces on bones from Mauran and Wallertheim illustrates uniform strategies of marrow bone breakage (Gaudzinski 1996b, figs 7–8). The positioning of the blows are oriented to take advantage of natural breakage and they were positioned at the weakest part of the bone. This method of bone fracture for the extraction of marrow can be seen too in the Holocene (Noe-Nygaard 1977).

In case of complex site histories, the analysis of a single faunal assemblage can lead to quite a range of interpretations. The interpretation of these bovid assemblages as being the result of repeated, focused, and selective exploitation of bovids by humans has to be seen as one uncomplicated variant within the range of possible interpretations.

Mauran appears to provide the most comprehensive impression of what Pleistocene bovid exploitation looked like as it has the best bone preservation. On the basis of aspects such as age structure, sexual composition of the bovid assemblage, season of occupation, and fracture marks on the bones, but also the lithic assemblage and the topographic setting of the site, a picture emerges that can be interpreted as showing controlled, focused, and selective hunting strategies by humans over a long period of time. It seems obvious that selection of the prey will have been influenced by the nutritional condition of the animals. It has already been noted (Gaudzinski 1996b) that every single aspect of this scenario can also be

interpreted in a different way. Prime-adult mortality could equally be regarded as a lag-mortality structure derived from an original living structure and subsequently modified by selective destruction of juvenile teeth. But even if the simultaneous death of many animals is suggested at Mauran, the high bovid MNI nevertheless points to repeated activities and selective behaviour of some sort in choosing only bovids.

Studies of the sex-structure indicate a pattern comparable to that of a bovid herd during the rutting season, and seasonal determinations point to occupation during summer and autumn. Both factors could indicate nonselective hunting. Taking into account that occupation of the site occurred repeatedly, as indicated by different degrees of bone abrasion and bone weathering, the sex and seasonal determinations do not seem useful in answering questions about the selectivity or non-selectivity of hunting strategies. Because seasonal determination is based on analysis of wear stages of milk teeth, only those seasons when calves died can be positively identified.

The Mauran evidence can also be interpreted according to a different scenario but, irrespective of whether or not it is possible to demonstrate selective exploitation, it is difficult to recognise an agent responsible for the death of the bovids other than big-game hunting by humans.

Bovid assemblages comparable to those of the Middle Palaeolithic are not known for the Upper Palaeolithic, although the Amvrosievka and Zolotovka sites in Russia could be exceptions. At the former a bovid bone bed was unearthed, probably resulting from recurring hunting events (Krotova and Belan 1993). Since detailed analysis is not yet finished it is impossible to estimate whether Amvrosievka represents a comparable subsistence tactic. The same is true for Zolotovka I (Praslov and Ščelinskij 1996).

Since nearly all Middle Palaeolithic bovid assemblages represent remains of *Bison priscus*, the absence of these assemblages during the Upper Palaeolithic could be the result of the extinction of this species in parts of Europe during the last glacial period.

Monospecific or species-dominated reindeer assemblages

For the Middle Palaeolithic there are not only bovid assemblages but also reindeer-dominated faunal accumulations coming from open-air sites. At the site of Salzgitter Lebenstedt on the north-west German plain a faunal assemblage correlated with the Early Weichselian Odderade Interstadial was discovered during the 1950s (Gaudzinski forthcoming; Preul 1991; Tode *et al* 1953) (Table 7.2). The assemblage is dominated by remains of *Rangifer tarandus* with a MNI of 86, calculated from

Table 7.2 Mammals identified from sites where reindeer predominate

species	Salzgitter Lebenstedt[1] MNI	NISP	Lommersum[2] MNI	NISP	Stellmoor[3] MNI	NISP	Meiendorf[4] MNI	NISP	Schussenquelle[5] MNI	NISP
Homo sp	2	5	–	–	–	–	–	–	–	–
Canis lupus	1	1	1	4	1	3	–	–	1	5
Vulpes vulpes	–	–	–	–	?	11	1	2	1	2
Alopex lagopus	–	–	1	1	–	–	–	–	1	9
Ursus arctos	–	–	–	–	–	–	–	–	2	2
Gulo gulo	–	–	1	2	–	–	–	–	2	2
Lynx lynx	–	–	–	–	1	1	–	–	–	–
Panthera spelaea	–	–	1	2	–	–	–	–	–	–
Mammuthus primigenius	17	410	1	61	–	–	–	–	–	–
Equus sp	8	227	10	402	1	4	1	8	3	15
Coelodonta antiquitatis	1	8	–	–	–	–	–	–	–	–
Sus scrofa	–	–	–	–	–	1	1	–	–	–
Rangifer tarandus	86	2130	36	2730	300	17083	69	1931	44	1292
Alces alces	–	–	–	–	2	9	–	–	3	8
Bison priscus	3	79	–	–	–	–	–	–	–	–
Bison bonasus	–	–	–	–	1	4	–	–	–	–

notes:

MNI   =   minumum number of individuals
NISP =   number of individual specimens

1   The MNI of 16 for *Mammuthus primigenius* was calculated from 27 molars
        which are now lost; the MNI based on post-cranial skeletal elements is 7
2   Data from Hahn 1989; *Mammuthus primigenius* was represented only by ivory fragments
3   Data from Bratlund 1996 and Eriksen 1996; large mammals from the Ahrensburgian horizon;
        the NISP for *Rangifer tarandus* does not include 5426 antler fragments
4   Data from Bratlund 1996 and Eriksen 1996; the NISP for *Rangifer tarandus* does not include
        320 antler fragments
5   Data from Schuler 1994

right unshed antlers. Postcranial elements such as the tibia and first phalanges give a MNI of 51. Evidence for human interaction with the bones consists of cut and fracture marks resulting from meat and marrow processing, as well as the presence of lithic and bone tools. The uniform and excellent state of bone preservation, a very low amount of carnivore modification (only 16 examples), selective exploitation of marrow-yielding bones excluding the metacarpals, the presence of bones from juvenile individuals, and the uniform state of the bases from unshed antlers indicate that most of the animals were probably killed in a single hunting episode. Considering the state of preservation and carnivore modification, the reindeer bones show a unique pattern in comparison to the skeletal elements from other species present at Salzgitter.

An age profile has been established for the reindeer population at this site on the basis of 74 complete hemimandibles (Fig 7.4). A clear dominance of 7–8 year old individuals and a near absence of elderly individuals can be observed. This age pattern might be interpreted as a prime-dominated or a lag-catastrophic mortality structure, indicating either ambush hunting by humans over a long period of time or a mass kill of animals. Since there are several arguments for the simultaneous death of many reindeer, interpretation of the age structure according to the latter scenario could also support the hypothesis of a single hunting event. The presence of mandibles from juvenile individuals as well as the uniform state of bases from unshed antlers point to an exploitation of reindeer during the summer to mid-autumn period.

Evidence from Salzgitter Lebenstedt shows that during the Middle Palaeolithic various strategies in big-game hunting were established. Focused and selective exploitation of big game as well as mass-kill encounters were apparently undertaken.

A comparable hunting strategy has been suggested for the Aurignacian by archaeozoological analysis of the faunal assemblage from Lommersum in Germany. The open-air site of Lommersum is situated at the southern edge of the Lower Rhine Basin near Düren in Germany (Hahn 1989). The assemblage, with a MNI of 36, is dominated by *Rangifer tarandus* (Table 7.2). At Lommersum faunal remains were also found in association with lithic and bone tools. Evidence for human interaction with the bones is indicated by the intensive fracturing of the reindeer bones. Only the phalanges, which might have been attached to the hide, survived complete. It has been suggested that the juveniles died between 10 and 12 months old, based on the analysis of wear patterns of teeth, indicating a single hunting event that took place between the end of March and mid June. A relatively short occupation of the site is also supported

by analysis of the lithics; the archaeological record gives no evidence for reoccupation of the site.

For the Lommersum reindeer an age profile was calculated on the basis of the teeth wear pattern of mandible and maxilla fragments (Fig 7.5). A clear dominance of individuals between three and a half and six years old is obvious, which might, as in the case of Salzgitter Lebenstedt, be interpreted as a prime-dominated age pattern or a lag-catastrophic mortality pattern.

The Final Palaeolithic assemblage from the Ahrensburgian level at Stellmoor also suggests periodical mass killing during the summer to autumn. The site is situated in the Ahrensburger tunnel valley of Germany. The faunal assemblage is also dominated by reindeer remains with a MNI of 300 (Table 7.2). Massive communal hunting drives are indicated by the high MNI, by hunting lesions (Bratlund 1990) pointing to the use of bow and arrow (Rust 1943) (underlined by the presence of arrows in the archaeological find horizon), by selective and incomplete butchering of carcasses, as well as by the population structure of the kill (illustrated by age and sex analysis of the animals) (Bratlund 1996).

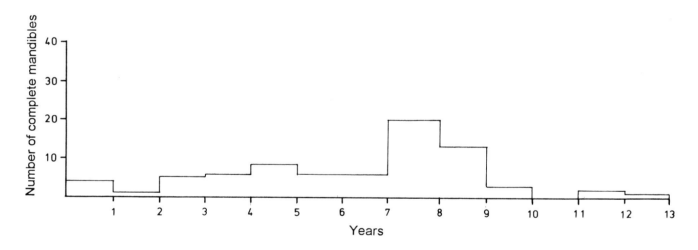

Fig 7.4 Age profile for Rangifer tarandus *from Salzgitter-Lebenstedt*

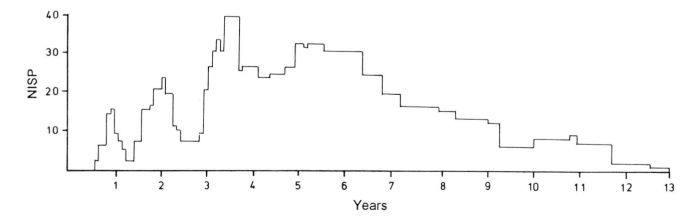

Fig 7.5 Age profile for Rangifer tarandus *from Lommersum (Hahn 1989, fig 11.13)*

The site of Meiendorf, also located in the Ahrensburg tunnel valley of Germany shows that hunting strategies for obtaining reindeer were not only restricted to periodical mass killing episodes. Reindeer dominated the faunal assemblage within the Hamburgian level with a MNI of 69. According to population structure and carcass exploitation, these remains are considered to reflect kills of strategic hunting camps occupied during the autumn period where the animals were targeted partly in drives, and partly by stalking (Bratlund 1996). A comparable mode of big-game hunting has been postulated for Magdalenian settlements that are also dominated by reindeer remains, such as the Schussenquelle (Schuler 1994) where reindeer is represented with a MNI of 44 (Table 7.2).

Faunal evidence from the Middle, early Upper and late Upper Palaeolithic give no indication that the mode of reindeer exploitation changed through time. This is true even though the organic record testifies to big changes in weaponry over this period. A bone tool has been discovered at Salzgitter Lebenstedt that could be interpreted as a projectile point (Fig 7.6). At Lommersum antler points are present (Hahn 1989). During the Magdalenian tradition accurate distance weapons such as spearthrowers were used (Stodiek 1993) and finally for the Final Palaeolithic the use of bow and arrow is attested (Rust 1943). Although one can assume that improved weaponry led to a more efficient exploitation of game animals this cannot be seen in the faunal record. In contrast, changes in carcass exploitation become clearly visible. In comparison to the other assemblages considered here the faunal evidence from Stellmoor (Ahrensburgian horizon) shows highly organised processing of reindeer carcasses; labour-intensive segments such as neck and sacrum were only rarely exploited.

Fig 7.6 Bone tool from Salzgitter Lebenstedt; scale 1:1

Monospecific or species-dominated horse assemblages

The famous site of Solutré in France shows that monospecific exploitation of a single gregarious species was not only practised at the beginning or end of the Upper Palaeolithic. This site displays a stratigraphic succession from the Aurignacian to the Magdalenian tradition and during all phases horse is the dominant species. Thorough analysis of Solutré is presently underway, published species lists indicating the total number of identifiable bones as well as MNI are preliminary and not representative of the whole site. The topography of the region and site, evidence for seasonality, scarcity of artefacts and evident structures, and selective exploitation of the carcasses as well as horse ethology suggest the bone accumulation at Solutré reflects episodic hunting of migrating horses by driving and corralling, from late spring to early autumn, with the preferential killing of adult individuals (Olsen 1989). Analysis of horse remains from the Magdalenian level in Sector I 11 indicates in addition a less dramatic method of hunting: the suggestion is that the horses were ambushed as they skirted around the base of the rock at Solutré (Turner 1996).

Especially for the Magdalenian, horse-dominated faunal assemblages have been reported from open-air sites such as Gönnersdorf and Andernach (Street 1993) in the Central Rhineland of Germany, and Oelknitz in Thuringia (Musil 1985). No archaeozoological studies or details of the mode of meat procurement have yet been published for any of the three sites.

Dominance of horses in faunal assemblages is not restricted to the Upper Palaeolithic. At the early Weichselian site Zwoleń in Poland horses dominate the faunal assemblage with a MNI of 30 (Gautier 1988; Schild and Sulgostowska 1988). Since analysis of the faunal assemblage is not yet published no further discussion is possible.

Conclusion

For the Middle and early Upper Palaeolithic periods our knowledge about subsistence tactics based on detailed case studies is very fragmentary. For many bone assemblages evidence of human interference can be shown, but it is often very difficult to specify the form of this human interaction more closely. Comparison of different assemblages is often hampered by an insufficient methodology. However, the presence of monospecific or species dominated faunal assemblages and their changes through time provide a promising area for future research. These bone accumulations have the advantage that prey species as well as the mode of procurement can be defined quite clearly. There are big chronological and geographical gaps between these faunal records which

will not necessarily be filled with material from new excavations but rather with material from sites already in our
archives. Because the nature of these assemblages is to a
large extent unknown, the following suggested directions
for future research on them are preliminary.

Big-game hunting was regularly undertaken after the
Eemian Interglacial. Herd animals were hunted either by
stalking of single individuals or in mass-kill events or by
a combination of both. Several Middle Palaeolithic as
well as Upper Palaeolithic assemblages provide evidence
for seasonally restricted exploitation of game. Although
the organic record indicates changes in weaponry that
can be interpreted as improvements, the faunal record
does not suggest more efficient big-game exploitation.

Changes in the mode of big-game hunting, either at
the transition from Middle to Upper Palaeolithic, or at
the beginning of the late Upper Palaeolithic period are
not evident from monospecific faunal assemblages.
Changes in subsistence tactics become clearly visible for
the first time during the Final Palaeolithic. These changes
do not find their expression in the qualitative or quantitative composition of bone assemblages, nor in an obvious change in hunting tactics but changes can be
observed in carcass processing. Evidence from Stellmoor
indicates highly organised processing of prey; labour-
intensive carcass parts were only rarely exploited. In this
way the Stellmoor assemblage differs considerably from
most of the Magdalenian bone assemblages that have
been mentioned above, which are characterised by complete and highly standardised processing of meat and
marrow. Whether such standardisation, which is also
known in Magdalenian lithic assemblages, is restricted to
this period is as yet an open question.

Until recently it was believed differences between the
Middle and the Upper Palaeolithic were clear. While the
Middle Palaeolithic represented the material culture of
Neandertal man, the Upper Palaeolithic record was considered to result from *Homo sapiens sapiens*. The human
record from the Levant of *Homo sapiens sapiens* associated
with a Middle Palaeolithic lithic assemblage dated at
around 90,000 BP (Stringer *et al* 1989; Vandermeersch
1981) was only one discovery that changed the perception of the Middle to Upper Palaeolithic transition. In
addition, similarities in the Middle and early Upper
Palaeolithic species-dominated faunal records had been
demonstrated by Chase during the 1980s. Based on several Middle Palaeolithic faunal assemblages, coming
mainly from cave sites, he suggested that we must look
'elsewhere' to find an explanation for the Middle to
Upper Palaeolithic transition (Chase 1989, 333).

On the basis of the faunal material from the early
Upper Palaeolithic site of the Abris du Flageolet, it has
been suggested that changes in subsistence tactics
occurred not at the Middle–Upper Palaeolithic transition,

but at the beginning of the late Upper Palaeolithic (Enloe
1993). The fauna from level V is characterised by a dominance of *Rangifer tarandus*, which seem to have been targeted during the winter by individual ambush kills. The
presence of this species is considered to be due to climatic factors, rather than to a planned mass kill of a target species as is known from several French Magdalenian
sites, eg Pincevent (David and Enloe 1993; Enloe and
David 1989). The faunal assemblage from La Flageolet is
interpreted as the result of a mode of subsistence more
like that of foragers than systematic collectors. This foraging mode of meat procurement is characterised by
encounter hunting and immediate consumption, rather
than planned hunts of larger numbers of animals associated with storage for long term consumption. As a result
of the La Flageolet find, an adaptive shift at the beginning
of the late Upper Palaeolithic was postulated (Enloe
1993; see also Pike-Tay and Bricker 1993). However, a
subsistence strategy comparable to that of the
Magdalenian was also used during the Middle and early
Upper Palaeolithic, as indicated by the monospecific faunal assemblages presented above.

The reason why subsistence strategies during the
Upper Palaeolithic seem to be so different from those of
the Middle Palaeolithic may be that for the former
description is based on organic remains from a very few,
and in some ways unique, sites such as the huge
Magdalenian settlements at Pincevent in France,
Gönnersdorf, Andernach, and Oelknitz in Germany with
specialised reindeer or horse faunas. The fact that these
assemblages consist of thousands of bones entangled in
complex occupation histories, which we are only able to
disentangle to a certain degree, is one factor that hampers
fast publication. As pointed out by Conkey (1985), it is
only our view of the Upper Palaeolithic as a cultural
entity that permits us to consider these assemblages as
representative for the whole Upper Palaeolithic period.

For the future, work is in progress on almost all of the
assemblages mentioned above. It is hoped that these
results will equip us with more detailed information for
the more definitive interpretations of the continuity
and/or change visible in Middle to Late Palaeolithic faunal assemblages. As mentioned above, what is needed is
not new excavation but fuller studies of existing finds;
this is where resources should be concentrated in the
short to medium term. At present, studies on faunal
analysis are very often one-sided and restricted to the
testing of specific models, to a large degree caused by the
highly specialised orientation of the individual
researches. What we urgently need in the long term is the
development of a more appropriate methodology for faunal analysis, which can only be obtained by detailed and
comprehensive studies of all facets of archaeological sites
including the individual site history as well as the lithics.

References

Adam, K-D, 1951 Der Waldelefant von Lehringen, eine Jagdbeute des diluvialen Menschen, *Quartär*, **5**, 72–92

Audouze, F, and Enloe, J, 1991 Subsistence strategies and economy in the Magdalenian of the Paris Basin, France, in *The Late Glacial in north-west Europe: human adaptation and environmental change at the end of the Pleistocene*, (eds N Barton, A J Roberts, and D A Roe), CBA Res Rep, **77**, 63–71, London

Auguste, P, 1992 Etude archéozoologique des grands mammifères du site Pléistocène moyen de Biache-Saint-Vaast (Pas-De-Calais, France): apports biostratigraphiques et palethnographiques, *L'Anthropol*, **96**, 49–70

Baales, M, and Street, M, 1996 Hunter-gatherer behaviour in a changing Late Glacial landscape: Allerød archaeology in the central Rhineland, Germany, *J Anthropol Res*, **52**, 281–316

Barber, H, 1941 Untersuchungen über die chemischen Veränderungen von Knochen bei der Fossilisation, *Palaeobiolog*, **7**, 217–35

Bartholomew, G A, and Birdsell, J B, 1953 Ecology and the protohominids, *Amer Anthropol*, **55**, 481–96

Berger, J, 1983 Ecology and catastrophic mortality in wild horses: implications for interpreting fossil assemblages, *Science*, **220**, 1403–4

Binford, L R, 1981 *Bones: ancient men and modern myths*, New York

Binford, L R, 1984 *Faunal remains of Klasies River Mouth*, New York

Binford, L R, 1985 Human ancestors: changing views of their behaviour, *J Anthropol Archaeol*, **4**, 292–327

Binford, L R, 1988 Etude taphonomique des restes fauniques de la Grotte Vaufrey, in *La Grotte Vaufrey à Cenac et Saint-Julien (Dordogne): Paléoenvironnements, chronologie, et activités humaines* (ed J-P Rigaud), Mémoires de la Société Préhistorique Française, **19**, 535–64, Bordeaux

Brain, C K, 1981 *The hunters or the hunted? An introduction to African cave taphonomy*, Chicago

Bratlund, B, 1990 Rentierjagd im Spätglazial. Eine Untersuchung der Jagdfrakturen an Rentierknochen vom Maiendorf und Stellmoor, Kreis Stormarn, *Offa*, **47**, 7–34

—, 1996 Hunting strategies in the Late Glacial of northern Europe: a survey of the faunal evidence, *J World Prehist*, **10**, 1–48

Bunn, H, Harris, J W K, Isaak, G, Kaufulu, Z, Kroll, E, Schick, K, Toth, N, and Behrensmeyer, A K, 1980 FxJj50: an Early Pleistocene site in northern Kenya, *World Archaeol*, **12**, 109–36

Callow, P, and Cornford, J M, (eds), 1986 *La Cotte de St. Brelade 1961–1978*, Norwich

Chase, P G, 1989 How different was Middle Palaeolithic subsistence? A zooarchaeological perspective on the Middle to the Upper Palaeolithic transition, in *The human revolution: behavioural and biological perspectives on the origin of modern humans*, (eds P Mellars and C Stringer), 321–37, Edinburgh

Clark, J D, 1959 *The prehistory of southern Africa*, Baltimore

Conard, N J, 1992 *Tönchesberg and its position in the Paleolithic prehistory of northern Europe*, Monographien des RGZM, **20**, Bonn

Conkey, M W, 1985 Ritual Communication, social elaboration, and the variable trajectories of paleolithic material culture, in *Prehistoric hunter-gatherers: the emergence of cultural complexity* (eds T D Price and J A Brown), 299–323, New York

David, F, and Enloe, J G, 1993 L'Exploitation des animaux sauvages de la fin du Paléolithique moyen au Magdalénien, in *Exploitation des animaux sauvages a travers le temps*, VIe Colloque international de l'Homme et l'Animal, Société de Recherche interdisciplinaire, 30–47, Juan-les-Pins

de Mortillet, G, 1890 *Origines de la chasse, de la pêche, et de l'agriculture, I, chasse, pêche*, Paris

Dubard, M, 1995 Séquences de ttransition climatique en domaine fluviatile et karstique dans la région de Nice (A.–M., France), en rapport avec l'eustatisme, *Quaternaire*, **6**, 99–105

Enloe, J G, 1993 Subsistence organization in the early Upper Palaeolithic: reindeer hunters of the Abri du Flageolet, Couche V, in *Before Lascaux: the complex record of the early Upper Palaeolithic* (eds H Knecht, A Pike-Tay, and R White), 101–16, Boca Raton

Enloe, J G, and David, F, 1989 Le remontage des os par individus: le partage du renne chez les Magdaléniens de Pincevent (La Grande Paroisse, Seine-et-Marne), *Bull Soc Préhist Française*, **86**, 275–81

Eriksen, B V, 1996 Regional variation in Late Pleistocène subsistence strategies: southern Scandinavian reindeer hunters in a European context, in *The earliest settlement of Scandinavia* (ed L Larson), Arch Lundensia, **24**, 7–21, Stockholm

Farizy, C, David, F, and Jaubert, J, 1994 Hommes et bisons du Paléolithique moyen à Mauran (Haute Garonne), *Supplément à Gallia Préhistoire*, **30**, Paris

Feyfar, O, 1958 Einige Beispiele der Benagung fossiler Knochen, *Anthropozoikum*, **7**, 145–9

Gaudzinski, S, forthcoming Knochen und Knochengeräte der mittelpaläolithischen Fundstelle Salzgitter-Lebenstedt (Deutschland), *Jahrbuch des RGZM*

—, 1995 Wisentjäger in Wallertheim: zur Taphonomie einer mittelpaläolithischen Freilandfundstelle in Rheinhessen, *Jahrbuch des RGZM*, **39**, 245–424

—, 1996a Review of M Stiner, *Honor among thieves*, *Antiquity*, **70**, 227–9

—, 1996b On bovid assemblages and their consequences for the knowledge of subsistence patterns in the Middle Palaeolithic, *Proc Prehist Soc*, **62**, 19–39

Gaudzinski, S, and Turner, E, 1996 The role of early humans in the accumulation of European Lower and Middle Palaeolithic bone assemblages, *Curr Anthropol*, **37**, 153–6

Gautier, A, 1988 Preliminary notes on the fauna of the Middle Palaeolithic site at Zwoleń (Poland), in *L'homme de Néandertal, Vol 6* (ed M Otte), 69–73, Liège

Grayson, D K, 1996 Review of M Stiner, *Honor among thieves*, *Amer Antiq*, **61**, 815–16

Grayson, D K, and Delpech, F, 1994 The evidence for Middle Palaeolithic scavenging form couche CIII, Grotte Vaufrey (Dordogne, France), *J Archaeol Sci*, **21**, 359–375

Hahn, J, 1989 Genese und Funktion einer jungpaläolithischen Freilandstation: Lommersum im Rheinland, *Rheinische Ausgrabungen*, **19**, Köln

Haynes, G, 1991 *Mammoths, mastodons, and elephants*, Cambridge

Hoffecker, J F, Baryshnikov, G, and Potapova, O, 1991 Vertebrate remains from the Mousterian site of Il'skaja I (northern Caucasus USSR): new analysis and interpretation, *J Archaeol Sci*, **18**, 113–47

Jaubert, J, Lorblanchet, M, Laville, H, Slott-Moller, R, Turq, A, and Brugal, J P, 1990 Les chasseurs d'auroche de La Borde, *Documents d'archéologie française*, **27**, Paris

Jaubert, J, Brugal, J-P, and Quinif, Y, 1994 Tour de Faure: Coudoulous I et II, *Bilan Scientifique de la région Midi-Pyrénées, 1993*, 144–6

Jaubert, J, Brugal, J-P, and Mourre, V, 1995 Tour de Faure: Coudoulous I, *Bilan Scientifique de la région Midi-Pyrénées, 1994*, 160–62

Justus, A, 1988 Die Steinartefakte der Ausgrabungen auf den Wannen-Vulkanen bei Saffig/Neuwieder Becken, unpubl Magister thesis, Univ Köln

Justus, A, and Urmersbach, K-H, 1987 Mittelpaläolithische Funde vom Vulkan 'Wannen' bei Ochtendung, Kreis Mayen-Koblenz, *Archäologisches Korrespondenzblatt*, **17**, 409–17

Kahlke, R-D, 1994 Die Entstehungs-, Entwicklungs-, und Verbreitungsgeschichte des oberpleistozänen Mammuthus-Coelodonta-Faunenkomplexes in Eurasien (Großsäuger), *Abhandlungen der Senckenbergischen Naturforschenden Gesellschaft*, **546**, Frankfurt am Main

Klein, R G, 1995 Neanderthal carnivory, *Science*, **267**, 1843–4

Klein, R G, Allenwarden, K, and Wolf, C, 1983 The calculation and interpretation of ungulate age profils from dental crown heights, in *Hunter-gatherer economy in prehistory* (ed G Bailey), 47–57, London

Klein, R G, and Cruz-Uribe, K, 1984 *The analysis of animal bones from archeological sites*, Chicago

Korby, F E, 1941 Le 'charriage à sec' des ossements dans les cavernes, *Ecologae geologicae helvetiae*, **34**, 319–20

Krotova, A A, and Belan, N G, 1993 Amvrosievka: A unique Upper Palaeolithic site in eastern Europe, in *From Kostenki to Clovis* (eds O Soffer and N Praslov), 125–47, New York

Kučera, C, 1927 Pokusy o tleni kosti, *Biologické spisy vysoké skoly zverolékarské, Brno, ČSR*, **6**, 105–20

Lee, R B, and Devore, I (eds), 1968 *Man the hunter*, Chicago

Levine, M A, 1983 Mortality models and the interpretation of horse population structure, in *Hunter-gatherer economy in prehistory* (ed G Bailey), 23–46, London

Lioubin, V P, and Baryshnikov, G F, 1984 L'activité de chasse des plus anciens habitats du Caucase (Acheuléen, Moustérien), *L'Anthropol*, **88**, 221–9

Lister, A, 1990 Taxonomy and biostratigraphy of Middle Pleistocene deer remains from Arago, Pyrénées-Orientales, France, *Quaternaire*, **3–4**, 225–30

Lupo, K D, 1994 Butchering marks and carcass acquisition strategies: distinguishing hunting from scavenging in archaeological contexts, *J Archaeol Sci*, **21**, 827–37

Lyman, R L, 1987 On the analysis of vertebrate mortality profiles: sample size, mortality type, and hunting pressure, *Amer Antiq*, **52**, 125–42

—, 1994 *Vertebrate taphonomy*, Cambridge

Mania, D, Thomae, M, Litt, T, and Weber, T, 1990 Neumark-Gröbern. *Beiträge zur Jagd des Mittelpaläolithischen Menschen*, Veröffentlichungen des Landesmuseums für Vorgeschichte in Halle, **43**, Berlin

Marcy, J-L, Auguste, P, Fontugne, M, Munaut, A-V, and Van Vliet-Lanoë, B, 1993 Le gisement Moustérien d'Hénin-sur-Cojeul (Pas-de-Calais), *Bulletin de la Société Préhistorique Française*, **90**, 251–6

Mellars, P, 1989 Major issues in the emergence of modern humans, *Curr Anthropol*, **30**, 349–85

Murray, P D T, 1936 *Bones: a study of the development and structure of the vertebrate skeleton*, Cambridge

Musil, R, 1985 *Die Fauna der Magdalénien-Siedlung Oelknitz*, Weimarer Monographien zur Ur- und Frühgeschichte, **17**, Weimar

Narr, K J, 1956 Der Urmensch als Natur und Geisteswesen, *Saeculum*, **7**, 243–88

Noe-Nygaard, N, 1977 Butchering and marrow fracturing as a taphonomic factor in archaeological deposits, *Paleobiol*, **3**, 218–37

Olsen, S L, 1989 Solutré: a theoretical approach to the reconstruction of Upper Palaeolithic hunting strategies, *J Human Evol*, **18**, 295–327

Perkins, D, und Daly, P, 1968 A hunters village in Neolithic Turkey, *Sci Amer*, **219**, 96–106

Pike-Tay, A, and Bricker, H M, 1993 Hunting in the Gravettian: an examination of evidence from south-western France, in *Hunting and animal exploitation in the Lower Palaeolithic and Mesolithic of Eurasia* (eds G L Peterkin, H M Bricker, and P Mellars), Archeological Papers of the American Anthropological Association, **4**, 127–43, Washington DC

Praslov, N D, and Ščelinskij, V E, 1996 *Verchnepaleolitičeskoe poselenie Zolotovka I na nižnem Donu*, St Petersburg

Preul, F, 1991 Die Fundschichten im Klärwerksgelände von Salzgitter-Lebenstedt und ihre Einordnung in die Schichtenfolge des Quartär, in *Der altsteinzeitliche Fundplatz Salzgitter-Lebenstedt* (eds R Busch and H Schwabedissen), Fundamenta, **11**(2), 9–100, Köln

Rogers, F, 1924 Mineralogie and petrography of fossil bones, *Bull Geol Soc Amer*, **35**, 535–57

Rust, A, 1943 *Die Alt- und Mittelsteinzeitlichen Funde von Stellmoor*, Neumünster

Santonja, M, and Villa, P, 1990 The Lower Palaeolithic of Spain and Portugal, *J World Prehist*, **4**, 45–93

Schäfer, J, 1990 Der altsteinzeitliche Fundplatz auf dem Vulkan Schweinskopf-Karmelenberg, unpubl PhD thesis, Univ Köln

Schild, R, and Sulgostowska, Z, 1988 The Middle Palaeolithic of the North European plain at Zwoleń: preliminary results, in *L'homme de Néandertal, Vol 8*, (ed M Otte), 149–67, Liège

Schuler, A, 1994 *Die Schussenquelle: eine Freilandstation des Magdalénien in Oberschwaben*, Materialhefte zur Archäologie in Baden-Württemberg, **27**, Stuttgart

Soergel, W, 1922 *Die Jagd der Vorzeit*, Jena

Stiner, M C, 1990 The use of mortality patterns in archaeological studies of hominid predatory adaptions, *J Anthropol Archaeol*, **9**, 305–51

—, 1994 *Honor among thieves: a zooarchaeological study of Neandertal ecology*, Princeton

Stodiek, K, 1993 *Zur Technologie der jungpaläolithischen Speerschleuder*, Tübinger Monographien zur Urgeschichte, **9**, Tübingen

Stopp, M, 1993 Taphonomic analysis of the faunal assemblage, in *The Lower Paleolithic site at Hoxne, England*, (eds R Singer, B G Gladfelter, and J J Wymer), 138–49, Chicago

Straus, L G, 1983 From Mousterian to Magdalenian: cultural evolution viewed from fasco-cantabrian

Spain and pyrenean France, in *The Mousterian legacy* (ed F. Trinkaus), BAR, Int Ser, **164**, 74–111, Oxford

—, 1987 Hunting in late Upper Palaeolithic western Europe, in *The evolution of human hunting* (eds M H Nitecki and D V Nitecki), 147–76, New York

Straus, L,G, and Heller, C W, 1988 Explorations of the twilight zone: the early Upper Palaeolithic of Vasco-Cantabrian Spain and Gascony, in *The early Upper Palaeolithic: evidence from Europe and the Near East* (eds J F Hoffecker and C A Wolf), BAR, Int Ser, **437**, 97–134

Street, M J, 1993 Analysis of Late Palaeolithic and Mesolithic faunal assemblages in the Northern Rhineland, Germany, unpubl PhD thesis, Univ Birmingham

Stringer, C, Grün, R, Schwartz, H, and Goldberg, P, 1989 ESR dates for the hominid burial site of Es Skuhl in Israel, *Nature*, **338**, 756–8

Stringer, C, and Gamble, C, 1993 *In search of the Neanderthals*, London

Thieme, H, 1997 Lower Palaeolithic hunting spears from Germany, *Nature*, **385**, 807–10

Thieme, H, and Veil, S, 1985 Neue Untersuchungen zum eemzeitlichen Elefanten-Jagdplatz Lehringen, Ldkr. Verden, *Die Kunde*, NF **36**, 11–58

Thode, A, 1953 Einige archäologische Erkenntnisse aus der paläolithischen Freilandstation von Salzgitter-Lebenstedt, *Eiszeitalter und Gegenwart*, **3**, 192–215

Turner, E, 1996 An analysis of the horse remains from the Magdalenian level in sector I11 (Q 69, 79 et 89) at Solutré, *Cahier Archéologiques de Bourgogne*, **6**, 131–40

Valensi, P, 1996 Taphonomie des grands mammifères et palethnologie à la Grotte du Lazaret (Nice, France), Anthropozoologica, **23**, 13–28

Vandermeersch, B, 1981 *Les hommes fossiles de Qafzeh (Israel)*, Paris

Vereščagin, N K, and Kolbutov, A A, 1957 Ostatki životnych na must'erskoj stojanke pod Stalingradom i stratigrafičeskoe položenie paleolitičeskogo sloja, *Trudy Zoologičeskogo instituta Akademii Nauk, SSSR*, **22**, 75–89

Vereščagin, N K, 1967 *The mammals of the Caucasus*, Jerusalem

Washburn, S L, and Lancaster, C S, 1968 The evolution of hunting, in *Man the hunter*, (eds R B Lee and I Devore), 293–303, Chicago

Wasmund, E, 1926 Biocoenose und Thanatocoenose, *Archiv für Hydrobiologie*, **17**, 1–116

Weigelt, J, 1927 *Rezente Wirbeltierleichen und ihre paläobiologische Bedeutung*, Leipzig

Zamjatnin, S N, 1929 Station moustérienne a Ilskaja, Province de Kouban (Caucase du Nord), *Revue Anthropol*, **39**, 282–95

Zamjatnin, S N, 1961 Stalingradskaja paleolitičeskaja stojanka, *Kratkie soobščenija o dokladach i polevych issledovanijach instituta Archeologii Akademija Nauk SSSR*, **82**, 5–36

Zapfe, H, 1939 Untersuchungen über die Lebensspuren knochenfressender Raubtiere, mit besonderer Berücksichtigung der Hyäne, *Anzeiger der Akademie der Wissenschaften Wien*, **7**, 33–5

Zapfe, H, 1940 Lebensspuren der eiszeitlichen Höhlenhyäne, *Palaeobiologica*, **7**, 111–46

8 What do we want to know? Questions for archaeological science from the Mesolithic to the Iron Age

by Richard Bradley

Abstract

Archaeological scientists have sometimes been accused of investigating problems that contribute little to the core of the discipline. Some of those criticisms are unfair, as other papers in this volume show. But if the present situation could be improved it is incumbent on the archaeological community to say where they would like research to be concentrated. This paper offers a personal agenda for prehistoric studies from the end of the Mesolithic period to the middle of the Iron Age. It focuses on those areas in which scientific analysis might shed light on current controversies. Among these are: the origins of agriculture in Britain; the movement of human populations between Britain and Continental Europe; the extent of settlement and land use at different points in the prehistoric sequence; the balance between mobility and sedentism; nutrition, public health and dietary change; the relationship between the production and consumption of artefacts; and the main areas of chronological uncertainty in the prehistoric sequence.

This paper is an agenda for archaeological science in Britain from the Mesolithic period to the middle of the Iron Age. Because it is a personal statement, I retain the informal style of the conference paper and restrict bibliographical references to those scholars who are mentioned by name.

I must start by explaining the premises on which the paper is based. Archaeological science can be characterised as the systematic study of the physical properties of ancient material. Whether these are artefacts, seeds, pollen grains, or bones, their analysis depends on more general principles that have been devised outside archaeology itself. Those principles rely on physical constants, and it is a prerequisite of such methods that these studies can be repeated by another investigator with the same results. What is archaeological about this procedure is the source of the material being studied: it is of unusual age, and very often this poses special problems. It may be fragmentary or poorly preserved, and it may have undergone natural alteration between its deposition and its recovery.

Archaeology uses such evidence as a means to an end that cannot be described as science in itself. It is the study of the past using physical remains, but the human behaviour that is the real subject of enquiry would not have exhibited the same regularities as the materials studied in the laboratory. It follows that archaeological

science must take one of two paths. It must either be limited to the precise documentation of the physical residues of the past, or it must step outside the scientific arena entirely and employ its findings in the less predictable task of writing human history. That is not to say that such an exercise is lacking in any discipline, but history and science are not identical, and in archaeology one has to be the servant of the other. Which is the right relationship? In contrast to some of the processual archaeologists of the 1960s and 70s, I believe that science can do no more than contribute to the writing of human history. In place of 'science-based archaeology' I prefer to think in terms of a 'science-assisted archaeology'. But that assistance is crucial.

It follows that my agenda is not concerned with the development of new techniques or the analysis of new kinds of material. I prefer to ask historical questions that science may assist in answering; but lest I appear to be too half-hearted in my espousal of archaeological science, let me say from the outset that these are questions that science alone has the potential to resolve. Mainstream archaeologists have already failed to provide adequate answers to these questions. All we can do at the moment is formulate them more precisely as targets for scientific research.

Some years ago English Heritage published a policy for archaeology in this country that placed a special emphasis on a number of important transitions in the past (English Heritage 1991). I am sorry to say that understanding of those events has not improved since then. Archaeological science may be of material assistance here.

What were the major changes in British prehistory? With just one exception, these were not the period divisions on which so many research policies have been based. The transition from the Mesolithic to the Neolithic remains a pivotal issue, but it is very doubtful indeed whether the first adoption of metalwork was an equally important event. The same surely applies to the beginning of ironworking, whereas the major change that is so visible in the British landscape came part way through what we persist in calling the Bronze Age. There was another in the later years of the Iron Age. My brief excludes the Late Iron Age but it does take in other transitions of equal significance. The irony is that we hardly know them at all.

The Mesolithic–Neolithic transition reflects all of these difficulties, but in an extreme form. Everyone has an opinion on this subject, but no one possesses sufficient information. The issues themselves are quite simple, for they are historical questions. How significant and how widespread is the evidence for economic changes at this time? How much continuity can be seen between the human impact on the Earlier Neolithic landscape and the more controversial changes to the natural environment dating from the late Mesolithic? Were the changes in methods of food production synchronous with changes in material culture? Indeed, where is the latest Mesolithic to be found? And now that the elm decline has lost its cultural status, can we even tell from environmental evidence when the Neolithic period started?

There are many possibilities to be explored, but some confusion has been caused by the way in which archaeologists and pollen analysts have deferred to one another's interpretations until it is not quite clear how we should use their evidence. If we accept that the period division has an economic basis, we need to pay more attention to the earliest finds of cereal pollen. If it is to be marked by changes of material culture, it is essential that radiocarbon dating be directed towards the difficult task of characterising the latest Mesolithic; we can hardly believe the present distribution of dates, which places virtually all the evidence within the jurisdiction of Historic Scotland. It is perverse, to say the least, that we can identify the latest Mesolithic clearances in the pollen record but can barely identify artefacts of the same date on the ground.

These difficulties are absolutely central to our understanding of some wider issues. Why is it that the adoption of domesticates is so difficult for archaeological scientists to pin down? Do environmental archaeologists possess enough spatial resolution to distinguish between mobile and sedentary patterns of exploitation at this time? I ask because of the paradoxical situation that we can find sites with many thousands of artefacts dating from perhaps 5000 BC but can hardly recognise the occupation sites created a thousand years later. That runs completely counter to our intuitive understanding that Mesolithic land use was less sustained than the first exploitation of domesticates. Ian Simmons has recently published an extensive study of the environmental impact of later Mesolithic groups on the environment of upland Britain (Simmons 1996) It would be worth examining rather later deposits in the same amount of detail. Did the adoption of domesticates involve a major change in the ways in which the environment was used? The key to such questions may be provided by radiocarbon dating, for all too often in the past episodes of prehistoric land use have been located by reference to archaeological orthodoxies.

If we are to resolve these issues we shall need to be proactive. Field archaeologists have made it an article of faith that all their observations should be recorded objectively and given equal weight. That is why excavation reports so often fail as pieces of research. If certain issues seem to be vitally important at the moment, why not investigate them at the expense of other topics? Where Neolithic domestic material exists, surely it would be worth investing more heavily in the seeds and animal bones than in the pottery and flints. In similar circumstances it might be better to excavate waterlogged deposits for their environmental information rather than the monuments in their vicinity, which may tell us nothing new. Above all, we should concentrate on deeply stratified sites with relevant information rather than those that were used during a single phase. Grahame Clark's work in the Fenland during the 1930s set an example of well targeted research that has rarely been emulated, and has still not been surpassed. Surely the riches revealed by the Fenland Survey include sites where this work could be carried out, for unless we can achieve more fine-grained analyses than we have carried out up to now, this most important transition will remain in darkness.

Other possible approaches are on the horizon, but their usefulness may be limited by problems of sample size. It may be possible to extract DNA from human skeletal remains, but until we find Mesolithic cemeteries like those in Continental Europe (and we have no reason to suppose that they existed here) we shall be able to study the Neolithic population without knowing how far it diverged from the genetic makeup of insular hunter-gatherers. The same will also be true of any attempts to use human bone to study prehistoric diet. Perhaps more could be achieved in the short term by the routine analysis of surviving residues in Neolithic pottery.

The same problems recur in different guises later in the prehistoric sequence. The environmental record needs to be more carefully assessed since there is absolutely no consensus about the nature and extent of farming during the Later Neolithic; nor is it by any means obvious whether it increased in importance in the Early Bronze Age. These are not entirely empirical questions, as they have very much wider implications for the ways in which we write prehistoric archaeology. Is it true that the creation of enormous monuments in the Later Neolithic was financed by an agricultural surplus? There are certainly changes in the distribution of settlements and monuments at this time, but to what extent was the economy based on cereals rather than animal products? If there were a larger number of sedentary settlements, why has it been so difficult to find them? And why should wild plant remains play such a prominent part among the food remains that have been studied? In order to answer these questions, we must be proactive yet again, looking deliberately for samples of pollen, seeds, insects, and plant remains that will enable us to address these questions. It will also be important to consider the dietary evidence provided by human bones, for by this phase many suitable samples are available. Again there is an important role for analysis of the residues inside Later Neolithic ceramics.

Earlier in this paper I expressed the view that the transition between the Late Neolithic and the Early Bronze Age might have been less significant than was once supposed, but this dogmatic statement should not be taken at face value. There are two key issues here, each with persuasive proponents. First, there are the questions raised by the adoption of Beakers and metalwork. These have been debated almost entirely in terms of archaeological theory, yet we may soon be able to test the arguments for genetic continuity among the British population using the evidence of DNA. Why are we not taking that opportunity? I fear that it is because the question itself is unfashionable, yet it does bear on a second interpretation that has equally important implications. Some years ago Peter Fowler argued that it was during the Beaker phase that we find evidence for agricultural intensification, including an increased investment in cereal growing and the first creation of field systems (Fowler 1983). I am doubtful about both of these ideas, but the first of these hypotheses has certainly been supported by carefully conduced research in the Netherlands, and it is surely time to test this hypothesis using the same techniques that I have advocated for the Neolithic period. This could also shed light on another influential but entirely untested proposition: Andrew Fleming's suggestion that the dramatic increase in wealth seen in Early Bronze Age communities was based on a pastoral economy (Fleming 1971).

During later phases there is much less difficulty in deciding the character of the subsistence economy: it is the pattern of stable mixed farming that so many prehistorians had expected to encounter in the Neolithic period. In this case the evidence from animal bones, plant remains, and from the landscape itself is unequivocal, but that is not to suppose that all the problems have been solved. At least three key issues remain to be investigated systematically. First, there are the influential arguments of Colin Burgess that after a period of widespread exploitation that began during the Early Bronze Age large parts of upland Britain could no longer sustain human settlement (Burgess 1992). As he himself said, this interpretation appears to conflict with the pollen record. We need to resolve that problem. Part of the difficulty, I suspect, is that the Early Bronze Age settlements are dated by their pottery. A first stage might be to subject their chronology to scrutiny using radiocarbon dating.

A second related issue is to investigate the timing of economic intensification in the landscape, using radiocarbon-dated pollen cores. Some years ago the situation seemed clear – the landscape was reorganised around the needs of productive agriculture during the Middle and Late Bronze Ages – but this easy generalisation has worn very thin indeed, and substantially similar developments seem to be distributed across different regions over nearly a thousand years. Thus the intensification that took place on Dartmoor during the Early Bronze Age did not reach some regions until the Late Bronze Age or Iron Age. Early developments in East Anglia have few close counterparts in the Midlands until the mid first millennium BC.

The last issue is the explanation of changes in the landscape. Here the major factor is often identified as population pressure, but it is difficult to test this model on a large enough scale, especially during the Early Iron Age, where such ideas figure prominently in the work of Barry Cunliffe (1991). That is because so few settlements sites can be dated by their surface remains. The history of field systems and land boundaries remains extremely sketchy, and during the crucial period a further complication is provided by a plateau in the radiocarbon calibration curve. It follows that population densities are best extrapolated from some form of proxy evidence. One might be the extent of clearance in the pollen record, and another could be build-up of alluvial and colluvial deposits. Both have the advantage that they provide stratigraphic sequences that cut across the 'dark age' in the calibration curve. We might also look for evidence of dietary stress, using the evidence of human bones.

As all these examples show, there are considerable advantages in organising work on an explicitly comparative basis. Mesolithic specialists may be concerned with the extent to which the human population made an impact on the natural environment. I would like to know how that impact compared with the effects of Neolithic or Early Bronze Age people. I would also like to know whether there were any horizons of change in the exploitation of resources or whether, as I suspect, the pattern of development differed significantly from one region to another.

If such a project is to be useful, it must be coupled with a more securely based chronology for artefacts and monuments, and with a much better understanding of the processes by which those objects were made. Otherwise the results of archaeological science will still be cut off from the remainder of discipline. I shall start with chronology, for what seems to be a simple question of sequence soon becomes implicated in a more complex historical narrative. It is on the chronology of different phenomena that influential interpretations depend.

I shall quote just two examples of the way in which interpretations and chronologies intertwine. The first concerns the Later Neolithic period. Here there are two main styles of pottery in England – Peterborough Ware and Grooved Ware – and both seem to have been succeeded by the adoption of Bell Beakers of Continental origin; whether there was a substantial overlap remains uncertain at the moment. All three of these basic styles can be subdivided, although in every case their internal sequence is contentious. More important, these ceramic styles have different associations. Peterborough Ware and Beakers can be associated with round barrows and with individual burials, whereas Grooved Ware is especially associated with henge monuments. If those two styles were in use over the same period, as the apparent resemblance between Peterborough Ware and Early Bronze Age Collared Urns suggests, then it seems likely that they were used in different ways. Some time ago Thorpe and Richards suggested that the people who used Peterborough Ware practised a form of 'prestige goods economy' in which personal position was symbolised by access to exotica. Grooved Ware users, on the other hand, had a rather different form of social organisation in which differences of power and status were based on access to the supernatural; this would account for the close links between this tradition and henge monuments (Thorpe and Richards 1984). For these authors the adoption of Beakers from the Continent could be explained by the dynamics of the Peterborough Ware network, which set a considerable premium on the acquisition of non-local goods. It also explained why early Beakers were uncommon in henges.

There was a time when this model seemed to solve several problems; now it creates many more. The main difficulty is that the radiocarbon chronology for these three styles is unsatisfactory. Grooved Ware and Peterborough Ware may have run in parallel, but it is just as likely that they were used in sequence, in which case the links with Collared Urns would have to be rejected. In the same way, it is possible that Beaker pottery replaced either or both of these styles and that there was little overlap between them. Each reconstruction of the chronology of these ceramics has quite different social implications and, as Gibson and Kinnes (1997) have shown, none of them is securely based.

The second chronological question concerns the dating of the Wessex Early Bronze Age. I am not so concerned with the relationship between Wessex and Continental Europe as I am with the domestic settlements of this period. Do the last Wessex graves overlap with the creation of field systems, urnfields, and enclosed settlements, as the radiocarbon dates suggest, or are we dealing with another sequence? In one model, the Wessex Culture might have collapsed, to be replaced by a series of undifferentiated agricultural settlements; in another, it would have been the intensification of food production that supported the lavish consumption of wealth in funerary ritual. The fact is that neither model can command much support, for the available dates are too few and too imprecise. Again what seems to be a matter entirely of chronology involves fundamental problems of explanation. The same is true of the application of scientific techniques to many other problems in prehistory.

The other area of uncertainty concerns the characterisation of artefacts. Again the differences of opinion seem to be of a very specialised nature, and as such are really the province of the scientists. For example, how far was pottery (or its contents) exchanged in Neolithic society, and how far are we observing the movement of the raw materials? Is the fingerprinting of stone axes based on satisfactory evidence? Could axes of similar petrology have originated from different sources, and might some of these artefacts have been made from glacial erratics. How reliable are our methods for sourcing Bronze Age artefacts?

What might seem to be methodological questions of this kind are too important to be left unanswered. We attempt to characterise prehistoric artefacts, not because they 'are there', nor because it provides an opportunity for developing new techniques of analysis. What matters is a crucial historical issue. How far were social relations in prehistory mediated through long distance exchange? How far should the distributions of artefacts be explained in utilitarian terms? Did any of these processes come under political control?

In recent years there have been some welcome developments in this field, but for the most part they have not come from archaeological science, which has been rather too silent on such issues. There have been studies of the circumstances under which particular kinds of artefacts were consumed, and there have also been investigations of the sites where they were made. Yet we seem reluctant to take these issues sufficiently seriously. Most of the British flint mines have been ploughed out, and the stone axe quarries are eroding away. It is only recently that we have even begun to follow the lead of our Irish colleagues in locating early copper mines. Surely the most logical point from which to track the movement of artefacts across the landscape is the place where they were made. O'Brien's work (this volume) shows the merits of this approach. It should not be limited to studies of metalwork. Prehistorians cannot wait for their colleagues to agree on the right methods of analysis. It is time that they took the lead.

I am aware that I have asked many questions and offered very few answers. I have said less about our knowledge than our ignorance, but this is surely the time for prehistorians like myself to say what we want from archaeological science. For that reason I disagree with Julian Thomas's attack on the intellectual basis of the discipline (Thomas 1990). If we want scientists to write history, it is up to us to make sure that they are asking the right kinds of questions. There are as many agendas as there are archaeologists studying the past. I am grateful for this opportunity to tell the reader what *I* would like to know.

References

Burgess, C, 1992 Discontinuity and dislocation in later prehistoric settlement: some evidence from Atlantic Europe, in *L'habitat et l'occupation du sol a l'Age du Bronze* (ed C Mordant), 21–40, Paris

Cunliffe, B, 1991 *Iron Age communities in Britain*, 3 edn, London

English Heritage 1991 *Exploring our past: strategies for the archaeology of England*, London

Fleming, A, 1971 Territorial patterns in Bronze Age Wessex, *Proc Prehist Soc*, **37**(1), 138–66

Fowler, P, 1983 *The farming of prehistoric Britain*, Cambridge

Gibson, A, and Kinnes, I, 1997 On the urns of a dilemma: radiocarbon and the Peterborough problem, *Oxford J Archaeol*, **16**, 65–72

Simmons, I, 1996 *The environmental impact of later Mesolithic cultures*, Edinburgh

Thomas, J, 1990 Silent running: the ills of environmental archaeology, *Scott Archaeol Rev*, 7, 2–7

Thorpe, I, and Richards, C, 1984 The decline of ritual authority and the introduction of Beakers into Britain, in *Neolithic studies* (ed R Bradley and J Gardiner), 67–84, Oxford

9 Detection of human impact on the natural environment: palynological views

by Kevin J Edwards

Abstract

Pollen data are used extensively in archaeology, both to provide information about the environmental context for early human communities and to illuminate landuse practices. The implications arising from pollen analysis have been, and continue to be, far-reaching. There is still a need, however, for archaeologists to be more aware of the potential offered by palynology; many of them are aware of the limitations.

If the findings of palynology are accepted, then the explanatory and predictive power offered by it already have the potential to answer a number of the questions posed by archaeologists. As significantly, pollen data used proactively can provide valuable challenges to the archaeologist in terms of remedying deficiencies arising from the invisibility and lack of continuity in the archaeological record.

There is still a need for advances in palynological methodology, including the wider utilisation of complementary techniques such as tephrochronology, the AMS dating of pollen and statistical approaches. More adventurous interpretational tools are also desirable.

Introduction

For more than half a century, awareness of the potential of palynology to provide a measure of human impact upon the natural environment has been substantial. In 1929, the founder of modern pollen analysis, Lennart Von Post, had suggested that frequencies of cereal pollen could be used to determine the expansion of tilled areas (quoted in Iversen 1941, 48). Firbas's demonstration of cereal pollen detection in 1937 (Firbas 1937) was followed in 1941 by Iversen's classic paper on the *landnam* or clearance phase phenomenon. Since these times, an enormous number of publications have focused upon the anthropogenic factor in vegetation history; as long ago as 1981, the bibliography of Simmons and Tooleys' edited volume *The environment in British prehistory* contained about 265 palynological papers, mostly from English and Irish sites, and a quantity that represented only key papers to that date. Tipping's (1994) survey of Scottish woodland history cites some 200 relevant papers, while Caseldine's (1990) survey of environmental archaeology in Wales mentions about 150 pollen-analytical publications.

Off-site pollen data – those obtained from peat bogs and lakes at varied distances from archaeological sites – are now available for large areas of northern Europe, and the casual observer might be forgiven for believing that saturation coverage is available for much of the British Isles. Despite the existence of hundreds of pollen diagrams, the quality of available data leaves much to be desired, especially data obtained many years ago. On-site pollen data – of the sort often obtained from archaeological soil contexts – can be of great use for elucidating site history and conditions, but can be extremely difficult to interpret.

The broad findings from pollen studies are so ingrained in the archaeological and environmental psyches that I think we take them for granted. There is, for instance, the evidence of the migration and presence of trees at different time periods (clearly of great significance if we are concerned with the environmental context of Mesolithic peoples); there are the indisputable beginnings of major clearance during, variously, the Neolithic, the Bronze Age, and the Iron Age; there is the interplay between arable and pastoral activities; and for upland areas especially, there is the inexorable spread of blanket mires. Superimposed upon these patterns is a wealth of information allowing inferences concerning, for instance, the use of fire and other landscape impacts by hunter-gatherers, coppicing and leaf-foddering as part of woodland management regimes, and pre-elm decline cereals with the implications for early agriculture.

That there are limitations to palynology is well known, precisely because palynology has been exemplary in tackling methodological problems arising from its techniques and interpretations (cf Faegri and Iversen 1989; Moore *et al* 1991). The sheer number of palynologists has also enabled a continuous examination of the method in a way that has not been possible in most other specialisms associated with archaeological science; this certainly applies to microscope-based studies with fewer practitioners, such as of diatoms, insects, or phytoliths.

The fact that many of the results of palynological research are so well established may blind us to the fact that much more work needs to be done. Indeed, the ubiquity of the pollen method, the relative ease with which beginners can at least start to count pollen, the elegance of the findings, and a failure to appreciate the nuances of pollen inference, may all have contributed to a complacency regarding the nature of the discoveries associated with it and the continuing need for more data and basic research. It is possible to cite a continuum of quotations that puts some of this into perspective. Thus, at a basic level, there are the statements from ecologist David Bellamy (1972, 17, 20) that:

All that posterity needs is a peat borer and a tame palynologist ... the pollen people have been doing their homework and have schemes which account for just about everything ...

There is Neil Roberts's claim (1989, 22) that:

Palynology is the single most important branch of palaeoecology for the Late Pleistocene and Holocene.

Belief in the method reaches possibly grandiloquent heights with the assertion of limnologist Ed Deevey (1967, quoted in Birks 1993, 166):

Von Post's simple idea, that a series of changes in pollen proportions in accumulating peat was a four-dimensional look at vegetation, must rank with the double helix as one of the most productive suggestions of modern times.

Archaeologist Stig Welinder pronounced that (1988, 129):

Pollen analysis is a science fascinatingly devoid of epistemological theory compared to modern archaeology.

While one distinguished palynologist avers that for him (Birks 1993, 166):

many of the current and future challenges in Quaternary pollen analysis lie at the conceptual interface between vegetation science and palaeoecology, rather than between pollen analysis and ... local site archaeology ...

It is not the aim of this paper to extol the virtues of palynology for archaeology, but rather to indicate where advances in on- and off-site pollen analysis have and can be made.

Successes and answers?

If the general usefulness of pollen-analytical results is taken as given, then that removes the need to dwell on the findings, many of them of both general and site-specific interest, from innumerable sites in Britain and elsewhere. They become of particular interest, however, if they can be applied to questions asked by non-environmental, social archaeological colleagues.

Without conducting an opinion poll, it is difficult to be sure of central questions asked of the palynologist (either directly by pollen, or indirectly as a problem aimed at the environmental fraternity in general). Richard Bradley (this volume) asks some of them, and others were asked in a series of papers delivered at a joint Quaternary Research Association/Association for Environmental Archaeology conference (Edwards and Sadler forthcoming). Questions associated with the themes considered below recur frequently. Each of these will be tackled briefly from the point of view of recent findings, which in this writer's view are both of interest and worthy of development. Some related issues are considered elsewhere (Edwards forthcoming).

The role of fire in the Mesolithic

A copious literature relating to palynologically-inferred fire in the Mesolithic and at other periods exists (cf Bennett *et al* 1990; Clark and Royall 1995; Edwards 1990; Patterson *et al* 1987; Simmons 1996) and an equally extensive ethnographic literature is available (eg Cronon 1983; Lewis 1981; Mellars 1976). An interesting question arises, however, as to the significance of the microscopic charcoal record. Various papers have produced data in conflict with known catchment fire histories (MacDonald *et al* 1991; Whitlock and Millspaugh 1996); others have presented patterns that, along with the accompanying pollen, are ecologically highly plausible (Edwards 1996; Odgaard 1992; Turner *et al* 1993).

An example of the differing perspectives that might apply comes from work in the Outer Hebrides when compared to data from a wider area of Europe. Detailed charcoal and pollen data from the South Uist site of Loch an t-Sil (Fig 9.1) reveal two phases of woodland reduction at *c* 8040 and *c* 7870 BP, lasting 130 (phases b(i) and b(ii)) and 70 (phase d) radiocarbon years respectively. These are associated with increases in Poaceae (grasses), *Calluna* (heather), and charcoal, and with decreases in undifferentiated ferns (Pteropsida monolete indet. = Filicales) and royal fern (*Osmunda regalis*). The reduction in birch and hazel may be anthropogenic in origin and the expansions in grass and heather could indicate their spread into cleared areas. Whether the extension of browse in order to attract animals was the intention, or a useful by-product of cropping woodland or burning a trashed ground layer, remains unknown. The sustained charcoal peaks do not have to indicate woodland removal by fire or burning as part of management practice (eg muirburn or brushwood burning), but simply the burning of felled wood for heating or cooking purposes (cf Edwards 1990). This site and others like it (Edwards 1996; Edwards *et al* 1995) are of special interest because there is no archaeological evidence for Mesolithic peoples in the Outer Hebrides – a topic addressed below. The possibility remains that most, if not all of the phenomena evident at Loch an t-Sil, have natural causes.

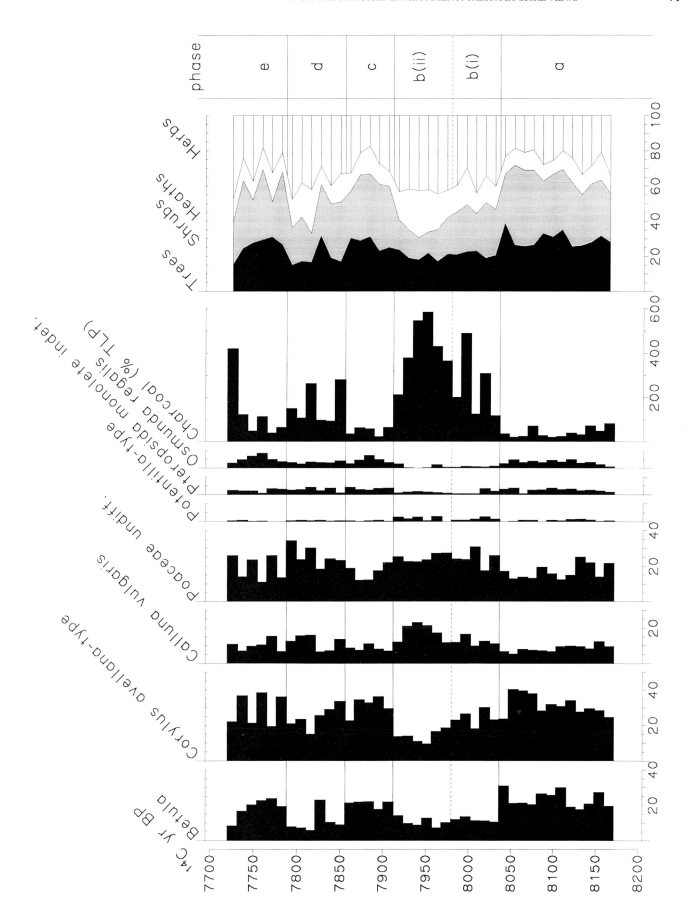

Fig 9.1 Selected pollen and spore taxa from Loch an t-Sìl, South Uist showing possible phases of Mesolithic impact beginning at 8040 and 7870 BP; there is no archaeological evidence for a Mesolithic presence in the Outer Hebrides (after Edwards 1996)

Richard Tipping (1996) takes the fire records from South Uist and elsewhere in northern Scotland, produces a single cumulative summary curve, and compares the results with an 'effective' precipitation curve for north-west Europe based on such palaeoclimatic data as lake-level fluctuations and peat stratigraphies (Fig 9.2). The averaged charcoal data display a marked increase in representation from *c* 8000 BP, with a doubling of registered fire incidence from the previous period. Tipping doubts that human agency could have contributed to such a dramatic increase and concludes that a more likely cause was a combination of the development of potentially combustible heathland and a climatic shift to increased aridity. The extent to which such a model can be transported to more southerly areas is clearly worthy of investigation.

Studies of biomass burning based upon changes in combustion by-products measured in the Greenland ice cores also provide new perspectives (Chylek *et al* 1992; Legrand *et al* 1992). They suggest, for instance, an enhancement in burning between the periods 5000–> 6000 BP, 1150–3250 BP, 350–750 BP, and 0–150 BP following wildfire events in eastern Canada especially, but also including major inputs from northern Europe (probably >10% in the GISP2 core, Taylor *et al* 1996). The burning introduces fire by-products such as organic compounds, ammonium, and soot into the atmosphere, and tropospheric transport and precipitation may eventually lead to the deposition of materials in the accumulating Greenland ice sheet. Prior to 6000 BP, major changes in air masses associated with the down-wasting of the Laurentide ice sheet, complicate the interpretations as to fire sources. The applicability of such results to local patterns of burning may be minimal– indeed, it might be wondered whether any patterns are contained in background charcoal rain levels, but are obscured by the signal from local anthropogenic fires.

Fire studies are a major source of palynological investigation and more of these are necessary, especially modern charcoal trapping experiments. The importance of fire to hunter-gatherer and early agricultural economies is essentially unknown for Britain and many other areas. The evidence from palynology really is fundamental to this history.

Agricultural origins and the Mesolithic–Neolithic transition

The beginnings of agriculture, in the sense of cereal cultivation, are always likely to be of major concern to archaeology. They have been of marginally less importance to environmentally-oriented palynologists who have traditionally been concerned with the phenomenon of woodland clearance rather than necessarily looking for signs of agriculture, which may be absent anyway (as far as cereal and diagnostic weed pollen are concerned), and which may not coincide with woodland reduction.

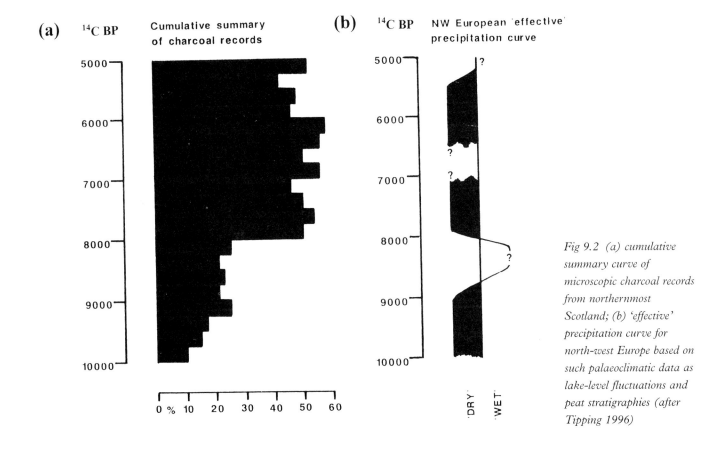

Fig 9.2 (a) cumulative summary curve of microscopic charcoal records from northernmost Scotland; (b) 'effective' precipitation curve for north-west Europe based on such palaeoclimatic data as lake-level fluctuations and peat stratigraphies (after Tipping 1996)

Spread of cultivation

A few years ago (Edwards and MacDonald 1991), it was suggested that pollen data might be used in a similar way to archaeological and plant macrofossil evidence in an exercise of the type made famous by Ammerman and Cavalli-Sforza (1971; 1984). Bravely, Willis, and Bennett (1994) have since done this using the rather limited number of pollen data sets from the Balkans, not without comment (Edwards *et al* 1996; Magri 1996). The utility of such procedures on a Europe-wide scale, where the temporal compass is larger than the imprecisions on radiocarbon dates, may be justifiable. The application of the approach might even be applicable to Britain, or, arguably, a region of the island given certain strict conditions, viz availability of deposits, a sufficient density of sites and acceptably well defined agricultural horizons (eg the first appearance of cereal pollen, or as a surrogate, the first agriculturally related changes in arboreal or herbaceous pollen taxa). Meeting these requirements would be very time-consuming, even if optimising techniques were employed (Bowler and Hall 1989; Edwards and McIntosh 1988; Edwards *et al* 1986; Gish 1994). Early cultivation, of course, may not have taken place in major clearings – it may have been a feature of forest farming in which small garden plots were involved (Edwards 1993; Göransson 1986); an implication of this would be that sites become even more difficult to detect.

Early agriculture

Linked to all this, in a north-west European context, is the phenomenon of pre-elm decline cereal-type pollen. Ever since attention was drawn to such pollen grains in Britain and Ireland (Edwards and Hirons 1984; Groenman-van Waateringe 1983), many more have been found. The separation of cereal from wild grass pollen grains is very difficult (Andersen 1979; Dickson 1988) and the interpretation of the evidence from pollen profiles must be carefully qualified (Edwards 1989; O'Connell 1987). What is also becoming apparent is that certain near-coastal pollen sites are producing cereal-type pollen deposited thousands of years prior to the *Ulmus* decline (eg in the Outer Hebrides, Edwards and Whittington 1997; Fossitt 1996), almost certainly representing large pollen grains from coastal grasses such as *Ammophila arenaria* (marram) and *Leymus arenarius* (lyme-grass), and there is no suggestion that these are reflecting anthropogenic influences.

Notwithstanding this, there is probably a message from inland areas, at least about early agriculture, that should be taken on board: that woodland-based cultivation was taking place in Britain and elsewhere up to a millennium prior to the usually first seen appearance of cereal pollen in elm decline times (from *c* 5100 BP [3830 cal BC], Fig 9.3).

Acceptance of this would pose a discovery problem for the archaeologist: where are the likely ephemeral occupation sites of the first agriculturalists? The warning must be given, of course, that the more people become aware of the existence of pre-elm decline cereal-type pollen, then the greater the likelihood of them being recorded as such (rather than simply as undifferentiated Poaceae), whether they are derived from the Cerealia or from wild species (if that is a relevant distinction [cf Edwards 1988; Zvelebil 1994]). Ultimately, proof of such early agriculture may need to come from excavation and/or macrofossils, assuming that the dating evidence is also secure.

The charcoal decline

A number of analysed sites are revealing a sharp decline in microscopic charcoal at or close to the elm decline (cf Fig 9.3). This phenomenon has been discussed elsewhere (Edwards 1988; Edwards and MacDonald 1991; Edwards and McIntosh 1988; Simmons 1996) but, in general, has been little remarked. The significance of this needs investigation. The reduction means that less charcoal is reaching the pollen site. Can this be interpreted

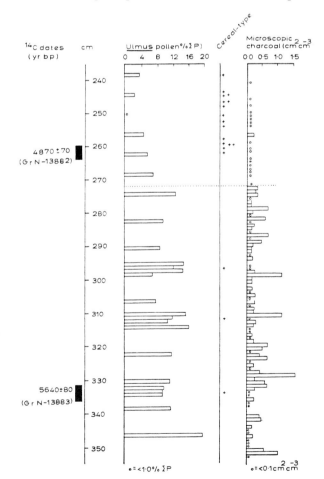

Fig 9.3 Elm pollen, cereal-type pollen, and microscopic charcoal records from Rhoin Farm, Kintyre; the elm decline is shown by the dotted line (after Edwards 1991)

simply as an economy based predominantly on hunter-gathering (with a preponderance of camp-fires and conceivably burning for browse), giving way to nucleated farming sites where domestically-produced charcoal, of lower abundance than previously, predominates and where the charcoal sources were typically more distant from hunter-gatherer ones (which tended to be close to subsequent charcoal sampling sites, ie mires and lakes)? This may have implications not just for the balance of activities, but if refined or proven, could represent a reliable indicator locally of a move away from the fire regimes typical of hunter-gathering times. Could this be, in fact, one of the better measures of the Mesolithic–Neolithic transition? More published charcoal data, especially from England, is urgently required.

The nature of agricultural activity

Arable/pastoral ratios

The nature of agricultural activity is central to much archaeological explanation and it has an extensive palynological literature. While continuing attempts to characterise pollen assemblages by arable/pastoral ratios may be refined (cf Fenton-Thomas 1992; Pratt 1996), there is no getting away from the fact, recognised some time ago by most people involved in such exercises (eg Maguire 1983; Turner 1964), that such reconstructions are imprecise, both because of difficulties involved in justifying a taxon as a specific indicator type (cf Behre 1981) and because the pollen productivity and catchment area characteristics of an assemblage can be so varied. An inferential bias in favour of pastoralism needs to be guarded against (Caseldine and Hatton 1996; Edwards 1979). A trend from apparent pastoral to arable regimes, or *vice versa*, may be quite convincing, however, and it would not be surprising if statistical methods of the type used to investigate the significance of diversity in minor taxa, such as rarefaction analysis (Birks and Line 1992), could not be adapted to provide insights for the assessment of agricultural regimes.

Woodland management

It was the Swedish palynologist Hans Göransson (1987) who said that a model that includes only herbaceous anthropogenic pollen indicators and that excludes the pollen sum of broad-leaved trees during the Stone Age is a useless one. As if in recognition of this, woodland management is increasingly discussed by palynologists. Coppicing, pollarding, shredding, and leaf-foddering (Rackham 1980; 1988) are all management tools that optimise woodland resources, which could have an impact upon pollen production and which might be evident in pollen diagrams (cf Andersen 1988; Edwards 1993; Göransson 1986; Smith 1970; Troels-Smith 1984). Progress in efforts to detect these practices may

well lie in modern pollen rain studies, based on the supposition that woodland management is likely to lead to initial bursts of flowering and pollen production. The latter could be discernible via studies of annual pollen accumulation rates (pollen influx). An attempt to identify woodland management is that of Stevenson and Harrison (1992) who used canonical correspondence analysis to compare fossil with modern analogue data from Spain. The persistence of apparent regeneration phases (Edwards 1979; Göransson 1986), often with single dominant tree types untroubled by competition for unusually long periods (Edwards 1993; Göransson 1986; Tipping 1994) could indicate that a protected, managed woodland is in existence. Once again, this is a phenomenon that pollen influx studies might reveal.

Modern pollen studies

Behre's 1981 paper emphasised the ecological amplitudes of many cultural pollen indicators. Groenman-van Waateringe (1986) showed that *Plantago lanceolata*, the archetypal anthropogenic indicator, can, in certain circumstances, be a useful indicator of arable activity. More recently (Groenman-van Waateringe 1993), she has shown how, in an initial clearing, there is a burst of flowering for grasses, but as grazing continues and intensifies, grass pollen production falls, giving the appearance of a closing forest cover. Palynological interpretations must become more sophisticated if these situations are to be tackled. Awareness of such effects, however, demands far more carefully designed modern pollen studies and probably a greater willingness to embrace statistical procedures (cf Gaillard *et al* 1992).

The movement of population across territories

Application of 'wave of advance' type activities by pollen analysts (see above) may be considered to provide also an indication of population movement. If this is thought too grandiose a claim, then small areas may be viewed on a site by site basis. A major problem is that a lot of pollen diagrams would be required to provide patterns of spread acceptable to the palynologist. In any case, convincing patterns of population movement for small areas based on excavation data, would need to be based on an equally dense grid of sites to satisfy most scientists. It might be thought provocative, but appropriate pollen and radiocarbon data could be more forthcoming, more quickly and at a lower price than a series of excavations – with the environmental data as a bonus!

The extent of settlement and landuse at different times

The areal extent of settlement and/or farmland will exercise some control over the quantity of pollen reaching a depositional site; for instance, an extensively cleared area of woodland, replaced by buildings and mixed farmland will be reflected by reduced woodland pollen and an increase in the pollen of crops, pasture, and disturbed areas. A single pollen site will be able to indicate that such activities were taking place over a given period of time, but only in clearly differentiated ecological situations will it be able to show where that activity was occurring (cf Oldfield 1963), and it will probably be unable to demonstrate that it was taking place in different parts of the pollen catchment area at different times (eg as part of a process of landuse rotation or of shifting cultivation); nor will it allow discernment as to whether a distant large impact, as opposed to a nearby small one, was under consideration. These conundra are discussed at length elsewhere (eg Edwards 1979; 1982; 1991), but in defence of the pollen data from single sites, the ability to show that clearance and agriculture were taking place for a specified length of time is a very powerful one.

An elegant, if time-consuming way of attempting to overcome the limitations of the single profile study, is to use multiple profiles in a so-called 'three-dimensional' investigation, whereby pollen sites located in different parts of the pollen catchment area will detect the spatial variation in human activity to be added to the dimensions of abundance and time (Behre and Kučan 1986; Molloy and O'Connell 1995; Turner 1970; 1975). The reliability of this will depend on the density of sites and the precision of the chronological framework. What this boils down to, of course, is the availability of resources to produce extra detailed pollen data and, normally, to obtain a sufficiently large number of radiocarbon dates. An interesting development of this is the use of multiple pollen sites for a constrained time period (Segerström 1991) and this is discussed later.

The detection of mobile populations

Some comment has already taken place about the transition from hunter-gathering to agriculture, and the Mesolithic–Neolithic transition and the movement of population. Sedentism may be more evident in the pollen record because of the scale of impact upon woodland pollen taxa and the response from herbaceous species. Mobility of populations mean that the detection of probably minor disturbances (disregarding game driving by fire) becomes very difficult, even if high resolution analyses are carried out (Turner and Peglar 1988). The significance of minor taxa in this respect is displayed in the work associated with summer transhumance camps in Norway by Kvamme (1988) and Moe et al (1988), on forest reindeer herding in Sweden by Aronsson (1991) and on Saami forest-based hunter-gathering winter sites in Finland by Hicks (1993). Both Kvamme and Hicks demonstrate the need for pollen sites to be located close to the activities being investigated if anthropogenic impact is to be detected.

Taxonomy, economic plants, and diet

Apart from the basic division between arable crop production and animal husbandry, the limitation on refining the detection of foodstuffs is pollen taxonomy (Table 9.1). This is certainly capable of improvement. For reasons of confidence or strategy, many palynologists do not take identifications to the lowest taxonomic level. Lactuceae (or Compositae liguliflorae) is seen as sufficient and conveys enough for some purposes as splitting the taxon further to say Cichorium intybus-type or Sonchus oleraceus-type. The pollen catalogue of Bennett (1994) shows what can be done by optical means as do the continuing series of publications in the Northwest European pollen flora (eg Clarke and Jones 1977; Punt and Maloteaux 1984). The necessity of using the electron microscope is not seen as paramount by most palynologists – or not unless there is a specific problem to be investigated (cf Edwards 1981). Similarly, most investigators will not be concerned to measure Cannabaceae grains in order to differentiate Cannabis sativa (hemp) from Humulus lupulus (hop) (Whittington and Gordon 1987), for the context and behaviour of the pollen curves is assumed to provide the required level of certainty (Whittington and Edwards 1989).

An ever-present concern is likely to be that of separation within the cereals (see above), and specific identification may not be solvable even with the aid of the electron microscope (cf Köhler and Lange 1979; Watson and Bell 1975). Vicia faba (broad bean) and non-cultivated species accommodated within Vicia sylvatica-type represent another difficult taxon, although separation is possible given good type material (cf Greig 1994). A willingness to tackle difficult, often herb-rich polleniferous media, such as latrine fills or urban contexts (Krzwinski et al 1983), cannot fail to illuminate the records and limitations from more customary off-site locations.

The lowlands

Many pollen data derive from upland, northern, and western locations. The Midlands, and eastern and southern England have a lower density of sites. This is exacerbated by the lack of lakes and intact mires (though see eg Peglar 1993; Peglar and Birks 1993; Van de Noort and Ellis 1995). The study of valley mires (Day 1993; Scaife 1982) and dolines (Waton 1982) can go some way to alleviating the situation. The potential importance of the lowlands and river valleys to early settlement is coming increasingly under palynological survey. In this respect, researches on riverine deposits in the eastern Midlands (Brown 1992), on the pre-Anglian fluvial deposits at High Lodge, Suffolk (Hunt 1994), on

Table 9.1 Plants of potential economic importance in the Mesolithic of north-west Europe[1] and levels of pollen taxonomic precision[2]

Scientific name	Common name	Product(s)	Pollen
Corylus avellana	hazel	nuts	*Corylus avellana*-type
Crataegus spp	hawthorn	leaves/fruit	*Sorbus*-type
Fagus sylvatica	beech	nuts	*Fagus sylvatica*
Juglans regia	walnut	nuts	*Juglans regia*
Malus spp	crab apple	fruit	*Sorbus*-type
Prunus avium	wild cherry	fruit	*Sorbus*-type
Pyrus spp	wild pear	fruit	*Sorbus*-type
Quercus spp	oak	acorns	*Quercus*
Fragaria vesca	wild strawberry	leaves/fruit	*Potentilla*-type
Ribes nigrum	blackcurrant	fruit	*Rubus rubrum* type[3]
Rosa spp	wild rose	fruit	*Rosa*
Rubus chamaemorus	cloudberry	fruit	*Rubus chamaemorus*
Rubus spp	bramble/raspberry	fruit	*Rubus* undiff
Sambucus nigra	elder	fruit	*Sambucus nigra*
Empetrum nigrum	crowberry	fruit	*Empetrum nigrum*
Vaccinium spp	bilberry	fruit	*Vaccinium*-type
Atriplex spp	orache	seeds	Chenopodiaceae
Chenopodium spp	goosefoot	seeds	Chenopodiaceae
Galeopsis tetrahit	common hemp-nettle	leaves	*Stachys*-type
Persicaria bistorta-type	common bistort	leaves	*Persicaria bistorta*-type
Poaceae (Gramineae)	grasses	seeds	Poaceae
Polygonum spp	knotweed	seeds	*Polygonum*-type
Potentilla anserina	silverweed	roots	*Potentilla*-type
Rumex crispus	curled dock	leaves	*Rumex sanguineus*-type
Stachys palustris	woundwort	roots	*Stachys*-type
Stellaria media	chickweed	leaves	*Cerastium*-type
Taraxacum officinale	dandelion	leaves	*Cichorium intybus*-type
Urtica dioica	common nettle	leaves	*Urtica dioica*
Vicia spp	vetch	seeds	*Vicia cracca;V. sylvatica*-type
Alisma plantago-aquatica	water plantain	rhizomes	*Alisma*-type
Menyanthes trifoliata	bog bean	rhizomes	*Menyanthes trifoliata*
Nuphar lutea	yellow water-lilly	seeds	*Nuphar*
Nymphaea alba	white water-lily	tubers/seeds	*Nymphaea alba*
Phragmites australis	common reed	rhizomes	Poaceae
Trapa natans	water chestnut	nuts	*Trapa natans*
Typha latifolia	bulrush	rhizomes	*Sparganium emersum*-type

[1] based on Price 1989
[2] after Bennett 1994
[3] after Moore *et al* 1991

alluvial fills in Kent and Sussex (Burrin and Scaife 1984; Waller 1993; 1994) and on meander infills in more westerly locations (Brown 1988; Wiltshire forthcoming) may be noted.

It is quite clear that such problems as highly variable pollen sources, catchment areas and preservation, and disturbed and intermittent sedimentation may afflict sample sites. The potential importance of such sites, however, must surely justify more research in an effort to understand their dynamics and in an attempt to overcome their deficiencies. The study of riverine deposits has a long history in Continental Europe (eg Planchais 1987; Wasylikowa 1986) and in North America (Solomon *et al* 1982).

Soil pollen studies

It will be apparent that the discussion thus far has focused upon the evidence and potential provided by off-site pollen data. This neglect of on-site, often archaeological context data from soils and other minerogenic deposits is a function of the availability of data considered to be of primary use for environmental and cultural reconstructions. If it is necessary to demonstrate a concern for the malaise associated with soil pollen studies, there are glimmers that its future may be brighter, even if it is not dazzling. Perseverance by archaeopalynologists is necessary, though, because archaeologists often work with soils, and because the pollen contained within excavated materials must have some significance. Rather than continuing to neglect on-site studies, I would like to cite some examples of interesting work, and to point things a little towards the future.

Processes

The American researcher Gerald Kelso (1994) takes as his starting point the observation of Dimbleby (1985) that pollen in forested areas percolates through the profile at a rate of 10mm in *c* 30 years. He then looks at data from archaeological sites and former agricultural fields in the north-eastern United States.

The William Pepperrill Site is located on Appledore Island off the coasts of Maine and New Hampshire. The soil stratum dates based on archaeological evidence are compared with the historical dates based on such distinct palynological events as the chestnut (*Castanea dentata*) blight of 1925, human abandonment of the island in 1912 (shown by a fall in ragweed [*Ambrosia*] and dandelion type [Lactuceae] pollen and a rise in grass frequencies), and the establishment of a hotel in 1849 shown by a fall in grass pollen and rises for ragweed and dandelion. These types of data enabled Kelso to calculate that pollen was moving down-profile at a rate of 10mm in 4.2 years.

Although it may be unwise to compare these results with those from wooded environments, they show that some open soil sites have very rapid pollen percolation compared to the supposed patterns in wooded sites. An implication for prehistoric situations is that the often-found rapid degeneration of pollen with depth may show that the pollen survival was not of great longevity. Thus, the pollen spectra found under earthworks or ploughwash may reflect short periods of activity covering perhaps a few centuries only and that the pollen spectra even some hundreds of millimetres beneath monuments could actually derive from the activities of those constructing the prehistoric sites.

Survival

Related issues are involved in a high resolution palynological and soil micromorphological study of old ground surfaces beneath Early Bronze Age round cairns on Biggar Common in the Scottish Borders (Tipping *et al* 1994). The results suggest that pollen significantly predating burial was removed from the soil by processes of pollen deterioration. The plentiful palynomorphs in the top few score millimetres are believed to have been closely contemporaneous with human activity. The abundance of this 'fresh' pollen led to a swamping of older assemblages, characterised by deteriorated palynomorphs, and the spectra could be interpreted plausibly because they were not as poorly preserved. The authors maintain that the study offers a way 'of establishing with increased rigour the "validity" of soil pollen analyses' (ibid, 401).

Spatial studies

In a study of mor (acid) humus layers in northern Sweden, Segerström (1991) tested the hypothesis that such horizons can be used for identifying ancient arable fields in a boreal coniferous region. These humus layers are very thin (20–30mm), and it is also supposed from historical documentation that cultivation took place on a few occasions between 300 and 700 years ago. The results of the soil pollen analyses from Kroktjärnen show a very clustered pattern for cereal-type and other taxa characteristic of cultivated ground. Six control sites and many others around the presumed cultivated area had <2% cultural indicator pollen. The method thus appears to have been able to delimit a former arable area with considerable precision. The wider applicability of this otherwise elegant approach may be limited unless organic topsoils, perhaps buried beneath slopewash, can be first uncovered.

Landscape scale soil palynology

Three-dimensional pollen analysis accommodates the spatial component in landscape history. The fact that it is carried out on mire sites is a disadvantage because it is always 'off-site', even if it is based on a mire that is perhaps surrounded by occupation areas. There are examples where the peat (and sometimes underlying soils) forms part of the landscape mosaic in which archaeological remains are plentiful (cf Bakker and Groenman-van Waateringe 1988; Keith-Lucas 1986; Molloy and O'Connell 1991; 1995), although the peat generally post-dates the archaeological monuments.

One way of extending this work and of overcoming the constraints of off-site studies, is to investigate the soils associated more intimately with the occupation area. These usually consist of minerogenic rather than highly organic mor humus deposits, however, and their properties are problematic for pollen taphonomy and subsequent interpretation. Notwithstanding this, and in association with probable Neolithic and Bronze Age field and settlement systems in Shetland, attempts are being made to study soils from beneath a blanket peat cover on a landscape scale (cf Whittington and Edwards forthcoming).

The problem of dating these events, other than being able to determine the latest dates provided by basal blanket peats where present, is a serious impediment to reconstructing landuse history. The potential to overcome this is described in the section on the AMS dating of soil pollen.

Prediction and continuity

Environmental approaches in archaeology are too often relegated to post-excavation study rather than providing direction to archaeological investigation and palynology is no exception. Unlike many monument- and artefact-dominated data sets, pollen records, especially if obtained from off-site depositional contexts, are often continuous and can be employed predictively. Pollen analyses may provide not only a fuller picture of environmental and cultural change, but they also highlight lacunae in the archaeological record, where the vicinity of pollen sites is often devoid of finds and monuments relating to specific periods. Palynology can then produce plausible and challenging data that help to pose questions and to isolate problems for the archaeologist.

The recurrent nature of the phases of woodland reduction and regeneration, and indications of their longevity, are unlikely to be revealed by traditional archaeological methods. Archaeologists are often faced with the inconvenient fact that their sites alone may give little idea of the extent and intensity of human activity in prehistoric and later times. The degree of exploitation of the cultural landscape in terms of vegetation types and change, the extent of cultivation, the arable/pastoral mix, soil status, and erosion (especially where supported by sedimentological data [cf Edwards and Rowntree

1980; Whittington *et al* 1990]) are all kinds of information that palynologists are often able to contribute to the ecological history of sites and areas.

The deliberate use of palynology as a predictive tool is largely unknown in archaeology (though see Cloutman and Smith 1988; Finlayson *et al* 1973; Kvamme 1988; Whittington and Edwards 1994). In the example provided above of five records from South Uist, of possible Mesolithic landscape impacts in the Outer Hebrides, the value of palynology is emphasised because there is no archaeological evidence for such an early human presence. Similar data can be evinced from Shetland (Bennett *et al* 1992; Edwards 1996). Caithness and Orkney were once seen as Mesolithic-free zones, a situation that pertains no longer (Saville 1996; Wickham-Jones 1994). Assuming that some material remains of Mesolithic peoples exist in these areas of 'invisibility', then they are likely to be beneath peat, sand, and sea.

The widespread discoveries of pre-elm decline cereal-type pollen grains up to about a millennium earlier than Neolithic field monuments provide a comparable case (see above). For a later period, palynological analyses in north Lancashire suggest widespread clearance in the Late Iron Age, while little seems to be known about the Iron Age/Romano-British period in the region (Middleton *et al* 1995). Less spectacular are the innumerable palynological instances of vegetational disturbance and clearance in all parts of the Britain and Ireland in periods for which the local archaeological records are mute.

An archaeological perspective on prediction is when it informs the choice of pollen site locations. Thus, decisions might be based on model predictions of activity locales – on and around coasts and hills as foci for animal migration routes in the Palaeolithic and Mesolithic perhaps, or on high ground for the study of Neolithic ritual sites compared with lower slope locations for contemporaneous agriculture. The possibilities are obviously considerable – or would be given a surfeit of well-distributed deposits.

Advances

A remit for participants in this endeavour was to take a strategic look at the contributions and potential of archaeological science to archaeology, but from an archaeological rather than a scientific viewpoint. Arguably, the 'chicken and egg' syndrome precludes a strict adherence to such a stricture. The identification of new and unanswered archaeological questions that archaeological science has the potential to answer may often only occur once a technology is available to inspire the asking of relevant questions. This becomes apparent from a consideration of a number of the following topics.

Dating

Thanks to the increasing number of studies with large numbers of radiocarbon dates, site chronologies are adequate – or they are usually accepted as so within the constraints of funding. A comparison of maps in Lowe and Tipping (1994), however, shows that that even though more than 328 pollen diagrams for the post-5000 BP period are available from Scotland, dates may be available for only one third of these, many with only a single ^{14}C date for the last five millennia, the period that experienced most vegetational disturbance. Birks's maps for England (1989) also show surprisingly large areas of the country without sufficiently good detail for isopollen mapping exercises. There is no room for complacency here and there are plenty of reasons for more intensive studies featuring better dating support, even in areas popularly considered to have been saturated with pollen analysts.

Tephropalynological approaches

Radiocarbon dating is, of course, crude when compared with another tool, which is becoming more widely used, especially in northern Britain: tephrochronology. Tephra, the microscopic glass shards produced by volcanic eruptions and deposited rapidly, provides, when present, a very accurate tool for dating. Microprobe analysis of shard chemistry can enable identification to specific eruptions and the precise correlation of tephra layers across vast areas (Dugmore *et al* 1995). Tephra isochrons thus furnish temporally precise horizons, and pollen associated with them effectively provides snapshots of past vegetation and environments to be compared with the chronological precision of a Pompeii (Blackford *et al* 1992; Dugmore *et al* 1996; Edwards *et al* 1994; Hall *et al* 1994).

It must not be assumed, however, that tephra is 'everywhere'; that when found it can be easily characterized geochemically; that it is vertically distributed in the neatest of fashions without problems of particle redistribution; or, in the case of prehistoric eruptions, that it can be dated more precisely than the best ^{14}C-based estimates (cf Dugmore *et al* 1995; Pilcher *et al* 1995) – though, of course, each tephra layer is as temporally-precise an entity as one is likely to find in many mid-latitude situations. Moreover, many of the most archaeologically important sites are not going to be in areas of tephra-rich peat bog!

AMS dating of soil pollen

The dating of pollen is still an infrequent activity and has been pursued in the context of lake and peat deposits, which in certain circumstances may produce anomalous dates (Brown *et al* 1989; Regnéll 1992). It is a very time-consuming procedure and requires meticulous laboratory care; many would consider that the time taken for extraction may not justify the final results unless a key dating problem could not be investigated otherwise (eg by dating macrofossils).

An important problem can focus upon testing various of the productive hypotheses put forward by Geoffrey Dimbleby (1961) over 30 years ago. One priority area is to date the soil pollen levels containing high quantities of hazel and ivy grains in order to test their assignation to Mesolithic times (Dimbleby 1985; Keef *et al* 1965; Simmons and Dimbleby 1974); another might be to assess the age of pollen in calcareous soils (Dimbleby and Evans 1974). Attempts are now being made at Sheffield to extract thousands of individual pollen grains from soils by micromanipulation techniques (cf Long *et al* 1992) and then to date the pollen by AMS. The whole activity is still fraught with problems of extracting sufficient pollen to provide a date and the uncertainties of temporal integrity associated with pollen movement within the solum. Nevertheless, the optimisation of such approaches may provide a dating life-line for other investigations employing soil pollen data.

Statistical approaches

Unless a simple concern with the presence or absence of a taxon is considered adequate, then statistics must be regarded as a basic part of palynology, even if the analyst simply sticks with percentage data. Many practitioners, of course, also employ multivariate statistics in order to extend the explanatory range of their material (cf Birks and Gordon 1985; Birks and Line 1992; Edwards and Berridge 1994; Odgaard 1992). Given the extensive use of the computer packages TILIA and TILIA•GRAPH (Grimm 1991), which contain programmes for the ordination techniques of correspondence analysis (CA) and detrended correspondence analysis (DCA or DECORANA), it is surprising that more use is not made of such approaches. This suggestion applies also to the versatile package CANOCO (ter Braak 1987) – the program TRAN (Juggins 1992) will transform pollen data saved in TILIA (ASCII) format into Cornell condensed format suitable for CANOCO; and to PSIMPOLL (Bennett 1992), which *inter alia* contains routines for principal components analysis (PCA), rarefaction analysis (rfa), and pollen confidence limits (pcl). Figure 9.4 displays some of these computational relationships.

A statistical approach to pollen and spore data, which is relatively simple but which could provide more information than is normally produced by ordination, is to examine the data from *within* long profiles rather than looking at whole profiles, which might include, for instance, both Late- and Postglacial assemblages, thus obscuring events of cultural interest. This was attempted

PSIMPOLL ⇐ **TILIA** ⇒ **CA, DCA**

⇓   ⇓

PCA, rfa, pcl   **TRAN**

⇓

CANOCO ⇒ **PCA, CA, DCA**

Fig 9.4 Some of the computer routines accessible from data produced in TILIA (see text for details)

at Kilconquhar Loch, Fife (Whittington and Edwards 1995), with interesting results for changing landuse regimes. Thus, for one of the pollen zones at the site (KQ1-3n, Fig 9.5), and taking into account the changes in ordination plots and pollen assemblages, it was suggested that *Hordeum* (Ho: barley type) and *Avena/Triticum* (A/T: oats/wheat type) were growing separately, while *Cannabis* (Can: hemp) was part of a crop rotation with oats/wheat. Gramineae (Gr: grasses) might be seen as temporary ley as part of a rotation, or as fallow, which might explain the proximity of *Plantago lanceolata* (Pl: ribwort plantain). The expansion in the grass and plantain pollen curves may indicate that grass sown for animal feed was becoming more important than arable agriculture, or that soil impoverishment was forcing crop rotation and/or fallow. The nearness of Compositae tubuliflorae (Tub) to *Hordeum*-type may indicate the infestation of barley crops with corn marigold (*Chrysanthemum segetum*). 'Guld' or 'gool' was the bane of medieval agriculturalists from at least the fifteenth century onwards in Scotland (Franklin 1952) and the removal of corn marigold could increase corn yields ten-fold.

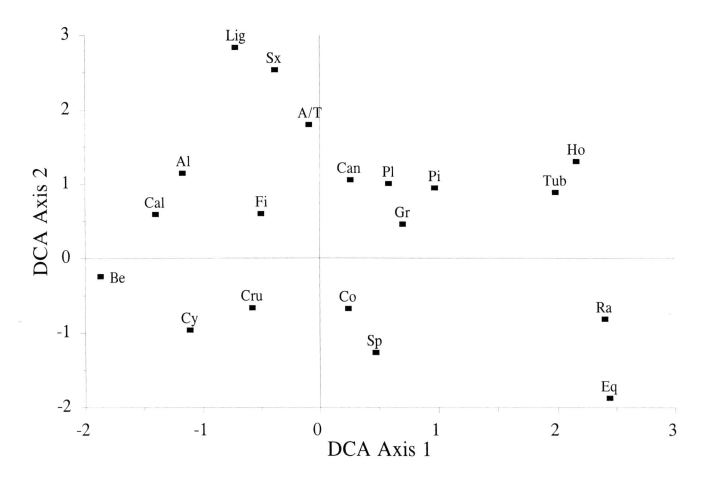

Fig 9.5 Ordination (detrended correspondence analysis) plots of pollen taxa from within zone KQ1-3n at Kilconquhar Loch, Fife (after Whittington and Edwards 1995) (see text for details)

Databases and GIS

The advent of the North American and European Pollen Databases (NAPD and EPD) have made accessible an enormous volume of pollen data. On a more local scale, there is the Scottish Palaeoecological Site Index (SPSI) currently under development and which provides background information on many Scottish pollen sites. The North East England Pollen Database (NEEPD) not only contains background information on more than 200 pollen sites from the area, but also contains actual pollen data based on the EPD format (Pratt 1996). Following construction of the NEEPD, Pratt went on to link it to the ArchInfo geographical information system (GIS) for various Holocene time slices and has produced pollen maps/surfaces for important taxa and groups of taxa. Her map of Gramineae for the period

1000–500 cal BC (Fig 9.6) shows that grassland had an easterly dominance over nort-eastern England, with its lowest representation in the Pennine uplands to the west; this would have implications for assessing the extent of pastoral activity in this period. The labour involved in constructing these databases and GISs is formidable, and they are often far from easy to use, but they could have a bright future if applied innovatedly.

Interpretation

Apart from advances in palynological methodology, including the wider utilisation of complementary techniques such as those deriving from statistics and sedimentology, more adventurous interpretational tools are also desirable. Two recent examples from either end of the interpretational spectrum might be mentioned.

Ternary ordination plots

Triangular (ternary) diagrams depicting pollen data have been used by both Green and Dolman (1988) and by Regnéll (1989) to provide summary views of pollen data. Kathryn Pratt (1996) has also adopted this form of data representation as a consequence of work on the NEEPD. Her triangular ordination plots are an attempt to relate archaeological sites to the types of vegetation inferred from averaged pollen data. Many assumptions and caveats are involved and it is impossible even to attempt to address them here. It might be deduced from Figure 9.7 that archaeological sites of the Late Bronze Age period are not just associated with areas in which clearance indicators are frequent (note the 40+ sites with around 80% herbaceous pollen towards the top of the diagram), but that large numbers are also to be found where tree and shrub percentages are high (lower left apex). In the second case, it may suggest that there was still a considerable amount of woodland in the pollen catchment areas close to the archaeological sites, and this could encourage inferences of forest farming or a preference for areas containing a good balance of natural resources.

These constructions may meet the agreement of Welinder (1988, 129), who notes that traditional pollen diagrams are less adequate for 'displaying the sophisticated dynamics in local diagrams', and Butler (1995, 20) who sees their use as one that enables more patterns to emerge, thus providing differing perspectives in pursuit of a post-processual agenda.

Post-processual palynolgy

Simon Butler (1995, 15) has examined the possibilities of adopting 'some post-modern concepts' and attempts to 'define some of their implications for empirical practice in palynology'. He claims (ibid, 20) that:

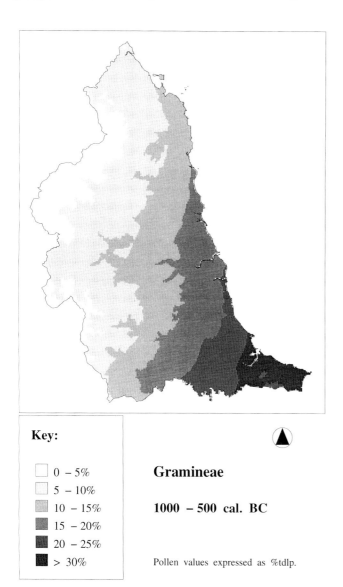

Key:

☐ 0 – 5%
☐ 5 – 10%
▨ 10 – 15%
▨ 15 – 20%
▨ 20 – 25%
▨ > 30%

Gramineae

1000 – 500 cal. BC

Pollen values expressed as %tdlp.

Fig 9.6 GIS-based map of interpolated grass pollen percentages averaged for the period 1000–500 cal BC in north-eastern England (after Pratt 1996); pollen values expressed as % of total dry land pollen

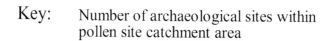

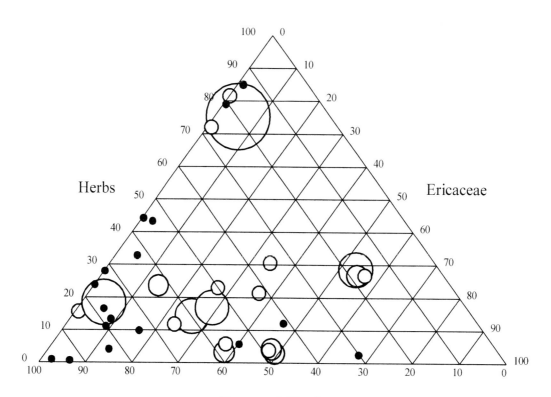

Fig 9.7 Triangular ordination plots showing the relationship between number of archaeological sites within the assumed catchment area of each pollen site and averaged arboreal, herb, and heath (Ericaceae) pollen values for the period 1000–500 cal BC in north-eastern England (after Pratt 1996)

In practice the exploration of these wider meanings essentially involves asking new questions; questions concerning the social and symbolic significance of plants and landscapes as much as their ecological-economic and functional significance. In this way, post-processual palynology calls for and contributes to both closer integration of palynology and archaeology, and broader understandings of the interrelationships between nature and humanity.

A fundamental point for Butler is that if the present-day world (including palynological reconstructions) is relative to the way it is perceived, then the perceptions of past peoples must be relative to their, rather than our, perceptions of it. Pollen data are supposedly used to provide evidence for real environments of the past and not for perceived ones. Examples of assumed social and symbolic dimensions to perceptions in the past, including inter-relationships with nature, are followed by the implications for the palynologist. These range from the interesting (ibid, 18):

A scarcity of woodland has often led to laws protecting trees, so that what a palynologist might regard as insignificant in quantitative ecological terms (ie a low tree pollen count) actually takes on a significance in social terms.

to seeming despair (ibid, 19):

We look for associations and patterns in the pollen and archaeological records that allow us to talk about the nature of a real, material environment and its practical utility and functional relationships with society. This is the meaning we give to pollen data, and we thus effectively reduce the meaningful dimensions to the means of [pollen] production.

and eventually to hope (ibid, 20):

contextualising pollen data along meaningful dimensions requires familiarising ouselves with a broader range of archaeological evidence than we normally consider relevant, speculating freely about the meanings we give to pollen data, and giving more attention to interpretation and reflection.

Any approach that poses reasonable questions has something to offer. It is probably not asking too much, however, to hope that post-processual approaches would accord with O'Connor's (1991, 2) sentiments:

To throw off the shackles of a systematic analysis of the material evidence, and to reject the requirement

that an interpretation should at least not be wholly inconsistent with such evidence as is available, would leave archaeology open to a plethora of speculation, fantasy, and outright codswallop.

and many palynologists and users of pollen data will be satisfied that (ibid, 40):

A pollen analysis will not of itself explain whether early Post-Glacial Europeans had a precocious grasp of dialectical materialism or picked their noses, but it will contribute an impression of how, to modern eyes, the landscape in which those people moved, acted, and thought might have looked. It will also reflect, to a greater or lesser extent, the actions of those people and of the wider biota of which they were a part.

Whether post-processual palynology will have anything useful to add to traditional modes of interpretation or is, with apologies to Queen and to Van Morrison, an indication that *I want to break free* or an effort to enter *Into the mystic*, remains to be seen.

Acknowledgements

I would like to thank Kathryn Pratt for allowing me to present material from her unpublished PhD thesis and two anonymous referees for their helpful comments.

References

Ammerman, A J, and Cavalli-Sforza, L L, 1971 Measuring the rate of spread of early farming in Europe, *Man*, **6**, 674–88

—, 1984 *The Neolithic transition and the genetics of population in Europe*, Princeton

Andersen, S T, 1979 Identification of wild grass and cereal pollen, *Danmarks Geologiske Undersøgelse Arbog 1978*, 69–92

—, 1988 Changes in agricultural practices in the Holocene indicated in a pollen diagram from a small hollow in Denmark, in *The cultural landscape – past, present, and future* (eds H H Birks, H J B Birks, P E Kaland, and D Moe), 289–99, Cambridge

Aronsson, K-Å, 1991 *Forest reindeer herding AD 1–1800: an archaeological and palaeoecological study in northern Sweden*, Archaeology and Environment, **10**, Department of Archaeology, Univ Umeå

Bakker, J A, and Groenman-van Waateringe, W, 1988 Megaliths, soils, and vegetation on the Drenthe Plateau, in *Man-made soils,* (eds W Groenman-van Waateringe and M Robinson), BAR, Int Ser, **410**, 143–81, Oxford

Behre, K-E, 1981 The interpretation of anthropogenic indicators in pollen diagrams, *Pollen Spores*, **23**, 225–45

Behre, K-E, and Kučan, D, 1986 Die Reflektion archäologisch bekannter Siedlungen in Pollendiagrammen verschiedener Entfernung – Beispiele aus der Siedlungskammer Flögeln, Nordwestdeutschland, in *Anthropogenic indicators in pollen diagrams* (ed K-E Behre), 95–114, Rotterdam

Bell, M, and Limbrey S (eds), 1982 *Archaeological aspects of woodland ecology*, BAR, Int Ser, **146**, Oxford

Bellamy, D, 1972 *Bellamy on botany*, London

Bennett, K D, 1992, *PSIMPOLL computer program*, Department of Plant Sciences, Univ Cambridge

—, 1994 *Annotated catalogue of pollen and pteridophyte spore types of the British Isles*, Cambridge

Bennett, K D, Boreham, S, Sharp, M J, and Switsur, V R, 1992 Holocene history of environment, vegetation, and human settlement on Catta Ness, Lunnasting, Shetland, *J Ecol*, **80**, 241–73

Bennett, K D, Simonson, W D, and Peglar, S M, 1990 Fire and man in post-glacial woodlands of eastern England, *J Archaeol Sci*, **17**, 635–42

Birks, H J B, 1989 Holocene isochrone maps and patterns of tree-spreading in the British Isles, *J Biogeogr*, **16**, 503–40

—, 1993 Quaternary palaeoecology and vegetation science: current contributions and possible future developments, *Rev Palaeobot Palynol*, **79**, 153–77

Birks, H J B, and Gordon A D, 1985 *Numerical methods in Quaternary pollen analysis*, London

Birks, H J B, and Line, J M, 1992 The use of rarefaction analysis for estimating palynological richness from Quaternary pollen-analytical data, *The Holocene*, **2**, 1–10

Blackford, J J, Edwards, K J, Dugmore, A J, Cook, G T, and Buckland, P C, 1992 Icelandic volcanic ash and the mid-Holocene Scots pine (*Pinus sylvestris*) pollen decline in northern Scotland, *The Holocene*, **2**, 260–65

Bowler, M, and Hall, V A, 1989 The use of sieving during standard pollen pre-treatment of samples of fossil deposits to enhance the concentration of large pollen grains, *New Phytol*, **111**, 511–15

Brown, A G, 1988 The palaeoecology of *Alnus* (alder) and the postglacial history of floodplain vegetation: pollen percentage and influx data from the West Midlands, United Kingdom, *New Phytol*, **110**, 425–36

—, 1992 Paleochannels and palaeolandsurfaces: the geoarchaeological potential of some Midland (UK) floodplains, in *Archaeology under alluvium* (eds S Needham and M Macklin), 185–96, Oxford

Brown, T A, Nelson, D E, Mathewes, R W, Vogel, J S, and Southon, J R, 1989 Radiocarbon dating of pollen by accelerator mass spectrometry, *Quat Res*, **32**, 205–12

Burrin, P J, and Scaife, R G, 1984 Aspects of Holocene valley sedimentation and floodplain development in southern England, *Proc Geol Assoc*, **95**, 81–96

Butler, S, 1995 Post-processual palynology, *Scott Archaeol Rev*, **9/10**, 15–25

Caseldine, A, 1990 *Environmental archaeology in Wales*, Lampeter

Caseldine, C, and Hatton, J, 1996 Early land clearance and wooden trackway construction in the third and fourth millennia BC at Corlea, Co Longford, *Biology and Environment: Proc Roy Ir Acad*, **96B**, 11–19

Chyleck, P, Johnson, B, and Hong, W, 1992 Black carbon concentration in a Greenland Dye-3 ice core, *Geophys Res Letters*, **19**, 1951–3

Clark, J S, and Royall, P D, 1995 Particle-size evidence for source areas of charcoal accumulation in Late Holocene sediments of eastern North American lakes, *Quat Res*, **43**, 80–89

Clarke, G C S, and Jones, M R, 1977 The north-west European pollen flora, 15: Plantaginaceae, *Rev Palaeobot Palynol*, **24**, 129–54

Cloutman, E W, and Smith, A G, 1988 Palaeo-environments in the Vale of Pickering. Part 3: environmental history at Star Carr, *Proc Prehist Soc*, **54**, 37–58

Cronon, W, 1983 *Changes in the land: Indians, colonists, and the ecology of New England*, New York

Day, S P, 1993 Woodland origin and 'ancient woodland indicators': a case study from Sidlings Copse, Oxfordshire, UK, *The Holocene*, **3**, 45–53

Deevey, E, 1967 Introduction, in *Pleistocene extinctions* (eds P S Martin and H E Wright), 63–72, New Haven

Dickson, C A, 1988 Distinguishing cereal from wild grass pollen: some limitations, *Circaea*, **5**, 67–72

Dimbleby, G W, 1961 Soil pollen analysis, *J Soil Sci*, **12**, 1–11

—, 1985 *The palynology of archaeological sites*, London

Dimbleby, G W, and Evans, J G, 1974 Pollen and land-snail analysis of calcareous soils, *J Archaeol Sci*, **1**, 117–33

Dugmore, A J, Newton, A J, Edwards, K J, Larsen, G, Blackford, J J, and Cook, G T, 1996 Long-distance marker horizons from small-scale eruptions: British tephra deposits from the AD 1510 eruption of Hekla, Iceland, *J Quat Sci*, **11**, 511–16

Dugmore, A J, Shore, J S, Cook, G T, Newton, A J, Edwards, K J, and Larsen, G, 1995 Radiocarbon dating tephra layers in Britain and Iceland, *Radiocarbon*, **37**, 379–88

Edwards, K J, 1979 Palynological and temporal inference in the context of prehistory, with special reference to the evidence from lake and peat deposits, *J Archaeol Sci*, **6**, 255–70

—, 1981 The separation of *Corylus* and *Myrica* pollen in modern and fossil samples, *Pollen Spores*, **23**, 205–18

—, 1982 Man, space and the woodland edge: speculations on the detection and interpretation of human impact in pollen profiles, in Bell and Limbrey 1982, 5–22

—, 1988 The hunter-gatherer/agricultural transition and the pollen record in the British Isles, in *The cultural landscape – past, present, and future* (eds H H Birks, H J B Birks, P E Kaland, and D Moe), 255–66, Cambridge

—, 1989 The cereal pollen record and early agriculture, in *The beginnings of agriculture* (eds A Milles, D Williams and N Gardner), BAR, Int Ser, **496**, 113–35, Oxford

—, 1990 Fire and the Scottish Mesolithic: evidence from microscopic charcoal, in *Contributions to the Mesolithic in Europe* (eds P M Vermeersch and P Van Peer), 71–9, Leuven

—, 1991 Using space in cultural palynology: the value of the off-site pollen record, in *Modelling ecological change* (eds D R Harris and K D Thomas), 61–73, London

—, 1993 Models of mid-Holocene forest farming for north-west Europe, in *Climate change and human impact on the landscape* (ed F M Chambers), 133–45, London

—, 1996 A Mesolithic of the Western and Northern Isles of Scotland? Evidence from pollen and charcoal, in *The early prehistory of Scotland* (eds T Pollard and A Morrison), 23–38, Edinburgh

—, forthcoming Palynology and people: observations on the British record, *Quat Proc*

Edwards, K J, and Berridge, J M A, 1994 The Late-Quaternary vegetational history of Loch a'Bhogaidh, Rinns of Islay SSSI, Scotland, *New Phytol*, **128**, 749–69

Edwards, K J, Buckland, P C, Blackford, J J, Dugmore, A J, and Sadler, J P 1994 The impact of tephra: proximal and distal studies of Icelandic eruptions, *Münchener Geographische Abhandlungen*, **B12**, 79–99

Edwards, K J, Halstead, P, and Zvelebil, M, 1996 The Neolithic transition in the Balkans – archaeological perspectives and palaeoecological evidence: a comment on Willis and Bennett, *The Holocene*, **6**, 120–22

Edwards, K J, and Hirons, K R, 1984 Cereal pollen grains in pre-elm decline deposits: implications for the earliest agriculture in Britain and Ireland, *J Archaeol Sci*, **11**, 71–80

Edwards, K J, and MacDonald, G M, 1991 Holocene palynology: II. Human influence and vegetation change, *Progr Phys Geogr*, **15**, 364–91

Edwards, K J, and McIntosh, C J, 1988 Improving the detection rate of cereal-type pollen grains from *Ulmus* decline and earlier deposits from Scotland, *Pollen Spores*, **30**, 179–88

Edwards, K J, McIntosh, C J, and Robinson, D E 1986 Optimising the detection of cereal-type pollen grains in pre-elm decline deposits, *Circaea*, **4**, 11–13

Edwards, K J, and Rowntree, K M, 1980 Radiocarbon and palaeoenvironmental evidence for changing rates of erosion at a Flandrian stage site in Scotland, in *Timescales in geomorphology* (eds R A Cullingford, D A Davidson and J Lewin), 207–23, Chichester

Edwards, K J, and Sadler, J P (eds), forthcoming Holocene environments of prehistoric Britain, *Quat Proc*

Edwards, K J, and Whittington, G, 1997 Vegetation history, in *Scotland: environment and archaeology, 8000 BC–AD 1000* (eds K J Edwards and I B M Ralston), 63–82, Chichester

Edwards, K J, Whittington, G, and Hirons, K R, 1995 The relationship between fire and long-term wet heath development in South Uist, Outer Hebrides, Scotland, in *Heaths and moorland: cultural landscapes* (eds D B A Thompson, A J Hestor, and M B Usher), 240–48, Edinburgh

Faegri, K, and Iversen, J, 1989 *Textbook of pollen analysis*, 4 edn by K Faegri, P E Kaland, and K Krzywinski, Chichester

Fenton-Thomas, C, 1992 Pollen analysis as an aid to the reconstruction of patterns of land-use and settlement un the Tyne-Tees region during the first millennia BC and AD, *Durham Archaeol J*, **8**, 51–62

Finlayson, W D, Byrne, R A, and McAndrews, J A, 1973 Iroquoian settlement and subsistence patterns near Crawford Lake, Ontario, *Bull Can Archaeol Assoc*, **5**, 134–6

Firbas, F, 1937 Der Pollenanalytysche Nachweis des Getreidebaus, *Zeitschrift für Botanik*, **31**, 447–78

Fossitt, J A, 1996 Late Quaternary vegetation history of the Western Isles of Scotland, *New Phytol*, **132**, 171–96

Franklin, T B, 1952 *A history of Scottish farming*, London

Gaillard, M-J, Birks, H J B, Emanuelsson, U, and Berglund, B E, 1992 Modern pollen land/use relationships as an aid in the reconstruction of past land-uses and cultural landscapes: an example from south Sweden, *Veg Hist Archaeobot*, **1**, 3–17

Gish, J W, 1994 Large fraction pollen scanning and its application in archaeology, *Amer Soc Stratigr Palynologists Contrib Ser*, **29**, 93–100

Göransson, H, 1986 Man and the forests of nemoral broad-leaved trees during the Stone Age, *Striae*, **24**, 145–52

—, 1987 Comments on early agriculture in Sweden. On arguing in a circle, on common sense, on the smashing of paradigms, on thistles among flowers, and on other things, *Norweg Archaeol Rev*, **18**, 43–5

Green, D G, and Dolman, G S, 1988 Fine resolution pollen analysis, *J Biogeogr*, **15**, 685–701

Greig, J, 1994 Pollen analyses of latrine fills from archaeological sites in Britain; results and future potential, *Amerssoc Stratigr Palynologists Contrib Ser*, **29**, 101–14

Grimm, E C, 1991 *TILIA and TILIA·GRAPH*, Springfield, Illinois

Groenman-van Waateringe, W, 1983 The early agricultural utilization of the Irish landscape: the last word on the elm decline?, in *Landscape archaeology in Ireland* (eds T Reeves-Smyth and F Hamond), BAR, **116**, 217–32

—, 1986 Grazing possibilities in the Neolithic of the Netherlands based on palynological data, in *Anthropogenic indicators in pollen diagrams* (ed K-E Behre), 187–202, Rotterdam

—, 1993 The effects of grazing on the pollen production of grasses, *Veg Hist Archaeobot*, **2**, 157–62

Hall, V A, McVicar, S J, and Pilcher, J R, 1994 Tephra-linked landscape history around 2310 BC of some sites in Counties Antrim and Down, *Biology and Environment: Proc R Ir Acad*, **94B**, 245–53

Hicks, S, 1993 Pollen evidence of localized impact on the vegetation of northernmost Finland by hunter-gatherers, *Veg Hist Archaeobot*, **2**, 137–44

Hunt, C O, 1994 Palynomorph taxonomy in the fluvial environment: an example from the Palaeolithic site at High Lodge, Mildenhall, UK, *Amerssoc of Stratigr Palynologists Contrib Ser*, **29**, 115–26

Iversen, J, 1941 Landnam i Denmarks stenalder [Land occupation in Denmark's Stone Age], *Danmarks geologiske Undersøgelse*, **II**, **66**, 1–68

Juggins, S, 1992 *TRAN computer program*, Environmental Change Research Centre, Department of Geography, Univ College London

Keef, P A M, Wymer, J J, and Dimbleby, G W, 1965 A Mesolithic site on Iping Common, Sussex, England, *Proc Prehist Soc*, **31**, 85–92

Keith-Lucas, M, 1986 Vegetation development and human impact, in *Scord of Brouster: an early agricultural settlement on Shetland, excavations 1977–1979* (eds A Whittle, M Keith-Lucas, A Milles, B Noddle, S Rees, and J C C Romans), Oxford Univ Comm Archaeol Monogr, **9**, 92–118, Oxford

Kelso, G K, 1994 Pollen percolation rates in Euroamerican-era cultural deposits in the north-eastern United States, *J Archaeol Sci*, **21**, 481–8

Köhler, E, and Lange, E, 1979 A contribution to distinguishing cereal from wild grass pollen grains by LM and SEM, *Grana*, **18**, 133–40

Krzywinski, K, Fjelldal, S, and Soltvedt, E C, 1983 Recent palaeoethnobotanical work at the Mediaeval excavations at Bryggen, Bergen, Norway, in *Site, environment, and economy* (ed B Proudfoot), BAR, Int Ser **173**, 145–69, Oxford

Kvamme, M, 1988 Pollen analytical study of mountain summer-farming in western Norway, in *The cultural landscape – past, present, and future* (eds H H Birks, H J B Birks, P E Kaland, and D Moe), 349–67, Cambridge

Legrand, M, De Angelis, M, Staffelbach, T, Neftel, A, and Stauffer, B, 1992 Large perturbations of ammonium and organic acids content in the Summit-Greenland ice cor: fingerprint from forest fires? *Geophys Res Lett*, **19**, 473–5

Lewis, H T, 1981 *A time for burning*, Boreal Institute for Northern Studies, Univ Alberta, Occasional Publication, **17**, Edmonton

Long, A, Davis, O K, and De Lanois, J, 1992 Separation and ^{14}C dating of pure pollen from lake sediments: nanofossil AMS dating, *Radiocarbon*, **34**, 557–60

Lowe, J J and Tipping, R M, 1994 *A national archive of palaeoenvironmental records from Scotland: a pilot study*, Scottish Natural Heritage Research, Survey and Monitoring Report, **30**, Edinburgh

MacDonald, G M, Larsen, C P S, Szeicz, J M, and Moser, K A, 1991 The reconstruction of boreal forest fire history from lake sediments: a comparison of charcoal, pollen, sedimentological, and geo-chemical indices, *Quat Sci Rev*, **10**, 53–71

Magri, D, 1996 The Neolithic transition and Palaeoecology in the Balkans: a comment on Willis and Bennett, *The Holocene*, **6**, 119–20

Maguire, D J, 1983 The identification of agricultural activity using pollen analysis, in *Integrating the subsistence economy* (ed M Jones), BAR, Int Ser, **181**, 5–18, Oxford

Mellars, P A 1976 Fire ecology, animal populations, and man: a study of some ecological relations inships in prehistory, *Proc Prehist Soc*, **42**, 15–45

Middleton, R, Wells, C E, and Huckerby, E, 1995 *The wetlands of north Lancashire*, North West Wetlands Survey 3; Lancaster Imprints 4, Lancaster

Moe, D, Indrelid, S, and Fasteland, A, 1988 The Halne area, Hardangarvidda: use of a high mountain area during 5000 years – an interdisciplinary case study, in *The cultural landscape – past, present, and future* (eds H H Birks, H J B Birks, P E Kaland, and D Moe), 429–44, Cambridge

Molloy, K, and O'Connell, M, 1991 Palaeoecological investigations towards the reconstruction of woodland and land-use history at Lough Sheeauns, Connemara, western Ireland, *Rev Palaeobot Palynol*, **67**, 75–113

—, 1995 Palaeoecological investigations towards the reconstruction of environment and land-use changes during prehistory at Céide Fields, western Ireland, *Probleme der Küstenforschung im südlichen Nordseegebiet*, **23**, 187–225, Oldenberg

Moore, P D, Webb, J A, and Collinson, M E, 1991 *Pollen analysis*, Oxford

O'Connell, M, 1987 Early cereal-type pollen records from Connemara, western Ireland and their possible significance, *Pollen Spores*, **29**, 207–24

O'Connor, T P, 1991 Science, evidential archaeology, and the new scholasticism, *Scott Archaeol Rev*, **8**, 1–7

Odgaard, B V, 1992 The fire history of Danish heathland areas as refelcted by pollen and charred particles in lake sediments, *The Holocene*, **2**, 218–26

Oldfield, F, 1963 Pollen-analysis and man's role in the ecological history of the south-east Lake District, *Geografiska Annaler*, **45**, 23–40

Patterson, W A, III, Edwards, K J, and Maguire, D J, 1987 Microscopic charcoal as a fossil indicator of fire, *Quat Sci Rev*, **6**, 3–23

Peglar, S M, 1993 The development of cultural landscapes around Diss Mere, Norfolk, UK, during the past 7000 years, *Rev Palaeobot Palynol*, **76**, 1–47

Peglar, S, and Birks, H J B, 1993 The mid-Holocene Ulmus fall at Diss Mere, south-east England – disease and human impact? *Veg Hist Archaeobot*, **2**, 61–8

Pilcher, J R, Hall, V A, and McCormac, F G, 1995 Dates of Holocene Icelandic eruptions from tephra layers in Irish peats, *The Holocene*, **5**, 103–10

Planchais, N, 1987 Impact de l'homme lors du remplissage de l'estuaire du Lez (Palavas Herault) mis en evidence par l'analyse pollinique, *Pollen Spores*, **29**, 73–88

Pratt, K E, 1996 *Development of methods for investigating settlement and land-use using pollen data: a case study from North-East England, circa 8000 cal BC–cal AD 500*, unpubl PhD thesis, Univ Durham

Punt, W, and Maloteaux, M, 1984 The north-west European pollen flora, 31: Cannabaceae, Moraceae, and Urticaceae, *Rev Paleobot Palynol*, **42**, 23–44

Rackham, O, 1980 *Ancient woodland: its history, vegetation and uses in England*, London

—, 1988 Trees and woodland in a crowded landscape – the cultural landscape of the British Isles, in *The cultural landscape – past, present, and future* (eds H H Birks, H J B Birks, P E Kaland, and D Moe), 53–77, Cambridge

Regnéll, J, 1989 *Vegetation and land use during 6000 years: palaeoecology of the cultural landscape at two lake sites in southern Skåne, Sweden*, Lundqua Thesis, **27**, Lund

—, 1992 Preparing pollen concentrates for AMS dating: a methodological study from a hard-water lake in southern Sweden, *Boreas*, **21**, 373–7

Roberts, N, 1989 *The Holocene: an environmental history*, Oxford

Saville, A 1996 Lacaille, microliths and the Mesolithic of Orkney, in *The early prehistory of Scotland* (eds T Pollard and A Morrison), 213–24, Edinburgh

Scaife, R G, 1982 Late-Devensian and early Flandrian vegetation changes in Southern England, in Bell and Limbrey 1982, 57–74

Segerström, U, 1991 Soil pollen analysis: an application for tracing ancient arable patches, *J Archaeol Sci*, **18**, 165–75

Simmons, I G, 1996 *The environmental impact of later Mesolithic cultures*, Edinburgh

Simmons, I G, and Dimbleby, G W, 1974 The possible role of ivy (Hedera helix L.) in the Mesolithic economy of western Europe, *J Archaeol Sci*, **1**, 291–6

Simmons, I G, and Tooley, M J (eds) 1981 *The environment in British prehistory*, London

Smith, A G, 1970 The influence of Mesolithic and Neolithic man on British vegetation, in *Studies in the vegetational history of the British Isles* (eds D Walker and R G West), 81–96, London

Solomon, A M, Blasing, T J, and Solomon, J A, 1982 Interpretation of floodplain pollen in alluvial sediments from an arid region, *Quat Res*, **18**, 52–71

Stevenson, A C, and Harrison, R J, 1992 Ancient forests in Spain: a model for land-use and dry forest management in south-west Spain from 4000 BC to 1900 AD, *Proc Prehist Soc*, **58**, 227–47

Taylor, K C, Mayewski, P A, Twickler, M S, and Whitlow, S I, 1996 Biomass burning recorded in the GISP2 ice core: a record from eastern Canada, *The Holocene*, **6**, 1–6

ter Braak, C J F, 1987 *CANOCO – a FORTRAN Program for Canonical community Ordination by [Partial] [Detrended] [Canonical] Correspondence Analysis (Version 2.0)*, TNO Institute of Applied Computer Science, Wageningen

Tipping, R, 1994 The form and fate of Scotland's woodlands, *Proc Soc Antiq Scotl*, **124**, 1–54

—, 1996 Microscopic charcoal records, inferred human activity and climate change in the Mesolithic of northernmost Scotland, in *The early prehistory of Scotland* (eds T Pollard and A Morrison), 39–61, Edinburgh

Tipping, R, Carter, S, and Johnston, D, 1994 Soil pollen and soil micromorphological analyses of old ground surfaces on Biggar Common, Borders Region, Scotland, *J Archaeol Sci*, **21**, 387–401

Troels-Smith, J, 1984 Stall-feeding and field-manuring in Switzerland about 6000 years ago, *Tools and Tillage*, **5**, 13–25

Turner, J, 1964 The anthropogenic factor in vegetational history: I Tregaron and Whixall Mosses, *New Phytol*, **63**, 73–90

—, 1970 Post-Neolithic disturbances of British vegetation, in *Studies in the vegetational history of the British Isles* (eds D Walker and R G West), 97–116, London

—, 1975 The evidence for landuse by prehistoric farming communities: the use of three-dimensional pollen diagrams, in *The effect of man on the landscape: the Highland Zone* (eds J G Evans, S Limbrey, and H Cleere), CBA Res Rep, **11**, 86–95, London

Turner, J, Innes, J B, and Simmons, I G, 1993 Spatial diversity in the vegetational history of North Gill, North Yorkshire, *New Phytol*, **123**, 599–647

Turner, J, and Peglar, S M, 1988 Temporally-precise studies of vegetation history, in *Vegetation history* (eds B Huntley and T Webb III), 753–77, Dordrecht

Van de Noort, R and Ellis, S (eds), 1995 *Wetland heritage of Holderness: an archaeological survey*, Kingston upon Hull

Waller, M P, 1993 Flandrian vegetational history of south-eastern England. Pollen data from Pannel Bridge, East Sussex, *New Phytol*, **124**, 345–69

—, 1994 Flandrian vegetational history of south-eastern England: stratigraphy of the Brede valley and pollen data from Brede Bridge, *New Phytol*, **126**, 369–92

Wasylikowa, K, 1986 Plant macrofossils preserved in prehistoric settlements compared with anthropogenic indicators in pollen diagrams, in *Anthropogenic indicators in pollen diagrams* (ed K-E Behre), 173–85, Rotterdam

Waton, P V, 1982 Man's impact on the chalklands: some new pollen evidence, in Bell and Limbrey 1982, 75–91

Watson, L, and Bell, E M, 1975 A surface-structural survey of some taxonomically diverse grass pollens, *Austral J Bot*, **23**, 981–90

Welinder, S, 1988 Review of H Göransson, Neolithic man and the forest environment around Alvastra Pile Dwelling, *Norweg Archaeol Rev*, **21**, 129–30

Whitlock, C, and Millspaugh, S H 1996 Testing the assumptions of fire-history studies: an examination of modern charcoal accumulation in Yellowstone National Park, USA, *The Holocene*, **6**, 7–15

Whittington, G, and Edwards, K J, 1989 Problems in the interpretation of Cannabaceae pollen in the stratigraphic record, *Pollen Spores*, **31**, 79–96

—, 1994 Palynology as a predictive tool in archaeology, *Proc Soc Antiq Scotl*, **124**, 55–65

—, 1995 A Scottish broad: historical, stratigraphic, and numerical studies associated with polleniferous deposits at Kilconquhar Loch, in *Human impact and adaptation: ecological relations in historical times* (eds R Butlin and N Roberts), 68–87, Oxford

—, forthcoming Landscape scale soil pollen analysis, *Quat Proc*

Whittington, G, Edwards, K J, and Cundill, P R, 1990 *Palaeoenvironmental investigations at Black Loch, in the Ochil Hills of Fife, Scotland*, O'Dell Memorial Monogr, **22**, Aberdeen

Whittington, G, and Gordon, A D, 1987 The differentiation of the pollen of *Cannabis sativa* L. from that of *Humulus lupulus* L, *Pollen Spores*, **29**, 111–20

Wickham-Jones, C R, 1994 *Scotland's first settlers*, London

Willis, K J, and Bennett, K D, 1994 The Neolithic transition – fact or fiction? Palaeoecological evidence from the Balkans, *The Holocene*, **4**, 326–30

Wiltshire, P E J, forthcoming Palynological analyis of palaeochannel silty peats at Grove Farm, Market Lavington, Wiltshire

Zvelebil, M, 1994 Plant use in the Mesolithic and its role in the transition to farming, *Proc Prehist Soc*, **60**, 35–74

10 The study of food remains in prehistoric Britain

by Tony Legge, Sebastian Payne,
and Peter Rowley-Conwy

Abstract

In recent years considerable advances have been made in the study of food remains from prehistoric Britain. Methodological advances have been made in many directions, especially in the development of new techniques, in our understanding of site formation processes, and in interpretation and synthesis.

We are still held back, however, by a shortage of well-preserved material from well-sampled sites: economic prehistorians should consider initiating and directing projects designed to fill lacunae. We need to be more ready to address difficult central questions, to integrate different approaches, and to approach the past with fewer assumptions; and we need to spend more effort on synthesis and dissemination. The ritual lament that the writers of archaeological books know far too little about our results means that specialists should write more for non-specialist readers.

Introduction

Food production, food preparation, and diet, though prosaic, are of obviously vital importance to any society, and especially to a pre-industrial one. It is, for this reason, all the more salutary to recognise that in spite of undoubted advances in our methods of study over the past 50 years, our understanding of food production and diet in prehistoric Britain has not advanced as far as we might have hoped. Advances there have certainly been – in methodology and in interpretation; but we still have problems in addressing and answering simple central questions.

Methodologies: recent advances

There have been significant methodological advances on two main fronts: actualistic studies ranging from the ethnoarchaeological to the experimental, and improved approaches to the analysis and interpretation of archaeological materials.

Our understanding of charred plant remains has benefitted greatly from actualistic studies. Work by Hillman (1981; 1984) and Jones (1984) on traditional crop processing methods in the eastern Mediterranean has a wider geographical relevance as all societies cultivating wheat and barley face the same problems converting a harvested crop into an edible meal. The various processing stages (using pre-industrial technology) produce recognisable and distinct waste products. One that is commonly encountered is a fine sieve residue; the sieving was intended to remove crop contaminants smaller than cereal grains, so chaff fragments, weed seeds and the smallest cereal grains are the result. This waste is often thrown on the fire where it may become charred and thus can be recovered by flotation. In composition it is completely different from cleaned grain intended for consumption but charred by accident.

The taphonomy of these charred plant remains has also been examined. Boardman and Jones (1990) carried out experiments showing that cereal grains survive burning and become charred at a wider range of temperatures than does chaff. This may affect arguments based on the presence or absence of chaff at particular sites. Useful experimental work has also been done by van der Veen and Palmer (1997) on emmer and spelt wheat yields under different husbandry regimes.

Actualistic work has also been undertaken with regard to animal bones. For example, tooth eruption ages and wear stages have been studied in modern goats (Deniz and Payne 1982) and in wild boar (Bull and Payne 1982), and in the case of the goats and sheep, linked to husbandry practices so that the relative importance of meat, milk, and wool may be elucidated (Payne 1973). The potential of dental microwear as a tool for investigating the use of different forms of grazing and fodder has been investigated by Mainland (1995) with encouraging preliminary results. Experimental replication of bone fracture has been carried out by Outram (forthcoming), enabling assessment of both the degree of utilisation of within-bone nutrients and the previous treatment of the bone (eg boiling, roasting).

Turning now to archaeological work, various aspects may be commented on. Seasonality studies have been carried out on wild animals at various sites. Early work emphasised the presence or absence of migratory species, mostly birds and fish, and the growth cycle of deer antlers (Star Carr is a good example of the latter: Fraser and King 1954). These were not without their problems: birds and fish may occur in the 'wrong' season, are often minor components of the faunal spectrum, and need not be captured at the same time of year as the land mammals at the same site. Antler is not primarily a food indicator but is a useful raw material and may be transported or exchanged, and thus not indicate the season of occupation of the site on which it is found. This was the case at Star Carr: the antlers indicated winter and spring, while all other indicators such as tooth eruption pointed to the summer, suggesting that antlers were indeed retained in circulation for some months at least; in addition, the red deer postcranial bones indicated an even sex ratio, while the antlers implied a heavy dominance of males, a further indication that antler was receiving special treatment (Legge and Rowley-Conwy 1988). Seasonality studies using the major resources present at a site are clearly to be preferred. An example was the Oronsay shell middens, where otoliths of saithe indicated that different sites were occupied at different times of year (Mellars and Wilkinson 1980).

The scarcity of Mesolithic sites in Britain limits the number of examples, but the same approaches can of course also be applied to domestic animals in later periods: tooth eruption and bone growth provided tight seasonal patterns suggestive of sacrificial activities at two Roman temples in southern England (Legge *et al* 1992). Marine mammals have not been examined from this perspective in Britain, but current work elsewhere suggests that these taxa too can produce good results (Hodgetts forthcoming).

Studies of the husbandry of domestic animals in Britain are also bedevilled by the scarcity of Neolithic and Bronze Age faunal remains. Sheep and goat are relatively uncommon in these periods, but cattle have been studied using methods similar to those for sheep and goat described above (see eg Halstead 1985; Legge 1981; 1992). The Bronze Age cattle bones at Grimes Graves were interpreted by Legge (op cit) as resulting from a dairy economy: the large numbers of very young animals and the predominance of females among the adults suggested most male calves were being culled to make the milk available for humans. Others have however suggested that the pattern may result from inadequate husbandry practices (Entwhistle and Grant 1989; Noddle 1989), a point contested by Legge (1989; 1992).

Examining the adult sex ratio, Legge (1981) argued that the predominance of adult female cattle in the faunas of causewayed camps may also be indicative of a dairy economy. A study of the mandibles from the Hambledon Hill and Stepleton causewayed camps shows that mature cattle predominate in the assemblages, and bone measurements demonstrate that most were females. It seems that the cattle were surplus animals brought to the causewayed camps from domestic sites and used for food; the predominance of mature females can be explained as the cull from herds that were largely of this composition. Certainly there is little evidence for younger male cattle at the prime age for meat production.

Pigs are also common on later Neolithic sites, particularly Durrington Walls, where domestic pigs appear to have been 'ritually hunted' and then feasted upon (Albarella and Serjeantson forthcoming). One priority

for future research is to excavate Neolithic settlements and see how closely the previously excavated animal remains from non-domestic causewayed camps and henges reflect the domestic economy. Animal bone assemblages become more common in the Iron Age with some, such as that from Danebury (Grant 1984), being very large indeed. Comparison between sites is often difficult, however, because different researchers often use different methods and present and group their data in different ways; however, significant inter- and intra-regional patterns in the culling of cattle and sheep do appear when the data are recalculated in a consistent manner (Hambleton forthcoming).

Plant remains are also relatively scarce in the Neolithic and Bronze Age, becoming more common in the Iron Age. Until recently, there was relatively little cereal evidence from northern England even in Iron Age times, a fact that led some to postulate an entirely pastoral economy run by 'Celtic cowboys' (Piggott 1958, 25; also Frere 1978; and van der Veen and O'Connor, this volume). This interpretation has been comprehensively disproved by systematic botanical work (van der Veen 1992). Iron Age subsistence in the north definitely included a very major cereal component. Whether Neolithic and Bronze Age economies were heavily reliant on cereals or made greater use of wild foods is currently under discussion. Some interpret samples of wild plant seeds as evidence for the use of forest products (Entwhistle and Grant 1989; Jones 1980; Moffett *et al* 1989), while others argue that cereals were always fundamental to the economy (Legge 1989; Rowley-Conwy forthcoming). As with the question of dairying, this is partly a methodological problem, and partly a question of how we view past peoples: were they necessarily less skilful than farmers of more recent times? With regard to cereal cultivation, recent finds of early Neolithic buildings at Balbridie (Fairweather and Ralston 1993) and Lismore Fields (Jones forthcoming) that were apparently full of cereals when they burnt down is good evidence in favour of major reliance on cereals in this period. Scord of Brouster on Shetland produced examples of both cleaned grain and processing waste from late Neolithic levels (Milles 1986), testifying to the importance of agriculture – not surprising in view of the 2.5ha field system in which the site lies.

This brief discussion of methods would be incomplete without reference to recovery methods. The importance of adequate recovery of faunal remains was demonstrated long ago (eg Payne 1972), and a method for the mass recovery of plant remains was presented in the very same volume (Jarman *et al* 1972). Most excavations now make at least some attempt at water-sieving for animal and plant remains; however, large-scale sampling producing adequate samples is still regrettably uncommon. Most samples of Neolithic and Bronze Age plant remains come from the equivalent of just a bucket or two of soil (eg most of those listed by Moffett *et al* 1989). This practice inevitably produces small samples that are hard to interpret, and has been a major cause of the lack of knowledge of Neolithic and Bronze Age agriculture. Larger flotation samples are essential if this is to be remedied.

Problems of synthesis

The above discussion has made the point that methodology is a developing field; in many cases we have methods available that will solve outstanding problems when we obtain the appropriate data. Some broader questions and problems, however, still look intractable. Two of these can be suggested as topics that urgently need more work. One is the reconstruction of the entire diet – in particular the less visible parts of the diet. It is easy enough to use animal bones to provide a reasonable guess at what meats were eaten, and even to add in hazel nuts from their shells and blackberries from their pips. But the frequency – or scarcity – of cereal remains does not help very much in assessing how important these were in the diet relative to meat; and what of rhizomes and tubers, which leave almost no visible trace in the archaeological record?

Some lines of investigation are beginning to appear – for instance, stable isotope ratios in human bone – though less work has been done in Britain than in some other regions (eg Schwarcz and Schoeninger 1991; see Mays 1997 for similar work in Britain in later periods). Attempts to integrate more closely work on animal bones, plant remains, and human skeletons, however, are all too rare; they probably offer one way in which we can and should improve our approach to the problem. Important advances have also been made in developing other new methodologies that will assist here, most strikingly in analytical techniques and at the molecular level. These include, for instance, the work of Evans and of Evershed on residue analyses (Evershed *et al* 1992) and especially of lipids; the work of Samuel (1996) on recognising the residues of brewing and bread-making; and, in particular, major advances in work on ancient DNA, which offers new and direct information about genetic relationships and the past movements of people, of domestic stock, and of crop plants (NERC 1998).

Another important development has involved our approach to understanding food production systems. It is only a slight exaggeration to suggest that we have spent too much of the past 50 years trying to impose our preconceptions and preferred current theories on the past. Fifty years ago, we expected to find a slow unidirectional development from simple and inefficient precursors, and so tended to look for and see simpler versions of recent 'traditional' practice. Some recent syntheses have tended to follow this pattern (eg Thomas 1992). Increasingly, however, we have been prepared to recognise that past practice may have been very different from present practice, reflecting different priorities, quite different environmental conditions, and technologies which, though in some respects more limited, reflected considerable knowledge and skill – people in the past were no less intelligent, and had just the same capacity to observe and to learn from experience. The subsistence economy of the British Neolithic, for instance, may have depended on using forest grazing in open woodland of a kind that no longer exists. This has no modern analogues and the best way to understand it is by trying, without preconception, to reconstruct that environment and what people were doing, when appropriate using models that predict archaeological outcomes that can be tested against the data.

Another subject which is still full of problems, in spite of increasing awareness and research, is site formation processes. Better understanding of the nature of the archaeological record, and of the losses and biasses in that record, is clearly central to any understanding of the past; several aspects related to the reconstruction of diet are discussed below.

First, as mentioned above, is the question of whether the relative scarcity of charred cereal remains from some Neolithic sites a real scarcity? – or is it because they do not survive, or simply because we are failing to recover them? The same questions may be asked about fish bones. Improved sampling and recovery is important.

Just as important, or even more so, is the integrated study of different materials. Experiments on the mechanisms of destruction, before, during, and after burial (eg the experimental earthworks at Overton Down and Wareham, Bell *et al* 1996), together with the integrated study of different materials, offers the opportunity of recognising situations where the preservation of one class of material can be used with greater confidence to suggest that the absence of another is real, or that the apparent scarcity of another probably implies much larger amounts, and should provide hypotheses that we can then try to test, for instance, using isotope ratios or organic residues.

Second, incomplete and idiosyncratic publication of data often makes potentially rewarding comparisons impossible to carry out. Most faunal analysts are convinced that the frequency of anatomical parts in faunal assemblages is telling us something – even if we are not always sure what. One approach worth exploring is the comparison of multiple archaeological assemblages – but this is rarely possible because data, if presented at all, are presented in so many ways and with so little discussion of method that most publications are of little use in this.

The destruction of bones by domestic dogs is commonly invoked, but is this the sole cause of inter-element variation in all cases? Some have measured bone mineral density using densitometry in an attempt to predict which elements should succumb to dog gnawing – sheep, for example, have been tested by Lyman (1984; 1994). In one recent study of a series of heavily gnawed assemblages of sheep and goat, survivorship was, however, not as predicted by density (Rowley-Conwy 1997), but matched closely that observed in the classic actualistic experiment of Brain (1967; 1981), where a known number of goat skeletons were processed by humans and then scavenged by dogs. This example highlights once again the value of such work, which in this case at least appears more useful than more 'high-tech' studies.

Legge (1992, 34–7) has drawn attention to the differential survival of bones in well-preserved midden samples in relation to their fusion ages and the pattern of age-related predation upon the mammalian population. Gross percentages of bone survival are misleading unless the population age distribution is taken into account. Those bones that fuse early in life are usually well represented in archaeological samples, while those that fuse later in life are usually poorly represented. This is due to the simple fact that more of the former group were discarded when fused than was the case for the latter group and a marked increase in element density is caused by the fusion process (Brain 1967). If tooth eruption and bone fusion ages are known for the species under consideration, a correction can be made for this bias, and this may result in a very different understanding of bone representation in the sample under study. Obviously the consideration of predation ages is crucial in making comparisons of bone representation between sites, whether the species concerned are wild or domestic.

Third, the problem of 'structured' or 'ritual' activities and deposition involves animal bones and plant remains no less than artefacts and structures. In some cases interpretation may be fairly clear, for example the domestic pigs at Durrington Walls had in some cases been shot with arrows, and patterns of burning suggest that the carcasses were roasted whole; there can be little doubt that this is not normal domestic consumption (Albarella and Serjeantson forthcoming). But in other cases the issue is less clear, as in the status of the burials of complete carcasses at Danebury, which Grant (1984) interprets as structured deposition, but which Wilson (1992) interprets more prosaically as waste disposal. At some sites different parts of the evidence may suggest differing interpretations; for example, the animal bones from the pits at Down Farm were regarded as the result of structured deposition (Legge 1991), as were some other classes of material, but the plant remains were apparently not (Jones 1991). That such differences in interpretation occur should be regarded as encouraging rather than surprising, showing that studies of animal bones and plant remains are increasingly approaching a whole range of archaeological questions, including some not traditionally associated with such work – surely a very positive development.

Conclusion

In conclusion, a number of deliberately simple suggestions are offered.

Of prime importance is the need for more excavations where plant and animals remains are well preserved and well sampled. The shortage of such sites places major limitations on our understanding of prehistoric Britain. The ritual lament that we lack key data means that economic prehistorians should consider initiating and directing projects designed to fill lacunae.

In studying the plant and animal remains we recover from prehistoric sites, it is important to ask and to focus on major questions, however difficult, rather than ignore them. The primary example here is trying to look at the relative importance of cereals, other plant foods, meat and, if it was used, milk. Second, it is important, through the study of process, both to gain a better understanding of the archaeological record and of the necessary biological background – as archaeologists, this is work that we need to be prepared to carry out ourselves, and to see funded from archaeological resources. Third, it is important to recognise that what happened in the past may be entirely unfamiliar, and that our best chance of understanding it is to try, with an open mind, to reconstruct it rather than impose a preconception or theory on it – in this sense, we should take a deliberately empiricist and atheoretical position. Fourth, greater emphasis needs to be placed on integrated study, using a range of different materials and techniques to try to come at the same problem from different directions. Sites with large amounts of relatively well preserved and diverse material are of particular importance in this context and, in the present state of knowledge, we would argue that it is better to concentrate more of the available resource on a few sites of this kind rather than spread it over large numbers of more poorly preserved sites.

Finally, greater priority should be given to synthesis and dissemination. Too high a proportion of our effort goes into producing specialist appendices to excavation reports: the ritual lament that the writers of general archaeological books know far too little about our results means that specialists should write more for non-specialist readers.

Acknowledgements

We are grateful to Justine Bayley, Mike Corfield, Dominique de Moulins, Simon Mays, and Terry O'Connor for helpful comments on earlier drafts of this paper.

References

Albarella, U, and Serjeantson, D, forthcoming A passion for pork: butchery and cooking at the British Neolithic site of Durrington Walls, in P Miracle (ed), forthcoming

Barrett, J, Bradley, R, and Hall, M (eds), 1991 *Papers on the prehistoric archaeology of Cranbourne Chase*, Oxbow Monogr, **11**, Oxford

Bell, M, Fowler, P J, and Hillson, S W, 1996 *The experimental earthwork project 1960–1992*, CBA Res Rep, **100**, York

Boardman, S, and Jones, G, 1990 Experiments on the effects of charring on cereal plant components, *J Archaeol Sci*, **17**, 1–11

Brain, C K, 1967 Hottentot food remains and their bearing on the interpretation of fossil bone assemblages, *Scientific Papers of the Namib Desert Research Station*, **32**, 1–7

—, 1981 *The hunters or the hunted?*, Chicago

Bull, G, and Payne, S, 1982 Tooth eruption and epiphysial fusion in pigs and wild boar, in B Wilson, *et al* (eds), 1982, 55–71

Deniz, E, and Payne, S, 1982 Eruption and wear in the mandibular dentition as a guide to ageing Turkish Angora goats, in B Wilson, *et al* (eds), 1982, 155–205

Entwhistle, R, and Grant, A, 1989 The evidence for cereal cultivation and animal husbandry in the southern British Neolithic and Bronze Age, in A Milles, *et al* (eds), 1989, 203–15

Evershed, R P, Heron, C, Charters, S, and Goad, L J, 1992 The survival of food residues: new methods of analysis, interpretation, and application, *Proc Brit Acad*, **77**, 187–208

Fairweather, A D, and Ralston, I B M, 1993 The Neolithic timber hall at Balbridie, Grampian Region, Scotland: the building, the date, the plant macrofossils, *Antiquity*, **67**, 313–23

Fraser, F C, and King, J E, 1954 Faunal remains, in *Excavations at Star Carr* (ed J G D Clark), 70–95, Cambridge

Frere, S, 1978 *Britannia: a history of Roman Britain*, rev edn, London

Grant, A, 1984 Animal husbandry, in *Danebury: an Iron Age hill fort in Hampshire* (ed B Cunliffe), CBA Res Rep, **52**, 496–548, London

Halstead, P, 1985 A study of the mandibular teeth from Romano-British contexts at Maxey, in *Archaeology and environment in the lower Welland Valley*, volume 1 (ed F Pryor, C French, D Crowther, D Gurney, G Simpson, and M Taylor), E Anglian Archaeol Rep, **27**, 219–24, Cambridge

Hambleton, E, forthcoming Comparative studies of faunal assemblages from Iron Age Britain, unpubl PhD thesis, Univ Durham

Higgs, E S (ed), 1972 *Papers in economic prehistory*, Cambridge

Hillman, G, 1981 Reconstructing crop husbandry practices from charred remains of crops, in R Mercer (ed), 1981, 123–62

—, 1984 Interpretation of archaeological plant remains: the application of ethnographic models from Turkey, in W van Zeist and W Casparie (eds), 1984, 4–41

Hodgetts, L, forthcoming The use of ethnography and the development of younger Stone Age archaeology in north Norway, in *Ethnography, history, and environmental archaeology*, Proceedings of the 18th Annual Conference of the Association for Environmental Archaeology, held in Limerick in September 1997

Jarman, H N, Legge, A J, and Charles, J A, 1972 Retrieval of plant remains from archaeological sites by froth flotation, in E S Higgs (ed), 1972, 39–48

Jones, G, 1984 Interpretation of plant remains: ethnographic models from Greece, in W van Zeist and W Casparie (eds), 1984, 43–61

—, forthcoming Charred plant remains from the Neolithic settlement at Lismore Fields, Buxton, in *Lismore Fields* (ed D Garton), London

Jones, M, 1980 Carbonised cereals from Grooved Ware contexts, *Proc Prehist Soc*, **46**, 61–3

—, 1991 Down Farm, Woodcutts: the carbonised plant remains, in J Barrett, *et al* (eds), 1991, 49–53

Legge, A J, 1981 Aspects of cattle husbandry, in R Mercer (ed), 1981, 169–81

—, 1989 Milking the evidence: a reply to Entwhistle and Grant, in A Milles, *et al* (eds), 1989, 217–42

—, 1991 The animal remains from six sites at Down Farm, Woodcutts, in J Barrett, *et al* (eds), 1991, 54–100

—, 1992 *Excavations at Grimes Graves, Norfolk, 1972–1976, 4: animals, environment, and the Bronze Age economy*, London

Legge, A J, and Rowley-Conwy, P A, 1988 *Star Carr revisited: a re-analysis of the large mammals*, London

Legge, A J, Williams, J, and Williams, P, 1992 The determination of season of death from the mandibles and bones of the domestic sheep (*Ovis aries*), in *Archeologia della pastorizia nell'Europa meridionale, vol II* (eds R Maggi, R Nisbet, and G Barker), Rivista di Studi Liguri A, **57**, 49–65, Bordighera

Lyman, R L, 1984 Bone density and differential survivorship of fossil classes, *J Anthropological Archaeol*, **3**, 259–99

—, 1994 *Vertebrate taphonomy*, Cambridge

Mainland, I, 1995 Dental microwear as evidence for prehistoric diet: the potential of qualitative analysis, in *Aspects of dental biology: palaeontology, anthropology, and evolution* (ed J Moggi-Cecchi), 159–66, Florence

Mays, S, 1997 Carbon stable isotope ratios in medieval and later human skeletons from northern England, *J Archaeol Sci*, **24**, 561–7

Mellars, P, and Wilkinson, M, 1980 Fish otoliths as evidence of seasonality in prehistoric shell middens: the evidence from Oronsay, *Proc Prehist Soc*, **46**, 19–44

Mercer, R (ed), 1981 *Farming practice in British prehistory*, Edinburgh

Milles, A, 1986 Charred remains of barley and other plants from Scord of Brouster, in *Scord of Brouster: an early agricultural settlement on Shetland, excavations 1997–1979* (eds A Whittle, M Keith-Lucas, A Milles, B Noddle, R Rees, and J C C Romans), Oxford Univ Comm Archaeol Monogr, **9**, 119–22, Oxford

Milles, A, Williams, D, and Gardner, N (eds), 1989 *The beginnings of agriculture*, BAR, Int Ser, **496**, Oxford

Miracle, P (ed), forthcoming *Consuming passions and patterns of consumption*, Cambridge

Moffett, L, Robinson, M A, and Straker, V, 1989 Cereals, fruits, and nuts: charred plant remains from Neolithic sites in England and Wales and the Neolithic economy, in A Milles, *et al* (eds), *1989*, 243–61

NERC 1998 *Molecular signatures from the past*, Project summaries, Ancient Biomolecules Initiative Grand Finale, held in London, January 1998

Noddle, B, 1989 Flesh on the bones: some notes on animal husbandry of the past, *Archaeozoologia*, **3**, 25–50

Outram, A, forthcoming Bone fracture and within bone nutrients: an experimentally based method for investigating levels of marrow extraction, in P Miracle (ed), forthcoming

Payne, S, 1972 Partial recovery and sample bias: the results of some sieving experiments, in E S Higgs (ed), 1972, 49–64

—, 1973 Kill-off patterns in sheep and goats: the mandibles from Aşvan Kale, *Anatolian Stud*, **23**, 281–303

Piggott, S, 1958 Native economies and the Roman occupation of north Britain, in *Roman and native in north Britain* (ed I A Richmond), 1–27, London

Rowley-Conwy, P, 1997 The animal bones from Arene Candide (Holocene sequence): final report, in *Arene Candide: functional and environmental assessment of the Holocene sequence* (ed R Maggi), Memorie dell'Istituto Italiano di Paleontologia Umana, ns **5**, 153–277, Rome

—, forthcoming Through a taphonomic glass, darkly: the importance of cereal cultivation in prehistoric Britain, in *Taphonomy and interpretation* (eds S Stallibrass and J Huntley), Oxford

Samuel, D, 1996 Archaeology of ancient Egyptian beer, *J Amer Soc Brew Chem*, **54**, 3–12

Schwarcz, H, and Schoeninger, M J, 1991 Stable isotopic analyses in human nutritional ecology, *Yearbook of Physical Anthropology*, **34**, 283–321

Thomas, J, 1992 *Rethinking the Neolithic*, Cambridge

van der Veen, M, 1992 *Crop husbandry regimes*, Sheffield Archaeol Monogr, **3**, Sheffield

van der Veen, M, and Palmer, C, 1997 Environmental factors and the yield potential of ancient wheat crops, *J Archaeol Sci*, **24**, 163–82

van Zeist, W, and Casparie, W (eds), 1984 *Plants and ancient man*, Rotterdam

Wilson, B, 1992 Considerations for the identification of ritual deposits of animal bones in Iron Age pits, *Internat J Osteoarchaeol*, **2**, 341–9

Wilson, B, Grigson, C, and Payne, S (eds), 1982 *Ageing and sexing animal bones from archaeological sites*, BAR, **109**, Oxford

11 Some thoughts on using scientific dating in English archaeology and building analysis for the next decade

by Alex Bayliss

Abstract

Two methods overwhelmingly dominate scientific dating applications in England, certainly for those periods after the last glaciation. These are dendrochronology and radiocarbon, both of which have seen significant developments over the last few years.

Dendrochronology has progressed steadily towards filling the gaps in the temporal and spatial coverage of reference chronologies. Increased funding for the repair of standing buildings is creating demand for conservation-led analysis to inform conservation decisions. Progress on prehistoric material is inevitably slower, as samples are less readily available. However there is now an oak chronology from the present to around 5000 BC, although this is still very poorly replicated.

The most important recent development for the use of radiocarbon in archaeology, has been the advent of mathematical modelling for the interpretation of results along with associated archaeological information. The routine application of these techniques allows far greater precision to be obtained from radiocarbon dating—frequently date ranges of less than a century at 95% confidence are obtainable, opening up whole new areas of potential. Research into the dating of new materials also appears to be promising, and so generally more problems can now be resolved using scientific dating techniques.

Introduction

Reliable dating is fundamental to the study of the past. It allows us to compare sites, structures, and artefacts of similar date. This helps us untangle those differences observed in the material evidence that arise from chronological factors from those that have other causes. This ability to compare like with like is critical, not only for the academic understanding of the past, but also for the assessment of significance and so for the formulation and application of strategies for conservation (eg Semple Kerr 1996).

Looking forwards is always fraught with uncertainties, and so this paper is limited in scope so that it does not drown in a mire of generality and speculation. Instead I have attempted to present some ideas on how the 'routine' application of scientific dating to help solve the day-to-day problems of the conservation community, both of archaeologists and architectural historians, will change and develop over the next five to ten years. The ideas presented have arisen from the experience gained by the author in the Ancient Monuments Laboratory collaborating with project teams on the provision and use of scientific dating for English Heritage-funded programmes of work. This includes archaeology commissions (English Heritage 1991a; Olivier 1994; Olivier 1995; Wainwright 1993; and http://www.engh.gov.uk/ArchRev/) and building recording and analysis commissioned to inform statutory and grant casework. This experience is therefore confined to England and is almost entirely post-Mesolithic in date. For this reason no attempt is made to consider the problems of dating palaeolithic archaeology (see instead Housley this volume) or to discuss scientific advances whose impact will be felt largely outside the UK (eg Southern Hemispheric radiocarbon calibration; McCormac *et al* forthcoming).

Because I am concerned here with the practical application of scientific dating by the conservation community over the next few years, there is also little discussion of directions in fundamental scientific research. Inevitably it takes some time for 'technology transfer' to be effected: for new and effective solutions to become widely applied to conservation problems. This is particularly true where, as is increasingly the case in England, the vast majority of such questions arise in projects that are completed outside the university sector (Morris 1993), for example in architectural practices or archaeological units. By contrast the majority of fundamental scientific research and methodological developments do occur in higher education establishments.

At present the two most widely used techniques of scientific dating applied in England are dendrochronology and radiocarbon dating, although other methods are used and can be very effective in specific circumstances. In particular archaeomagnetic dating of hearths and kilns found on archaeological sites can be helpful, and more rigorous approaches to the problem of calibration may improve the accuracy of quoted dates over the next few years (Batt 1997). Although research continues into several aspects of luminescence dating, quoted errors are still in the region of 5–10%, which limit the utility of the technique. Nevertheless optically stimulated luminescence, in particular, may occasionally prove useful in situations where little else is datable (Rees-Jones and Tite 1997). Considerable work is still required on this technique, however, so at the moment such work is probably best regarded as collaborative research rather than 'routine' application. Except for these rather rare and specific examples, it is likely that the familiar techniques of radiocarbon and tree-ring dating will remain the most widely applied methods for the near future.

There are two major factors that will affect how scientific dating techniques are applied to questions raised by the historic environment over the next few years. Firstly, a range of scientific and methodological advances will enable questions to be tackled that were previously beyond the scope of the available methods. Secondly, changes in planning procedures (DoE 1990; DoE and DNH 1994) and the availability of grant monies (National Heritage Act 1997; National Lottery Act 1993, §36) mean that it is likely that a relatively high percentage of dating applications will be in support of repair/conservation strategies or development projects, rather than part of purely research programmes. Of course, if adequately disseminated, information gathered for these reasons can contribute greatly to the wider academic understanding of the past.

Dendrochronology

The built heritage

The last decade has seen a great increase in the number of standing buildings dated using the results of tree-ring analysis on constructional timbers (*Vernacular Architecture* passim; Fig 11.1). Research has reached the stage where the first reviews of the impact of precisely dated buildings on our understanding of the built heritage can be attempted (Pearson 1997). The mid 1980s saw the first dendrochronology and building recording projects designed specifically to address chronological aspects of constructional features and building typology (eg Pearson 1994; Suggett 1996). Although undoubtedly such thematic and research-driven work will continue, it is likely that the number of buildings dated to

Fig 11.1 Taking a core for tree-ring analysis at Stokesay Castle

solve immediate and isolated questions arising from repair and conservation cases will increase.

Planning policy guidance: planning and the historic environment (PPG15; DoE and DNH 1994) states that

> [applicants for listed building consent] should provide the local planning authority with full information, to enable them to assess the likely impact of their proposals on the special architectural or historic interest of the building and on its setting.

In a small percentage of cases, it is likely that historical and structural analysis will be insufficient and that tree-ring dating will be a necessary part of this information (ALGAO 1997). In some cases dendrochronology is crucial in identifying unsuspected phases of repair, or surviving timberwork from earlier construction (Fig 11.2). This is often apparent from an informed examination of the remaining structure, although this is not always so. The understanding of the historic sequence of a building is fundamental to decisions about repair and conservation. This is reflected in the increasing adoption of *The conservation plan* (Semple Kerr 1996) and the consequent emphasis on an explicit methodology for the consideration of cultural significance. The emphasis is on the importance of adequate information *before* conservation decisions are made.

Another factor influencing the number of 'one-off' applications of tree-ring dating over the next few years is simply the increased funding available for the heritage sector from the Heritage Lottery Fund. So far this funding has impacted largely on the built heritage, although recent legislation allows a wider range of projects to be considered for funding, including archaeology (National Heritage Act 1997).

Regional oak chronologies

The last decade has also seen considerable progress in the construction of regional master chronologies for many parts of England in the historic period (eg Bridge 1988; Haddon-Reece and Miles personal communication; Laxton and Litton 1988; Laxton and Litton 1989; Tyers 1993). These are very important because they enable a much larger percentage of samples to be successfully dated. A number of English tree-ring laboratories continue to work in areas where there are gaps in the spatial or chronological coverage of master sequences, or where these are weak because they contain relatively little data.

The situation in the extreme south-west of England, in Devon and Cornwall, can be taken as an example of the progress that is continuing to be made on this front. Buildings sampled or dated in Devon before 1994 are

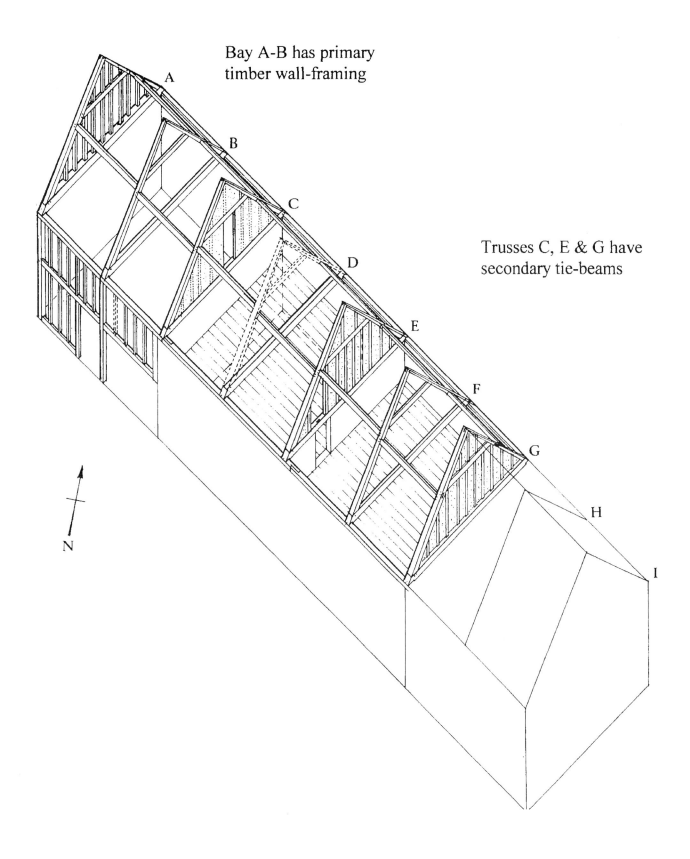

Bay A-B has primary
timber wall-framing

Trusses C, E & G have
secondary tie-beams

*Fig 11.2 Axonometric projection showing the surviving elements of the seventeenth-century roof construction at the Stable Building
at Forty Hall Farm, Enfield, Middlesex: the secondary tie-beams in Trusses C, E, and G have been dated by dendrochronology to
AD 1476–1499 (Bridge 1997)*

shown in Table 11.1. With the exception of Exeter Cathedral, it can be seen that the number of timbers that have produced absolute dates from this part of the country is very disappointing: only about 20% of those sampled. This compares with, for example, an average of 70% for tree-ring samples from English buildings published in the most recent volume of *Vernacular Architecture* (Bridge 1996; Howard *et al* 1996a–d; Miles 1996b; Miles and Haddon-Reece 1996a–c). During a particularly depressing period in 1994, only five out of 60 timbers sampled in Devon and Cornwall produced absolute dates.

This problem provided the impetus for a research project led by Cathy Groves of the Sheffield Dendrochronology Laboratory, jointly funded by English Heritage and Devon County Council, to build a local reference chronology by sampling buildings selected specifically for their potential for dendrochronology, rather than because they needed dating for reasons of management or conservation. The first stage of this work is nearing completion, with absolute dates for eleven buildings produced and approximately 54% of sampled timbers dated (Groves forthcoming a; forthcoming b). This improved, but still relatively low percentage of dated samples, along with the restricted spatial distribution of dated sites (Fig 11.3), and the large number of buildings assessed for dendrochronology but rejected as unsuitable at present, means that much more work is required in this region before tree-ring dating can be relied upon to solve the questions presented by conservation casework on a regular basis.

Table 11.1 Medieval and post-medieval buildings sampled for dendrochronology in Devon and Cornwall before 1994

building	location	sampled	dated
Berry Pomeroy Castle (Groves and Hillam 1993a)	SX839623	5	1
Christow: Reed Farm (Morgan 1980)	SX835837	1	1
Cullacott: Werrington (Miles 1996a)	SX303880	33	4
East Leigh: Elmside (Hillam and Groves 1991a)	SX698052	7	1
Eastleigh Manor: Westleigh (Miles 1994a)	SX488280	12	1
Exeter: Bowhill (Hillam 1991a)	SX906916	12	4
Exeter: Cathedral (Mills 1988)	SY921925	169	79
Exeter: Guildhall (Bridge 1986)	SY919926	2	2
Hatherleigh Church spire (Hillam and Groves 1991b)	SS542046	7	0
Molenick: St Germans (Miles 1994b)	SX612335	15	0
South Yarde: Rose Ash (Groves and Hillam 1993b)	SS711212	8	7
Tiverton Castle (Haddon-Reece unpubl)	SS711212	1	1
West Challacombe: Combe Martin (Groves and Hillam 1993c)	SS586475	9	0

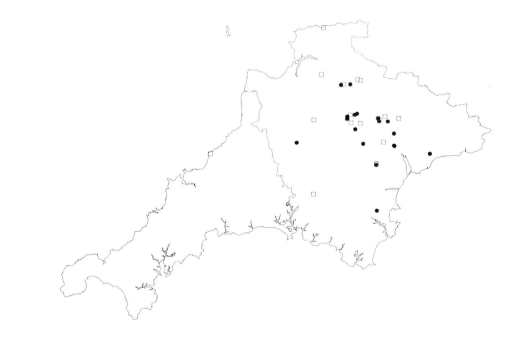

Fig 11.3 Location of dated (●) and sampled but undated (□) buildings in Devon and Cornwall up to August 1997

Prehistoric oak chronologies

If there are weaknesses in the regional and chronological coverage of reference chronologies in the historic period, the situation for prehistory is much worse (Fig 11.4). Although the prehistoric sequence is very poorly replicated and has to rely on samples spread over the whole country (Brown and Baillie 1992), progress has been made most notably with the dating of the Sweet Track to 3807/3806 BC (Hillam *et al* 1990). Because it is not yet possible to produce regional master sequences for different parts of the country for prehistory, success rates are much lower than for the historic period. More recent archaeological successes include dating Flag Fen (Neve 1992), the Goldcliff boat (Hillam forthcoming a), and prehistoric woodland off the coast at Wootton Quarr, Isle of Wight (Hillam 1991b; 1994; see Fig 11.5); but sites which have failed to produce absolute dates include the Dover Boat (Parfitt 1993) and Shinewater Park (Denison 1995).

Unlike the problems of missing or weak reference chronologies in the historic period, it is very difficult to take a proactive approach in prehistory. As all material is waterlogged and therefore only sporadically accessible, analysis is largely dependent on what is uncovered through excavation. However in the next few years it is likely that progress can be made by using material recovered from threatened coastal sites (Fulford *et al* 1997).

Oak sapwood estimates

The availability of reference chronologies is fundamental to enable the absolute dating of tree-ring samples. However the date of the last measured ring is not necessarily the same as the date when the timber was felled. Frequently, in the absence of bark edge on the sample or group of samples, a sapwood estimate is required to provide an *estimated felling date* (Baillie 1982, 54–7; 1995, 21–5; Hillam forthcoming b). For much of the last decade national estimates have been used in most applications (Hillam *et al* 1987; Hughes *et al* 1981), although regional estimates for the high medieval and early post-medieval periods have been calculated for a few regions such as Kent (Howard *et al* 1993). Further regional sapwood estimates are likely to be suggested over the next few years (Groves forthcoming a; forthcoming b; Miles 1997), and although the use of estimates based on a larger number of samples should allow users to have more confidence in the resultant estimated felling dates, it is unlikely to increase significantly the precision of

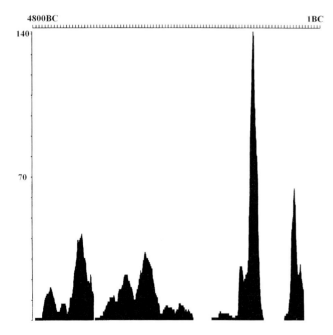

Fig 11.4 *Histogram showing the number of dated prehistoric oak samples from England and Wales per calendar year BC (samples measured in Belfast are not included): the earliest peak is comprised mostly of the Sweet Track, the second of Thorne Moors, and Wootton Quarr, the third is dominated by Flag Fen but also includes other Bronze Age sites, and the last consists of timbers from Fiskerton and Goldcliff*

Fig 11.5 *Measuring the tree-ring widths on a sample of waterlogged wood*

tree-ring dates that lack bark edge. In some instances structures can only be dated to within 50 years or so by tree-rings, and our interpretation must allow for this.

Other species of wood

Oak is the basis of British dendrochronology and is by far the most common timber encountered in buildings and on archaeological sites. However in many other European countries the analysis of other species, particularly conifers, is common. The potential of non-oak species for dating in Britain has been long recognised (Groves and Hillam 1988), and various attempts have been made to analyse other species, particularly from archaeological and sub-fossil contexts (Morgan 1987). Most of these attempts have not produced absolute dating, although recently there have been very promising developments in dating beech from archaeological contexts (Tyers 1997a; 1997b) and some success in dating sub-fossil pine (Brown 1991; Chambers et al 1997; Boswijk forthcoming).

From the high Middle Ages onwards, oak became more expensive and more difficult to obtain for building work. This led to the importation of oak timber, mainly from the Baltic (eg Hillam and Tyers 1995) and the use of other species. In some parts of the country elm was commonly used (eg Pearson 1994), as were imported conifers. The occurrence of conifer timbers in standing buildings increases dramatically during the eighteenth century and soon became more common than oak. Consequently comparatively few post-seventeenth-century buildings have been dated by tree-rings. This situation may well change over the next decade or so, as imported conifers become datable (Fig 11.6). On-going work funded by English Heritage at Sheffield University is promising (Groves 1993; Groves forthcoming b), with several known-age assemblages being successfully analysed. As practically none of the conifers used in historic buildings in England are native, this success is very largely owing to the generosity of fellow researchers in Europe, and beyond, who have allowed access to their

Fig 11.6 Tree-ring sample from a conifer timber

dated reference material. Potentially this work is extremely important. A few years may greatly affect the significance of industrial buildings in particular (Fig 11.7), and in such situations precise tree-ring dating may materially affect management and conservation decisions.

Although the dating of non-oak species is not yet routine, a great deal of promising applied research is underway. This means that the dating of other species should become more common in the next decade.

Tree-rings beyond dating

As a footnote to this section, it should be noted that dating is not the sole output of tree-ring analysis. A wealth of information about past climate (Baillie 1992; 1995), woodland management practices (Tyers *et al* 1994), and timber supply (Hillam and Groves 1996; Simpson 1996) can be interpreted from tree-ring data. As datasets expand over the next few years and increasing collaboration between laboratories continues, undoubtedly more research will also explore these avenues.

Radiocarbon dating

Mathematical modelling

For much of the 1990s research has been continuing into methods for the explicit mathematical modelling of the chronology of archaeological sites, combining the evidence from radiocarbon measurements with relative dating provided by stratigraphy and other absolute dating techniques, such as coins and dendrochronology (Bronk Ramsey 1995; forthcoming; Buck *et al* 1991; 1992; 1996; Buck, Christen *et al* 1994; Buck, Litton *et al* 1994; Christen *et al* 1995).

This methodology enables us to go beyond the simple calibration of a radiocarbon result, which provides an estimate of the date of the sample that has been analysed. Instead we can explicitly incorporate our interpretation of how a sample, or series of samples, relates to an archaeological event of interest and estimate the date when that event occurred. This practice requires a major conceptual shift in how users regard and apply radiocarbon dating. The measurement that is

Fig 11.7 The House Mill, Bromley-by-Bow, a complex industrial building largely constructed from conifers that have recently been sampled for dendrochronology

provided by the dating laboratory is no longer necessarily the answer to the archaeological question, but rather simply another piece of evidence to fit into the jigsaw of interpretation.

An example may make this process clearer. Figure 11.8 shows a simplified version of the chronological model that was used to provide an estimate of the date of digging the main ditch at Stonehenge. Readers who are interested in the dating of the site should refer to the full publication (Allen and Bayliss 1995; Bronk Ramsey and Bayliss forthcoming; and http://www.engh.gov.uk/stoneh/) and discussion of the modelling process (Bayliss *et al* 1997).

The diagram illustrates two important points. The combination of the calibrated radiocarbon dates and the archaeological evidence, in this case stratigraphy and knowledge from experimental archaeology about the mechanisms of ditch silting, enables more precise estimates to be made of the calendar date of the samples which were analysed. The probability distributions of these estimates are shown in black in Figure 11.8; distributions of the simple calibrated measurements, without taking account of the archaeological information, and shown in outline. So, for example, the estimated date range for antler pick 2804 (UB-3788) is *cal BC 3045–2955 (95% confidence)*, rather than the simple calibrated date range of cal BC 3095–2920 (95% confidence).

The probability distribution of the estimated date labelled '*ditch construction*' in Figure 11.8, is an explicit quantitative estimate of the date of the digging of the main ditch at Stonehenge. It has been calculated using all 15 radiocarbon measurements, combined with the archaeological evidence we have about the relative date of these samples and their relationship to the ditch digging. It is not a 'radiocarbon date'. It is not even a modified 'radiocarbon date'. It is something new. This is signified by the use of *italics* to distinguish estimated date ranges, which include other information, from simple calibrated radiocarbon dates (Mook 1986).

So, how will this new methodology impact on practical applications of radiocarbon dating over the next decade? Firstly, there is the potential for more precise dating for many archaeological sites and problems. Ongoing work at the Ancient Monuments Laboratory suggests that on average perhaps 80% of excavations produce archaeological sequences and samples that could benefit from this approach, and that the routine application of modelling techniques may produce a gain in precision of 25–35% (ie estimated date ranges spanning 200 calendar years rather than simple calibrated ranges spanning 300) (see Bayliss and Bronk Ramsey forthcoming for more detailed discussion).

This additional precision in chronology does not necessarily require the analysis of additional samples, nor does the radiocarbon necessarily need to be measured

more precisely. What is required, however, is explicit and rigorous consideration of the question that we wish to answer by using radiocarbon measurements, the material which is available for dating, and the sampling strategy required to achieve the objective of the dating programme. So, secondly, this practice requires rather more staff time in designing and implementing the dating programme, although this is amply justified by the additional information gained from the same number of determinations. These gains are certainly not evenly spread, however, with some sites gaining very little additional precision and others gaining a great deal. Estimated date ranges of about 100 calendar years, however, seem to be achievable reasonably frequently in the Neolithic and later periods.

But dates are just numbers. If we wish to utilise this potential for greater precision, why do we want to do so? The answer must be to address new, explicitly defined questions that have previously been beyond the range of our scientific techniques. For example, an environmental sequence from Market Lavington, Wiltshire, has recently had sampling levels dated to within a century or so (Wiltshire forthcoming). This is precise enough to enable the vegetational changes observed within the pollen assemblage to be interpreted within the framework of the adjacent middle Saxon settlement site. Greater precision will undoubtedly make radiocarbon analysis more useful in historic and proto-historic periods. Indeed it may also increase the utility of other analytical techniques in this period, where their use has previously been limited by an inability to produce a sufficiently precise dating framework to allow detailed interpretation in a historic context (see Bell this volume).

In prehistory the challenge is different. New and exciting questions may certainly come within view (see Bradley this volume), but a tighter chronological understanding of some sites may well exacerbate 'suck-in and smear' problems, where a precisely dated set of data tends to be used to 'explain' loosely-dated older material and where truly synchronous events go unrecognised, or misinterpreted as phases of activity, because of the inevitable scatter on radiocarbon measurements (Baillie 1991).

Research priorities and any resultant sampling strategies need to take account of the different scales of chronological information available for interpretation.

It is also necessary that the potential and practical realities of this alliance between radiocarbon dating and the mathematical modelling of chronological problems is recognised and exploited by archaeological projects funded through the planning framework. It is crucial, both that sufficient financial resources are identified and that adequate time is programmed for suitable sampling strategies to be adopted. This situation is undoubtedly difficult as the details of the dating potential of a site are

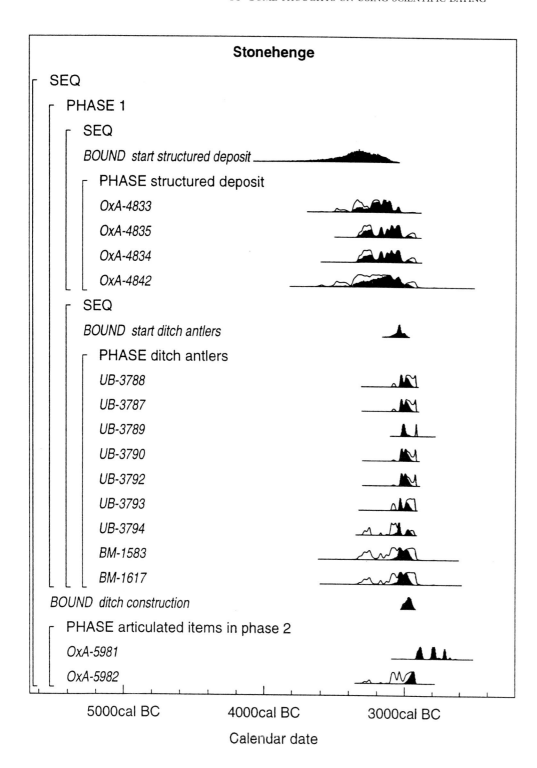

Fig 11.8 Probability distributions of dates from Phase 1 at Stonehenge: each distribution represents the relative probability that an event occurs at some particular time. For each of the radiocarbon dates two distributions have been plotted, one in outline, which is the result of simple radiocarbon calibration, and a solid one, which is based on the chronological model used; the 'event' associated with, for example, the radiocarbon date UB-3788 is the growth of the antler concerned. The other distributions correspond to aspects of the model: we have assumed that the material in the structured deposit started to be accumulated at some point defined as 'start structured deposit' and must have finished by the point at which the dig was actually dug ('ditch construction'); the acquisition of the antlers also forms a similar sub-phase starting at 'start ditch antlers'; we also use the additional information that the articulated material from Phase 2 must post-date the 'ditch construction' event. The large square brackets down the left hand side along with the OxCal keywords defined the overall model exactly

often not apparent until well into the analysis phase of a project (English Heritage 1991b).

It is likely that there are a range of solutions to this dilemma, and that the onus must lie with both curator and contractor to agree to a pragmatic response in each case.

Measurement precision

The last few years have seen an improvement in the precision of radiocarbon measurements, particularly those from AMS laboratories (Fig 11.9). It is debatable how much further these errors can be reduced, however, as sample chemistry becomes the principal limit on accuracy (Aerts-Bijma *et al* 1997). Small sample, high-precision dating (Wilson *et al* 1996) has also become

available. Since this has reduced the amount of material needed for such analyses by a factor of five (200g of bone, not a kilogram), the opportunities for applying the technique in archaeology have been greatly increased.

It is important that measurement precision is not confused with precision in the calibrated date. The relationship between the two is not direct, but very much dependent on the shape of the radiocarbon calibration curve in different periods. Archaeologists must therefore learn to use precise measurements efficiently – where the additional effort needed for the science is repaid by a useful increase in archaeological knowledge. Again, a date is just a number, and the question must be 'what more will it tell us?'.

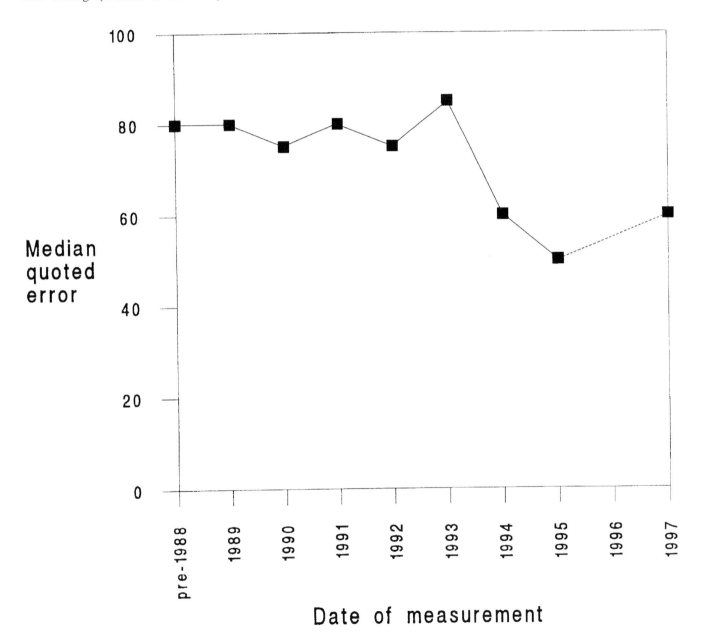

Fig 11.9 Graph showing the median error term quoted on AMS measurements funded by English Heritage 1986–1997 (n=581). Almost all samples were processed by the Oxford Radiocarbon Accelerator Laboratory. The value for 1996 has been interpolated because a major technical fault at the dating laboratory led to very few results being received in that year

New materials for dating

Routine mathematical modelling of chronological questions and higher measurement precision are available now, although obviously there are likely to be extensions and refinements to the methods over the next few years. Research, however, is also being carried out into dating a number of new materials using radiocarbon.

The dating of pure pollen from sediments has probably received most attention (Brown *et al* 1992; Long *et al* 1992; Regnell 1992), although the difficulties of sample separation are still formidable and so there is some way to go before such analysis will be available outside a purely research environment. Some work has also been started on the possibility of dating mortar samples (Heinemeier *et al* 1997), although this again needs more research before it can be tackled routinely.

The material possessing the most exciting potential for archaeology, however, is probably single bio-molecules, particularly lipids. The extraction of this group of chemicals for dating is beginning to receive much attention from a number of different areas of application. Work principally on oceanographic samples suggests that the problems of extracting sufficient quantities of pure sample by preparative capillary gas chromatography can be overcome and that accurate dating will be possible (Currie *et al* 1997; Eglinton *et al* 1996; Eglinton *et al* forthcoming). Potentially, this has wide application in archaeology, as the molecular residues already shown to be present in excavated ceramics (Charters *et al* 1997; Evershed and Tuross 1996) could be isolated and the actual use of ancient pottery dated directly. Work on this technique for archaeological application is in progress at the Universities of Bristol and Oxford (Evershed and Hedges personal communication).

Conclusion

In the 1990s there have been great changes in the planning framework in which English archaeology and our historic environment are managed. These have impacted on the use of scientific dating by archaeologists and other conservation professionals. In particular the rapid increase in the number of field evaluations (see for example Darvill *et al* 1995, fig 25) and the need for information before conservation decisions are made has led to a demand for dating within ever tighter deadlines. While this new framework presents a challenge to those who provide dates, technical developments are allowing an ever larger proportion of the chronological questions that users wish to pose to be resolved by scientific dating methods. This can only be welcome, as accurate chronology is fundamental to the interpretation, presentation, and conservation of archaeology and the built heritage.

Note on the citation of radiocarbon dates

The radiocarbon dates cited in the text has been calibrated according to the method of Stuiver and Reimer (1986) and the dataset of Pearson *et al* (1986). The range cited *in italics* is not a simple calibration, but derives from the mathematical modelling of the dating of Stonehenge (Allen and Bayliss 1995; Bronk Ramsey and Bayliss forthcoming).

Acknowledgements

The effective use of scientific dating in the heritage is a partnership between users and the dating laboratories. This paper has therefore been heavily influenced by many colleagues from both backgrounds. Particular thanks are due to Cathy Groves and Jennifer Hillam of the Sheffield Dendrochronology Laboratory for commenting on the text and providing the information shown in Figures 11.3 and 11.4 in advance of full publication, to Andy Wittrick of English Heritage for Figure 11.2, and to Christopher Ramsey of the Oxford Radiocarbon Accelerator Unit for being an unflagging ally in the transfer of routine mathematical modelling to the archaeological community.

References

Aerts-Bijma, A Th, Meijer, H A J, and van der Plicht, J, 1997 AMS sample handling in Groningen, *Nuclear Instruments and Methods in Physics Research B*, **123**, 221–5

Allen, M J, and Bayliss, A, 1995 Appendix 2: Radiocarbon dating, in *Stonehenge in its landscape: twentieth-century excavations* (R Cleal, K E Walker, and R Montague), EH Archaeol Rep, **10**, 511–35, London

ALGAO (Association of Local Government Archaeological Officers), 1997 *Analysis and recording for the conservation and control of works to historic buildings: advice to local authorities and applicants*, Bedford

Baillie, M G L, 1982 *Tree-ring dating and archaeology*, London

—, 1991 Suck-in and Smear: two related chronological problems for the 90s, *J Theoretical Archaeol*, **2**, 12–16

—, 1992 Dendrochronology and past environmental change, *Proc British Academy*, **77**, 5–23

—, 1995 *A slice through time*, London

Batt, C M, 1997 The British archaeomagnetic calibration curve: an objective treatment, *Archaeometry*, **39**, 153–68

Bayliss, A, and Bronk Ramsey, C, forthcoming Practising contextual archaeology in a processual manner: some experiences of the routine use of mathematical modelling for the interpretation of radiocarbon dates

Bayliss, A, Bronk Ramsey, C, and McCormac, F G, 1997 Dating Stonehenge, in *Science and Stonehenge* (eds B Cunliffe and C Renfrew), *Proc Brit Acad*, **92**, 39–59

Boswijk, G I, forthcoming Palaeoforest reconstruction and the development of raised mire at Thorne Moors in the Humberhead Levels, South Yorkshire and North Lincolnshire, unpubl PhD thesis, Univ Sheffield

Bridge, M C, 1986 Tree-ring dates obtained by Martin Bridge while at Portsmouth Polytechnic: list 19, *Vernacular Architect*, **17**, 53–4

—, 1988 The dendrochronological dating of buildings in southern England, *Medieval Archaeol*, **32**, 166–74

—, 1996 Tree-ring dates: London Guildhall University (list 69), *Vernacular Architect*, **27**, 91–2

—, 1997 Tree-ring analysis of timbers from build-ings at Forty Hall, Enfield, London, *Anc Mon Lab Rep*, **103/107**

Bronk Ramsey, C, 1995 Radiocarbon calibration and analysis of stratigraphy, *Radiocarbon*, **37**, 425–30

—, forthcoming Probability and dating, *Radiocarbon*

Bronk Ramsey, C, and Bayliss, A, forthcoming Dating Stonehenge, Computer applications and quantitative methods in archaeology (eds K Lockyer and V Mihăilescu-Bîrliba), BAR, Int Ser

Brown, D M, 1991 Studies on *Pinus sylvestris L.*, from Garry Bog, County Antrim, unpubl Msc thesis, Queen's Univ Belfast

Brown, D M, and Baillie, M G L, 1992 Construction and dating of a 5000 year English bog oak tree-ring chronology, in *Tree rings and Environment*, LUNDQUA Rep, **34**, 72–5

Brown, T A, Farwell, G W, Grootes, P M, and Schmidt, F H, 1992 Radiocarbon AMS dating of pollen extracted from peat samples, *Radiocarbon*, **34**, 550–6

Buck, C E, Cavanagh, W G, and Litton, C D, 1996 *Bayesian approach to interpreting archaeological data*, Chichester

Buck, C E, Christen, J A, Kenworthy, J B, and Litton, C D, 1994 Estimating the duration of archaeological activity using ^{14}C determinations, *Oxford J Archaeol*, **13**, 229–40

Buck, C E, Kenworthy, J B, Litton, C D, and Smith, A F M, 1991 Combining archaeological and radiocarbon information: a Bayesian approach to calibration, *Antiquity*, **65**, 808–21

Buck, C E, Litton, C D, and Scott, E M, 1994 Making the most of radiocarbon dating: some statistical considerations, *Antiquity*, **68**, 252–63

Buck, C E, Litton, C D, and Smith, A F M, 1992 Calibration of radiocarbon results pertaining to related archaeological events, *J Archaeol Sci*, **19**, 497–512

Chambers, F M, Lageard, J G A, Boswijk, G, Thomas, P A, Edwards, K J, and Hillam, J, 1997 Dating prehistoric bog-fires in northern England to calendar years by long-distance cross-matching of pine chronologies, *J Quaternary Sci*, **12**, 253–6

Charters, S, Evershed, R P, Quye, A, Blinkhorn, P W, and Reeves, V, 1997 Simulation experiments for determining the use of ancient pottery vessels: the behaviour of epicuticular leaf wax during boiling of a leafy vegetable, *J Archaeol Sci*, **24**, 1–7

Christen, J A, Clymo, R S, and Litton, C D 1995 A Bayesian approach to the use of ^{14}C dates in the estimation of the age of peat, *Radiocarbon*, **37**, 431–42

Currie, L A, Eglinton, T I, Benner, B A, Pearson A, 1997 Radiocarbon 'dating' of individual chemical compounds in atmospheric aerosol: first results comparing direct isotopic and multivariate statistical apportionment of specific polycyclic aromatic hydrocarbons, *Nuclear Instruments and Methods in Physics Research B*, **123**, 475–86

Darvill, T, Burrow, S, and Wildgust, D-A, 1995 *Planning for the past: volume 2, an assessment of archaeological assessments, 1982–91*, London

Denison, S, 1995 New Flag Fen-like site found in East Sussex, *British Archaeol*, **10**, 4

DoE (Department of the Environment), 1990 *Planning policy guidance: archaeology and planning* [PPG 16], London

DoE and DNH (Department of the Environment and Department of National Heritage), 1994 *Planning policy guidance: planning and the historic environment* [PPG 15], London

Eglinton, T I, Aluwihare, L I, Bauer, J E, Druffel, E R M, and McNichol, A P, 1996 Gas chromatographic isolation of individual compounds from complex matrices for radiocarbon dating, *Analytical chemistry*, **68**, 904–12

Eglinton, T I, Pearson, A, Benitez-Nelson, B C, McNichol, A P, Ertel, J R, Bauer, J E, and Druffel, E R M, forthcoming ^{14}C measurements of individual sedimentary organic compounds: a tool for developing refined sediment chronologies and understanding source inputs, *Radiocarbon*

English Heritage, 1991a *Exploring our past: strategies for the archaeology of England*, London

English Heritage, 1991b *Management of archaeological projects*, London

Evershed, R, and Tuross, N, 1996 Proteinaceous material from potsherds and associated soils, *J Archaeol Sci*, **23**, 429–36

Fulford, M, Champion, T, and Long, A, 1997 *England's coastal heritage*, London

Groves, C, 1993 Tree-ring analysis of a wood assemblage from Tilbury fort, Essex, 1988–9, *Anc Mon Lab Rep*, **20/93**

—, forthcoming a Dendrochronological research in Devon: phase 1—the pilot study, *Anc Mon Lab Rep*

—, forthcoming b The dating and provenancing of imported conifer timbers in England: the initiation of a research project, in *Archaeological Sciences 1995: proceedings of a conference on the application of scientific methods to archaeology* (eds A Sinclair, E Slater, and J Gowlett), Oxbow Monogr Ser

Groves, C, and Hillam, J, 1988 The potential of non-oak species for tree-ring dating in Britain, in *Science and Archaeology, Glasgow 1987* (eds E A Slater and J O Tate), BAR, **196**, 567–79, Oxford

—, 1993a Tree-ring analysis of oak timbers from Berry Pomeroy Castle, near Totnes, Devon, 1992, *Anc Mon Lab Rep*, **19/93**

—, 1993b Tree-ring analysis of oak timbers from South Yarde, Rose Ash, Devon, 1992, *Anc Mon Lab Rep*, **36/93**

—, 1993c Tree-ring analysis of oak timbers from West Challacombe, Combe Martin, Devon, 1992, *Anc Mon Lab Rep*, **37/93**

Heinemeier, J, Jungner, H, Lindroos, A, Ringbom, A, von Konow, T, and Rud, N 1997 AMS ^{14}C dating of lime mortar, *Nuclear Instruments and Methods in Physics Research B*, **123**, 487–95

Hillam, J, 1991a Tree-ring analysis of timbers from Bowhill House, Exeter, Devon, *Anc Mon Lab Rep*, **4/91**

—, 1991b The dating of oak timbers from Wootton Creek, Fishbourne, Isle of Wight an interim report, *Anc Mon Lab Rep*, **47/91**

—, 1994 The dating of oak timbers from Wootton Quarr Survey, Isle of Wight, *Anc Mon Lab Rep*, **10/94**

—, forthcoming a Tree-ring analysis and dating of Iron Age oak timbers from the Goldcliff excavations, Gwent, *Anc Mon Lab Rep*

—, forthcoming b *Guidelines for dendrochronology*, EH/AML Guideline, London

Hillam, J, and Groves, C, 1991a Tree-ring analysis of oak timbers from Elmside, East Leigh, Crediton, Devon, *Anc Mon Lab Rep*, **43/91**

—, 1991b Tree-ring analysis of oak timbers from St John the Baptist's church, Hatherleigh, Devon, *Anc Mon Lab Rep*, **45/91**

—, 1996 Tree-ring research at Windsor Castle: aims and initial results, in *Tree-rings, environment, and humanity* (eds J S Dean, D M Meko, and T W Swetnam), 515–23, Arizona

Hillam, J, Groves, C M, Brown, D M, Baillie, M G L, Coles, J M, and Coles, B J, 1990 Dendrochronology of the English Neolithic, *Antiquity*, **64**, 210–20

Hillam, J, Morgan, R A, and Tyers, I, 1987 Sapwood estimates and the dating of short ring sequences, in *Applications of tree-ring studies: current research in dendrochronology and related areas* (ed R G W Ward), BAR, Int Ser, **333**, 165–85, Oxford

Hillam, J, and Tyers, I, 1995 Reliability and repeatability in dendrochronological analysis: tests using the Fletcher archive of panel-painting data, *Archaeometry*, **37**, 395–405

Howard, R E, Laxton, R R, and Litton, C D, 1993 Nottingham University Tree-ring Dating Laboratory results: RCHME joint northern medieval roofs survey (list 50), *Vernacular Architect*, **24**, 45–6

—, 1996a Tree-ring dates: Nottingham University Tree-ring Dating Laboratory, general list (list 65), *Vernacular Architect*, **27**, 78–81

—, 1996b Tree-ring dates: Nottingham University Tree-ring Dating Laboratory, Derbyshire, Peak Park, and RCHME dendrochronological survey 1995–6 (list 66), *Vernacular Architect*, **27**, 81–4

—, 1996c Tree-ring dates: Nottingham University Tree-ring Dating Laboratory, buildings of the religious estates in medieval Durham 1994–5 (list 67), *Vernacular Architect*, **27**, 85–6

—, 1996d Tree-ring dates: Nottingham University Tree-ring Dating Laboratory, Sherwood forest oak: a dendrochronological survey (list 68), *Vernacular Architect*, **27**, 87–90

Hughes, M K, Milson, S J, and Legett, P A, 1981 Sapwood estimates in the interpretation of tree-ring dates, *J Archaeol Sci*, **8**, 381–90

Laxton, R R, and Litton, C D, 1988 *An East Midlands master tree-ring chronology and its use for dating vernacular buildings*, University of Nottingham, Dept Classical and Archaeol Stud Monogr Ser, **3**, Nottingham

—, 1989 Construction of a Kent master chronological sequence for oak, 1158–1540 AD, *Medieval Archaeol*, **33**, 90–8

Long, A, Davis, O K, and de Lanois, J, 1992 Separation and ^{14}C dating of pure pollen from lake sediments: nanofossil AMS dating, *Radiocarbon*, **34**, 557–60

McCormac, F G, Hogg, A G, Higham, T F G, Baillie, M G L, Palmer, J G, Xiong, L, and Brown, D, forthcoming Spatial and temporal variation of radiocarbon in tree rings: some preliminary results, *Radiocarbon*

Miles, D W H, 1994a The tree-ring dating of Eastleigh manor, Westleigh, Devon, *Anc Mon Lab Rep*, **41/94**

—, 1994b The tree-ring dating of Molenick farmhouse, St Germans, Cornwall, *Anc Mon Lab Rep*, **40/94**

—, 1996a The tree-ring dating of the old farmhouse at Cullacott, Werrington, Cornwall, *Anc Mon Lab Rep*, **11/96**

—, 1996b Tree-ring dates: Historic Building and Monuments Commission for England (English Heritage) (list 70), *Vernacular Architect*, **27**, 93–5

—, 1997 The interpretation, presentation, and use of tree-ring dates, *Vernacular Architect*, **28**, 40–56

Miles, D W H, and Haddon-Reece, D, 1996a Tree-ring dates: general list (list 71), *Vernacular Architect*, **27**, 95–7

—, 1996b Tree-ring dates: Hampshire dendrochro-nology project (list 72), *Vernacular Architect*, **27**, 97–102

—, 1996c Tree-ring dates: Shropshire dendrochro-nology project phase four (list 72), *Vernacular Architect*, **27**, 95–7

Mills, C, 1988 Dendrochronology of Exeter and its application, unpubl PhD thesis, Univ Sheffield

Mook, W G, 1986 Business meeting: Recommendations /Resolutions adopted by the Twelfth International Radiocarbon Conference, *Radiocarbon*, **28**, 799

Morgan, R, 1980 Tree-ring dates for buildings, *Vernacular Architect*, **11**, 22

—, 1987 Tree-ring studies in the Somerset Levels, unpubl PhD thesis, Univ Sheffield

Morris, R, 1993 Archaeology a casualty of the market? *British Archaeol News*, **8**, 1–2

National Heritage Act 1997 Chapter 14, London

National Lottery Act 1993 Chapter 39, London

Neve, J, 1992 An interim report on the dendrochron-ology of Flag Fen and Fengate, *Antiquity*, **66**, 470–5

Olivier, A C H, 1994 *Archaeology Review 1993–4*, London

—, 1995 *Archaeology Review 1994–5*, London

Parfitt, K, 1993 The Discovery of the Bronze Age Boat, *Canterbury's Archaeology 1992–3*, 15–18

Pearson, G W, Pilcher, J R, Baillie, M G L, Corbett, D M, and Qua, F, 1986 High-precision ¹⁴C measurement of Irish oaks to show the natural ¹⁴C variations from AD 1840–5210 BC, *Radiocarbon*, **28**, 911-34

Pearson, S, 1994 *The medieval houses of Kent: an historical analysis*, London

—, 1997 Tree-ring dating: a review, *Vernacular Architect*, **28**, 25–39

Rees-Jones, J, and Tite, M S, 1997 Optical dating results for British archaeological sediments, *Archaeometry*, **39**, 177–87

Regnell, J, 1992 Preparing pollen concentrates for AMS dating: a methodological study from a hard-water lake in southern Sweden, *Boreas*, **21**, 373–7

Semple Kerr, J, 1996 *The conservation plan*, 4 edn, Sydney

Simpson, G, 1996 Documentary and dendrochrono-logical evidence for the building of Salisbury cathedral, *British Archaeological Association Conference Transactions*, **17**, 10–20

Stuiver, M, and Reimer, P J, 1986 A computer program for radiocarbon age calculation, *Radiocarbon*, **28**, 1022–30

Suggett, R, 1996 The chronology of late medieval timber houses in Wales, *Vernacular Architect*, **27**, 28–37

Tyers, I, 1993 Tree-ring dating at Cressing Temple, and the Essex curve, in *Cressing Temple: a Templar and Hospitaller manor in Essex* (ed D Andrews), 77–83

—, 1997a Tree-ring analysis of beech and oak timbers from the Tower of London moat, *ARCUS Rep*, **293**

—, 1997b Dendrochronological analysis of beech timbers from the Magor Pill I wreck, Gwent, *ARCUS Rep*, **261**

Tyers, I, Hillam, J, and Groves, C, 1994 Trees and woodland in the Saxon period: the dendrochrono-logical evidence, in *Environment and economy in Anglo-Saxon England* (ed J Rackham), 12–24, York

Wainwright, G J, 1993 *Archaeology Review 1992–3*, London

Wilson, J E, McCormac, F G, and Hogg, A G 1996 Small sample high-precision ¹⁴C dating: characterisation of vials and counter optimisation, in *Liquid Scintillation Spectrometry 1994* (eds G T Cook, D D Harkness, A B MacKenzie, B F Miller, and E M Scott), Arizona

Wiltshire, P, forthcoming Palynological analysis of the palaeochannel silty peats, in *Excavations at Grove Farm, Market Lavington, Wiltshire, 1986–90* (P Williams and R Newman), Salisbury

12 Approaches to the study of metal in the insular Bronze Age

by William O'Brien

Abstract

This paper focuses on recent advances made in the study of metal supply during the insular Bronze Age. Long-standing research problems in this area are reviewed, with particular attention to the scientific characterisation of metal sources, the interpretation of production evidence, and the identification of exchange patterns. New approaches to these research areas are explored with reference to a project on Copper Age metallurgy currently underway in south-west Ireland.

Introduction

Whether as an agent of economic growth or an expression of social relations, metal has long been central to how we view the Bronze Age. For V G Childe and those influenced by his ideas, the Bronze Age was a world of economic force, of markets and customers, where metal supplied by smiths and traders represented not only technological progress, but contributed to the growth of personal wealth and power, expressed ultimately in the rise of chiefdom societies. In the diffusionist explanation of social change, the flow of metal was a central mechanism in promoting inter-regional contact and dependence. The successful development of metallurgy seemed to encapsulate those qualities of inventiveness, entrepreneurship, and individualism long associated with this period of prehistory.

In recent decades, this view of metal as a prime mover in Bronze Age societies has changed somewhat as new theoretical approaches place a different emphasis on the social role of this innovation. Metal is still widely regarded as a critical resource for this period, playing a dynamic role in society by promoting or maintaining the rise of elites through resource control and prestige goods networks. Some would argue that we have lost perspective on the true significance of this innovation in Bronze Age times, blinded in part by the high profile of the metalwork record today.

Clearly, the study of metal still has much to inform us about life in Bronze Age times, whether viewed narrowly in terms of technical achievement or explored to reveal broader social meanings behind production, exchange, use, and deposition. To realise this potential, it is important to understand that the interpretations we derive from scientific studies are ultimately grounded in current theoretical debates on the organisation of society in the Bronze Age. In these shifting sands, it is useful to consider how new methodologies can assist in furthering our understanding of various technical, economic, and symbolic dimensions.

My concern in this paper is to examine the contribution that archaeological science has made to the study of some 2000 years of Bronze Age metallurgy in Britain and Ireland. This examination will require some element of review to identify the main research trends over almost two centuries of interest shown by the scientific community. This interest, as with conventional archaeological approaches, has largely focused on finished metalwork, its technical production, and its economic context. As the artefactual side of Bronze Age research has declined in recent years, so too has the level of scientific enquiry. The explanation lies partly in those same root problems that have dogged artefact-based approaches to the insular Bronze Age – problems of context and association, weak chronology, and poor understanding of metal use and deposition.

This is not an issue of resources or scientific achievement, rather one of application and research direction. There have been important advances in recent years, both conceptually in how we approach metal in the Bronze Age and archaeologically in terms of increased understanding of mining and deposition. And yet, the contribution of science to this research often appears opportunistic in its application and overly specialist in publication. While excellent artefact studies have been presented in recent years, there is currently a lack of synthesis at many levels. It is thus timely to review the contribution which archaeological science has made in the study of early insular metallurgy and to consider future research directions in this field.

Archaeological science and ancient metallurgy

The concerns of archaeological science in relation to the study of ancient metal are well known and can operate at many levels. Most attention focuses on purely metallurgical studies aimed at understanding various aspects of metal production and fabrication, as inferred through chemical composition and microstructure (see Northover 1985 for details). As well as technological enquiries, scientific studies can be used to examine many other aspects surrounding and affecting the lifecycle of a metal object, from sourcing and exchange, to use-wear analysis and the study of depositional environments. This brings in contributions from many areas, among them geology, mineralogy, isotope geochemistry, and conservation science.

In terms of the broader definition of 'archaeological science', we can distinguish between those scientific studies that bear directly on the production and use of

metal, and those that serve to illustrate the wider context within which this took place. Thus, we may also
include the impact of radiocarbon dating in this field,
the contribution of environmental sciences and remote
sensing, statistics, and computer modelling. That this is
one of the most interdisciplinary fields of research in
modern archaeology can be both a strength and a weakness, demanding clear focus to avoid fragmenting into
disciplinary particularisms.

Research trends

The scientific investigation of ancient metals is a major
research area world-wide. This field has developed as a
specialist subdiscipline, partly serving archaeology, but
with its own research agenda heavily committed to the
history of technology. This specialism has been a
strength, drawing on the experience of many dedicated
researchers with the necessary blend of foundry experience and analytical know-how. Yet this has inevitably
distanced many projects from a broader archaeological
context and the call for closer collaboration through
integrated research has long been heard (eg Slater 1985,
45). It is possible to cite several instances over the past
two decades where archaeologists have collaborated
closely with research scientists in approaches to Bronze
Age metal. These collaborations are increasingly anthropologically informed, though as recently highlighted by
Budd and Taylor (1995), much research still proceeds
by applying modern 'industrial' perspectives to metal in
the ancient past.

Scientific approaches to the study of Bronze Age
metal in Britain and Ireland have a long history, dating
back to early antiquarian speculation on the fabrication
of these objects. In 1774, Alchorn, George III's assay
master, analysed two Bronze Age swords from Ireland
(Pownall 1786), and two decades later George Pearson
carried out some detailed experiments with a view to
determining the composition of a range of objects
(Pearson 1796). Scientific analyses are also a feature of
many nineteenth-century enquiries (eg Mallet 1853)
and feature in Evan's monumental study of Bronze Age
metalwork published in 1881 and in Coffey's (1901)
examination of early copper celts. The principal concern
of these early studies was to discuss metal composition
in terms of alloying practice and hence explore sourcing
of copper and tin. We see growing interest in the techniques by which Bronze Age metal artefacts were fash-
ioned. Gowland's (1899; 1906) work, drawing on
archaeological, anthropological, and scientific sources,
deserves special mention here, as does the research of
Herbert Maryon (1938).

The development of new analytical techniques such
as spectrographic methods early in this century saw

scientific investigation of ancient metal carried out routinely in many European countries. By the 1950s, scientific studies began to be integrated with the prevailing
typological approach. The work of Hugh Coghlan and
his colleagues in the Ancient Mining and Metallurgy
Committee of the Royal Anthropological Institute of
Great Britain and Ireland is of particular importance
here. Coghlan's analyses and scientific experiments, initially approached from a techno-historical perspective,
were soon given added value by his collaboration with
Humphrey Case. Their 1957 paper on early copper metallurgy in Britain and Ireland was followed by important
papers (Case 1966; Coghlan et al 1963) in a period of
sustained research lasting into the 1970s (Allen et al
1970), followed in recent decades by initiatives from the
British Museum (Craddock 1979; Needham et al 1989)
and Oxford University (Northover 1980).

The 'golden grail' of provenance

In addition to technology and the character of regional
metalworking traditions, a further strong incentive to
research has been efforts to link compositionally similar
artefacts to particular ore sources and thus identify
trade and exchange. Central to the established notion of
a European Bronze Age is the role played by trade and
other forms of cultural contact in promoting social and
economic change. The possibility of linking metal artefacts to their metal sources, in a Europe where those
same natural resources are not evenly distributed, has
long interested researchers in both scientific and conventional archaeology. This led to several analytical
studies in Europe in the post-war period (eg Pittioni
1957), from which emerged the major Stuttgart programme (Hartmann 1970; 1982; Junghans et al 1960;
1968; 1974), which included a significant number of
British and Irish results. British efforts in this area
include the early research by Coghlan and his collabo-
rators and subsequent programmes undertaken by the
British Museum and Oxford University (above). In
terms of metal sourcing, these scientific studies must
have been encouraged by the success of the stone axe
petrology programme conducted in Britain in recent
decades (Clough and Cummins 1979).

Following what was perceived to be the limited success of the Stuttgart initiative in terms of its central goals,
recent scientific research into Bronze Age metalwork has
been directed to new areas. The focus in provenance
studies has shifted away from trace element analysis to
the study of lead isotopes, most notably the work of the
Oxford laboratory in the Aegean (Gale and Stos-Gale
1982) and recently for the insular Bronze Age (Rohl
1996). The current interest in lead isotope studies ultimately relates to certain fundamental difficulties associated with the source provenancing of metal, which

conventional analyses were unable to resolve. The critical debate surrounding this research in recent years, most recently aired in *Antiquity* (Budd *et al* 1996; Tite 1997), suggests that a scientific panacea remains some way off.

Archaeological contributions

For much of this century, artefact research in the form of typology, with emphasis on chronology and periodisation, has been the dominant archaeological approach to the study of Bronze Age metal across Europe. With the development of radiocarbon and decline of the prevailing culture history approach, the value of this work is now widely questioned and is currently in decline. Of lasting significance is the contribution made by typological studies to defining the character and geographical spread of regional metalworking traditions. While metalwork studies have moved in new directions in recent years, most notably concerned with symbolism and deposition, some researchers have sought to advance typological approaches through a scientific interface (eg Needham *et al* 1989). This has demonstrated how conventional artefact information can be successfully integrated with scientific studies to define typo-compositional groupings of metal circulation in the Bronze Age.

One obvious way to move beyond artefact-based approaches to the study of Bronze Age metal is to try to develop a greater fieldwork perspective. This has already begun to some extent with the investigation of mine sources and a slowly growing settlement record from hillforts and other contexts in Britain and Ireland. The discovery of maritime wreck sites such as those at Moor Sand, Salcombe, Devon and at Langdon Bay, Dover, Kent (Muckleroy 1981) adds significantly to our understanding of metal trading in the Bronze Age. Significant problems remain, most notably the almost total absence of settlement contexts for metal production and use from the first 1000 years of insular metallurgy.

The past 15 years have also seen an increased understanding of the resource base of Bronze Age metallurgists in these islands, most notably in the study of early copper mines (summarised in Crew and Crew 1990; O'Brien 1996; Timberlake 1994). Advances here have been confined to two specific source regions, namely mid-north Wales and south-west Ireland, with little progress on the contribution of other British or Irish ore fields to copper supply. Our understanding of the lead, tin, and gold resource base is very poor, as is our insight into early metal sourcing in Cornwall, most probably a pivotal area in terms of tin supply and interregional metal exchange during the Bronze Age.

Even more problematic is the continuing paucity of evidence for the production and exchange of metal in this period. Archaeological contexts for the first 1000 years of metallurgy remain sparse; there is, however, a

slowly growing settlement record for the later Bronze Age in both Britain and Ireland. In recent decades, a range of habitation and other site types have been identified, marked by the presence of clay mould fragments and related artefacts. Where scientifically investigated, these sites have occasionally provided clear evidence of a workshop, although precise detail on furnace structures and internal site organisation is often lacking. The better known examples include a number of large hilltop enclosures, such as Llyn Bryn-dinas, Powys (Musson *et al* 1992), Rathgall, Co Wicklow (Raftery 1971), and Dun Aonghasa, Co Galway (Cotter 1993). Other habitation contexts include lake platform sites such as Lough Eskragh, Co Tyrone; settlements such as the Lough Gur complex (O Riordain 1954) and the important site of Jarlshof in the Shetlands (Hamilton 1956), and coastal occupation such as Dalkey Island, Co Dublin (Liversage 1968); and work centres such as Grimes Graves, Norfolk (Needham *et al* 1991).

Such sites as Jarlshof, Llyn Bryn-dinas, and Rathgall are important examples with workshops where artefact can be linked to hearth and furnace structures indicative of on-site casting and fabrication. With many other sites, for example Runnymede (Needham 1991), workshops must be inferred from the circumstantial evidence of artefact discoveries. Other sites where crucibles and moulds have been discovered, for example at Killymoon, Co Tyrone (Hurl 1995) and Dainton in Devon (Needham 1980), have a poorly understood archaeological context. Also of interest is the small number of Bronze Age sites where metalworking activity can be linked to the expression of ritual beliefs. Deposits of a likely votive nature include the presence of sword mould fragments at the King's Stables ritual pond site in Co Armagh (Lynn 1977) and the discovery of raw metal outside the entrance to a megalithic tomb at Toormore, Co Cork (O'Brien *et al* 1989/90). The deposition of Middle Bronze Age stone moulds in megalithic tombs in Ireland (*ibid*) may also be included in this list, while many would place a ritual interpretation on so-called 'scrap hoards' of later Bronze Age date.

Despite these discoveries there are still many gaps in our understanding of metal in the insular Bronze Age, whether it be in sourcing, production and supply, or consumption and deposition. For some crucial areas, such as like furnace technology, our knowledge is almost non-existant. Recent discoveries at Ross Island, Co Kerry (O'Brien 1995) include the first copper smelting furnaces known from this period in Ireland or Britain, while a single droplet from this site is the first piece of raw smelted metal to be discovered on a smelting site. This is a remarkable paucity of production evidence when set against the rich metalwork record in copper, bronze, and gold for all periods of the insular Bronze Age.

The organisation of Bronze Age metalworking, from the sourcing of raw material to the subsequent supply of finished metalwork remains poorly understood. These archaeological problems must of course be placed against the well-known difficulties that beset the Bronze Age settlement record, particularly for the second millennium BC. This explains to some extent why the study of Bronze Age metallurgy has declined in recent decades once the potential of an artefact-based approach was felt to have been exhausted. It follows that the development of a vigorous fieldwork dimension, whether through the investigation of mine sites, metalworking locations, or artefact depositional environments, is an obvious way to energise research in this field.

Science in archaeometallurgy

In the sections that follow, I wish to examine how scientific approaches can contribute to the study of Bronze Age metal at different levels, beginning with the production process and its wider context. Before doing so, it is important to reflect on the nature of this metallurgy and the degree to which it was ever driven by rational scientific principles. This has been explored in a recent paper by Budd and Taylor (1995), who question the orthodox industrial approach so often used to model early metallurgy and urge greater consideration of magico-religious dimensions. This follows a growing number of contributions from the ethnographic record in recent years, going back to Rowlands (1971) and more recently Herbert (1984), which demonstrate that the study of primitive metallurgy even from a technological perspective must never be divorced from its social context.

The consequence of viewing Bronze Age metallurgy as proto-scientific and specialist by nature is that we place this activity firmly within a narrow economic sphere of the past. This encourages a certain rational approach to analysis where scientific methodologies can be employed to produce hard 'results' in pursuit of apparently 'objective' conclusions. That this objectivity is usually compromised by the absence of reliable contextual details is a continuing problem for archaeological scientists studying Bronze Age metalwork. At issue is not the reliability or sophistication of scientific analyses, but the inferences to be drawn from this information in the interpretation of primitive metalworking.

Modelling the resource base

'Ore' and 'resources'

Consideration of metal supply in the Irish-British Bronze Age has long been influenced by deterministic models, which emphasise the industrial context of this production. Of particular prevalence is the view that different types of metal source became available as technology evolved to meet a burgeoning demand for metal. Consideration of the resource base used by early metallurgists in Europe has long emphasised the optimisation of resources. We see different mineral sources coming 'on line' as the necessary technology develops to exploit them. Thus, we move from an early exploitation of native metals to, in the case of copper, the extraction of supergene mineralisation and finally, the use of sulphide mineralisation in a sequence believed to mirror the geological occurrence of copper mineralisation.

This model has been encouraged by the conceptualisation of Bronze Age metal supply in terms of industries working to near-market conditions. A view of Bronze Age metallurgy as '...a single self-propagating industry, isolated from external factors and motivated by its own logic' (Slater 1985, 48) is now increasingly seen to be simplistic as we move to more anthropologically informed perspectives on the organisation of primitive metalworking. As Slater points out, most archaeological debate today views technology as secondary to broader social and economic influences in the organisation of Bronze Age metallurgy.

Increasingly, this view of metal sourcing as technologically constrained is being replaced by a social perspective that emphasises territorial control of resources and metallurgical knowledge. It is now clear that the sequence through which metallurgy developed in the Near East and Balkans is not appropriate to the inception and development of metallurgy in Britain and Ireland over a much shorter time-frame. The Bronze Age copper mining record from Britain and Ireland reveals an ability to process different ore types from a range of geological environments by 2000–1500 BC (O'Brien 1995; 1996). We also see important differences of scale between different mine operations, with several able to establish dominant positions in metal supply in different periods. This is probably true of Ross Island copper mine with regard to the supply of early arsenical copper in Ireland, while large mines like the Great Orme mine in Wales were probably major sources in later Bronze Age times.

In citing large 'productive' mine operations like Ross Island and the Great Orme, it is easy to lose sight of the many minor occurrences of surface mineralisation exploited in different periods of the Bronze Age. The Mount Gabriel-type mines spread across the Mizen and Beara peninsulas of south-west Ireland are a case in point. Here we see a proliferation of surface workings in the 0–15m depth range, exploiting a low-grade copper mineralisation consisting mainly of supergene malachite with a very small sulphide component (O'Brien 1994). The use of such a 'resource' in the Bronze Age is very informative in terms of how early metallurgists viewed mineral deposits. In early publications (eg O'Brien *et al* 1990), the use of this ore was viewed against a background of regional exhaustion of accessible oxidation zone mineralisation, with local metallurgists forced to work sedimentary copper-bed locations such as Mount Gabriel almost as a 'desperation resource'. In this model, technology is the main constraint on metal sourcing, caused by an inability to process sulphide mineralisation at this time (1700–1500 BC) in the insular Bronze Age.

Until recently, it was widely held in Europe that sulphide mineralisation first came to be worked quite late on in the Bronze Age owing to an 'industrial depression' caused by the depletion of oxide zone deposits (Charles 1985). Of particular influence here is a geological model of mineral zonation with depth in metallic orebodies, which we now know should not be used literally to model ore availability in prehistory. The discovery in 1992 of the Ross Island Beaker copper mine in southwest Ireland convinced me that the initial Mount Gabriel interpretation was not correct. The former site provides clear evidence of an ability to process sulphide mineralisation, chalcopyrite, and tennantite copper ores, from as early as 2400 BC, several centuries before the Mount Gabriel-type mining is known to have commenced in this region.

We now see in the insular Bronze Age an ability to exploit a range of mineralisation types in different geological settings. While only certain ore deposits were physically accessible, geology and technological capability were not the only determinants of resource availability in this period. The exploitation of mine operations such as Mount Gabriel must instead be explained in terms of the territorial ownership of and access to resources and the desire of different groups to become involved in metal production. Social perspectives such as these offer a greater insight than generalising techno-historical explanations into the availability of copper and other metals in prehistory.

Despite recent advances in the understanding of Bronze Age copper mining, it is not generally possible to assess the contribution of different mine sources to the overall metal pool. This relates to the issue of source provenancing of finished metalwork, which has generally been addressed by attempting to extrapolate back from artefact compositions to mine ore sources. The problems here are well known, relating mainly to the complex partitioning of chemical elements in the transformation from ore to metal and subsequent recycling. It is widely acknowledged that a poor understanding of the resource base used by Bronze Age metallurgists has greatly undermined the efforts of analytical programmes in terms of metal sourcing.

The recognition of a growing number of Bronze Age copper mines in recent years now offers much potential for scientific investigation in this area.

Approaches to source characterisation

The scientific study of mineralisation is obviously central to attempts at source characterisation of metal, both in terms of understanding background chemistry and isotopic ratios, and the technology required to treat different ore fractions. Metalliferous ore deposits are well known to be heterogeneous in terms of mineral and chemical composition, occurring within a wide range of geological environments and subjected to varying levels of supergene alteration. The problem of characterising polyminerallic deposits has long been appreciated, going back to Coghlan's early work, yet this has not discouraged efforts to characterise metallic deposits in terms more appropriate to the study of hard rocks.

The analysis of metal ores used in antiquity is usually approached quantitatively, with the aim of identifying characteristic trace element or stable isotope 'signatures'. This type of scientific 'finger-printing' generally makes fundamental assumptions about the composition of ore-bodies, their internal chemistry and mineralogy, which are rarely justified. The study of Bronze Age ore sources has been marked by an absence of determinative mineralogy work, for which quantitative analysis is no substitute. Sampling strategies have often been hopelessly inadequate and many studies fail to take ore treatment procedures sufficiently into account, to make the all-important distinction between naturally occurring mineralisation and processed ore.

While the geological study of mineral deposits in Britain and Ireland offers an important basis for research, we need a more archaeologically informed approach to understanding the Bronze Age resource base. The role of the archaeologist is fundamental, as information derived from modern resource survey will not always be relevant to a consideration of ore deposits used in prehistory. This may be simply illustrated by reference to an early sampling programme that examined potential sources of copper in Bronze Age Britain and Ireland (Butler in Coghlan *et al* 1963). Using ore samples derived from museum collections and major mine sites, the study managed to miss entirely the Mount Gabriel-type mineralisation of south-west Ireland. As stated above, Mount Gabriel emphasises that we must be very careful in assumptions made about what constitutes 'ore' in prehistory.

In studying the mineralogy and chemistry of ore mineralisation, sampling procedure is of the utmost importance. Sampling in connection with research into ancient metallurgy is often random and highly opportunistic, with no clear insight into what constituted 'ore' for a given period of extraction. It is usually focused on deposits of processed spoil, which are a common feature of ancient mine sites. Unless excavation has been carried out, surface sampling is usually not chronologically specific and by their residual nature, spoil tips will not be representative of ore as mined in prehistory. More detailed work must be carried out before we can begin to study mineral associations to ascertain what fractions could have been exploited and at what grades.

In the Ross Island copper mine project currently underway in south-west Ireland (O'Brien 1995), a more comprehensive programme of ore sampling has been developed, involving close collaboration between bedrock geologist, ore mineralogist, and the archaeological team. This work, coordinated by Robert Ixer of Birmingham University, involves sampling from different environments within the site, by chip collection and drilling of mineralisation *in situ*, as well as the collection of mineralised samples from secure excavation contexts. It is only through recovery from radiocarbon-dated contexts that we will be able to state with any confidence which mineral fractions were exploited at different times in the mining history of this polyminerallic deposit.

In conclusion, a more rigorous approach to the characterisation of mineral ore deposits is necessary if we are to achieve a meaningful understanding of the resource base used by Bronze Age metallurgists. This can be pursued through improved collaboration with earth science specialists within the context of integrated mine studies and sampling initiatives. The failure to undertake this basic research will significantly affect the progress of any subsequent scientific studies, be they concerned with provenancing or production technology.

Resource use: the Bronze Age mining record

Rigorous sampling is all very well, but unless we achieve a detailed understanding of the early mine record, it will be difficult to know which mineral occurrences are relevant to metal production in different periods. There is an urgent need to increase our knowledge of the utilisation of metal sources in the insular Bronze Age. This information cannot be inferred with any confidence from compositional analysis of finished metalwork, while for geological reasons, the contribution of isotopic studies is also likely to be limited in a British-Irish context. These scientific studies may in some cases point to potential sources of Bronze Age metal, which can then be targeted for archaeological investigation. We need to develop recent advances made in the study of early copper mining, to broaden the chronological as well as the geographical spread of extraction sites, not only for copper, but for gold, tin, and lead as well. Archaeological

science can contribute to what is essentially a fieldwork challenge, by assisting in the discovery and investigation of ancient mine sites. The potential for this involvement has been amply demonstrated by interdisciplinary studies carried out in recent years at the Great Orme and Cwmystwyth in Wales, and at Mount Gabriel and Ross Island in Ireland.

Radiocarbon dating, more than any other area of archaeological science, has been central to recent progress in this field. The principal success here has been in the absolute dating of Bronze Age copper mines in two specific source regions, namely south-west Ireland (Brindley and Lanting 1990) and mid-north Wales (Ambers 1990). A number of observations may be made here:

1 Further fieldwork is required to extend the geographical spread of these early copper mines into other metalliferous regions. The research programme currently funded by the Leverhulme Trust at Alderley Edge is an important step here. Further initiatives are required for other metalliferous areas of Britain, most importantly Cornwall and Scotland. A greater appreciation by State authorities in Britain and Ireland of the extent of early mining heritage is essential here. Furthermore, the study of early metal mines is unnecessarily regarded as a specialist area and could be easily moved closer to mainstream Bronze Age studies through greater involvement of archaeologists and prehistorians.

2 The application of radiocarbon dating has been limited to copper mines of late third and second millennia BC date. With the possible exception of the Great Orme, no major copper mine source is known for the insular Late Bronze Age. This may reflect a real problem of archaeological visibility caused by changes in mining technology. Alternatively, it may represent a major shift in metal supply, with greater input by continental sources and more developed recycling networks. The latter are unlikely to account entirely for the enormous metal consumption in this period in both Britain and Ireland.

With almost a millennium of mining and prospecting experience behind them and possessing obvious metallurgical skills, there is no technological reason why Late Bronze Age groups could not have continued to exploit insular ore sources. Social factors may be relevant here, for example the political tension and interregional warfare suggested by the rise in fortified settlement and weapon production in the first millennium BC. A breakdown of social stability may have adversely affected some mining and metal production efforts and it would also be very interesting to know what impact Celticisation and the adoption of iron metallurgy had on these same activities. By using compositional data from

Late Bronze Age metalwork, it may be possible to target specific ore-bodies for archaeological scrutiny and thus begin to tackle this problem.

3 There have been few advances in the identification of early lead, tin, and gold sources. The archaeological record of alluvial gold and tin extraction in areas of long mining history, such as Cornwall, is highly problematic. Scientific approaches to the sourcing of gold and tin must be a research priority to further our understanding of these metals and move beyond the kind of generalisation so common in the literature. The current investigation of gold sources in Ireland, through detailed geological sampling and scientific analysis (Warner 1995), is possibly the only research currently underway in this field. The latter is a good example of the type of inter-disciplinary collaboration necessary to advance knowledge in this field.

To address these problems requires dedicated fieldwork programmes, which must involve a strong commitment to archaeological excavation. The ore deposits to be targeted should have been accessible to Bronze Age miners in terms of geology and mineralogy, offer possible correlations with metalwork compositions, and ideally be associated with circumstantial evidence of primitive mining in the documentary or artefact record. What is also needed is the application of radiocarbon dating on a scale not previously seen, to investigate the internal chronology of multi-period mines. This is an important feature of the current Ross Island investigation, where a programme of dating involving some 50 determinations is underway. This involves multi-context dating in an attempt to identify archaeologically invisible mine horizons. Central to the study is large-scale AMS dating of animal bone food waste, as well as conventional dating of charcoal residues from mining, ore treatment, and habitation activities.

With this radiocarbon programme in progress, the main success to date has been the discovery of a horizon of early medieval metal production at Ross Island. On completion, it is hoped to examine the time-scale of extraction within this mine site. By understanding the duration of specific mining initiatives, it will be possible to address questions pertaining to the organisation of mining in the Bronze Age. Calibration and statistical treatment of these radiocarbon results should yield a refined chronology for this mine site, which in turn may allow more meaningful estimates of production.

Further developments in mine chronology lie in the area of tree-ring studies, first attempted in the Mount Gabriel complex (McKeown 1994). This is an area with considerable potential once more waterlogged mine contexts are investigated. Other scientific approaches,

such as archaeomagnetism and luminescence, may also find limited applications in the dating of specific mine contexts.

In conclusion, we need to make the whole consideration of Bronze Age metallurgy more time-specific and move away from generalisation to a situation where different mine sites are linked chronologically as well as metallurgically to specific metalworking traditions. The potential for correlation here is illustrated by the increasingly refined typo-compositional groupings, which can now be identified for different periods of the insular Bronze Age (eg Needham *et al* 1989, fig 4). Radiocarbon dating of metalwork contexts, whether through new discoveries or the investigation of old findspots, will further refine typology-based chronologies leading to greater correlation with mine activity.

The search for production evidence

In studying the insular Bronze Age, we must place a rich and technically advanced artefact record in one of the most metalliferous regions of western Europe, against a production record that in terms of mines, smelting sites, and fabrication centres was virtually unknown up to recent times. Our understanding of metal production in all periods of the Bronze Age is very limited and clearly this is an area where scientific studies have much to offer in terms of site discovery and process investigation. The problem remains the continuing paucity of production evidence in the form of furnaces, slags, crucibles, and associated refractories relating to all stages of metal production. While scrap hoards testify to widespread recycling from early in the Bronze Age, the sourcing and logistics of this metal collection and the circumstances surrounding deposition are poorly understood.

The absence of smelting evidence in both artefact and site form is a particular feature of the insular Bronze Age. This is also seen in other European regions, which contrast with the Bronze Age record from Austria and the Mediterranean zone, where metal production can have a high visibility marked by slag deposits, furnace installations, and roasting areas. The absence of Bronze Age copper slag deposits in Britain and Ireland may be explained either in terms of technology or archaeological visibility. In recent years Craddock (1990) has suggested that the absence of slag deposits is a direct consequence of a widely used metallurgical process that was both low-temperature and non-slagging. He argues that this type of smelting regime is supported by the low iron content of finished metalwork in the insular Bronze Age. There may well be other explanations to account for the absence of these residues from the archaeological record, for example the crushing and water flotation of slags to extract entrapped metal prills. On the other hand, the absence of metallurgical structures such as furnaces almost certainly reflects limited field survey and excavation.

Before scientific and technological arguments can be accepted, more intensive archaeological fieldwork is necessary to examine the character of our metal production record. Based on evidence from centres in Austria, an obvious starting point for this research must the investigation of Bronze Age copper mines. Fieldwork here is complicated by the environmental setting of many sites (peat cover on Cwmystwyth and Mount Gabriel) or the large-scale destruction of evidence by later mining (Great Orme, Parys Mountain, and Ross Island). One obvious contribution that archaeological science can make is in the area of remote sensing, specifically geophysical survey. A number of studies in recent years (eg Desvignes and Tabbagh 1995, 132) highlight the potential of survey techniques such as magnetic susceptibility and gradiometry in the detection of pyrodynamic activity areas.

Recent research carried out as part of the Ross Island project has highlighted the difficulties of geophysical imaging in ancient mine landscapes. Techniques such as ground probing radar have been applied with little success in an effort to image underground mine workings. In our investigation of the adjacent work camp, magnetic, electromagnetic, and resistivity survey methods were unable to penetrate through masking spoil deposits to investigate the Beaker work surfaces containing metallurgical pit features. Test-pit investigation of magnetic susceptibility anomalies on the site periphery did, however, detect two spreads of plate slag with pit furnaces and associated refractories. While the latter were subsequently dated to the early medieval period, this discovery illustrates the potential of geophysical methods in the search for metallurgical areas in and close to ancient copper mines.

In the right environment, such techniques as magnetic susceptibility survey have the ability to image metallurgical work surfaces even where no significant slags were produced or discarded. This is an obvious area where archaeological science can contribute to a problem that seriously hampers our understanding of Bronze Age metallurgy. Large-scale geophysical survey and subsequent test excavation in the environs of known and possible Bronze Age mine sites offers much potential for progress.

Understanding the production record

Recently, several archaeological scientists have emphasised the primitive character of metal production in the insular Bronze Age (Budd *et al* 1992; Craddock 1990; Pollard *et al* 1990). Partly in reaction to the dearth of production evidence, there is a growing belief that early metal production in Britain and Ireland may not be comparable to the large-scale slagging output seen in other parts of Europe in this period. These researchers have suggested that the smelting processes involved may have been much simpler, low temperature affairs, with low metal output and little in the way of an archaeological record today. Leaving aside the scientific feasibility of these models, it must be asked if a model of low-temperature furnace technology is really consistent with the fabrication skills evident in Bronze Age metalwork? The difficulty with much of this research is that it seeks to come up with rational scientific explanations for what may well be shortcomings in the archaeological record.

In fact, there has been no systematic surface excavation in the environs of ancient mine sites in Britain. In Ireland, excavation close to mine workings and spoil tips was first attempted in the Mount Gabriel project, but the scale of investigation here was too limited for significant metallurgical discoveries to be made. Recently, the investigation of some 700 square metres of a surface work camp at Ross Island has led to the discovery of a metal processing record associated with copper mining and the users of Beaker pottery in the period *c* 2400–1900 BC. Excavation of this site revealed a concentration of pit features and surface sediments clearly associated with heat treatment of arsenical copper ore (tennantite).

The interpretation of this record is complicated by the absence of metallurgical residues, with only a few possible slag fragments and metal droplets recovered. The absence of slag is a particular problem when attempting to understand the nature of these metallurgical processes. The evidence survives in a form with which the laboratory scientist is not accustomed to working, namely pit features associated with burning, stake structures, and soft sediment deposits. As this site dates to an early stage in insular metallurgy, it is uncertain how representative this type of archaeological record will prove to be. Clearly, whether hard metallurgical residues like slags are produced or not, the physical record of copper smelting and related activities does survive in a form readily retrievabale by archaeologists.

In the absence of slags and other residues, archaeological scientists may have to develop new approaches to understanding primitive metal production at such sites as Ross Island. These will have to include the consideration of soft sediment archaeology and a much greater role for experimentation. At Ross Island, it is hoped to initiate a programme of field and laboratory experimentation, in an attempt to replicate this type of archaeological record. The metallurgy of this site remains problematic, but we are now at least moving in the right direction: from ore to metal in a production site environment.

Rigorous research experimentation and process modelling of the type initiated by Merkel (1990) for Timna or Doonan (1994) for Austria has been largely absent from recent approaches to insular Bronze Age metallurgy. Much experimentation today comes across as very generalised, lacking any firm archaeological context and employing parameters that are either largely imaginative or derivative. What we need are programmes of experimentation framed within specific mine studies, where the behaviour of particular ore types linked to Bronze Age mining can be scrutinised in a controlled way. This would enable some meaningful studies to be made on the partitioning of trace elements during smelting, using ore samples representative of material mined in antiquity and not the mineral grade material so often used. This type of mine-based experimentation would provide some valuable, if problematic, data-sets that could then be compared usefully with local and regional artefact compositions. Experimentation must not be confined to laboratory-based research, which can sometimes produce scientifically feasible process models that bear little reality to the resource base of Bronze Age metallurgy or its archaeological record.

Fabrication and use

The scientific study of Bronze Age metalwork has always been marked by a concern with fabrication techniques. While provenancing studies have held the limelight, this is an area of research somewhat neglected in recent decades, particularly when we consider the metalwork record at our disposal. The potential of metallography here is considerable, in terms of understanding the thermal history and mechanical properties of artefacts, alloying practice, finishing techniques, and use-wear analysis. Yet metallography appears to be a neglected area of archaeological science, with few practitioners and few problem-oriented studies in evidence today. More broadly based research of the type carried out by Coghlan and his colleagues (Coghlan *et al* 1963) and by Peter Northover (1982) is urgently required. Clearly, the attitude of museums is increasingly important, compelling us to come up with more imaginative reasons to carry out destructive analysis.

Most metallographic studies carried out today focus on individual finds, with the result that this information can lack broader contexts within the same or allied metalworking traditions. This technique offers much potential in clarifying the technical nature of 'workshop traditions' in the insular Bronze Age. In the absence of settlement evidence, metallographic methods can usefully complement conventional artefact studies and experimentation, to put together some picture of the prevailing workshop skills in different periods. There is

much potential in pursuing metallography in association with use-wear studies, which in turn can be tied into depositional environments. Another approach lies with mine-based research programmes, currently being explored in the Ross Island project with the assistance of Peter Northover. Once again, we need to return to the spirit evident in Hugh Coghlan's work where artefact research of this kind was pursued vigorously in laboratory analysis and in experiment.

Functional analysis of metal implement and weapon types is clearly a neglected area wthat can be usefully tied into fabrication experiments, use-wear, and residue studies. The precise use and tooling patterns left by many implement types are unknown, as are the functional implications of many typological groupings. The performance of weapons under combat conditions has also scarcely been researched, the potential here demonstrated by a project underway in the University of Sheffield exploring the relationship between sword damage and deposition (Bridgford 1997). There is much scope for broad-ranging, problem-oriented investigations of this kind, where various areas of archaeological science can usefully contribute to conventional artefact studies (see Ramsey 1995 for recent discussion on the latter).

Environmental context

I also wish to refer briefly to the potential contribution of environmental science to the study of Bronze Age metal. This is a relatively new field of research, concerned with understanding both the landscape setting of mining and metal production and with the environmental impact of these same activities. We may also include here the study of use-contexts and depositional environments for Bronze Age metal, from the study of tooling marks in bog trackways (Coles and Coles 1986) to the formation of Runnymede-type alluvial deposits (Needham 1991).

Of particular interest is the contribution that palynology and wood studies can make to understanding the environmental impact of Bronze Age mining and metal production. This area of research is being developed in Britain by Tim Mighall of Coventry University, who has undertaken studies at Copa Hill in Wales and Mount Gabriel in Ireland (Mighall and Chambers 1993; 1994). In these projects, it has proven possible to investigate the impact of mining on local woodland cover in terms of fuel supply. This pollen research can be integrated with the study of waterlogged and charred wood from early mines to shed light on possible woodland management. The application of tree-ring studies to the study of waterlogged fuel assemblages from Bronze Age mines has much potential to examine the environmental context and seasonality of mining and metal production. Other research areas include the production of charcoal as a metallurgical fuel and the long-term effects of fuel collection in promoting landscape change through alteration of vegetation patterns and blanket bog growth.

Several other fields of environmental science can usefully contribute to understanding the wider context of metallurgy and metal use in the Bronze Age. These range from animal bone studies relevant to food economy and mining tools (eg Dutton and Fasham 1994), to geochemical investigation of metallurgical environments and the analysis of geobotanical indicators (eg Brooks and Johannes 1990, 15–63).

Metal supply and exchange

Returning to metal supply and exchange, the search for more advanced scientific provenancing methods will doubtless continue through the current lead isotope debate and beyond. This technique, combined with compositional data, may ultimately permit provenancing of metal to specific source regions, though mine characterisation may prove more elusive. Copper Age production in south-west Ireland may well be one instance where some measure of success is achieved. The apparent consistency of Irish metal over the first 300–500 years of metallurgy points to the use of arsenical ore sources, which Coghlan and Case (1957) suggested were probably located in this region. This is now supported by the discovery of the Ross Island mine in Co Kerry, which certainly contributed to the supply of this arsenical metal and may well have been the dominant source. The working of a tennantite copper source here in the period 2400–1900 BC correlates well with the currency of early arsenical copper in these islands (Northover 1980; 1982). Unpublished research by Brenda Rohl (personal communication) of the Isotrace Laboratory, Oxford, points to a possible lead isotope correlation between early arsenical copper in western Britain and Ross Island.

With widespread recycling from very early in the Bronze Age, the inevitable pooling of metal from different mine sources on both sides of the Irish Sea and additional input from time to time of continental metal, must greatly complicate matters in terms of artefact provenancing. This is not to say that the considerable effort invested in compositional analyses has been wasted, as we are at least able to outline the circulation of different metal types through the Bronze Age even if the geographical source of this metal remains unclear. With greater emphasis on metal circulation as opposed to sourcing, scientific analyses have much potential to shed light on recycling practice and the movement of different metal types. Where a refined chronology is available,

analytical data can be used to trace major developments in regional metal use (eg Needham et al 1989). By over-emphasising the inter-regional character of metal supply in the Bronze Age, we ignore many useful linkages that might possibly be made at the local level.

Typo-compositional groupings will remain relevant to the study of Bronze Age metalworking traditions, particularly as more information on Bronze Age metal sources becomes available. Also relevant to the study of metal supply is the scale of production apparent at Bronze Age mine centres across Britain and Ireland. This has proved a difficult area of enquiry and we now know that early estimates for such centres as Mount Gabriel greatly exaggerated the capacity of these mines to produce metal (O'Brien 1994, table 12). Future production estimates will have to be based on a reliable survey record, detailed geological assessment of the ore body in question, and a refined radiocarbon chronology for its exploitation.

While there is a definite reaction today against the idea of highly organised, concentrated 'industry' in the Bronze Age, not all metal production in this period may necessarily have been small-scale and localised. This is not the impression one gets at the Great Orme, though as with other centres it is difficult to infer on the basis of physical size alone the scale or organisation of production at mines worked over a long period. Chronological control is essential if we are to assess the release of metal from these centres and their relative contribution to overall metal supply in the Bronze Age. Clearly, we should expect significant differences in scale of production between different mine centres, although the implications in terms of wider metal supply are not clear.

The study of metal supply may still offer considerable insight into Bronze Age trade and cultural exchange. An important step towards identifying the scale and character of metal exchange networks has come from Stuart Needham's (forthcoming) contribution to the 1996 Dijon conference. In modelling the flow of metal from production centres, he has usefully explored the relationship between supply and consumption for Bronze Age groups actively engaged in recycling. This and earlier perspectives on displacement and deposition (Needham 1993) emphasise the many complexities that underlie metalwork distribution patterns and provide a theoretical foundation for future science-assisted efforts to understand metal sourcing and circulation.

Conclusion

In recommending future research directions for the study of Bronze Age metallurgy, one could be tempted to suggest that laboratory advances will eventually lead to major breakthroughs in areas such as provenancing and process reconstruction. Certainly, methodological innovation will continue to set much of the agenda in this field, if only because of the way archaeological science is now structured in Britain. While acknowledging the sophistication of modern scientific approaches, one is struck by how few advances have really been made in early insular metallurgy since the work of Coghlan and his colleagues four decades ago. The blame for this lies squarely with conventional archaeology and its passive approach to the archaeological record of Bronze Age metal and metalworking. The future must lie in new forms of collaborative research, in addressing marked deficiencies in the archaeological record and in applying such tried and tested analytical techniques as metallography to specific research problems.

Yet we must be sure what questions we really want to address. The understanding of process – metal production and fabrication – will continue to be a priority, while use-wear studies will assume an increasing importance as research into deposition continues apace.

Source provenancing of metal remains a problem area and indeed we may usefully ask, as the Bradford group did in a recent *Antiquity* paper (Budd *et al* 1996), whether the effort is really worth all the research energy. Given the complex character of copper in its natural state and the transformation it undergoes from ore to metal, with all the complications of alloying and recycling, it is doubtful whether many of the hopes of provenancing will ever be realised. The long-term contribution of elemental and stable isotope analysis may be a greater understanding of metal circulation and recycling rather than specific mine sourcing. Identifying metal circulation patterns or even specific mine-artefact connections is only a first step towards explaining their broader significance. Recent research into displacement and deposition highlights the many problems that efforts to join up metalwork dots on the archaeological landscape are likely to meet in attempts to reconstruct synchronous metal supply networks.

Any current failings of scientific approaches in the study of Bronze Age metallurgy have less to do with the sophistication of analytical techniques and more to do with approach and application. Archaeological science in Britain is driven by innovation, with considerably less emphasis in terms of funding given to the application of existing methodologies like metallography. Scientific studies in this field are, for the most part, opportunistic and the absence of an active fieldwork dimension limits the scope of these enquiries in terms of broader archaeological significance.

Several recent studies highlight the potential of integrating conventional and scientific artefact analyses with fieldwork investigation of depositional contexts (eg Needham 1990; 1991; Musson *et al* 1992). The future

must lie in a more active investigation of production sites, settlements, and other depositional environments. Where the latter are absent, the scientific investigation of artefact find-spots through geophysics and excavation may offer future insight into metal production, use, and deposition. While fieldwork in the past was usually site-specific in reaction to fortuitous artefact discoveries, there is considerable potential in a broader landscape-based approach to the study of Bronze Age metal. In addition, mine studies can play a key role by allowing us to focus on the utilisation of specific mineral deposits and extrapolate chronologically and metallurgically to wider Bronze Age manufacturing traditions – ore to metal and not the reverse!

By introducing a fieldwork dynamic to the study of Bronze Age metal, it will prove increasingly possible to contextualise our scientific results. It should also be possible to broaden the scope of archaeological science beyond the purely metallurgical approach to realise the potential of remote sensing and environmental studies. Of central importance is the need for archaeologists to become more directly involved in the search for this archaeological record and to initiate programmes of collaborative research with scientists in specialist fields. Funding mechanisms are crucial here, and it may be that existing structures in Britain do not exploit the key role that the prehistorian can play at the project design stage, or the contribution that the field archaeologist can make in generating new data sources. Greater involvement of these groups will help to place scientific results within a broader context and establish greater relevance to current issues and problems in prehistory. Fieldwork collaborations will also qualitatively improve the database with which laboratory scientists have to work.

As well as project-based approaches, it may desirable to structure science-assisted research through specialist study groups or initiatives comparable to the Implement Petrology Committee of the Council for British Archaeology. These approaches might serve to promote collaborative research programmes and expand publication opportunities. It is also important to raise the profile of this subject in university teaching and research, where a significant decline has been observed in recent years (Burgess and Coombs 1979, i). The development of imaginative teaching courses that highlight the many exciting strands of enquiry in this field is of considerable importance. Lastly, archaeological science can do much in the modern era to enhance museum presentation of Bronze Age metal and metalworking and thus contribute to public education and perception.

In conclusion, this paper has emphasised the many important contributions that science-assisted research can make to the study of metal in the insular Bronze Age. Archaeologists must now realise the potential of these approaches, while not allowing the concerns of laboratory science to dictate the agenda. Nor should we confuse the apparent objectivity of scientific procedures with the interpretation of resulting data. This paper reiterates the important role we know science can play in the study of ancient metallurgy, but suggests that this energy needs a broader environment within which to flourish. The successful integration of conventional archaeology and scientific approaches will ultimately provide a more meaningful understanding of metal and its place in Bronze Age life.

Acknowledgements

I am grateful to Stuart Needham and Richard Bradley for comments on this text and to Justine Bayley for editorial guidance. The views expressed remain of course those of the author alone.

References

Allen, I M, Britton, D, and Coghlan, H H, 1970 *Metallurgical reports on British and Irish Bronze Age implements and weapons in the Pitt-Rivers Museum, Oxford*, Oxford

Ambers, J, 1990 Radiocarbon, calibration, and early mining: some British Museum radiocarbon dates for Welsh copper mines, in Crew and Crew 1990, 59–63

Bridgford, S, 1997 The first weapons devised only for war, *Brit Archaeol News*, **22**, 7

Brooks, R R, and Johannes, D, 1990 *Phytoarchaeology*, Leicester

Brindley, A, and Lanting, J, 1990 Radiocarbon dates for the Mount Gabriel copper mines, in Crew and Crew 1990, 64

Budd, P, and Taylor, T, 1995 The faerie smith versus the bronze industry: magic versus science in the interpretation of prehistoric metal-making, *World Archaeol*, **27**, 133–43

Budd, P, Gale, D, Pollard, A M, Thomas, R G, and Williams, P A, 1992 The early development of metallurgy in the British Isles, *Antiquity*, **66**, 677–86

Budd, P, Haggerty, R, Pollard, A M, Scaife, B, and Thomas, R G, 1996 Rethinking the quest for provenance, *Antiquity*, **70**, 168–74

Burgess, C B, and Coombs, D G (eds), 1979 *Bronze Age hoards: some finds old and new*, BAR, **67**, Oxford

Case, H J, 1966 Were Beaker-people the first metallurgists in Ireland, *Palaeohistoria*, **12**, 141–77

Charles, J A, 1985 Determinative mineralogy and the origins of metallurgy, in *Furnaces and smelting technology in antiquity* (eds P T Craddock and M J Hughes), Brit Mus Occas Pap, **48**, 21–8, London

Clough, T, and Cummins, W (eds), 1979 *Stone axe studies*, CBA Res Rep, **23**, London

Coffey, G, 1901 Irish copper celts, *J Roy Anthropol Inst Great Britain and Ireland*, **31**, 265–79

Coghlan, H H, Butler, J R, and Parker G, 1963 *Ores and metals*, A report of the Ancient Mining and Metallurgy Committee, Royal Anthropological Institute, London

Coghlan, H H, and Case, H J, 1957 Early metallurgy of copper in Britain and Ireland, *Proc Prehist Soc*, **23**, 91–123

Coles, J, and Coles, B, 1986 *Sweet Track to Glastonbury: the Somerset Levels in prehistory*, London

Cotter, C, 1993 Western stone fort project: interim report, in *Discovery Programme Reports* (ed J Waddell), **1**, 1–19, Dublin

Craddock, P T, 1979 Deliberate alloying in the Atlantic Bronze Age, in *The origins of metallurgy in Atlantic Europe, Proceedings of the fifth Atlantic Colloquium* (ed M Ryan),369–85, Dublin

—, 1990 Copper smelting in Bronze Age Britain: problems and possibilities, in Crew and Crew 1990, 69–71

Crew, P, and Crew, S (eds), 1990 *Early mining in the British Isles*, Maentwrog

Desvignes, G and Tabbagh, A, 1995 Simultaneous interpretation of magnetic and electromagnetic prospecting for characterization of magnetic textures, *Archaeol Prospection*, **2**, 129–40

Doonan, R, 1994, Sweat, fire, and brimstone: pretreatment of copper ore and the effects on smelting techniques, *Hist Metall*, **28**, 84–98

Dutton, A, and Fasham, P, 1994 Prehistoric copper mining on the Great Orme, Llandudno Gwynedd, *Proc Prehist Soc*, **60**, 245–86

Evans, J, 1881 *The ancient bronze implements, weapons, and ornaments of Great Britain and Ireland*, London

Gale, N H, and Stos-Gale, Z A, 1982 Bronze Age copper sources in the Mediterranean: a new approach, *Science*, **216**, 11–19

Gowland, W, 1899 The early metallurgy of copper, tin, and iron in Europe, as illustrated by ancient remains and the primitive processes surviving in Japan, *Archaeologia*, **56** 267–322

—, 1906 Copper and its alloys in prehistoric times, *J Roy Anthropol Inst Great Britain and Ireland*, **36**, 11–38

Hamilton, J, 1956 *Excavations at Jarlshof, Shetland*, Ministry of Works Archaeological Reports, **1**, Edinburgh

Hartmann, A, 1970 *Prahistorische Goldfunde aus Europa: Spektraanalytische Untersuchungen und dere Auswertung*, Berlin

—, 1982 *Prahistorische Goldfunde aus Europa II: Spektraanalytische Untersuchungen und dere Auswertung*, Berlin

Herbert, E, 1984 *Red gold of Africa: copper in precolonial history and culture*, Wisconsin

Hurl, D, 1995 Killymoon: new light on the Bronze Age, *Archaeol Ireland*, **34**, 24–7

Junghans, S, Sangmeister, E, and Schröder, M, 1960 *Metallanalysen kupferzeitlicher und frübronzezeitlicher Bodenfunde aus Europa*, Berlin

—, 1968 *Kupfer und Bronze in der frühen Metallzeit Europas*, Berlin

—, 1974 *Kupfer und Bronze in der frühen Metallzeit Europas*, Berlin

Liversage, D, 1968 Excavations at Dalkey Island, Co Dublin, 1956–9, *Proc Roy Ir Acad*, **C, 66**, 53–233

Lynn, C, 1977 Trials excavations at the King's Stables, Tray townland, Co Armagh, *Ulster J Archaeol*, **40**, 42–57

Mallet, W, 1853 Report on the chemical examination of antiquities from the museum of the Royal Irish Academy, *Trans Roy Ir Acad*, **22**, 313–42

Maryon, H, 1938 The technical methods of the Irish smiths in the Bronze and Early Iron Ages, *Proc Roy Ir Acad*, **44C**, 181–228

McKeown, S, 1994 The analysis of wood remains from mine 3, Mount Gabriel, in O'Brien 1994, 265–80

Merkel, J, 1990 Experimental reconstruction of Bronze Age copper smelting based on archaeological evidence from Timna, in *The ancient metallurgy of copper* (ed B Rothenberg), 78–122, London

Mighall, T, and Chambers, F, 1993 The environmental impact of prehistoric mining at Copa Hill, Cwmystwyth, Wales, *The Holocene*, **3** 260–64

—, 1994 Vegetation history and Bronze Age mining on Mount Gabriel, in O'Brien 1994, 289–98

Muckleroy, K, 1981 Middle Bronze Age trade between Britain and Europe: a maritime perspective, *Proc Prehist Soc*, **47**, 275–97

Musson, C R, Britnell, W J, Northover, J P, and Salter, C J, 1992 Excavations and metalworking at Llyn Bryn-dinas hillfort, Llangedwyn, Clwyd, *Proc Prehist Soc*, **58**, 265–83

Needham, S P, 1980 An assemblage of Late Bronze Age metalworking debris from Dainton, Devon, *Proc Prehist Soc*, **46**, 177–216

—, 1990, *The Petters Late Bronze Age metalwork: an analytical study of Thames Valley metalworking in its settlement context*, Brit Mus Occas Pap, **70**, London

—, 1991, *Excavations and salvage at Runnymede Bridge, 1978: the Late Bronze Age waterfront site*, London

—, 1993 Displacement and exchange in archaeological methodology, in *Trade and exchange in prehistoric Europe* (eds C Scarre and F Healy), 161–70, Oxford

—, forthcoming Modelling the flow of metal in the Bronze Age, *Proceedings of the 1996 Dijon conference*

Needham, S P, Leese, M N, Hook, D R, and Hughes, M J, 1989 Developments in the Early Bronze Age metallurgy of southern Britain, *World Archaeol*, **2**, 383–402

Needham, S P, Longworth, I, Herne, A, and Varndell, G, 1991 *Excavations at Grimes Graves, Norfolk, 1972–6, Fasicule 3, Shaft X: Bronze Age flint, chalk, and metalworking*, London

Northover, J P, 1980 Bronze in the British Bronze Age, in *Aspects of early metallurgy* (ed W A Oddy), Brit Mus Occas Pap, **17**, 63–70, London

Northover, J P, 1982 The exploration of the long-distance movement of bronze in Bronze and Early Iron Age Europe, *Univ London Inst Archaeol Bull*, **19**, 45–72

Northover, J P, 1985 The complete examination of archaeological metalwork, in Phillips 1985, 56–9

O'Brien, W, 1994 *Mount Gabriel: Bronze Age mining in Ireland*, Galway

—, 1995 Ross Island and the origins of Irish-British metallurgy, in Waddell and Shee Twohig 1995, 38–48

—, 1996 *Bronze Age copper mining in Britain and Ireland*, Aylesbury

O'Brien, W, Ixer, R, and O'Sullivan, M, 1990 Copper resources in prehistory: an Irish perspective, in Crew and Crew 1990, 30–35

O'Brien, W, Northover, P, and Cameron, E, 1989/90 An Early Bronze Age metal hoard from a wedge tomb at Toormore, Co Cork, *J Ir Archaeol*, **5**, 9–17

O Riordain, S P, 1954 Lough Gur excavations: Neolithic and Bronze Age houses on Knockadoon, *Proc Roy Ir Acad*, **56**, 297–459

Pearson, G, 1796 Observations on some ancient metallic arms and utensils; with experiments to determine their composition, *Phil Trans Roy Soc London*, **18**, 38–61

Phillips, P (ed), 1985 *The archaeologist and the laboratory*, CBA Res Rep, **58**, London

Pittioni, R 1957 Urzeitlicher Bergbau auf Kupfererz und Spureanalyse, *Archaeol Austriaca*, **1**, Vienna

Pollard, A M, Thomas, R G, and Williams, P A, 1990 Experimental smelting of arsenical copper ores: implications for Early Bronze Age copper production, in Crew and Crew 1990, 72–4

Pownall, Govenor, 1786 An account of some Irish antiquities, *Archaeologia*, **III**, 355–6

Raftery, B, 1971 The Rathgall hillfort, Co Wicklow, *Antiquity*, **44**, 51–4

Ramsey, G, 1995, Middle Bronze Age metalwork: are artefact studies dead and buried?, in Waddell and Shee Twohig 1995, 49–62

Rohl, B, 1996 Lead isotope data from the Isotrace Laboratory, Oxford: Archaeometry data base 2, galena from Britain and Ireland, *Archaeometry*, **38**, 165–80

Rowlands, M, 1971 The archaeological interpretation of prehistoric metalworking, *World Archaeol*, **3**, 210–24

Slater, E, 1985 Sources and resources for non-ferrous metallurgy, in Phillips 1985, 45–9

Timberlake, S, 1994 Evidence for early mining in Wales, in *Mining before powder* (eds T D Ford and L Willies), 133–43, Matlock Bath

Tite, M, 1997 In defence of lead isotope analysis, *Antiquity*, **70**, 959–62

Waddell, J, and Shee Twohig, E (eds), 1995 *Ireland in the Bronze Age*, Dublin

Warner, R, 1995 Golden Bronze Age fingerprints, *Archaeol Ireland*, **9**, 22–3

13 Archaeological science and proto-historic societies

by Martin Millett

Abstract

There is sometimes still a tendency to assume that there is little new to learn about the period from the end of the Iron Age to the early Middle Ages because there are textual sources available. In truth, the sources have comparatively little to tell us about the changes in society that took place during this period when Britain became an integral part of a complex network of European societies. Archaeological science has already contributed greatly to current understandings of this period, but there is still much that it can offer. This paper outlines some of the principal achievements and suggests important avenues for further research. The emphasis is on how science can address central issues of broad historical relevance.

Introduction

It is frequently presumed, first, that we already know most that is of significance to be known about the period from the later Iron Age to the early Saxon period, and second, that any framework for study should be primarily founded upon information drawn from the written sources. I would reject both these notions and further suggest that a number of categories (eg oppida and towns) which have regularly been used in the past need critical re-evaluation before we can make much progress in research. Science-based archaeology has a much larger role to play in this re-evaluation, and thus in developing our understanding of this period, than has hitherto been perceived. Existing presumptions are too often based on ideas and syntheses that have not taken sufficient notice of progress already achieved through the application of methods drawn from the sciences. Notable work has been undertaken, especially in the fields discussed by the contributors to this section (eg by the English Heritage funded laboratories on bones and seeds from Romano-British towns). I leave it to them to report on this progress, but would emphasise how important it is that recent science-based work is more regularly assimilated into synthetic studies if we are to build on it for the future.

Equally, it is important that those working on science-based studies maintain an up-to-date understanding of current perspectives in the broader archaeological interpretation of particular periods. It is too easy for mutual ignorance to create divisions in understanding and for them to propagate an absence of communication. There is a very real danger too that the fragmentation of fieldwork as a result of 'contract' archaeology will increasingly mean that material is collected and analysed, and sometimes even published, in ignorance of previous work in a region and in an unthinking way and without any academic relevance.

Experience suggests that the most substantive research with enduring impact is either long-term and persistent (eg Marijke van der Veen's work on botanical remains from the north-east of England) and/or large-scale and carefully focused (eg the Danebury project). We in the UK have lessons to learn here from overseas experience. For example, the Pioneer Project in the Netherlands combines rescue and research within a common, long-term research-based framework (see, for example, Roymans and Theuws 1991; Roymans 1996).

As the aim of the conference was to evaluate the most significant contributions of 'science' to the discipline and to look forward, I would like to make some suggestions for the future. Here I think archaeologists should define questions which we think need addressing whether or not on current research agendas.

For the late Iron Age and Roman periods, I think the key focus should be on how to use the archaeological evidence more fully to enhance our understanding of the nature of society and the character of social change. This implies the investigation of three interrelated areas: the agricultural landscape, changes in exchange systems, and settlement characterisation.

The agricultural landscape

Given the clear evidence that life in these periods remained fundamentally based upon agriculture, biological evidence should play a leading role in any discussion about society. The key points to appreciate are that the manner in which economies such as Rome's functioned remains a matter for debate, and that biological evidence should play a greater role in the discussion. Perhaps more important, we need additional knowledge about economies of the later Iron Age–Roman and later Roman–early medieval transition periods. Currently there is simply too little information available from these periods (as illustrated by the recent regional review of the North: Huntley and Stallibrass 1995); without more data, specific questions are irrelevant. Thus an emphasis on sampling any excavated deposits of these periods, in order to establish whether biological material is present and has previously been ignored or whether it is genuinely absent, would help fill this gap. Lack of evidence may, after all, be one defining characteristic of these transitions.

We also need more attention focused upon the extent that biological data can be further deployed to investigate regional and chronological patterns of agricultural change. Within this period of social complexity and settlement differentiation I would like to see more emphasis placed on the extent to which movements of agricultural products can be characterised and understood. Such research should help focus on key issues, such as the victualling of towns and the movements of goods to support the Roman state. We should, however, question more carefully whether changes can be related to historical events such as the inclusion of Britain within the Roman world, changes within the Roman imperial system, or the Anglo-Saxon migrations. Too often these short-term events have been used unquestioningly to explain change when longer-term processes may be more appropriately invoked.

Exchange systems

In addition to the movement of agricultural goods, there were large volumes of pottery and other manufactured artefacts in circulation from the first millennium BC onwards. Various techniques of analysis have already enabled us not only to isolate the origins of particular artefact types but also to come towards a broader understanding of the changing patterns of exchange. However, we do need to question economic (or other) mechanisms, which are often invoked to explain changes, and to use the evidence more systematically and thoughtfully. Personally, I have grave doubts about the extent to which a market economy existed in these periods.

There are exciting prospects for new technical applications, but there is also a strong case to be made for the simple integration of the results from existing studies. Allen and Fulford (1996) have recently demonstrated how the results from a variety of published quantified pottery reports can be deployed to shed light on the economy through the distribution of a single pot fabric. Similar low-cost research, capitalising on existing data, should be a priority. Equally, the staggering intensification in the use of metals which characterises the period from the late Iron Age onwards should be the subject of synthetic research. It would be interesting to know how far existing studies of individual objects (and manufacturing sites) might enable us to develop a broader understanding of use-intensification and any concomitant changes in the technology and organisation of production. Such studies should also help in identifying gaps in our knowledge that could be examined by new research projects.

In a broader perspective we should enquire how far these data (together with the biological material) can be used to understand evolving human communities under the impact first of demand-intensification represented by Rome and then its decline as seen during the early medieval period. Surely the artefactual evidence could be used more effectively to identify socially meaningful patterns of consumption and exchange?

Finally, what can technology tell us about the organisation of the society which produced such a fantastic quality of metalwork in the early Anglo-Saxon period? Artefact studies do have the potential to address the big questions in the Iron Age–early medieval period if only they are asked.

Characterising settlement

Current ideas are very often based on the notion that settlement types are known and unproblematic. Thus such categories as town, villa, oppidum, hillfort (and later emporium) are commonly used in the literature without any apparent need being felt to define or question them. They have therefore too often developed a usage based on assumption rather than evidence. I see the combination of 'scientific' evidence and the results of fieldwork as crucial in questioning these definitions and in characterising the roles of both individual sites and broader classes within their landscapes.

Geophysical and geochemical surveys together with aerial photographic analysis of individual sites, ought to enable us better to understand both settlement sites and agricultural landscapes. Biological and artefact evidence used in combination with these should facilitate the characterisation of settlement roles and use. It is no longer good enough simply to assume that we know how particular types of site worked. This is not only important at the grand scale (eg what was a Roman town?) but equally at the domestic level (eg can we identify use patterns within a building; can we even tell whether it was a habitation?). Moving beyond basic taphonomic problems, questions which might be addressed include characterising the changing ways in which objects such as bones were used and disposed of within settlements –ultimately this might lead to new perspectives in the investigation of what is now called 'structured deposition'.

Conclusions

In this brief introduction I have not attempted to present anything like a comprehensive 'shopping list'. I do not believe that this would be appropriate as the richness of British archaeology depends on a diversity of approaches and good new ideas most often come from those with fresh approaches and new perspectives. Such innovative research should be supported even though not all of it can be expected to produce results. Science-based archaeology has already made a considerable contribution to our understanding of the human past in Britain but its practitioners perhaps need more confidence to be bold in proclaiming their achievements. I believe that its continuing vibrancy depends on communication between the full range of people with different approaches.

Against this background I would make three final points. First, we do need to recognise that more does not always mean better; in some areas we may already be seeing some diminishing returns. Second, we need bolder initiatives to work together on focused questions. Too often archaeology employs groups of individuals with particular skills who work alone rather than as research teams sparking ideas off each other. Finally, we need to recognise that there are differing scales of question on which excellent research can be undertaken. Much of the contemporary 'post-processualist' archaeological debate concerns the small scale (eg the house). Science-based archaeology has much potential to contribute to issues (such as the identification and investigation of cooking) but its practitioners do need to be more proactive in the theoretical debates.

Acknowledgements

I should like to thank Justine Bayley for inviting me to the conference and Andrew Millard and an English Heritage referee for their comments on a draft of this paper.

References

Allen, J R L, and Fulford, M G, 1996 The distribution of south-east Dorset Black Burnished Category 1 pottery in south-west Britain, *Britannia*, **27**, 223–82

Huntley, J P, and Stallibrass, S, 1995 *Plant and vertebrate remains from archaeological sites in northern England: data reviews and future directions*, Architectural and Archaeological Society for Durham and Northumberland Research Report, **4**, Durham

Roymans, N, (ed) 1996 *From the sword to the plough*, Amsterdam

Roymans, N, and Theuws, F, (eds), 1991 *Images of the past*, Amsterdam

14 The expansion of agricultural production in late Iron Age and Roman Britain

*by Marijke van der Veen
and Terry O'Connor*

Abstract

The late Iron Age and Roman period saw the creation of settlements not primarily involved in agricultural production, and this development is linked to an expansion of agriculture. We identify several different types of expansion, each leaving a distinct archaeological imprint. Both the process of adoption or rejection of new strategies and the choice of strategy are directly influenced by factors such as availability of land and labour and the social position of the farmer. The growing regionalisation of the country during the period concerned reflects variations in these factors across the country. We suggest that the identification and analysis of this regional diversity should be a key area for research during the next ten years, and that environmental archaeology needs to apply an analytical and explanatory approach to this problem while, at the same time, becoming more embedded within explanatory frameworks for social change.

Late Iron Age and Roman Britain

The time span considered here is the Iron Age and Roman period, approximately 500 BC to AD 400. During this time a number of cultural, sociopolitical, economic, and, perhaps, demographic changes occurred, any one of which may have had an impact on the agricultural systems in operation at that time. During the Iron Age we see a growing regionalisation of the country: regional patterns of settlement, social structure, subsistence strategy, and belief system emerge (Cunliffe 1991). Some regions are characterised by population nucleation and by a marked stratification of society, while others show considerably less change from the preceding period. Variations in population growth and pressure, access to resources, and physical distance from the continent have all been put forward as possible explanations for this development (Cunliffe 1991; Darvill 1987). From the late Iron Age, the growth of long-distance trade and the consequent increase in contact with the Mediterranean world resulted in considerable social and economic changes in the south-eastern part of the country and the growth of major ports and market centres (*oppida*). The Roman period is, of course, primarily characterised by the arrival of an occupying army and by the introduction of a different cultural and socioeconomic system. The latter was a gradual process, in part building on the earlier, indigenous Iron Age changes in social stratification and settlement pattern, while the burden of the occupying army fell largely on societies in the northern part of the country, probably emphasising already existing regional differences (Millett 1990). During this period we see the first appearance of towns and, perhaps, the development of a money-based market economy (Greene 1986).

Thus, during the period under study we see the creation of settlements not primarily involved in agricultural production (hillforts, *oppida*, Roman forts, towns) and the consequent need for surplus production in the rural areas in order to feed the people in the new settlements. There is considerable evidence that the density of settlement and intensity of land use increased around this time (Cunliffe 1991; Haselgrove 1989), and the evidence for agricultural expansion has been discussed in a series of syntheses (Grant 1989; Jones 1981; 1984; 1989; 1996; King 1978; 1984; Maltby 1996). Major regional differences in the degree and rate at which these changes occurred have been identified (Jones 1984; 1989), and it is recognised that both indigenous and external factors played a role in the expansion of agriculture and the adoption of innovations in this period (Jones 1989; Millett 1990). This is not the place to describe these developments in detail or to review the existing evidence; for this the reader is referred to the synthetic articles mentioned above. Here we aim to discuss some of the strategies available to farmers intent on expanding their production, the extent to which we are, at present, able to recognise these in the archaeological record, and the areas in which future research may usefully be focused.

Agricultural expansion, intensification, and extensification

Before discussing the options available to farmers responding to the need for surplus production, it is necessary to define some terms. In the literature we often see the use of the term 'intensification' of agriculture, generally meaning the expansion of agriculture. This term is in some ways unfortunate as, in an agricultural context, the term 'intensification' has a very specific and far more restricted meaning, denoting the opposite of extensification. Intensification, in the strict sense, signifies the increase of output per unit area by increasing the input, whether of labour or of other resources, while extensification signifies the increase of output per capita by increasing the area under cultivation without an associated increase in labour or other input. Both strategies result in a productive increase, but the implications in terms of land use and resource scheduling are quite different, and so, therefore, is their possible archaeological imprint.

Subtle differences in the way these terms are used do, however, exist. Boserup (1965) defined intensification as the change in the 'ratio of the area under crop to the total area under crop *plus* fallow' and saw intensification as the process of reducing the amount of land left fallow. She suggested that an increase in population forces a shift from extensive to intensive forms of agriculture, and that spatial variations in farming practices can, therefore, be explained by differences in population pressure. While this model has been very influential in archaeological discussions of past agriculture, its underlying assumptions make it inappropriate for Iron Age and Roman Britain, if only because societies in Iron Age and Roman Britain were not pure subsistence societies without outside contacts. Boserup saw intensification as a natural progression away from extensive forms of agriculture in response to population pressure, which may be the reason why the term intensification is often seen as synonymous with expansion; but this is not the way we use the term here (see below).

Boserup was, however, correct in identifying a relationship between population density and farming strategies; this relationship is apparent even in the modern, developed world (Grigg 1995, 158). The industrialised countries have seen a decline in the agricultural labour force since the nineteenth century, as a result of higher wages in industry and the mechanisation of farming, while the area under cultivation has remained constant, which has resulted in an increase in the amount of land per worker. But even here we see a link between population density and agricultural strategy (Grigg 1995, 151–8). In densely populated areas land is expensive but labour is abundant and relatively cheap, so the best choice is to maximise the output per unit area, by investing in input that increases yields (fertilizers, pesticides, herbicides) and concentrating on intensive forms of agriculture. In areas of lower population density land is relatively cheap, but labour expensive and here the best choice is to concentrate on maximising output per capita, by spending more on labour-saving machinery and less on inputs that increase yields. An example of the former is the Netherlands with its intensive pig rearing and its horticulture (flowers, bulbs, vegetables), and an example of the latter is Britain with its extensive sheep rearing in the uplands, or America with its extensive cereal growing.

To summarise, we use the following definition of the terms: intensive agricultural systems are those where the input per area and the return per area are high, but the return per capita is low (eg horticulture); extensive agricultural systems have low input per area and low return per area, but the return per capita is high (eg sheep rearing, large-scale cereal growing). Thus, following Grigg (1995), we see intensive and extensive forms of agriculture as different strategies, different responses to local conditions. Intensive and extensive farming systems are options or strategies available to farmers at any one time and place, and local conditions, be they social circumstances, availability of land, labour, or markets, determine which response is the more appropriate at any one time, recognising that farmers may switch from one to the other and back again, or adopt a combination of both for different parts of their production.

A thorough discussion of why changes in agricultural production take place is outside our remit, but we note that studies of modern farming communities show that innovations are not automatically accepted, even when the benefits are easily identifiable (Bayliss-Smith 1982; Grigg 1970; 1995; Spedding 1988), and a recognition of this phenomenon is essential to our understanding of the regional variation we see in Iron Age and Roman Britain. First of all, the specific characteristics of the innovation play a role: simple or gradual innovations are more easily adopted than complex or expensive ones, but there are both economic and social factors to consider too. Economists tend to believe that the adoption of innovations is largely determined by the farmer's economic assessment of the innovation, while sociologists argue, correctly, that the social circumstances and the psychological make-up of the farmer are the main determining factors as they have a major influence on the farmer's perception of the potential benefits of the innovation. Land ownership, personal wealth, size of the farm, and control over the decision-making process all influence farmers' ability to implement changes, while their readiness to adopt change is linked to personal characteristics such as age, education, social standing and integration, and business attitude (Bayliss-Smith 1982; Grigg 1970; 1995, 174; Husain 1979; Spedding 1988).

While many of these factors are linked to individual circumstances, some, admittedly broad, generalisations can be made. Boserup (1965) already identified that farmers in subsistence societies have different priorities from those in market economies. Subsistence societies typically show limited goals, an absence of specialisation, a slow rate of change, little response to price mechanisms, and a preference for leisure. The overall aim is to feed the family, and to minimise risk; many achieve this by growing 'a little bit of everything'. In a market economy, on the contrary, we see strong specialisation, an emphasis on cash crops and other commodities, surplus production, a rapid response to price fluctuations, and frequent innovations. Output and profit are maximised, principally through specialisation and innovation.

It is important to remember that these two examples are extremes at opposite ends of a continuum, and that within each society there are individuals who are able to respond to the need to change more rapidly and more readily than others. As well as that, even in market economies, feeding the family remains important. Thus the social and psychological make-up of the farmer and the structure of society in which farming communities find themselves, as well as availability of land and labour, directly influence the ability of farmers to react to new developments and the type of expansion they choose.

If we are to identify in Iron Age and Roman Britain when, where, and, ultimately, why farmers altered their agricultural strategies, we need, among other things, to be able to identify in the archaeological record the various forms that agricultural expansion can take. Here several types of expansion are considered:

- a general expansion of the area under cultivation and/or pasture, largely in response to population growth; this should not be confused with extensification, as it concerns the bringing into cultivation/pasture of new areas by new people and does not, necessarily, involve changes in crop/animal management

- an increase in yield within the existing area through a shift to new crops or animals, which may be higher yielding or offer other advantages; this should not be confused with intensification, as it does not necessarily involve changes in crop/animal management, though we recognise that changes in crops and animals can be the result of a change of management regime (see below)

- an increase in yield through a change in cultivation or management regime – intensive or extensive depending on local availability of land, labour, manure, and traction power; this may include changes in the ratio of animal to crop husbandry

- a change towards more specialised production, ie of cash commodities to sell through a market in order to engage with new exchange mechanisms where these existed

- a shift towards a non-domestic mode of production, ie production of staples primarily to fulfil demand elsewhere, over and above that of the family/village; intentional surplus production, not to be confused with surplus production that is used as risk buffering against bad years (see Bakels 1996)

To conclude, the expansion of agricultural production can take many forms, of which intensification and extensification are but two expedient responses. We would like to stress that the options identified above are neither exhaustive, nor mutually exclusive. Intensive and extensive strategies can take place on the same farm, are often associated with changes in crop or animal species, and can be combined with the introduction of a few cash commodities or a switch to a non-domestic mode of production, as we will see below. As mentioned above, regional and local differences in the availability of land, labour, and social structure will have influenced the degree to which these options were adopted and, therefore, the extent to which farmers and societies actively participated in the new developments and opportunities brought about by the invasion of the Roman army.

If we are to recognise and understand these regional differences, we need first to identify the archaeological imprint of these options and second to ensure that our database consists of a regional coverage of the resolution and quality required to pick up these differences.

Crop and livestock husbandry

This section considers the extent to which the options listed above can be identified in the archaeological record. While the aim is to refer to both plant and animal resources in each sub-section, it will be clear that both the nature of the source materials and the evidence available to date make this difficult and the balance between the botanical and faunal evidence is, consequently, unsatisfactory. Writing this article has highlighted not only the need for more integration of the different lines of evidence, over and above bones and seeds, but also the enormity of this task, especially as the chronological and spatial resolution of our database is still very poor.

The expansion of production

By the Iron Age and Roman period, much of the British countryside can be characterised as open land, and the existing evidence suggests that the amount of land given over to cultivation and grazing had gradually increased (though not at a constant rate) from the Neolithic period onwards, a process almost certainly due primarily to a growth in population. While pollen analysis demonstrates that this opening-up of the landscape was asynchronous across the country, it is possible to say, as a broad generalisation, that large-scale clearances were taking place across the entire country during the Iron Age and Roman period, but occurred earliest in the south and east and progressively later in the north and west (Bell 1996; Turner 1981). Recent palynological evidence from palaeochannels in lowland river valleys suggests that large-scale clearances in the lowlands may have occurred as early as the Late or even Middle

Bronze Age (Brown 1997, 215–18), corroborating existing evidence for marked regional variation and highlighting the value of applying pollen analysis to as wide a range of sediments as possible.

Linking changes in pollen diagrams to specific historical events remains problematic. Dumayne and Barber (1994; 1997), McCarthy (1995), and Tipping (1997), for example, have taken quite different views on the significance of 'clearance events' in pollen diagrams from sites close to Hadrian's Wall. This debate centres on whether ^{14}C dates are sufficiently precise to show whether a given clearance event was synchronous with, or consequent upon, the Roman arrival in the region, or happened a matter of decades earlier. With the availability of AMS dates, there is the need to re-analyse some pollen sequences with more ^{14}C dates of the relevant horizons, and to combine these with refined wiggle-matching and Bayesian calibration methods. It also remains difficult to identify whether the expansion of cleared land was primarily for arable or pastoral purposes. The use of so-called arable and pastoral indicators has become rather discredited (Behre 1986; Groenman-van Waateringe 1988; Maguire 1983), and this is clearly an area that merits further research.

The highly targeted use of pollen and land snail data from small catchments to locate areas being taken into grazing and cultivation and the increased emphasis on recognising the spatial scale of vegetational events through the pollen record (Bradshaw 1991) is to be welcomed, and this now needs to be combined with a clearer definition of the palynological attributes that characterise degrees of grazing pressure. In parallel, further detailed work on 'open country' land snail communities is urgently needed to allow more confident recognition of 'grazed grassland' communities. Recent work in this field has taken research away from naive use of sweeping analogue communities (eg Evans 1991) and focused development of the use that Rouse, Evans, and others (Evans *et al* 1992, Whittle *et al* 1993) have made of correspondence analysis and the more subtle recognition of mollusc taxocoenes offers the possibility of interpreting these 'open country' communities in ways that can contribute directly to the investigation of changing patterns of pastoral land use.

It is also possible that more information resides in 'failed soils', such as colluvial infills in valleys. Research such as that conducted by Allen (1988), Bell (1992), and Tipping and Mercer (1994) has suggested that cultivation of potentially unstable slopes through later prehistory is likely to have been a major trigger for accelerated colluviation, though caution is needed when associating accelerated colluviation with cultivation, and when assuming that permanent pasture is relatively stable. We need research into the small-scale geomorphological

consequences of increased grazing pressure, and a better understanding of whether it is cultivation, or the abandonment of cultivation, that triggers the destabilisation of soils and consequent colluviation. How such information might be manifested in colluvial deposits is not clear, though investigation of the magnetic and iron species (ie the forms of iron oxides, sesquioxides, and hydroxides) characteristics of the sediments may offer a way forward, particularly if combined with examination of sediment micromorphology, such as that undertaken by Macphail (1992) at Ashcombe Bottom, Sussex.

A different choice of crops and animals

In this section the evidence for changes in crops and animals that have been recorded for the period and the implications of these changes in terms of scales of production are discussed. To start with crops, two major changes in the choice of wheat crop have been identified. The switch from emmer wheat to spelt wheat during the Iron Age, and the switch from glume wheats (emmer and spelt) to free-threshing bread wheat during the early post-Roman period, are developments recorded in Britain, as well as other parts of western Europe (Jones 1981; 1984). Bread wheat (*Triticum aestivum*) is the main, if not only, species of wheat grown in Britain and western Europe today. It is likely that farmers who started to grow bread wheat early (ie during the late Iron Age or Roman period) may be correctly recognised as innovators and it is important to identify where in Britain this innovation first took place (Jones 1989).

The advantage of bread wheat over emmer and spelt is thought to be the easy removal of the chaff; this means a reduction in processing time after the harvest and a reduction in volume and weight on long distance transport (Green 1979 as quoted in Jones 1981; emmer and spelt were often transported as spikelets). Bread wheat has been found as early as the Neolithic, but the number of grains is always very low and the occurrences are sporadic; there is no evidence that it represented an important crop at that time. Traces of bread wheat have also been found on several Iron Age sites, but it remains difficult to assess the importance of this crop in this period, as there are problems with the dating evidence of some records and the correctness of the identifications in others. Two late Iron Age sites have been mentioned in the literature as having fairly substantial amounts of bread wheat: Bierton, Buckinghamshire, and Barton Court Farm, Oxfordshire (Jones 1981; 1984; 1986). The dating evidence for Bierton, however, has been questioned: the bread wheat may be of Saxon rather than Roman date (Mark Robinson personal communication), and it is possible that several more Iron Age records of bread wheat represent Saxon material, owing to the difficulty of distinguishing Iron Age and

Saxon pottery in some regions (Mark Robinson personal communication). Grains of bread wheat from two late Iron Age sites in north-east England, when radiocarbon dated, turned out to be medieval and modern in date (van der Veen 1992, 60, 74), although accelerator dates on bread wheat chaff from another Iron Age site in the same region did identify this material as late Iron Age in date (ibid, 61, 74). Furthermore, grains of bread wheat are difficult to distinguish from those of spelt wheat and hard wheat, a problem highlighted in a recent article (Hillman *et al* 1996), and there is some doubt over the correctness of published identifications based on grain rather than chaff (Dominique de Moulins personal communication).

The first time bread wheat is found in large quantities is during the Roman period, but most of these records are from non-agricultural settlements. There are too few archaeobotanical records from Romano-British settlements to be able to assess the case for importation versus local production. Thus, we are at present unable to trace the history of the cultivation of bread wheat in this country with any accuracy. Clearly, a re-evaluation of the existing records of bread wheat from Iron Age and Roman sites, using the latest morphological criteria as well as biomolecular and chemical methods, coupled with an extensive AMS dating programme, is urgently needed.

The existing record for the shift from emmer to spelt wheat is much better, but even here the regional resolution of the database is poor. While there are plenty of Bronze Age records of spelt wheat across the country, it is not until the Iron Age that emmer wheat was replaced by spelt wheat, though this switch was not universal in either space or time (Jones 1981; 1984; van der Veen 1992). The increased preference for spelt has been the subject of much discussion. Jones explained it by the fact that spelt can grow on the heavier clay soils and is hardier than emmer and, therefore, very suited to winter sowing, allowing a general expansion of agriculture through access to previously marginal soils and a new growing season (Jones 1981; 1984; 1996). The evidence from growing experiments at Butser Ancient Farm has always suggested that emmer and spelt had similar yields (Reynolds 1992), so differences in yield never entered these discussions. Recent results from a national wheat growing experiment do, however, provide a slightly different picture. Emmer and spelt were grown on experimental plots across the country for three years (1987–90; van der Veen and Palmer 1997), and the results indicate that spelt is higher yielding than emmer, and that this is statistically significant. This is different from the results at Butser Ancient Farm, where both species were grown in experimental fields for more than 15 years (Reynolds 1992); here there is no statistically significant difference in the yield between the two species.

This difference in results can be explained as follows: in the recent study it was clear that spelt was higher yielding than emmer when the temperatures in January were low, which confirms the hardiness of spelt referred to earlier. In warm winters the difference between the two species was negligible, but in cold winters spelt performed better, and a similar analysis of the Butser yield figures has corroborated this pattern. Thus, spelt outperforms emmer except in warm years and in certain parts of the country (eg at Butser where warm winters occur more frequently, van der Veen and Palmer 1997). The shift towards spelt wheat recorded in the Iron Age can, therefore, be related to one of three closely interrelated factors: its tolerance of heavier soils, its hardiness, and its higher yields, all three, of course, crop characteristics beneficial to farmers intending to expand their production.

The fact that clear regional variations have been identified in the timing of the switch to spelt wheat indicates that the choice of crop was more complex than just choosing a new crop for its yield, soil tolerance, or hardiness, something we already know from studies of modern farming communities (see above). It is important to emphasise here that these regional differences do not conform to the highland/lowland division of the country, as postulated in the past, but that differences in the uptake of spelt wheat have been recorded within these broad zones (eg between the Upper Thames Valley and Wessex; Jones 1984) and also within Cunliffe's regions (eg within the north-eastern zone; van der Veen 1992). This suggests that the need for expansion was not uniform across the country or within the regions as defined by Cunliffe (1991), or that not all farmers chose spelt wheat (ie cereals) as the method through which to expand their production. So far, however, the switch to spelt wheat has been regarded as a straightforward decision to start sowing a different species of crop. There is, however, evidence to suggest that the switch may have come about through a change in cultivation regime (see below).

It is more difficult to predict, and so to test, whether relative changes in the numbers of livestock species reflect particular production strategies. Domestic animals mostly provide more than one resource, and so a diachronic change, say, from cattle to sheep could represent a change in meat production, or could be a consequence of changes in the desirability of producing wool rather than cereals. An increase in the area of land cultivated for cereals would necessitate an increase in the numbers of cattle retained as plough oxen. That said, there are some chronological and regional variations in the relative abundance of different livestock that might be linked to production strategies. King (1978) summarised a large volume of published work up to that date, and set down a number of generalisations which are perhaps due for re-assessment. Roman sites with a military connection typically produce bone assemblages with a very high relative abundance of cattle bones, whereas Iron Age sites and Romano-British sites in less 'Romanised' areas typically show a higher proportion of sheep bones. King also notes that villas and later Roman sites typically produce a higher proportion of pig bones than do earlier Roman and 'native' sites. Although King's survey is 20 years old, subsequent work has tended to confirm these generalised patterns, although the reason for them has not been analysed in any detail.

At Thorpe Thewles, Rackham (1985; 1987) draws attention to a relative increase in sheep bones in the last Iron Age phase, and even suggests that taphonomic attrition may have depressed the amplitude of the increase. A smaller increase in sheep is also noted by Grant *et al* (1991) at Danebury, where the relative increase is largely at the expense of pigs, and comes, again, in the very last Iron Age phase. This is clearly not the beginnings of a move towards what was to become the 'typical' Roman pattern of exploitation, as most Roman assemblages from Britain are predominantly of cattle bones. A shift towards sheep would be consistent with an expansion into areas not suitable for cereal agriculture, or with an increased emphasis on the production of wool.

The predominance of cattle in Roman assemblages, however, might be more consistent with an increase in the production of cereals, with adult cattle becoming available as a source of meat largely as a side-product of cereal agriculture. If the shift to cattle was primarily for meat, then one might expect the cattle to be relatively young at death, which is not the case, and we might also expect pig bones to be relatively abundant. Pigs, after all, are the most efficient of the three common domesticates in terms of rapid meat production. However, pig bones tend to be relatively scarce on later Iron Age and early Roman sites.

At a fairly coarse level of analysis, then, the animal bone evidence is consistent with the evidence from plant macrofossils in indicating an increased emphasis on cereal production in the Roman period. Grant (1989) has argued this case, but suggests that the trend began in the Iron Age. This is difficult to confirm or refute on the available data, although the data from Thorpe Thewles and Danebury certainly suggest otherwise. A few sites have yielded well sealed bone assemblages from the very earliest stages of Roman occupation, but these are often very small. Thus the earliest assemblages from Segontium (Noddle 1993) and Silchester (Maltby 1984) show much the same predominance of cattle as the later phases at both sites. One fears that we have a problem of comparability between, for example, hill-forts, undefended Iron Age sites, Roman military sites,

coloniae, villas, and so on. There may be some evidence that the apparent increase in cereal production is matched by an increase in the keeping of cattle, but we need well stratified data from individual sites that extend from the Iron Age into the Roman period in order to get around this problem of comparability.

Intensive and extensive production regimes

By the middle of the first millennium BC the expansion of agriculture no longer consisted primarily of the growing population taking new areas into cultivation, ie the type of expansion identified above. Apart from the fact that, by this time, the expansion of production was affected by the lack of suitable new land, which resulted in the need to take into cultivation land that was previously regarded as marginal or unsuitable (Jones 1981), the expansion was now also no longer primarily a result of population growth, but included a response to social stratification and the development of non-agricultural sections of the population, and thus the need for surplus production, over and above that produced to buffer bad years. This required a new type of expansion, one that increased the amount of food available, and this could be done either within the existing area by increasing productivity (intensification), or by extending the area under cultivation without expanding the existing labour force or other input (extensification). This section tries to identify what archaeological traces these different strategies leave behind.

One way we can identify management regimes of crops is through analysing the arable weed assemblages associated with them (Behre and Jacomet 1991; Hillman 1991; G Jones 1992; M Jones 1988; Küster 1991). An example of a case study in which different management regimes were identified is that of six late Iron Age sites in north-east England (van der Veen 1992; 1995). The statistical analysis of the charred seed assemblages identified two groups of sites, which differed from one another in both the types of cereals cultivated and the weed flora associated with these crops. Group A sites are characterised by the presence of emmer wheat, some spelt wheat, barley, and arable weed species indicative of intensive soil working (digging or ploughing), weeding and manuring, and, consequently, fertile soil conditions, ie an intensive cultivation regime. Group B sites are characterised by spelt wheat, barley, and arable weed species indicative of limited soil working and manuring and, consequently, less fertile soil conditions, ie a more extensive cultivation regime (van der Veen 1992). Moreover, the differences between the two groups of sites were not limited to crops and weed species. The sites were located in different parts of the region, they were characterised by different types of settlement (defended/non-defended), social structure of society (different degrees of centralisation), and tribal affinity (Votadini/Brigantes; ibid). Thus, not only does this case study demonstrate that different cultivation strategies can be identified in the archaeobotanical record, but it also demonstrates that these differences can be related to archaeologically identifiable differences between the two societies. The latter aspect has been explored in more detail by Ferrell (1995; 1997), who identified differences in the spatial organisation of these societies (isolated versus integrated), which could be linked to the observed differences in modes of production.

It is interesting to note here that at both groups of sites barley was treated differently from wheat. In both cases it was associated with the poorest soil indicators, suggesting that the barley crop was grown under more extensive conditions than the wheat crop, highlighting differences in the relative status of these crops, and the fact that both cultivation regimes can be in operation on the same farm.

Another issue raised by the results of the case study is that of the choice of crop. We have so far assumed that farmers wanting to expand moved to growing spelt wheat, rather than emmer, but the evidence also allows a different hypothesis. At the Group A sites both wheat species, emmer and spelt, were associated with one another, suggesting that they were either grown as a mixture (maslin) or as separate crops receiving the same treatment. The evidence suggests that under an intensive cultivation regime (Group A) emmer is the dominant crop, while under a more extensive form of cultivation (Group B) spelt wheat is dominant. This could mean that emmer flourishes under an intensive system and that spelt competes better under a less intensive system, probably because of its tolerance for more marginal soils and its hardiness. If a farmer decided to expand by increasing the area under cultivation without an associated increase in available traction, manure or labour, then a gradual deterioration of the soil conditions in the fields would result. Thus, if a mixture of emmer and spelt was sown (and the archaeobotanical evidence suggests that this is likely) then, over the years, there would be a marked increase in the proportion of spelt within the fields at the expense of emmer, and emmer would ultimately disappear. The results from this case study suggest the hypothesis that a change in cultivation regime could bring about a change in the dominant wheat crop in the fields. If this is what happened, then the change-over from emmer to spelt wheat need not have been a conscious decision to change crops, but may have been the result of a change in cultivation regime (van der Veen 1995; van der Veen and Palmer 1997). Either way, the switch to spelt can be used as a marker to identify an expansion of agricultural production.

There is some evidence from Germany that corroborates the pattern identified here. Knörzer (1964; 1984) noted in the lower Rhineland not only a switch from emmer to spelt in the Iron Age and Roman period, but also an association of spelt wheat with arable weed species indicative of poor soil conditions, which he related to an increase in the scale of production and a consequent degradation in the soil conditions. There is, clearly, an urgent need for more detailed statistical analyses of other, comparable, data sets to test whether similar patterns can be identified elsewhere.

Differences between these management regimes relate to the amount of soil working and manuring in each and, therefore, to the degree to which animals are integrated within the productive system. Small-scale, intensive agriculture may need no more than a few cattle to cover the requirement for manure and traction, but may be combined with extensive hill-farming of sheep, while large-scale cereal production requires large numbers of cattle, especially when harvesting and when preparing soil for the following crop. It may not be a coincidence that the evidence for poor soil conditions found associated with the evidence for spelt and agricultural expansion in the later Iron Age co-occurs with evidence for an emphasis on sheep, eg Danebury and Thorpe Thewles. While these sheep offer wool and the utilization of agriculturally unproductive lands, they cannot help with the working of the fields or the ploughing-in of manure, and they appear in these two cases not to have provided enough manure themselves to maintain soil fertility. There are, however, at present too few sites where both the seed and bone assemblages are of sufficient quality to test this hypothesis in detail, and this is clearly a priority for the future.

The importance of dung in systems where crop yields need to be maximised would seem obvious enough, yet the subject has received scant attention in the context of British prehistory. Bakels (1997) has reviewed the evidence from continental Europe, and concludes that manuring has been practised from the Late Neolithic onwards. One of the more effective means of maximising crop yields while making maximum use of crop by-products as animal feed is to allow livestock (usually sheep, because of their ability to graze even very short plant growth) to graze the crop aftermath. The remaining stubble and weeds are of little use to humans, being expensive to collect, difficult to store, and of negligible food value to an omnivorous primate. Stubble and weeds, however, can be readily collected and stored in the form of livestock, and may then be utilised by people as meat or secondary products. In addition, the urine and dung of the livestock replace soil nutrients, especially nitrogen, removed with the crop. If livestock are spatially restrained (folded), the manuring can be highly concentrated, giving maximum benefit to the following year's crop. This procedure, commonly termed 'direct manuring', requires relatively small fields with well-defined boundaries, or the use of mobile boundaries analogous to modern wire or hurdle fences.

The so-called Celtic field systems often associated with later Iron Age and Romano-British settlement would seem to have been well suited to direct manuring. To test this, soil analyses within such systems should seek to detect high levels of total phosphorus, probably with moderate enhancement of magnetic susceptibility, but with the absence of dense finds of abraded pottery or other domestic debris. If manuring is largely indirect, through the application of household waste, then in a period such as the later Iron Age and Romano-British period, substantial amounts of pottery ought to have found their way onto field surfaces. If manuring was largely direct, straight from the sheep, then the amounts of pottery on field surfaces should have been much less. A third procedure, in which animals are stalled and soiled bedding is utilised as manure, would be more difficult to detect, unless through the identification in ancient anthrosols of plants or materials inconsistent with the location. The use of a low-utility plant such as heather (*Calluna vulgaris*) as animal bedding, for example, could result in macrofossils or pollen of that species being recovered from what would otherwise appear to be a cultivated field. What is required here is not so much new techniques as focused, problem-oriented application of existing techniques. To go one step further, the existence of intensive cereal production might also be confirmed by finding a correlation between sites with emmer and small fields with evidence for manuring.

While it may be difficult to identify intensive and extensive management systems from animal bone assemblages, integration of bone data with the evidence from plant remains offers a way forward, and other lines of evidence may be successfully used. Increasing the numbers of livestock grazing on a given area of land (intensification) is likely to require closer management and control of that land. Hay production is one example, and this is first attested in the Roman period (Greig 1984; Jones 1989; Lambrick and Robinson 1979); another is the construction of boundaries, exclosures, droveways, and the like, such as those structures which Pryor (1996) has recently reinterpreted in terms of Bronze Age stock management in the Fenland. Site and monument surveys of these often large-scale landscape features can be used to locate possible grazing areas, followed by extensive soil analyses of attributes such as total soil phosphorus and magnetic susceptibility. This approach has been applied to an upland study area near Malham, North Yorkshire, enabling areas of managed grazing and exclosures in which crops may have been grown in a late prehistoric landscape to be recognised (McIlwaine and O'Connor forthcoming). The few settlement sites in the area typically yield a mixture of 'native' and Roman pottery, perhaps indicating that the intensified management of this particular area of upland was a phenomenon of the Iron Age–Roman transition.

One such site excavated in 1997 appears to lie at the core of a 'managed landscape', and yielded mostly Roman pottery, including some *terra sigillata*, from what is otherwise a typical cluster of 'prehistoric' roundhouses. Midden material from the structure has produced a bone assemblage, not yet fully analysed, in which sheep predominate. Perhaps this site is another example of the emphasis on sheep noted in the late Iron Age phases at Thorpe Thewles and Danebury, but here in a Roman chronological context, and associated with a surrounding landscape laid out apparently to facilitate the management of livestock. We thus have to examine the animal bone evidence in two ways, as evidence for the integration of livestock with crop production, and as evidence for livestock production *per se*. While the available data may lack the desired quality and quantity, there is clearly ample scope for modelling different production strategies and their archaeological outcomes, and then using that essentially speculative exercise to inform the research designs of subsequent field research.

The creation of products for a market

It is very difficult not only to identify commodities produced for exchange, but also to separate these from surplus production as part of a non-domestic mode of production; the difference is one of scale. As a broad generalisation we can identify a first stage, where farmers produce staples on a subsistence level, but introduce the production of a few commodities in order to engage with new exchange mechanisms and acquire new goods, while the last stage represents the present day situation where the entire agricultural production of a farm is geared towards the demand of the market, rather than the needs of the family or community.

The first, admittedly tentative, evidence for the production of agricultural cash commodities dates to the Roman period; the apparently large-scale production of beer is a good example. Evidence for the production of malt comes from the so-called corn driers. They are first identified in the first century AD, but mostly date to the third and fourth centuries. They are now thought to have been multifunctional structures associated with both the production of malt and with the preparation of grain for large-scale storage and transport (Reynolds 1981; Reynolds and Langley 1979; van der Veen 1989; see also below). Charred grain assemblages from five corn driers (Bancroft villa, Buckinghamshire, Catsgore,

Somerset, Hibaldstow, Lincolnshire, Mucking, Essex, and Tiddington, Warwickshire) provided conclusive evidence that these structures were used to roast germinated grain for the production of malt, the main raw material in the manufacture of beer (van der Veen 1989). While beer must have been produced throughout prehistory, this is the first evidence that the production was organised on a scale that suggests something beyond domestic consumption. Martin Jones (1981) has suggested that the production of beer may be interpreted as a response of British farmers to seasonal problems of cash flow. By holding back part of the cereal harvest, beer could be brewed and sold all year round, at a higher price than the grain would have fetched at harvest time.

Other potential cash crops are vegetables, herbs and fruit. In the Roman period we find, for the first time, clear evidence for the cultivation of garden and orchard plants: dill, celery, asparagus, beet, cabbage, carrot, apple, medlar, cherry, plum, etc (Dickson 1994; Greig 1991; Murphy and Scaife 1991; Robinson 1981; 1992). This is not to say that none of these food plants were cultivated in the preceding periods (though the rarity of waterlogged assemblages from Iron Age and earlier contexts does pose problems here), but again there is a difference of scale. The abundance and frequency of these finds, often from military and urban sites, is suggestive of market gardening, and thus the development of an intensive form of production developed in response to the demand from the new, non-agricultural settlements. Evidence for a possible suburban market garden has been recovered at Balkerne Lane, Colchester (Crummy 1984, 138–41; Murphy and Scaife 1991), and evidence for Roman period vineyards at North Thoresby, Lincolnshire (Webster and Petch 1967) and Wollaston, Northamptonshire (Meadows 1996) has been recorded. The evidence for an increase in garden and orchard crops is not unique to Britain, but has been recorded in many other parts of the Roman empire (Kreuz 1995; Pals 1997; van Zeist 1991). A comprehensive review of all the new records of these species and the nature of the sites on which they are found, is desirable.

The analogous cash crops from animals may simply have been meat, or dairy produce such as cheese, which is far more difficult to track in the archaeological record. Again, the difference between subsistence and market production is essentially one of scale, although production of a surplus may lead to a more evident focus on one particular productive strategy, rather than a diversified 'risk management' strategy. For example, it could be argued that the practice of slaughtering animals while still young, as seen at some Roman sites (eg O'Connor 1988, 87–8) is a form of cash-cropping. The difficulty with recognising this strategy lies in the disentangling of,

for example, young lambs that represent 'surplus males' culled out of a dairy flock, from young lambs that have been raised and slaughtered as the intended 'crop'. None the less, the presence of young lambs in refuse in a town implies that they have been moved from the place of production, and that in turn implies some form of marketing or redistribution of the resource. The production of surplus meat for sale clearly implies the movement of livestock about the landscape, largely, though not necessarily exclusively, between country and town. The archaeological investigation of such movement brings us back to extensive landscape surveys, and the recognition of structures associated with droving, or with the holding of large numbers of stock. Possible means of recognising different regional populations of animals are discussed below.

We cannot currently recognise from the bones of a cow whether she was regularly milked or not. Clearly a cow or ewe that is allowed to breed regularly will pass through regular phases of lactation, and may differ only a little in this respect from one that has been routinely milked for human consumption. What we are looking for, in effect, is a means of recognising prolonged and intense lactation such as might be interpreted as milking by humans rather than suckling by offspring alone. The conventional use of age-at-death data may enable the recognition of samples drawn from populations with a demography apparently optimal for milk production, but that is only an indirect means of recognising the organised production of dairy produce that might have been encouraged by the development of markets.

Towards a non-domestic scale of production

The first indicators of surplus grain production identifiable in the archaeological record are probably the large subterranean storage pits and above-ground, four-poster granaries of the Iron Age hillforts, although these may partly represent evidence for risk-buffering rather than true surplus-production. By the Roman period, however, we find large granaries associated with all military establishments, an indication that surplus production has occurred elsewhere (Bakels 1996). While it remains a subject of much discussion and speculation whether the grain required to feed the Roman army came from within Britain or from abroad, we know that long-distance grain transport took place. The presence of foreign crops and/or weeds has demonstrated the import of grain in a number of instances. There are examples from London (Straker 1984), Caerleon (Helbaek 1964), and York (Williams 1979), and others from beyond Britain (eg Kuijper and Turner 1992; Pals and Hakbijl 1992; Pals et al 1989).

What is clear is that during the Roman period the transport and storage of grain took place on a scale altogether different from that of any previous period, and this is corroborated by the fact that the first evidence for serious damage of grain caused by grain weevils and beetles dates to this period (Buckland 1978; Kenward 1979). The reason that insect infestation was not a problem during the Iron Age or earlier can be explained by proposing that until the Roman period grain was stored in much smaller units, usually for domestic use only, and little bulk transport took place. In the few places where bulk storage was practised, eg at the hillforts, the grain (or at least some of it) was stored in sealed, underground pits, where the rapid accumulation of carbon dioxide proved lethal to the insects, thus inhibiting insect infestation (Buckland 1978).

Other evidence for large-scale cereal production can be found in the occurrence of corn-driers and large watermills (Spain 1984; van der Veen 1989). The appearance of so-called corn-driers has already been mentioned. Apart from their role in the production of malt, they are also associated with evidence for the preparation of grain for large-scale storage and transport (ie parching and drying; van der Veen 1989). Watermills have been identified at three sites along Hadrian's Wall – Chesters, Haltwistle, and Willowford (Spain 1984) – and there are, in some cases admittedly tentative, associations between corn-driers and watermills or large millstones at the Roman villa at Chew Park, Somerset (Rahtz and Greenfield 1977), Heronbridge, Cheshire, Littlecote Park villa at Ramsbury, Wiltshire, and Barton Court Farm Abingdon, Oxfordshire (Spain 1984). Both the drying and/or parching of grain prior to storage or transport and the milling of grain into flour have been carried out throughout prehistory, but on a domestic scale, without the need for specialised structures or using anything other than hand-operated querns. In the Roman period this changed, and the appearance of corn-driers and large mills heralds the first step in the direction of a non-domestic scale of production. What is needed is a systematic compilation of all this evidence, so that a detailed map can be constructed registering when and where these changes occurred and what regional variations can be identified.

If we are to recognise the keeping of increased numbers of livestock, two particular requirements may be proposed. The first is to be able to quantify, if only crudely, the amounts of bone in circulation at different sites or in different phases of a site. One of the biggest weaknesses of archaeological animal bone studies is our apparent inability to relate changes in the relative abundance of taxa to changes in the absolute abundance of one or more taxa (Grayson 1984; Ringrose 1993). Nonetheless, loci at which increased numbers of livestock have been slaughtered and butchered, though not necessarily those at which the livestock were raised, will

presumably have generated increased quantities of bone debris. The huge quantities of bone debris recovered from some Roman sites hint at large-scale production and movement of livestock. Piercebridge, for example, is estimated to have yielded at least 250,000 bones (Rackham and Gidney 1984). Although the factors of deposition and diagenesis, let alone excavation policy, will be major determinants of the size of recovered bone assemblages, the sheer quantities of bones at sites such as Piercebridge, Binchester, and Vindolanda do suggest the increased mobilisation of livestock in the Roman period.

Quantifying this increase is obviously problematic, but a way forward might be for further research into bone taphonomy to develop models of bone deposition and incorporation which treat bone fragments as large sediment clasts, irrespective of Linnaean taxonomy. A few researchers, notably Bob Wilson (1996), have made some progress in this direction, and have also shown how difficult a line of investigation it is. If more bone debris is generated by human activity at a particular location, then more of this category of clast is contributed to the depositional processes going on around the site. There are obviously many stages between the recovered assemblage and the number and density of the population from which it is derived; but surely some information about the latter must reside in the former? Despite the exigencies of disposal, redeposition, diagenesis and recovery, even to be able to make generalised, ordinal, statements such as that 'much more bone, and probably more livestock, was in circulation at this site in the later Iron Age phases than in the early phase' would be a step forward.

One further line of enquiry is to examine the utilisation of animal carcasses. It may not always be correct to interpret a change in the utilisation of animal carcasses solely in functional terms. Differences in tradition, and the enhancement of those traditions when different peoples come into contact, will produce patterning within the animal bone record which could on its own be mistaken for changes in butchery practice in response to a need to intensify utilisation, perhaps to generate a commodity for trade. Given that proviso, however, several Romano-British sites in this country and on the near Continent have given evidence of cattle carcasses being butchered to a pattern, with specific joints being processed *en masse*, and sometimes with large quantities of heavily-butchered bone suggesting a coordinated effort to retrieve every possible product from the butchered carcass (van Mensch 1974; van Mensch and Ijzereef 1977; O'Connor 1988). Detailed examination of bone assemblages of good stratigraphic and dating integrity, where recovery was well controlled, should be undertaken in order to determine whether such bone deposits are just a characteristic of Romano-British sites, and then mainly of military sites, or whether similar deposits can be recognised in Iron Age material as well. Careful attention will have to be paid to the burial context, and the possibility of non-functional behaviour constantly borne in mind.

Access to imported luxuries and other symbols of wealth

Another well recorded phenomenon in the Roman period is the presence of 'exotic' food items, which, though not representing local expansion of production, do identify long-distance trading contacts and demonstrate wealth. The seeds of grapes, figs, olives, dates, lentils, pine-nuts, cucumber, and coriander have been found in many urban excavations, as well as at Roman forts, and some of these have also turned up at Romano-British settlements (Dickson 1994; Greig 1991; Hall and Kenward 1990; Murphy 1997; Murphy and Scaife 1991; Willcox 1977). To these we can add, of course, the import of wine, olive oil, and fish sauce, as demonstrated by the amphorae found on many sites (eg Sealey and Tyers 1989). As with the garden and orchard crops, it is difficult to monitor the access to these luxury items owing to the rarity of suitable preservation conditions at sites of the preceding period. Some of the crops initially imported were subsequently cultivated within Britain itself, and like the garden and orchard plants their occurrence needs to be plotted in detail against type of site and date, in order to identify patterns of access to wealth and changes through time. While most of these imports concern plant foods, one rather charming rodent represents the animal world: the garden dormouse (*Eliomys quercinus*) has been found in Roman deposits in York and South Shields, though whether this creature was imported deliberately or accidentally remains problematic (O'Connor 1988, 105–10; Younger 1994). Ornamental gardens are also first recorded in the Roman period (Dickson 1994; Murphy and Scaife 1991; Pals 1997). As symbols of wealth they deserve mention here, but they are otherwise outside the scope of this article.

New approaches

Many of the archaeological questions discussed here require a more focused application of existing techniques, but some will benefit from new approaches. Here we briefly mention a few new developments that will play an significant role in the coming years.

The most important recent development is the rise of biomolecular archaeology, in particular the isolation and characterisation of ancient DNA and the use of chemical analyses such as gas chromatography and mass spectrometry (Brown *et al* 1993; Eglinton 1996;

Evershed 1993; Evershed *et al* 1992; Hillman *et al* 1993). These techniques could make a significant contribution to the identification of problematic archaeological remains, such as grains of bread wheat. Grains of free-threshing wheat found in Roman granaries cannot be identified to species (hexaploid or tetraploid) without associated chaff but, as bread wheat is the only free-threshing wheat cultivated in north-west Europe at the time, records have, in the past, sometimes been identified as belonging to bread wheat for that reason (eg van der Veen 1994). The grains could, of course, belong to durum wheat, a species more commonly grown in the Mediterranean, which raises the important issue of whether the grain for the Roman army in Britain came from within or outside the country. Interestingly, the preliminary analysis of some charred pottery residues from Roman Bearsden, Scotland, using infrared spectrometry, does point to the possible presence of durum wheat (Camilla Dickson and Frances McLaren personal communication), although the accuracy of this technique in identifying taxonomic and genetic differences still needs further, critical consideration.

With animals there are important questions of recognising regional populations, so as to be able to track past large-scale movements of livestock. One of the great weaknesses of archaeological bone studies is our apparent inability to 'provenance' livestock. We can propose a place of origin for a Northumbrian sceatta, or for a Neolithic polished stone axe, but seemingly not for a cow, which may have been moved hundreds of kilometres during its life as an item of trade and exchange. One means of investigating increased movement and trade of livestock during the later Iron Age and Romano-British periods may be through recognition of large-scale landscape features associated with droving, which returns us to the need for truly extensive sites and monuments mapping. Another approach may be through investigating the genotypes of livestock, principally by way of their phenotypic characters.

At the dawn of reliable agricultural history (about AD 1750), cattle and sheep formed local populations with distinctive characteristics, which presumably resulted from founder effect and a degree of genetic drift abetted by human selection of breeding animals. It is a reasonable presumption that similar regionally delimited populations existed in prehistory. In bringing about greater mixing of such populations, increased trade and exchange of livestock may have modified both the incidence and the local prevalence of particular genetically controlled traits. Research into local genotypes offers a means of investigating the existence and degree of endogamy of local populations, and of recognising the greater mixing of local populations that has been postulated. Genotype can be investigated directly by means of DNA analysis, though any such research needs to be very precisely targeted, and there is a clear need for greater realism in ancient DNA studies. Indirect investigation of genotype may be accomplished through markers such as discontinuous skeletal traits, a field of investigation that merits a far more thorough investigation than it has received to date. Some studies have shown quite distinct site-to-site variation in the prevalence of particular characteristics (Bond and O'Connor forthcoming; Noddle 1978), and the main thing that holds back further research in this area is the relative paucity of research on the prevalence and significance of discontinuous skeletal traits in modern populations. It is ironic, but by no means unusual, to have to say that a lack of appropriate research into modern skeletons is holding back research into ancient bones.

Recognising the uses to which livestock were put is a fruitful area for investigation. We have discussed above the difficulties inherent in recognising dairying. A conventional means of recognising the use of cattle and sheep for dairying has been through the analysis of age at death data, though the interpretations that result are often uncertain and ambiguous. The kill-off models that are conventionally applied to archaeological assemblages tend to be 'steady-state' models, in which herd or flock size is conserved rather than rapidly increased. We need new models, which are appropriate to a period of expansion and intensification, in which there may have been pressure to generate additional livestock for expansion and exchange (and as a buffer against military appropriation) as well as obtaining the range of primary and secondary products. These models need to be heuristic devices that allow the testing of values for different parameters, and, unlike Cribb's 'Flocks' model (Cribb 1984), to reflect the pressures of a fully-integrated agrarian system, not an explicitly pastoral system.

The mathematics of linear programming may be an appropriate foundation for such a model. A complicating factor is that differences in the intensity of management of different herds or flocks may have resulted in differences in the rate of attrition of the teeth, thus making age attribution more difficult. If sheep are grazed at high densities, the sward may be grazed down so far that significant quantities of soil are ingested. If the soil mineral material is particularly siliceous, this can appreciably accelerate the rate of attrition of the teeth, making a sheep appear to be 'older' on dental grounds than its actual age (Healy and Ludwig 1965; Healy *et al* 1967). Detecting inter-sample differences in attrition rate is not simple, but Bond and O'Connor (forthcoming) report a possible instance in medieval material from York.

An alternative approach is to examine the chemistry and histology of the bones themselves. First, Ca/Sr ratios in bone mineral are responsive to bone mineral turnover in lactating females. Some work has been undertaken to investigate the use of Ca/Sr ratios in cattle bones as a means of recognising possible dairy cows in archaeological assemblages (Mulville 1994). The results are inconclusive but not necessarily discouraging, and there is clearly potential for more work in this area. Second, lactating females mobilise and redeposit large amounts of bone tissue, and this process can leave distinctive histological traces in the skeleton. The detail depends on the season in which the animal is slaughtered, and thus at what point the cycle of bone demineralisation and remineralisation is interrupted. A radiographic approach has been proposed and tested, based on the thinning of cortical bone observed in some lactating female ungulates (Horwitz and Smith 1991). Though non-destructive, this approach has several fundamental weaknesses, which could be overcome to some extent through a more direct procedure based on thin-section examination. Radiographic examination may allow thinning of cortical bone to be recognised, but would not allow the discrimination of cortical bone loss through lactation from that resulting from general inanition or other, pathological, conditions. The examination of undecalcified bone thin-sections is an under-used procedure, and further research in this area is strongly encouraged.

The use of cattle as traction animals has been discussed, and is at the heart of the integration of livestock with cereal production. We might speculate that pressures towards increased crop production would lead to at least some cattle being used largely as draught animals, with a concomitant impact on their skeletons. Animal bone palaeopathology is a seriously under-developed subject; the presence of a particular hip arthropathy in cattle from a Neolithic site has been used as evidence that cattle were used for traction (Armour-Chelu and Clutton-Brock 1988), and others have drawn attention to a possible link between lower-limb pathology and traction (Bartosiewicz *et al* 1993; Higham *et al* 1981). The weakness with this research to date has been our poor characterisation and classification of arthropathies in non-human material, and our lack of data pertaining to prevalence in past populations. If we are to recognise increased use of cattle for traction through an increased prevalence of strain-related arthropathies, then we need to know exactly what the characteristic arthropathies are, and we need much better data on background prevalence of these conditions. A complicating factor is the possibility that some forms of arthropathy may be correlates of skeletal senescence, thus necessitating modern data on the relationship between the prevalence of different forms of arthropathy and the age structure of the population, and greater attention to the age structure of archaeological populations within which the prevalence of arthropathies is being investigated.

Fundamental to our recognition of ancient crop management regimes is a detailed knowledge of the behaviour of arable weeds in different 'man'-made environments. So far, research has concentrated on both autecological and phytosociological approaches, as well as on pattern recognition within archaeobotanical assemblages. Important new research has been initiated by Glynis Jones and colleagues (Charles *et al* forthcoming) measuring functional attributes of arable weeds and using these as indicators of the potential of species to cope within a particular (man-made) environment. This approach is completely new; it moves away from formal analogies, and as such avoids the problems associated with some of the previous methods. This new approach is highly original and extremely timely, as it forms a logical and essential progression of the research carried out so far and will provide a much-needed tool for the interpretation of archaeological evidence. By identifying the biological reason for particular weed associations one can start to reconstruct, using archaeobotanical evidence, cultivation regimes not available today, and thereby circumvent problems inherent in previous approaches. The results of this research project will, therefore, be of very considerable importance to our understanding of the choices made by farmers in Iron Age and Roman Britain.

Conclusions

In this paper we have tried to identify the types of strategies available to farmers intent on expanding their production and we have suggested that most of these can be identified in the archaeological record by using existing technologies, though we have also pointed to areas where new technologies could bring significant new contributions. What is needed most of all is a more focused, problem-orientated approach and a better integration between the various sources of data. This should, where possible, involve quantitative analyses of associations and relationships between the various 'markers' of agricultural expansion and wealth generation. For example, is there a correlation between spelt and cattle; between specialised slaughtering and non-agricultural settlements; between exotic foods and other wealth and Romanisation indicators; or between emmer wheat, small fields and manuring? Identifying patterning in space and time will allow us to start identifying areas (and individual sites) where innovations were implemented early, and areas where innovations were either implemented late or not at all. To a certain extent this information is already available; for example, we know that spelt wheat first became dominant in parts of the south and east of the country, and here we also find the earliest development of *oppida*, villas, towns, corn

driers etc, all markers of an expansion of agriculture, an increase in the scale of production, and the development of non-agricultural sections of the population. The southern and eastern parts of the country have, however, too often been treated as a uniform entity, even though we know this to be incorrect. Furthermore, we still know very little about the other parts of the country and what choices were made there.

Cunliffe (1991) identified five different regions within Iron Age Britain, using archaeological evidence. In the next ten years research needs to focus on the extent to which different agricultural practices coincide with these, whether any regional variation in the Iron Age continues into the Roman period, or whether the magnitude of the Roman occupation imposed its own divisions. As we have mentioned above, our database does not, at present, have a regional coverage of the resolution and quality required to address these issues. To remedy this we need archaeological fieldwork to be channelled towards regional projects outside the south and east of England, and funds to be directed towards a small number of large-scale research projects that aim to integrate the various lines of evidence we have discussed.

This integration of the different sources of data may be facilitated by using the concept of energy capture and flow. We have stressed the role of soil working and manuring in the different crop management regimes, and manuring can usefully be seen as a way of maximising the utility of grazing livestock, and of utilising otherwise unavailable energy sources (hill grazing and scrub) (Thomas 1983; 1989). The archaeological study of manuring has of necessity to bring together the study of the main source of manure (animals), the medium to which it is applied (soil), and the organisms that directly (plants) and indirectly (humans and soil biota) benefit from it. An energy flow paradigm must also consider fodder, a topic that has not received sufficient focus in the context of Roman and earlier Britain. The production of fodder crops, whether grazed directly or cut and stored, offers a means of managing the energy available through the year, both by maximising availability at certain times and by storing food to mitigate seasonal shortages.

We have repeatedly mentioned quantitative developments, whether as a prerequisite to detailed analyses of weed and crop associations, or to allow new models to be developed of energy flows and outputs in postulated agrarian systems. This is more than just the use of larger and better-quality datasets. We need a greater willingness to put guesstimated numbers into our models, in order to see if they work at all, or to test the susceptibility of a system to fluctuations in, for example, grain yield or cattle birth rate. We have argued that the expansion of production is a key question for the later Iron Age and Romano-British period. Expansion is a matter of quantities, so it follows that our attempt to model and understand that process has to be quantified as well. Not least, we may be able to identify which variables are the critical ones, where minor fluctuations produce major consequences, and so to redirect our questioning of the archaeological data.

In conclusion, we have highlighted the fact that there are many types of agricultural expansion, each of which leaves a different archaeological imprint. We have also emphasised the role of factors such as availability of land and labour, as well as the social position of the farmer in the process of adoption or rejection of new strategies and the choice of strategy. Variations in these factors across the country are likely to be responsible for the growing regionalisation that has been recorded during the period, the extent to which agricultural expansion took place, and the form it took. Research in the next ten years needs to identify and analyse this regional diversity in more detail as this process is crucial to our understanding of the long-term development of agriculture in the various regions of Britain. We suggest that such research is most likely to succeed if environmental archaeology moves from descriptive and comparative applications to more analytical and explanatory approaches while, at the same time, becoming more embedded within the explanatory frameworks for social change.

Acknowledgements

We would like to thank Julie Bond, Simon Clarke, Peter Murphy, Jane Webster, and Rob Young for helpful comments on an earlier draft.

References

Allen, M J, 1988 Archaeological and environmental aspects of colluviation in south-east England, in *Man-made soils* (eds W Groenman-van Waateringe and M Robinson), BAR, Suppl Ser, **410**, 67–92, Oxford

Armour-Chelu, A, and Clutton-Brock, J, 1988 Evidence for the use of cattle as draught animals at Etton, *Antiq J*, **65**, 297–302

Bakels, C C, 1996 Growing grain for others or how to detect surplus production, *J Europ Archaeol*, **4**, 329–36

—, 1997 The beginnings of manuring in western Europe, *Antiquity*, **71**, 442–4

Bartosiewicz, L, van Neer, W, and Lentacker, A, 1993 Metapodial asymmetry in draft cattle, *Internat J Osteoarchaeol*, **3**, 69–75

Bayliss-Smith, T P 1982 *The ecology of agricultural systems*, Cambridge

Behre, K-E ed, 1986 *Anthropogenic indicators in pollen diagrams*, Rotterdam

Behre, K-E, and Jacomet, S, 1991 The ecological interpretation of archaeobotanical data, in van Zeist *et al* (eds) 1991, 81–108

Bell, M G, 1992 The prehistory of soil erosion, in Bell and Boardman 1992, 21–35

—, 1996 Environment in the first millennium BC, in Champion and Collis 1989, 5–16

Bell, M, and Boardman, J, 1992 *Past and present soil erosion: archaeological and geographical perspectives*, Oxbow Monogr, **22**, Oxford

Bidwell, P and Speak, S, 1994 *Excavations at South Shields Roman Fort, vol 1*, Newcastle upon Tyne

Bond, J M, and O'Connor, T P, forthcoming *Bones from medieval deposits at 16–22 Coppergate and other sites*, The Archaeology of York, **15/5**, York

Boserup, E, 1965 *The conditions of agricultural growth, the economics of agrarian change under population pressure*, London

Bradshaw, R, 1991 Spatial scale in the pollen record, in Harris and Thomas (eds) 1991, 41–52

Brown, A G, 1997 *Alluvial geoarchaeology: floodplain archaeology and environmental change*, Cambridge

Brown, T A, Allaby, R G, Brown, K A, and Jones, M, 1993 Biomolecular archaeology of wheat: past, present, and future, *World Archaeol*, **25**, 64–73

Buckland, P C, 1978 Cereal production, storage, and population: a caveat, in *The effect of man on the landscape: the lowland zone* (eds S Limbrey and J G Evans), CBA Res Rep, **21**, 43–5, London

Champion, T C and Collis, J R, 1996 *The Iron Age in Britain and Ireland: recent trends*, Sheffield

Charles, M, Jones, G, and Hodgson, J, forthcoming FIBS in archaeobotany: functional interpretation of weed floras in relation to husbandry practices, *J Archaeol Sci*

Cribb, R, 1984 Computer simulation of herding systems as an interpretive and heuristic device in the study of kill-off strategies, in *Animals and archaeology 3: early herders and their flocks* (eds J Clutton-Brock and C Grigson), BAR, Int Ser, **202**, 161–70, Oxford

Crummy, P 1984 *Excavations at Lion Walk, Balkerne Lane, and Middlebrough, Colchester, Essex*, Colchester Archaeol Rep, **3**, Colchester

Cunliffe, B, 1991 *Iron Age communities in Britain*, 3 edn, London

Darvill, T C 1987 *Prehistoric Britain*, London

Dickson, C, 1994 Macroscopic fossils of garden plants from British Roman and medieval deposits, in *Garden history: garden plants, species, forms, and varieties from Pompei to 1800* (eds D Moe, J H Dickson, and P M Jorgensen), PACT, **42**, 42–72

Dumayne, L, and Barber, K E, 1994 The impact of the Romans on the environment of northern England: pollen data from three sites close to Hadrian's Wall, *The Holocene*, **4**, 165–73

Dumayne-Peaty, L, and Barber, K E, 1997 Archaeological and environmental evidence for Roman impact on vegetation near Carlisle, Cumbria: a comment on McCarthy, *The Holocene*, **7**, 243–6

Eglinton, G (ed), 1996 *ABI Newsletter*, **3**, November, Swindon

Evans, J G, 1991 An approach to the interpretation of dry-ground and wet-ground molluscan taxocenes from central-southern England, in Harris and Thomas (eds) 1991, 80–95

Evans, J G, Davies, P, Mount, R, and Williams, D, 1992 Molluscan taxocenes from Holocene overbank alluvium in southern central England, in *Alluvial archaeology in Britain* (eds S Needham and M G Macklin), 65–74, Oxford

Evershed, R P, 1993 Biomolecular archaeology of lipids, *World Archaeol*, **25**, 74–93

Evershed, R P, Heron, C, Charters, S, and Goad, L J, 1992 The survival of food residues: new methods of analysis, interpretation, and application. *Proc Brit Acad*, **77**, 187–208

Ferrell, G, 1995 Space and society: new perspectives on the Iron Age of north-east England, in *Different Iron Ages, studies on the Iron Age in temperate Europe* (eds J D Hill and C G Cumberpatch), BAR, Int Ser, **602**, 129–47, Oxford

—, 1997 Space and society in the Iron Age of north-east England, in *Reconstructing Iron Age societies* (eds A Gwilt and C Haselgrove), Oxbow Monogr, 228–38, Oxford

Grant, A, 1989 Animals in Roman Britain, in Todd 1989, 135–46

Grant, A, Rushe, C, and Serjeantson, D, 1991 Animal husbandry, in *Danebury, an Iron Age hillfort in Hampshire vol 5: the excavations 1979–1988: the finds* (B Cunliffe and C Poole), CBA Res Rep, **73**, 447–87, London

Grayson, D K, 1984 *Quantitative zooarchaeology*, London

Green, F J 1979 Medieval plant remains from Wessex, unpubl MPhil thesis, Univ Southampton

Greene, K, 1986 *Archaeology of the Roman economy*, London

Greig, J R A, 1984 The palaeoecology of some British hay meadows, in *Plants and ancient man* (eds W van Zeist and W A Casparie), 213–26, Rotterdam

—, 1991 The British Isles, in van Zeist *et al* (eds) 1991, 299–334

Grigg, D, 1970 *The harsh lands: a study in agricultural development*, London

—, 1995 *An introduction to agricultural geography*, 2 edn, London

Groenman-van Waateringe, W, 1988 New trends in palynoarchaeology in north-west Europe or the frantic search for pollen data, in *Recent developments in environmental analysis in Old and New World archaeology* (ed R E Webb), BAR, Int Ser, **416**, 1–19, Oxford

Hall, A R, and Kenward, H K, 1990 *Environmental evidence from the colonia*, The Archaeology of York, **14/6**, London

Harris, D R, and Thomas, K D (eds), 1991 *Modelling ecological change*, London

Haselgrove, C, 1989 The later Iron Age in southern Britain and beyond, in Todd 1989, 1–18

Healy, W B, Cutress, T W, and Michie, C, 1967 Wear of sheep's teeth IV: reduction of soil ingestion and tooth wear by supplementary feeding, *New Zealand J Agric Res*, **10**, 201–9

Healy, W B, and Ludwig, T G, 1965 Wear of sheep's teeth I: the role of ingested soil, *New Zealand J Agric Res*, **8**, 737–52

Helbaek, H, 1964 The Isca grain, a Roman plant introduction in Britain, *New Phytologist*, **63**, 158–64

Higham, C F W, Kijngam, A, Manly, B F J, and Moore, S J E, 1981 The bovid third phalanx and prehistoric ploughing, *J Archaeol Sci*, **8**, 353–65

Hillman, G, 1991 Phytosociology and ancient weed floras: taking account of taphonomy and changes in cultivation methods, in Harris and Thomas (eds) 1991, 27–40

Hillman, G, Wales, S, McLaren, F, Evans, J, and Butler, A 1993 Identifying problematic remains of ancient plant foods: a comparison of the role of chemical, histological, and morphological criteria, *World Archaeol*, **25**, 94–121

Hillman, G C, Mason, S, de Moulins, D, and Nesbitt, M, 1996 Identification of archaeological remains of wheat: the 1992 London workshop, *Circaea*, **12**, 195–210

Horwitz, L K, and Smith, P, 1991 A study of diachronic change in bone mass of sheep and goats from Jericho (Tel-es-Sultan), *Archaeozoologia*, **4**, 29–38

Husain, M, 1979 *Agricultural Geography*, Delhi

Jones, G, 1992 Weed phytosociology and crop husbandry: identifying a contrast between ancient and modern practice, *Rev Palaeobot and Palynol*, **73**, 133–43

Jones, M, 1981 The development of crop husbandry, in Jones and Dimbleby 1981, 95–127

— (ed), 1983 *Integrating the subsistence economy*, BAR, Int Ser, **181**, Oxford

—, 1984 Regional patterns in crop production, in *Aspects of the Iron Age in central southern England* (eds B Cunliffe and D Miles), Oxford Univ Comm Archaeol Monogr, **2**, 120–5, Oxford

—, 1986 The carbonised plant remains, in *Archaeology at Barton Court Farm, Abingdon, Oxon* (ed J D Miles), CBA Res Rep, **50**, fiche 9, London

—, 1988 The arable field: a botanical battleground, in *Archaeology and the flora of the British Isles* (ed M K Jones), Oxford Univ Comm Archaeol Monogr, **14**, 86–92, Oxford

—, 1989 Agriculture in Roman Britain: the dynamics of change, in Todd 1989, 127–34

—, 1996 Plant exploitation, in Champion and Collis 1996, 29–40

Jones, M, and Dimbleby, G, 1981 *The environment of man: the Iron Age to the Anglo-Saxon period*, BAR, **87**, Oxford

Kenward, H K, 1979 The insect remains, in Kenward and Williams 1979, 62–78

Kenward, H K, and Williams, D, 1979 *Biological evidence from the Roman warehouses in Coney Street, York*, The Archaeology of York, **14/2**, London

King, A C, 1978 A comparative study of bone assemblages from Roman sites in Britain, *Univ London Inst Archaeol Bull*, **15**, 207–32

—, 1984 Animal bones and the dietary identity of military and civilian groups in Roman Britain, Germany, and Gaul, in *Military and civilian in Roman Britain: cultural relationships in a frontier province* (eds T F C Blagg and A C King) BAR, **136**, 187–217, Oxford

Knörzer, K H, 1964 Über die Bedeutung von Untersuchungen subfossiler pflanzlicher Grossreste, *Bonner Jahrbücher*, **164**, 202–12

—, 1984 Pflanzenfunde aus fünf eisenzeitlichen Siedlungen im südlichen Niederrheingebiet, *Bonner Jahrbücher*, **184**, 285–315

Kreuz, A, 1995 Landwirtschaft und ihre ökologischen Grundlagen in den Jahrhunderten um Christi Geburt: zum Stand der naturwissenschaftlichen Untersuchungen in Hessen, *Berichte der Kommission für Archäologische Landesforschung in Hessen*, **3**, 59–91

Kuijper, W J, and Turner H, 1992 Diet of a Roman centurion at Alphen aan de Rijn, the Netherlands, in the first century AD, *Rev Palaeobot and Palynol*, **73**, 187–204

Küster, H, 1991 Phytosociology and archaeobotany, in Harris and Thomas (eds) 1991, 17–26

Lambrick, J, and Robinson, M, 1979 *Iron Age and Roman riverside settlements at Farmoor, Oxfordshire*, CBA Res Rep, **32**, London

Macphail, R I, 1992 Soil micromorphological evidence of ancient soil erosion, in Bell and Boardman 1992, 197–215

Maguire, D J, 1983 The identification of agricultural activity using pollen analysis, in Jones (ed) 1983, 5–18

Maltby, M, 1984 The animal bones, in *Silchester: excavations on the defences 1974–80* (ed M Fulford), Britannia Monogr Ser, **5**, 199–212, London

—, 1996 The exploitation of animals in the Iron Age: the archaeozoological evidence, in Champion and Collis 1996, 17–28

McCarthy, M R, 1995 Archaeological and environmental evidence for the Roman impact on vegetation near Carlisle, Cumbria, *The Holocene*, **5**, 491–5

McIlwaine, J J, and O'Connor, T P, forthcoming Archaeological fieldwork in New Close, Malham, 1994–7

Meadows, I, 1996 Wollaston: the Nene Valley, a British Moselle? *Current Archaeol*, **13**, 212–5

Millett, M, 1990 *The Romanization of Britain: an essay in archaeological interpretation*, Cambridge

Mulville, J, 1994 Milking, herd structure, and bone chemistry: an evaluation of archaeozoological methods for the recognition of dairying, unpubl PhD thesis, Univ Sheffield

Murphy, P, 1997 Plant macrofossils from a late Roman farm, Great Holts Farm, Boreham, Essex. Anc Mon Lab Rep, **7/97**, London

Murphy, P, and Scaife, R G, 1991 The environmental archaeology of gardens, in *Garden archaeology* (ed A E Brown), CBA Res Rep, **78**, 83–99, London

Noddle, B A, 1978 Some minor skeletal differences in sheep, in *Research problems in zooarchaeology* (eds D R Brothwell, K D Thomas, and J Clutton-Brock), Univ London Inst Archaeol Occas Pub, **3**, 133–42, London

—, 1993 Bones of larger mammals, in *Excavations at Segontium (Caernarfon) Roman fort, 1975–1979* (P J Casey, J L Davies, and J Evans), CBA Res Rep, **90**, 97–118, York

O'Connor, T P, 1988 *Bones from the General Accident site, Tanner Row*, The Archaeology of York, **15/2**, London

Pals, J-P, 1997 Introductie van cultuurgewassen in de Romeinse Tijd, in *De Introductie van onze Cultuurplanten en hun Begeleiders van het Neolithicum tot 1500 AD* (ed A C Zeven), 25–51, Wageningen

Pals, J-P, Beemster, V, and Noordam, A P, 1989 Plant remains from the Roman castellum Praetorium Agrippinae near Valkenburg (prov of Zuid Holland), *Dissertationes Botanicae*, **133**, 117–34

Pals, J-P, and Hakbijl, T, 1992 Weed and insect infestation of a grain cargo in a ship at the Roman fort of Laurium in Woerden (Province of Zuid-Holland), *Rev Palaeobot and Palynol*, **73**, 287–300

Pryor, F, 1996 Sheep, stockyards, and field systems: Bronze Age livestock in eastern England, *Antiquity*, **70**, 313–24

Rackham, D J, 1985 An analysis and interpretation of the sample of animal bones from Thorpe Thewles, Cleveland, Anc Mon Lab Rep, **4567**, London

—, 1987 The animal bone, in *The excavation of an Iron Age settlement at Thorpe Thewles, Cleveland, 1980–1982*, CBS Res Rep, **65**, 99–109, London

Rackham, D J, and Gidney, L J, 1984 Piercebridge Roman fort and environs: an analysis of a sample of animal bones from the collections excavated at Piercebridge Roman fort and vicus, unpubl archive report, Dept Archaeology, Univ Durham

Rahtz, P A, and Greenfield, E, 1977 *Excavations at Chew Valley Lake, Somerset*, DoE Archaeol Rep, **8**, London

Reynolds, P J, 1981 New approaches to familiar problems, in Jones and Dimbleby 1981, 19–49

Reynolds, P J, 1992 Crop yields on the prehistoric cereal types emmer and spelt: the worst option, in *Préhistoire de l'agriculture: nouvelles approches expérimentales et ethnographique* (ed P C Anderson) CNRS, Monographie de CRA 6, 383–93, Paris

Reynolds, P J, and Langley, J K, 1979 Romano-British corn-drying oven: an experiment, *Archaeol J*, **136**, 27–42

Ringrose, T J, 1993 Bone counts and statistics: a critique, *J Archaeol Sci*, **20**, 121–57

Robinson, M A, 1981 The Iron Age to early Saxon environment of the Upper Thames terraces, in Jones and Dimbleby 1981, 251–86

Robinson, M A, 1992 Environmental archaeology of the river gravels: past achievements and future directions, in *Developing landscapes of lowland Britain: the archaeology of the British gravels: a review* (eds M Fulford and E Nichols), Soc Antiq London Occas Pap, **14**, 47–62, London

Sealey, P R, and Tyers, P A, 1989 Olives from Roman Spain: a unique amphora find in British waters, *Antiq J*, **49**, 53–72

Spain, R J, 1984 Romano-British watermills, *Archaeol Cantiana*, **100**, 101–28

Spedding, C R W, 1988 *An introduction to agricultural systems*, London

Straker, V, 1984 First and second century carbonised cereal grain from Roman London, in *Plants and ancient man* (eds W van Zeist and W A Casparie), 323–9, Rotterdam

Thomas, K D, 1983 Agricultural and subsistence systems of the third millenium BC in north-west Pakistan: a speculative outline, in Jones (ed) 1983, 279–314

—, 1989 Hierarchical approaches to the evolution of complex agricultural systems, in *The beginnings of agriculture* (eds A Milles, D Williams, and N Gardner), BAR, Int Ser, **496**, 55–73, Oxford

Tipping, R, 1997 Pollen analysis and the impact of Rome on native agriculture around Hadrian's Wall, in *Reconstructing Iron Age societies* (eds A Gwilt and C Haselgrove), Oxbow Monogr, **71**, 239–47, Oxford

Tipping, R, and Mercer, R J, 1994 The history of soil erosion in the northern and eastern Cheviot Hills, Anglo-Scottish Borders, in *The history of soils and field systems* (eds S Foster and T C Smout), 1–25, Edinburgh

Todd, M, 1989 *Research on Roman Britain 1960–89*, Britannia Monogr Ser, **11**, London

Turner, J, 1981 The vegetation, in Jones and Dimbleby 1981, 67–73

van der Veen, M, 1989 Charred grain assemblages from Roman-period corn driers in Britain, *Archaeol J*, **146**, 302–19

—, 1992 *Crop husbandry regimes: an archaeobotanical study of farming in northern England 1000 BC–500 AD*, Sheffield Archaeol Monogr, **3**, Sheffield

—, 1994 The biological remains, in Bidwell and Speak 1994, 243–66

—, 1995 The identification of maslin crops, in *Res archaeobotanicae: international Workgroup for Palaeoethnobotany, proceedings of ninth symposium, Kiel 1992* (eds H Kroll and R Pasternak), 335–43, Kiel

van der Veen, M, and Palmer, C, 1997 Environmental factors and the yield potential of ancient wheats, *J Archaeol Sci*, **24**, 163–82

van Mensch, P J, 1974 A Roman soup kitchen at Zwammerdam? *Berichten van de Rijksdienst voor het Oudheidkundig Bodemonderzoek*, **24**, 159–65

van Mensch, P J, and Ijzereef, G F, 1977 Smoke-dried meat in prehistoric and Roman Netherlands, in *Ex Horreo* (eds B L van Beek, R W Brandt, and W Groenman-van Waateringe), 144–50, Amsterdam

van Zeist, W, 1991 Economic aspects, in van Zeist *et al* (eds) 1991, 109–30

van Zeist, W, Wasylikowa, K, and Behre, K-E (eds), 1991 *Progress in Old World palaeoethnobotany*, Rotterdam

Webster, P, and Petch, D F, 1967 A possible vineyard of the Romano-British period at North Thoresby, Lincolnshire, *Lincolnshire Hist Archaeol*, **2**, 55–61

Whittle, A, Rouse, A J, and Evans, J G, 1993 A Neolithic downland monument in its environment: excavations at the Easton Down long barrow, Bishops Canning, north Wiltshire, *Proc Prehist Soc*, **59**, 197–240

Willcox, G H, 1977 Exotic plants from Roman waterlogged sites in london, *J Archaeol Sci*, **4**, 269–82

Williams, D, 1979 The plant remains, in Kenward and Williams 1979, 52–62

Wilson, B, 1996 *Spatial patterning among animal bones in settlement archaeology: an English regional exploration*, BAR, **251**, Oxford

Younger, D A, 1994 The small mammals from the forecourt granary and the southwest fort ditch, in Bidwell and Speak 1994, 266–8

15 Changing the Roman landscape: the role of geophysics and remote sensing

by Vincent L Gaffney,
Christopher F Gaffney,
and Mark Corney

Abstract

Although the utility of geophysics for mapping archaeological remains has been recognised for a considerable time, it has rarely achieved a major analytical role. To a certain extent, the value of geophysical data as a potential cultural item has largely been ignored in favour of its exploratory role deriving from the utility of geophysics for non-invasive prospection, particularly in the context of archaeological assessment. It is also true that the range of techniques regularly applied has also been limited and their use has been relatively unimaginative. Furthermore, the level of confidence associated with the interpretation of most techniques can be described at best as unknown.

This situation is changing. In the first instance the range of techniques available has expanded, and these are not limited to ground-based surveys but also include multi- and hyper-spectral remote sensing technologies. The expansion in response types is also associated with the increasing availability of sophisticated image processing software and integrative systems. The consequence of such a situation is that remote sensing technologies are now available for synthesis within the larger archaeological domain as analytical, as well as exploratory, tools. The result of such a situation is that the data from survey can now be integrated within their larger cultural contexts. This paper reviews these trends, considers the implications derived from such developments, and illustrates them with reference to a number of major Iron Age and Roman projects.

Introduction

There can be little doubt that the development of remote sensing technologies has had a considerable impact on archaeological methodology and has, to some extent, been at the forefront of the general ascendancy of applied archaeological sciences in the last 30 years (Aspinall 1992). The positive reception afforded to geophysics may be due to the fact that most archaeologists find the use of 'black box' technology relatively intuitive and the output readily understandable. Archaeologists are generally happy with plans of interpreted features even if they are simply composed of lines, tones, and dots.

Throughout this period of development we have also seen the introduction of a significant number of techniques, passive and active, aerial or ground-based.

Interestingly, a brief consideration of techniques taken from a modern geophysical textbook would be familiar to those who pioneered archaeological geoprospection or to anyone who has perused the 1960s journal *Prospezioni Archeologiche*. Experience has shown us that there are many techniques that have more or less common use in our field practice. While some techniques are unique in their theory or use, many are interrelated, complementing both other non-invasive techniques and traditional excavation. Indeed, experience has demonstrated that a research design may require a battery of techniques or methods to reach a positive conclusion.

The value of geophysical techniques to archaeologists has, historically, been seen as their ability to locate specific archaeological features or artefacts, generally as a precursor to more traditional archaeological pursuits, most notably excavation. Consequently, one can observe that many of the early applications of ground-based remote sensing have been set apart by virtue of their scale. They covered relatively small areas and were largely site oriented. This has been attributed in part to technological limitations (Gaffney *et al* 1991). At a time when data capture was a manual event, and processing and display as much a concern of the drafting office as the geophysicist, the process of analysis was by definition a long drawn out affair, limiting considerably nascent applications. However, one should also note that early archaeological scientists were very much led by archaeologists and that archaeology itself was a very site-based discipline. As a result of this situation geophysical survey was regarded, essentially, as a means to provide a larger context for excavated features. The consequences of such a situation can be viewed at several levels.

Technologically there was considerable emphasis on hardware refinement both to improve the accuracy of the instrumentation and fundamentally to understand what specific geophysical responses related to. Also, and perhaps more relevant to this paper, technologists sought to improve methods of data capture and presentation (Kelly *et al* 1984).

The move towards the automation of data capture and the resulting routine collection of large-scale data sets has forced us to reconsider how we interpret geophysical results. The estimation of background levels and hence anomalous variation has become more difficult, particularly when confronted by hundreds of thousands of measurements. Filters and correlation techniques have become more common, while analysis using neural networks has been at the forefront of some innovative research (Scollar *et al* 1990; Sheen 1997).

However, these improvements alone do not necessarily equate with 'better', as some aspects of methodology are still underdeveloped. As an example, 1m spacing for resistance survey was an estimate that was thought likely to find representative features in the 1960s. Although still the norm in field application, this assumption is not always true, and the implementation of new resistance arrays may result in potentially large methodological changes.

In Britain, by the mid to late 1980s only two primary geophysical technologies were regularly employed: resistivity and magnetometry, more commonly known as resistance and gradiometry owing to the dominant variation on each theme. These techniques were proven to be relatively reliable and capable of significant automation. Following from this the use and, occasionally, the abuse of non-invasive techniques has been more widespread. Two other techniques that have become somewhat more prevalent are ground probing radar and magnetic susceptibility. In both cases it can be said that the prime mover in the increased use of these techniques has been applications based on PPG16 (DoE 1990) and that the main proponents of these techniques have been commercial firms rather than academic groups. This has led to inevitable conflicts of interest between assessing techniques and selling them in the market place. Despite this, both techniques have sound archaeological applications if the scale and the context of each problem is discrete.

Apart from technical innovations, equally important changes have occurred at an archaeological level. Geophysical prospection was, it has already been noted, primarily a site-centred technique. This, of course, was perfectly acceptable with respect to the general tenor of British archaeology during the 1960s and 1970s, but hardly reflects the broader theoretical perspectives of the 1980s and 1990s (Hodder 1986; Tilley 1994). Today, many archaeologists are increasingly concerned with analysis at a larger geographical scale, with the study of landscapes rather than sites. Whether one views this trend from a behavioural viewpoint or, for instance, as a symbolic landscape archaeologist, there are many good reasons to operate at scales above the level of the settlement, and although protagonists from such schools might deny it, the thread tying their work together is the need to provide a mosaic of archaeological features that is both spatially extensive and representative of the cultural repertoire. Given such a goal, remote sensing programmes, combined with analytical field survey, should be essential in providing the extensive database of cultural items critical for landscape research, and which lie beyond the scope of traditional excavation strategies.

The emerging capability of geophysical technology to carry out archaeological landscape prospection in line with current academic needs is clear; dozens of surveys provide examples of significant landscape data which otherwise might have been missed. Despite this potential, little exploratory remote sensing is carried out as part of a planned, cohesive academic strategy. Almost in spite of academic trends, the truth is that large-scale landscape projects that incorporate geophysics as an extensive technique are extremely rare in Britain, or indeed anywhere.

Examples of such work do exist, however, and we should consider how such procedures add to our larger knowledge, not simply of the position of archaeological features, but our understanding of the past in a more comprehensive manner.

Rural survey

The South Cadbury Environs Project, is one important example of an extensive landscape survey providing a balance to site-centred work (see http://www.bufau.bham.ac.uk/newsite/Projects/SC/southc.html). Here a landscape survey of an 18 square kilometre block of land is being carried out which has a significant geophysical element, planned as part of the investigation. The work by the universities of Birmingham and Glasgow is centred on the well known hillfort site, partly excavated by Leslie Alcock. Early excavations were, incidentally, also associated with a programme of exploration in which pioneering, extensive intra-site geophysics played a significant part with respect to the then novel soil conductivity meter (Howell 1966). Despite the intense archaeological activity at the site, the surrounding countryside had provided little evidence for significant, associated archaeological features. Work by Richard Tabor, however, has begun to provide a rich context for the hillfort, most dramatically at Sigwells, where the response has provided a mass of landscape features which the investigators have tentatively deconstructed to provide a prehistoric phase associated with ring ditches, enclosures and linear boundary features, two Roman phases demonstrating major landscape and settlement development, and a possible post-Roman phase incorporating ridge and furrow and a rectilinear enclosure.

A slightly different emphasis is provided by the RCHME Salisbury Plain Project. This has utilised directed geophysical survey as part of a larger landscape investigation. Here geophysics has been a major contributor to the resolution of specific landscape problems. Prior to the commencement of the project, the region had been regarded by Romanists as an undeveloped backwater, possibly an imperial estate. This suggestion, first made by Collingwood and subsequently repeated by all the major scholars of Roman Britain, was based on the apparent dearth of villas in the region.

Until five years ago only two villas were known in the immediate vicinity of the Plain. Recent fieldwork by the RCHME has revealed an extensive and well preserved Romano-British landscape consisting of villages (some over 20ha) integrated with field systems, trackways, and even dams to control water supply. It was felt that this landscape could only make sense if seen as a component of a village/estate-based economy as seen elsewhere on the Wessex chalklands.

Careful analysis of the archaeological record supplemented by the reconnaissance and study of the Plain and its immediate environs led to the identification of a number of potential villa sites along the foot of the scarp slopes and Avon valley. Unusually for this area, aerial photographs had failed to resolve this problem and a programme of geophysics was implemented. Three hitherto unknown villas have been located through this programme of work and a further four probable sites have been identified but for the time being remain unconfirmed until funding is available.

At Netheravon, in the Avon Valley, a winged corridor villa was located within a large enclosure of middle to late Iron Age date. Surface collection indicates occupation from the late Iron Age to fifth century AD and included a large quantity of coins, lead weights, and stylii. All are indicative of a major estate centre. Along the northern foot of the Salisbury Plain escarpment a major villa complex including a detached bath house was located adjacent to a Bronze Age ring ditch cemetery at Charlton (Fig 15.1) (Corney et al 1994). Ten km to the west of Lower Bayton Farm, Edington, a further villa was discovered which included a building of unusual form featuring a large apse. Thus a total of five villas are now confirmed around Salisbury Plain and a further four strongly suspected. The significance of the role of geophysics within this project cannot be over emphasised. It has allowed a radical interpretation of the Romano-British settlement pattern for the region and may also shed further light on the survival of Romano-British estate units into the Saxon and medieval periods. There is a marked coincidence between the villas located and the early Anglo-Saxon estates first noted by Desmond Bonney (1976). These discoveries, coupled with the excavated evidence on the villas sites indicating continuity into the sixth century AD, are enabling the writing of a new chapter in the archaeology and history of the late Roman and migration periods in central Wessex.

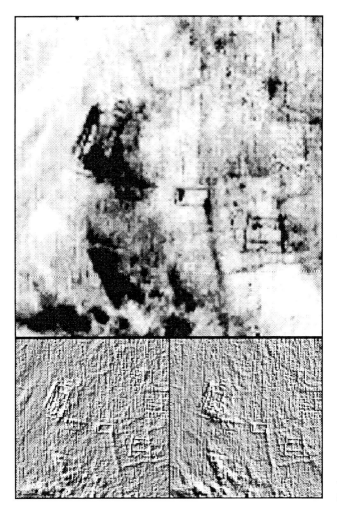

Fig 15.1 Villa and bathhouse at Charlton, Wiltshire

Urban survey

A dramatically different situation can be demonstrated at Viriconium Cornoviorum, the Roman city at Wroxeter (Barker 1990). Moving from essentially rural surveys we can now consider the results from survey of a major urban settlement covering *c* 78 hectares. The site is well known from the excavations led by Philip Barker and Graham Webster, and from the comprehensive plan derived from aerial photography (Barker *et al* 1997). The results of these extremely important studies have been the provision of a relatively well understood archaeological sequence for the town, from its origins as a legionary fortress through to Barker's remarkable evidence for post-Roman survival. Paradoxically, the impetus for a major geophysical reappraisal of the site has sprung from a study of its hinterland, funded by the Leverhulme Trust.

This study was designed to investigate the processes of Romanisation and urbanisation within the area of the Cornovii. Of particular interest was the apparent contrast between the highly Romanised urban centre at Wroxeter and the lack of Romanised settlement within its hinterland. Fieldwork designed to investigate the substantial absence of Romanised settlement suggests that this is a real phenomenon and not a problem of bias. While some settlements are heavily Romanised – for example the villa at Whitley Grange is a reasonably luxurious residence and has, as an aside, provided a mid fifth century magnetic date (http://www.bufau.bham.ac.uk/newsite/Projects/WH/Docs/nl11.html) – evidence for Romanisation has been limited or absent on other sites over most of the study area. Given the rural evidence, the situation within the town becomes more and not less critical. The extent of the settlement and the relative wealth of excavated urban buildings is problematic, particularly given the aerial photographic evidence which provided no evidence of structures over considerable areas within the town defences. Indeed, even the principal road system exhibited significant gaps. The bottom line was that it was rather difficult to gauge the Romanising effect of an urban area on the surrounding land if perhaps 40% of that urban zone was effectively uncharacterised, *terra incognita*; interpretation of the larger area became tied to a number of very basic questions related to the town itself.

In considering this situation, it is important to acknowledge that the study of Wroxeter is a landscape problem. The site itself possesses considerable topographical and archaeological variation. Moreover, few cities, until recent times, could really be divorced from their wider landscape and the Roman town, in particular, is best interpreted within this context (Lawrence 1994). Despite this, it is a peculiar fact that decades of discussion on the nature and relationship of town and

country by Roman archaeologists have rarely produced research programmes in Britain that have actually looked at this problem in an integral manner (Millett 1992).

It was clear that the situation at Wroxeter demanded a radical approach. There were cogent reasons to be circumspect with respect to aerial photographic evidence, while excavation over such an area was neither practical nor desirable. Geophysics suggested itself as the principal investigative methodology. To carry out such a major campaign it was necessary to organise an international academic network composed of British and foreign geophysicists and incorporating national bodies such as English Heritage and commercial groups including Geophysical Surveys of Bradford.

The interim results from the principal magnetometer survey, which was scheduled for completion during May 1997, provides the most extensive data set available to date (Fig 15.2). Some two million data points have been collected. This survey has provided exceptional evidence, and although the data primarily relates to the usual range of features that produce positive anomalies, the most significant and common response is a negative one linked to stone structural elements. Although common elsewhere in Europe, particularly on terra rosa soils, in Britain this response is rare, and may be attributed to relatively non-magnetic building stone within highly magnetically enhanced soils (Tite and Linington 1986).

Fig 15.2 General results from magnetometry survey at Wroxeter, Shropshire

Following this work, the city's street system has now largely been traced. There is also evidence for central elite buildings surrounded by, presumably, lower status (artisan) quarters (Fig 15.3). The latter areas provide little evidence for structures but possess sub-division of the insulae and demonstrate intense anthropogenic activity, presumably associated with settlement. The areas to the north are particularly intriguing (Fig 15.4). There is a considerable amount of open space, some of which may relate to industrial activity (the presence of kilns), but the suspicion is that the inclusion of such a large non-settlement area including the Bell Brook may also be indicative of agro-industrial activities such as tanning.

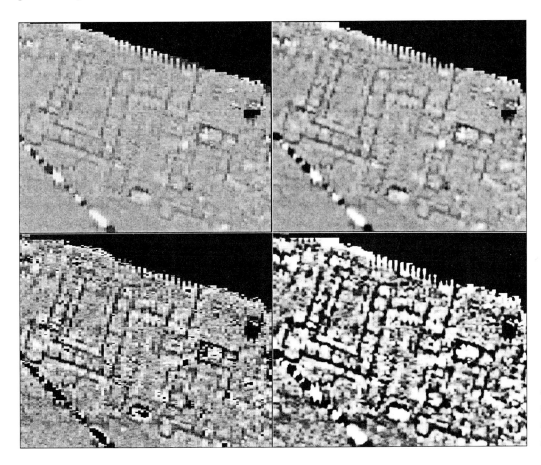

Fig 15.3 Magnetometry data illustrating a large stone building within the central area of Wroxeter, Shropshire

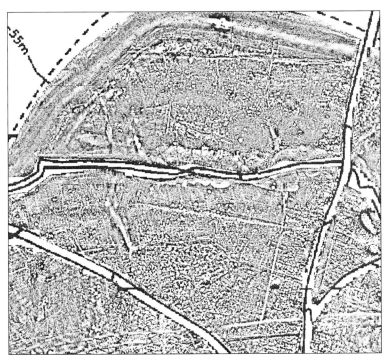

Fig 15.4 Magnetomer data from the north-western area of Wroxeter showing land divisions and possible industrial (kiln?) sites

A number of particular features deserve specific comment. The evidence for a possible church, 27m in length, is intriguing given Barker's suggestion that the town's late survival may be linked to the presence of a bishop (Fig 15.5). Equally important, given the gradiometer data, is the evidence for enhanced magnetic features associated with stone buildings in the north-eastern quarter of the town (Fig 15.6). These results seem most reasonably interpreted as evidence for a major fire, and one can conjecture, with very little real evidence of course, that such a major event might be linked to the fires recorded in the Forum, and perhaps associated with the collapsed market stalls found there (Atkinson 1942).

Apart from these individual points, the evidence for a considerable density of settlement in the town itself is provocative. Taken together the excavation and survey evidence points to a thriving urban community and this initially seems at odds with any general interpretation which regards Wroxeter as a precocious development or the Cornovii as a weakly stratified society. One must believe that the pre-existing, rural, agricultural, and, perhaps, industrial base largely supported a thriving urban core. The ability to direct communal wealth into the construction of the town at Wroxeter suggests the presence of a strong, centralised elite. This conclusion is strengthened by the apparent lack of any material benefit to the lower status rural sites within the city's hinterland. The complexity of this situation, however, is only emerging within the context of settlement density within the town as indicated by extensive geophysical survey.

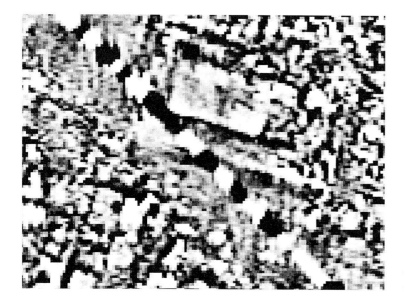

Fig 15.5 Magnetometry data showing a structure interpreted as a church at Wroxeter, Shropshire

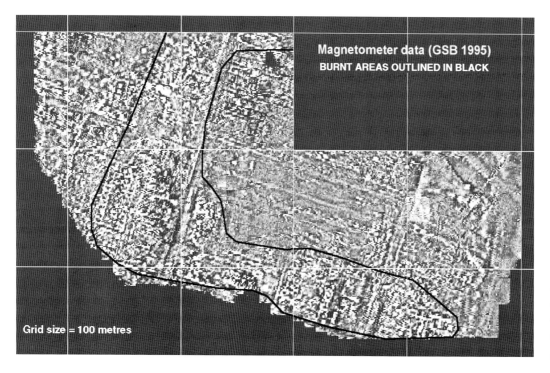

Fig 15.6 Stone buildings at Wroxeter associated with enhanced magnetic values and interpreted as evidence for a major fire

Site-based surveys

Up until this point we have concentrated upon the expanded role of geophysics at the largest spatial levels. In doing this, it is not the intention to suggest that site-based survey is used adequately or to its full potential.

The English Heritage Wessex Hillfort Project provides one good example of a site-based project (Payne 1996; Trow et al 1996) that considers geophysics as the prime methodology for the investigation of hillfort interiors. Using a planned sampling strategy, this project impressively attempts to rectify not only the historic excavation bias towards hillfort defences, but combines investigations into the nature of early and developed hillforts, spatial differentiation of function, regionally and at an intra-site level. Included in the research design is the exploratory assessment of a number of methods, including magnetic susceptibility, for rapid characterisation of hillfort interiors and settlement intensity. Clearly this is a measured response to problems that might have demanded massive investment in traditional excavation. More significant, however, is the fact that this project does not seek to provide a collection of geophysical anomalies that may, or may not, feed into archaeology's general fund of knowledge. Rather it proposes to solve substantive archaeological problems explicitly using geophysical data.

This is an important point because there are additional research avenues where geophysics can add supporting data or open alternative research routes at an intra-site level. There is the tendency among archaeologists to consider geophysics only in terms of the negative or positive archaeological features which are discovered, and this may be too simplistic. Morphological interpretation becomes

all in such circumstances, particularly if the results are not backed by excavation. Little consideration has been given to the exact archaeological interpretation of the response, except in the most functional of senses, for instance in the relationship between the shape of magnetometer response to specific features such as kilns.

At a functional level it is pertinent to note the potential for integration of surface soil studies within analysis. Repetitive activities can cause discrete changes to the properties of soil and can be differentiated using laboratory-based analysis. At Chesters Villa it proved possible to differentiate domestic from industrial areas through the magnetic properties of the soil. While industry, in particularly smelting and metalworking, engenders higher susceptibility than domestic activities, the latter also exhibit much lower magnetic viscosities. This demarcation was clearly seen in the results from Chesters and was confirmed on excavation by Fulford and Allen (1992) and has wider implications for field methodologies. A similar approach has been attempted on an Iron Age site at Guiting Power where differentiation has been made between habitation and stockade (Grove 1991), while, in general, the geophysical interpretation of stratified soil has also increasingly become of greater value (Boucher 1996; Linford 1994; Weston 1996).

Yet there is potential for even more sophisticated archaeological interpretation. We might consider equating machine response with cultural events and use the results within the overall archaeological interpretation. The gradiometer plot of an Iron Age enclosure at Norse Road, Bedfordshire provides an example of such a situation (Dawson and Gaffney 1995) (Fig 15.7). The plan of the site is particularly clear, with ditches showing as

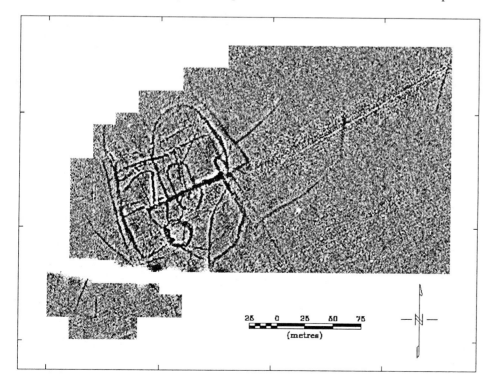

25   0   25   50   75

(metres)

—N—

Fig 15.7 Plot of an enclosure at Norse Road, Bedfordshire, from magnetometry data

positive anomalies declining away from the site. This is an extremely common phenomenon for Iron Age sites. While it seems reasonable to suggest that this response reflects domestic material within the ditches providing a magnetic response, we can interpret this simple phenomenon in a number of ways. As a behaviouralist one might suggest the data as evidence for simple rubbish disposal practice. Alternatively, we should at least consider that the dumping of material in Iron Age ditches and pits may be more than a simple rubbish disposal act. Work by a number of authors, most notably Hill (1995), has emphasised the peculiar nature of deposition on sites like this, so the nature, strength, and spatial variability of geophysical response may be a cultural as well as a physical phenomenon. The argument for such an interpretation at Norse Road is strengthened by the fact that the gradiometer response along the main D-shaped enclosure is spatially variable. This suggests that the dumping of settlement debris, which presumably governs instrument response, is differential, and therefore a cultural response. The importance of deposition in certain areas of enclosures has been noted at a number of sites, including Winnall Down, Hampshire (Hill 1994, fig 2.3). Apart from the suggestive nature of these results one wonders whether such phenomena might be detected during routine excavations without detailed soil analysis. The organic material which may engender such a response may be otherwise undetectable.

Air-based remote sensing

So far the primary emphasis has been on the role of ground-based remote sensing. Side-stepping aerial photography, which has a considerable literature, alternative air-based, non-photographic techniques, particularly multi-spectral remote sensing, should be considered. In the past this has been restricted in use and, at a practical level, management and interpretation of such data has frequently been a problem. The availability of relatively cheap mass storage and suitable commercial software for analysis, however, has overcome this situation. While the resolution of satellite-based digital data has previously been too coarse to be of practical value for archaeological prospection, air-based data solves some of these problems. It possesses greater resolution, enhanced numbers of bands, and modern georectification procedures enhance its value and efficiency.

Recent work by Dominic Powlesland at West Heslerton has begun to explore these possibilities (Powlesland *et al* 1997). Using aerial photography, ground-based geophysics and the NERC Daedalus multispectral scanner, this project has considered feature response over an area of nearly 48 square kilometres. While the detail provided from ground-based geophysics could not be replicated, multispectral evidence provides at least as much detail as aerial photography and can extend it in some areas. It has the advantage of providing continuous data sets over large areas while not relying on traditional, restrictive, oblique aerial photography formats.

Powlesland notes, however, that the technology used, while new for archaeologists, is already a decade old. We have not begun to explore the potential of hyperspectral data sets such as the 256 band output from NERC's compact airborne spectrographic imager. These instruments should be considerably more flexible analytically and provide data resolution to two metres or less in optimal circumstances. In archaeological terms, this may be sufficient for many features, as the important point about such images is the contribution of a feature to the overall pixel signal. There is a real need to assess this potential and inform the user community of its value and availability[1].

Methodological developments

So far the discussion has been of single instrumentation response to archaeological needs. While archaeology has tended to only use two techniques, however, a mature research design should consider the use of multiple strategies – in line with archaeological need. Here there is a problem. We have very few examples of large-scale, multi-technology surveys that can be used as a guide to the value of such suggestions.

Once again the work at Wroxeter provides some guidance. Within this project participants have been asked to consider variations in strategies that will enable larger-scale interpretation to be made. A French team, led by Albert Hesse, have developed a new close-spacing resistivity technique that will cover 1ha in a day (http://www.bufau.bham.ac.uk/newsite/Projects/WH/Tours/crg.html and Fig 15.8). The results are encouraging, confirming many of the gradiometer anomalies.

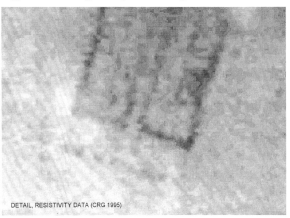

DETAIL, RESISTIVITY DATA (CRG 1995)

Fig 15.8 Detail of a stone building with portico at Wroxeter produced from automated resistivity survey

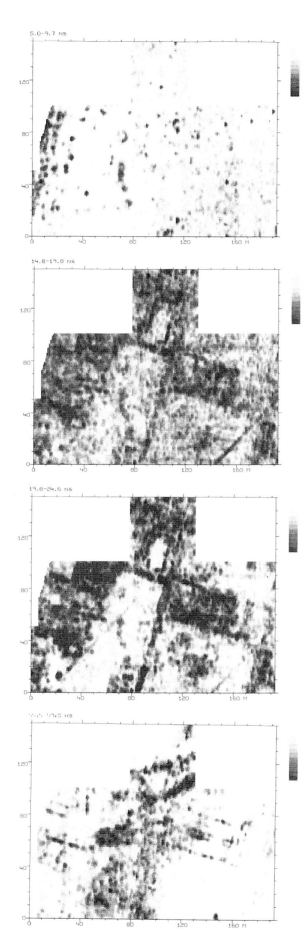

Fig 15.9 Time-sliced ground-probing radar data showing a stone structure at Wroxeter, Shropshire

Roger Walker of Geoscan has tried a different approach using a multiplexer system. This technique enables a suite of measurements to be taken, thereby assessing relative depths. A similar conceptual approach has been undertaken by Yasushi Nishimura and Dean Goodman (http://www.bufau.bham.ac.uk/newsite/Projects/WH/Tours/crg.html and Fig 15.9); they have resampled their vertical radar data sets to produce variations at different depths over a 3ha area. This is probably the largest survey of its kind ever attempted and yet only took four days in the field. Again, structural elements are clear. Alternative depth strategies have been evaluated using both electrical imaging and seismic studies by Geophysical Surveys of Bradford. In both cases understanding of the limitations of the techniques are now more advanced, which has helped identify their role within the project.

It should be emphasised that having moved into the domain of multi-technique survey, such work can only be attempted following development of commercial computer software, particularly relating to image processing and geographical information systems, along with the decreasing cost of hardware and mass storage. Despite these advances much of the work at Wroxeter remains highly experimental, and here there is another major problem. Although there has been a considerable amount of experimental work on machine response to individual features, we still lack detailed published or synthetic data on the field results of many techniques. This does not refer to work carried out in ideal conditions in the laboratory, but to the response of individual techniques to the highly variable landscape within which we actually work. This is ironic given the amount of geophysical work undertaken in Britain, especially in the planning arena. In these situations there is, frankly, almost total dependance on the experience of the individual surveyor when interpreting results; there is a striking lack of any shared formal knowledge generated by the discipline.

There are a number of possible research avenues that may remedy this. Firstly, comprehensive analysis of past results may be undertaken; such data sets do exist (http://www.eng-h.gov.uk/SDB/). Formal technical and applied research agendas, however, must also be formulated and funded. Another, not necessarily alternative, strategy involves the use of experimental sites for future work, where machine response or processing algorithms can be tested. By 'experimental' we mean the provision of archaeological test sites for remote sensing research which possess a wide variety of superficial deposits and structures, and which include a range of geologies and soils.

Wroxeter could be considered such a site. It is permanently protected and the archaeological history is well known. It provides a range of feature types including deeply and shallow stratified features and already possesses one of the most comprehensive remote-sensed surveys of its kind. Crucially, the site is also large and partially explored. This means that we have the rare luxury of possessing a reasonable idea of the character of features on the site while still possessing the majority of the original archaeological features for comparison. Having a number of such sites on the research agenda would be a valuable resource for those archaeological geophysicists who are applying to research bodies for funding for work on novel techniques.

If, however, the technical developments of the last two decades mean that remote sensing is reaching the stage where it could attempt many of the landscape questions being posed by academic archaeologists, the truth still is that most ground-based survey is undertaken in the hurly-burly of developer funding, where often the most exacting task asked of the geophysicist is to predict the presence or absence of potential remains. The shift from applied geophysics in the pure academic domain toward developer-led applications was at a crucial time when techniques, technology, and methodology had changed rapidly. Ironically, the changes that allowed British geophysicists to participate within the agenda of PPG16 were also those that should have allowed them to have participated in mature research agendas, incorporating sophisticated use of multiple technologies in research at the landscape level.

In common with the rest of archaeology, there is considerable doubt about whether this crude, *ad hoc* accretion of geophysical data is satisfying our own archaeological agendas – at any level. If we believe that archaeological understanding is enhanced by contextual landscape analysis, then fieldwork must be carried out at an appropriate level. In most cases this will only be achieved through programmes that incorporate remote sensing as part of a balanced research strategy. This aim is unlikely to be achieved through the current funding structure as developer funding is not likely for such work. This is dramatically emphasised in the recent publication on archaeological assessment, *Planning for the past* (English Heritage 1996, particularly vol 3, 34–5), which does not consider geophysics to any significant extent.

It is also unfortunate that applied archaeological geophysics seems to fall between the remit of many academic funding bodies with the result that it has tended to be taken for granted as a straightforward field methodology. From a personal viewpoint we have to say that if it was not for the enthusiasm of the geophysical groups participating within the Wroxeter Project, and more recently for an exceptional grant from the Roman Research Trust it would be difficult to see how the Wroxeter survey could have been implemented.

Yet even with this support there are many key research areas that still need addressing at this and virtually every other site, and a few of these are summarised in Table 15.1. Some of the problems are quite basic, reflecting the need for further research, but the solution of most would have considerable relevance to archaeologists operating in a wide variety of situations.

It is of course important to emphasise that some British projects at least are providing viable research agendas within which geophysics can participate, but we should be aware that the resources at our disposal are under utilised. We must strive to keep British archaeology at the forefront of both research and applied archaeogeophysics. It is an interesting fact that

Table 15.1 Primary technical problems at Wroxeter

problem	*observation*	*solution*
Depth estimation	Essential for deconstruction of complex sites and site management	Electrical pseudosection or radar work
Are 'blank' areas devoid of features?	Essential for demographic analysis etc	High sensitivity magnetometry
Are activity areas real?	Can we fully interpret the site without this information?	Integration of soil analysis
How real is the fire?	A good story but is it true?	Excavation or soil analysis
Are the results generally applicable?	We do not know enough about the geophysical responses elsewhere in Shropshire, nor beyond the county	Extensive research programmes of applied geophysics

a number of projects outside Britain, including some funded by British academic bodies, have been more responsive to the value of large-scale, directed use of geophysics within research programmes. For example, the British School at Rome's Tiber Valley Project includes a programme of remote sensing surveys of entire towns as part of its remit (http://britac3.britac. ac.uk/institutes/rome/archc.html). This bold move should be followed in Britain itself. However, the bottom line is not simply one of national pride. If we believe that remote sensed data has a real role within archaeological interpretation, or that landscape archaeology is worth carrying out, we have to consider the future role and funding of research and applied geophysics in detail. Archaeological geophysics must be integrated into the general domain of archaeological theory and problem solving. It has unique characteristics which will enhance our potential to understand the past, and mature research designs should reflect this. Single- or multiple-technique survey can lead as well as follow primary archaeological research. Roger Mercer (1985) once made a cogent and successful appeal for the development and implementation of analytical field surveys; unfortunately, geophysics seems to have been largely by-passed by such development. Clearly this clarion call must be repeated and extended to include remote sensing in its broadest sense. Without such an agenda it is extremely unlikely that we will achieve our broader academic aims.

Acknowledgments

The authors would like to thank the following individuals for their advice support and access to data during the writing of this paper: Dr A David, M Dawson, J Gater, Dr D Goodman, Dr A Hesse, P Linford, Y Nishimura, M van Leusen, Dr R White, and Dr R Walker. The authors acknowledge the crown copyright to the data from the Charlton site. Figures 15.8 and 15.9 are reproduced by permission of CNRS (Centre National pour la Recherche Scientifique) and Nara Cultural Properties Research Institute and the University of Miami, respectively.

Note

1 The Wroxeter Hinterland Project was granted NERC CASI hyperspectral data for exploratory analysis in 1995. Unfortunately, major technical problems at NERC resulted in non-delivery of the data during the three-year span of the project.

References

Aspinall, A, 1992 New developments in geophysical prospection, in *New developments in archaeological science* (ed A M Pollard), 233–244, Oxford

Atkinson, D, 1942 *Report on excavations at Wroxeter (the Roman city of Viroconium) in the county of Salop 1923–1927*, Oxford

Barker, P A (ed), 1990 *From Roman Viroconium to medieval Wroxeter*, Worcester

Barker, P A, White, R H, Pretty, K B, Bird, H, and Corbishley, M, 1997 *Wroxeter, Shropshire: excavations on the site of the baths basilica, 1965–90*, English Heritage Archaeological Report, **8**, London

Bonney, D J, 1976 Early boundaries and estates in southern England, in *English medieval settlement* (ed P H Sawyer), 41–51, London

Boucher, A R, 1996 Archaeological feedback in geophysics, *Archaeol Prospection*, **3**, 129–40

Corney, M, Gaffney, C F, and Gater, J A, 1994 Geophysical investigations at the Charlton villa, Wiltshire (England), *Archaeol Prospection*, **1**, 121–8

Dawson, M, and Gaffney, C F, 1995 The application of geophysical techniques within a planning application at Norse Road, Bedfordshire (England), *Archaeol Prospection* **2**, 103–15

DoE 1990 *Planning policy guidance note 16: archaeology and planning* [PPG16], London

English Heritage 1996 *Planning for the past*, London

Fulford, M, and Allen, M, 1992 Iron making at the Chesters Villa, Woolaston, Gloucestershire: survey and excavation 1987–91, *Britannia*, **25**, 175–211

Gaffney, C F, Gater, J A, and Ovenden, S M, 1991 *The use of geophysical techniques in archaeological evaluations*, IFA Technical Paper, **9**, Birmingham

Grove, R, 1991 Magnetic susceptibility and soil phosphate analysis of soils from the Bowsings site, Guiting Power, Gloucestershire, unpubl MSc thesis, Univ Bradford

Hill, J D, 1994 Why we should not take the data from Iron Age sites for granted: recent studies of intra-settlement patterning, in *The Iron Age in Wessex: recent work* (eds A FitzPatrick and E Morris), 4–9, Salisbury

—, 1995 *Ritual and rubbish in the Iron Age of Wessex: a study on the formation of a specific archaeological record*, BAR, **242**, Oxford

Hodder, I, 1986 *Reading the past: current approaches to interpretation in archaeology*, Cambridge

Howell, M, 1966 A soil conductivity meter, *Archaeometry*, **9**, 20–23

Kelly, M A, Dale, P, and Haigh, J G B, 1984 A microcomputer system for data logging in geophysical surveying, *Archaeometry*, **26**, 183–91

Lawrence, R, 1994 *Roman Pompeii: space and society*, London

Linford, N, 1994 Mineral magnetic profiling of archaeological sediments, *Archaeol Prospection*, **1**, 37–52

Mercer R, 1985 A view of British archaeological field survey, in *Archaeological field survey in Britain and abroad* (eds S Macready and F H Thompson), Soc Antiq London Occas Pap, n ser **6,** 8–24

Millett M, 1992 Rural integration in the West, in *Current research on Romanisation of the western provinces* (eds M Wood and F Queiroga), BAR, Suppl Ser, **575**, 1–8, Oxford

Payne, A, 1996 The use of magnetic prospection in the exploration of Iron Age hillfort interiors in southern England, *Archaeol Prospection*, **3**, 163–84

Powlesland, D, Lyall, J, and Donoghue, D, 1997 The application and integration of multi-sensor, non-invasive remote sensing techniques for the enhancement of the Sites and Monuments Record. Heslerton Parish Project, N Yorkshire, England, *Internet Archaeol*, **2**

Scollar, I, Tabbagh, A, Hesse, A, and Herzog, I, 1990 *Archaeological prospecting and remote sensing*, Cambridge

Sheen, N P, 1997 Interpretation of archaeological gradiometer data using a hybrid neural network, unpubl PhD thesis, Univ Bradford

Tilley, C, 1994 *A phenomenology of landscape: places, paths, and monuments*, Oxford

Tite, M S, and Linington, R E, 1986 The magnetic susceptibility of soils from central and southern Italy, *Prospezioni Archeologiche*, **10**, 25–36

Trow, S, Payne, A, David, A, Batchelor, D, Cunliffe, B, and Lock, G, 1996 Non-destructive assessment of the interiors of selected Wessex hillforts, unpubl project design

Weston, D, 1996 Soil science and the interpretation of archaeological sites: a soil survey and magnetic susceptibility of Altofts Henge, Normanton, West Yorkshire, *Archaeol Prospection*, **3**, 39–5

16 Ceramics and lithics: into the future

by David Peacock

Abstract

This paper compares the practice and potential of science (in its broadest sense) within the fields of ceramic and lithic studies, where past achievements and future needs are considered. It is argued that the study of pottery would benefit from a more rigorous application of quantitative methods. Stone is much neglected by comparison and here the concept of material vs surface is proposed. Each contains a different suite of information that can be elucidated by a combination of techniques of which one is the scientific characterisation of material. An integrated approach is advocated.

Introduction

In this contribution I would like to take stock of two of the most important types of find, pottery and stone. My objective is to assess the role currently played by archaeological science and to suggest new directions for the future. But science cannot stand alone – it must be seen in context and hence my comments will encompass more than just petrology, mineralogy, or chemistry. I will try to outline the way in which ceramic and lithic studies, as a whole, are developing.

Of the two areas of study there is no doubt that pottery is the senior. It has received the lions' share of attention and for decades has been regarded as a key focus of research in the late Iron Age and in the subsequent historic periods. Its traditional use as a dating medium has been augmented by an increasing use in the study of trade and exchange, on both a regional and interregional scale. The pots themselves may not have been inherently valuable, but because pottery survives it furnishes evidence of commercial currents or exchange mechanisms that may have been primarily concerned with more valuable commodities, many of which have a poor chance of survival in the archaeological record. It is also of value in assessing site function and in assessing levels of technological development. This broadening scope has lead to a greater interest in fabric and in quantification and it is these two facets which are the hallmark of the modern approach to pottery.

Ceramic studies

Ceramic studies are of two types. On the one hand there is the pottery report, the fundamental database for the study, and on the other hand there is the synthetic overview which seeks to analyse a particular ware or group of wares. Both involve, or should involve, archaeological science, but the nature of the involvement is, of necessity, different. The main objective of a pottery report is to convey the nature of the pottery as accurately as possible and in this careful scientific description of the fabric is as important as precise drawings to illustrate the typology. The former has always been a problem as I realised when I came to the subject from geology. It seemed to me that a pot was basically a sedimentary rock dynamically metamorphosed by the potters hand and thermally altered in the kiln. The basic scheme used by geologists in describing rocks should therefore be equally applicable to pottery. The approach that I suggested over 20 years ago seems to have stood the test of time although some of the parameters, such as the nature of the fracture, seem to be redundant. In recent years, however, there have been a number developments, funded by English Heritage, which seem to be particularly useful and auger well for the future. The first are a series of training courses on macroscopic approaches aimed at professional, largely archaeological unit, staff. We have now run four of these at Southampton: all were fully subscribed and the feedback from participants has been entirely positive. It is to be hoped that these will be a regular feature of the archaeological calendar. The other major innovation is the establishment of the National Roman Fabric reference collection, which will soon be accompanied by an invaluable handbook, written by Roberta Tomber and John Dore. All the major wares are carefully described, which means that in future, it will be unnecessary to reiterate this information, enabling a great saving of space to be made in pottery reports. Clearly, this initiative is to be welcomed and it is hoped that this approach will be widely emulated.

The general structure of pottery reports was established at the turn of this century by Bushe-Fox, and his method of presenting an illustrated catalogue gained popularity in the hands of workers such as Sir Mortimer Wheeler and Dame Kathleen Kenyon. The nature of pottery reports has changed very little since, which is rather disturbing because, surely by now, we should be witnessing some sort of evolution. The case for presenting page after page of pot profiles must weaken as the years go by and the old favourites appear time and time again. In samian studies, plain wares are not usually illustrated but simply referred to by their Dragendorff or other type numbers and we could now apply the same to the commonly traded coarse wares. The student wishing to reassess typology, would in any case have to resort to the original sherds as many pottery drawings are unreliable in detail, as I have found so often to my cost.

If data were to be presented in this way, it would open new possibilities for analysis and discussion. There would then be room to present the quantified data graphically and to undertake statistical analysis of trends and spatial distributions. The pottery report would become more analytical and would begin to address the questions which have always been the *raison d'être* of recording pottery. In scientific terms the need is for more, not less science, but perhaps with an increasing stress on computers and statistics. I am not suggesting that we should abandon traditional ways of doing things – new types always need illustration and description, but that we should be moving gradually and consciously towards the analytical pottery report, where graphs would be maximised and pot profiles minimised.

Other types of pottery work are not site-specific, but seek to examine individual wares and to interpret their distribution, usually in terms of trade. Some form of scientific analysis is usually mandatory unless the ware is unambiguous. The problem has always been that the analysis is usually structured around the techniques locally available rather than what is needed to solve the problem. The question should be one of ever increasing fineness of focus. We firstly examine the ware with the naked eye. If that fails, we use a binocular microscope. If there are still unresolved questions, we resort to thin sections and the petrological microscope; and if that fails to resolve the problem we use chemical analysis.

All too often, a sledge hammer is used to crack a nut, and what should be self-evident is proved by using expensive science. No names, no pack-drill, but one recent example, which involved an investment of £40,000, will suffice. Samples of this particular pottery were subjected to analysis using ICPS, which seemed to reveal a two types of chemical composition; but as this was uncertain, petrology was used as a back-up. There were indeed two petrological groups. Examination of the sherds, however, demonstrated that there were two macroscopically distinguishable types of ware. The analysis had merely demonstrated, at considerable cost, what could be seen by eye alone. This is an example of an Alice in Wonderland, through the looking-glass, back to front, approach.

The lesson is clear. Archaeometrical work needs to be part of a properly structured programme of investigation in which there is a progression from the simple to the more complex. On the other hand I hope we have now got away from what I call the 'bag of sherds syndrome', which all too often characterised early work on pottery. The scientist would be handed a bag of sherds from a locality, which he would then use to define the ceramic geochemistry of the site, without considering the possibility that some wares might be imported and others made locally. This practice may seem bizarre, but there are too many examples of it in archaeometrical literature published a decade or so ago.

Stone

Ceramic studies are basically alive, well, and flourishing, which is more than can be said for stone. Stone artefacts abound on archaeological sites, but seldom do they receive the attention they deserve. They are, after all, much easier to characterise than pottery and offer immense potential in the study of exchange, but they are of broader interest. In 1995/6 I was commissioned by English Heritage, to produce a report on the problems presented by stone artefacts and found them very much the Cinderella of the finds shed (Peacock forthcoming). As one unit director admitted, they had an unjustifiably low priority in his unit's work.

Stone, like pottery, is a natural material modified by human intervention, but there is a world of difference in the way the two materials are studied. There are lots of pottery specialists, but stone specialists seem to be geologists concerned only with identifying materials. Stone studies are about where pottery was half a century ago and there is an urgent need to develop this information resource.

Stone artefacts have two facets – the material and the surface – both of which contain information of different types. Material can inform us of origins and is hence important in assessing matters of trade and exchange. Most scientific work on stone focuses on characterising material and pinpointing origins and there is no doubt of the value of this work. At risk of appearing churlish, however, this is not enough. It is clear that we also need to consider the reasons for the choice of stone: what were the alternatives and why was that particular outcrop selected? In other words we need to consider the utilised material in relation to all similar outcrops.

A couple of examples will suffice. Recent work on the Neolithic axe factories of Great Langdale has demonstrated that while suitable material was widely available, it seems that rocks from the highest crags were preferred (Bradley and Edmonds 1993). Presumably the axes were perceived as having greater value because they came from a mountain top. Manufacture was not a matter of simple economics but seems to have been wrapped up in belief systems and other less tangible criteria. In a rather later period, something similar can be seen in the Roman exploitation of granodiorite in the Egyptian desert. I have argued elsewhere that the operation made no economic sense, because equally good rocks can be found in more accessible positions elsewhere (Peacock 1992). The rock seems to have been special because it came from the ends of the earth. It is only by considering alternative sources that we hope for cognitive insights.

An understanding of material also contributes to our understanding of style. Style is an amalgam of two determinants: material plus the cognitive processes of the stoneworker. Thus a sculptor working in granite will adopt different tools and methods than when working in marble. The two artefacts will differ in style because of the material.

On the other hand if we compare shepherd's cottages in the Pennines and, say, the Black Mountains, we have two structures which serve the same purpose and yet look totally different: they differ in style. The contrast is partly a result of the different properties of Flaggy Old Red Sandstone and massive Millstone grit, but part at least is due to the tradition and cultural background of the builders. If we are to understand a material we must assess its properties, not just the petrography and chemistry, but also its mechanical strength, jointing hardness, and general workability. If we could assess the geological constraints on style, we could, by a process of subtraction, get near to isolating cognitive and cultural parameters.

The concept of style is not just applicable to sculpture and architecture, since it also applies to portable artifacts, such as stone axes. Russell Coope (1979) long ago noted that finer rocks gave rise to slender axes, coarser ones to fatter ones. The picture is complicated by breakage and reuse, but the basic correlation between material and style is clear enough. It seems that coarser rocks are better worked by pecking with a point, finer ones by flaking, and that this contributes at least in part to stylistic differences.

The stone material is usually studied by geologists, stone surfaces by archaeologists, which is a pity because the two facets interrelate. Stone surfaces may have a wealth of information about the fashioning, use, and post-use history of the artefact. There may be evidence of quarrying and there will almost certainly be traces of the technology of fashioning. This has been little studied, but there is no excuse because Bessac (1986), a French stoneworker, has produced an exemplary guide to the traces his tools will leave on the stone surface.

There will also be evidence of use and use-wear studies are a well established branch of science. They have been applied largely to flint, but there is a need for them to be applied to a wider range of material. For example, many querns show asymmetric wear, which seems to be due to the way in which they were used. It could be that asymmetric wear results from to and fro motion perhaps as the quern handle is passed from one woman to another. An understanding of this could bear on the social context in which querns were used. There may also be traces of grain in the cavities of a quern, which may tell of the types of corn grown, just as there may be traces of metal on the surface of a whetstone giving evidence of its use.

The surface may also have evidence of post-use exposure. Lichen growth can in some cases be indicative of age and the micromorphology of the surface might also reveal evidence of date. As far as I am aware, however, little work has been done on changes in the micro texture of stone surfaces, although this might be archaeologically revealing.

I suggest that stone artefacts are a vast repository of information and we have only just begun to exploit it. There is ample work for archaeologists and scientists for many decades to come.

References

Bessac, J-C, 1986 L'outillage traditionnel du tailleur de pierre de l'Antiquité à nos jours, Paris

Bradley, R, and Edmonds, M, 1993 Interpreting the axe trade, Cambridge

Coope, G R, 1979 The influence of geology on the manufacture of Neolithic and Bronze Age stone implements in the British Isles, in Stone axe studies (eds T Clough and W Cummins), CBA Res Rep, 23, 98–101, London

Peacock, D P S, 1992 Rome in the desert: a symbol of power, Southampton

—, forthcoming The archaeology of stone: a report for English Heritage, (completed 1995)

17 Metals and metalworking in the first millennium AD

by Justine Bayley

Abstract

Archaeometallurgy has developed to the point where the identification of processes is relatively routine, though problems do still remain. It has become a specialist discipline, generally with limited impact on the overall interpretation of archaeological sites. The way forward must be in the broader interpretation of assemblages and their contexts. Metalworking did not exist separately from the society in which it was practised so the focus should be on workshops and industries rather than individual finds.

From the late Iron Age onwards there is an intensification in the use of metals which is marked not only by an increase in the quantity but in the range of metals utilised. Procedures for metal analyses are now routine and large datasets are available for certain artefact types. It is clear from these that alloy selection was not random. The impact of this data on finds study, however, has been less dramatic than for earlier periods. What is needed is a series of archaeological hypotheses about metal resources, trade, and utilisation that can be tested; existing data may provide some answers but for many, further analyses will be necessary.

Introduction

Metals and metalworking technology should be studied together as there is a mutual interdependence. The properties of metals result from the metallurgical processes that were used to produce and work them, while the limited range of known processes restricted the metals and alloys that could be used. Despite this, one aspect or the other is normally the focus of attention though some of the examples below demonstrate the greater rewards that can come from a broader approach.

Although there are metallurgical innovations in the first millennium AD the craftsmen's conservatism is also a major theme; once a reliable technique had been developed it continued in use, sometimes for thousands of years. Metallurgy can therefore only supply a limited number of chronological markers in this period.

Metalworking

The development of archaeometallurgy as a separate archaeological discipline began in earnest with the publication of Ronnie Tylecote's *Metallurgy in archaeology* (1962). Since then he and many others have produced a wide range of papers and books on various aspects of the discipline but the research they report has not been

evenly divided by geographical area, period, or process. Much effort has gone into the origins of metallurgy, into metal extraction, and into the development of iron technology. More recently, there have been major advances in the understanding of non-ferrous metalworking in the first millennium AD (eg Bayley 1992), though these developments are almost all in the secondary working of metals rather than in metal extraction.

In general, the focus of archaeometallurgical work has been on identifying processes; this is now relatively routine, though problems do still remain. As examples, we now know that brass was manufactured in Britain as early as the mid first century AD (Bayley 1984), that mercury gilding was a third-century innovation (Lins and Oddy 1975), and that new iron-smelting technologies were introduced in both the Roman and Saxon periods (Tylecote 1986).

Questions about how metallurgical processes worked have also been tackled, and systematic replication experiments have suggested some answers – but also usually posed further questions. Good examples are Crew's iron smelting experiments (eg Crew 1991), and Notton's (1974) salt parting of gold from silver; the turquoise-glazed appearance of his replica crucibles helped in the identification of subsequently excavated archaeological finds (Bayley 1991a).

Metallurgists have thus been able to tell excavating archaeologists something about what was happening on their sites – for example, that a blacksmith was at work – but what has normally been missing is any discussion or interpretation of this information, other than at a technical level. More surprisingly perhaps, the archaeologists too have failed to make much use of the available data. Cleere (1982) noted that:

> It is a melancholy fact that industry, the centre of modern economy and society, has hitherto been given scant attention by archaeologists studying the Roman period. This is somewhat surprising, since the economic basis of much of Roman civilisation ... rests to a very large extent on the existence of large-scale industrial enterprises.

His point is nearly as true now as when it was written – and much the same can be said for the post-Roman period too.

I believe that the prime question that archaeometallurgists should now be addressing is how their data can best be used. There are technical details that need to be sorted out and debated at a specialist level, but by reassessing existing data and offering archaeological interpretations of it we will be helping archaeology make better use of our discipline and we will be reincorporating it into the mainstream. Interpretations are possible at both intra- and inter-site levels, though with rather different types of information emerging.

When dealing with single sites it is still necessary to identify what was going on; but attempts should be made to say where on site the metalworking was carried out, and whether it was continuous for the whole life of the settlement or restricted to particular periods in its occupation. Answers should be sought to questions such as: Who were the metalworkers? Who were their customers? and, Why was metalworking being carried out there and then? Most important of all, methods for quantifying the scale of the metallurgical operations need to be developed. If that can be done, assessments of their economic importance, both absolutely and relative to other crafts and industries, will become possible.

Some of the data needed to answer these sorts of questions are already collected by either the excavating archaeologist or the metallurgist. The main problem is that our present level of integration and interpretation usually fails to bring the different data together. Neither collaborator realises that the other needs their information; either can fail to make an 'obvious' interpretation because they lack the necessary background or, worse still, do not realise that they have the data to answer an unasked question. One way to take matters forward is by better collaboration and teamworking, which can perhaps best be described as a shared awareness of possibilities, at all stages of projects from planning, through excavation, to post-excavation analysis. Excavators need to be more explicit in the questions they ask – their expectations at the moment are very low – and metallurgists must explain the type of information they need if they are to answer these questions.

It is common in current archaeological practice for finds to be considered in isolation, and for them to be segregated by material. The evidence for a particular metallurgical process may include ceramic, stone, slag, and a variety of metallic components; for full interpretation these must be considered together. It is also essential that the finds' relationships to each other and to associated features are adequately recorded. A greater, shared awareness of the likely components of a workshop assemblage increases the chance of one being recognised, and with it the likelihood that its various components will be retrieved and studied together. If excavators know in advance what to look for, they are more likely to notice and record or retrieve it. As an example, recent excavations by the Museum of London Archaeology Service (MoLAS) in Borough High Street, Southwark discovered two blacksmiths' workshops (Lynne Keys personal communication). The usual

quantities of smithing slag were found but, because the excavators knew what to look for, they also found localised deposits of hammer scale (the micro-slags produced by smithing) in and around some of the hearths they uncovered. The ironsmithing process could therefore be associated with the hearths and the structures within which they lay.

Some old excavations recorded most of the necessary information, but segregated the descriptions of finds and features, leading to only a basic level of interpretation. Frere's excavations in Insula XIV at St Albans can be cited as an example of this. A large number of crucibles were found, and published as pottery (Frere 1972, fig 141). Only recently have the metals being melted or refined in the crucibles been identified, and they were far more varied than had been supposed (Bayley 1991b). Plans of several phases of the shops/workshops were published and reconstructions of these buildings were made (Frere 1972, fig 5), but more information – on tools and metal artefacts and waste – was also published and this too could have been used.

Figure 17.1 is an attempt at a more detailed reconstruction using all this information, which also suggests answers to some of the questions asked above. The gaps in knowledge are more obvious in pictures than in words, as leaving a blank space in a picture is not an option. Not all the details are right, but by trying to make a drawing of this type one begins to realise what types of information are needed.

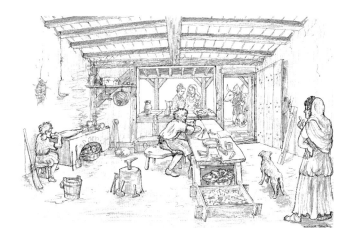

Fig 17.1 Reconstuction of a metal workshop, based on finds from insula XIV at Verulamium

The problem of quantification is certainly a difficult one, but not completely intractable. What are needed are new methodologies that will address this question; in developing them a start will be made in providing answers. When Lamm (1980) wrote about the migration period workshop site at Helgö in Sweden, where brooches and other small copper alloy castings were produced, she made no attempt in this direction, though analysis of the finds was then only at a preliminary stage. The site was isolated, occupied at a single period, rich in finds, and was nearly completely excavated, so it should be possible to make some attempt at quantifying production, even if only in estimating a minimum number of castings. From an outsider's viewpoint, this appears a simpler case than those of partial excavations of deeply stratified, multi-period sites (which are common in Britain) and where redeposition and residuality complicate interpretation.

At a regional or national level there is now sufficient data to start questioning the correlations of type of metalworking with type or location of site. Taking the example of Roman tin and pewter working (Fig 17.2), it is perhaps not surprising that evidence for tin working concentrates in Cornwall where tin ores are found. The evidence for pewter working has a more widespread geographical distribution, however, though these lead–tin alloys were used only in the later Roman period. A possible explanation for the concentration of sites on the Mendips is that it is the nearest lead source

Fig 17.2 Distribution map of Roman tin (•) and pewter (+) working finds in England

100 km

to Cornwall, but it is more difficult to identify reasons for the relatively large scale of pewter working in East Anglia or east Yorkshire. The answers here are likely to be social or economic rather than technical ones.

At the other end of the scale, copper alloy working is nearly universal (Fig 17.3), with evidence for both wrought and cast metalworking from all types of settlements: forts, vici, towns, villas, roadside settlements, and farmsteads. Iron smithing, though not smelting, was equally widely distributed. This distribution could be interpreted as reflecting a DIY attitude to craftsmanship, or a universal need for copper alloy and iron objects that was satisfied by itinerant metalworkers. While either interpretation may be plausible for common, small objects, some special products were probably not widely manufactured.

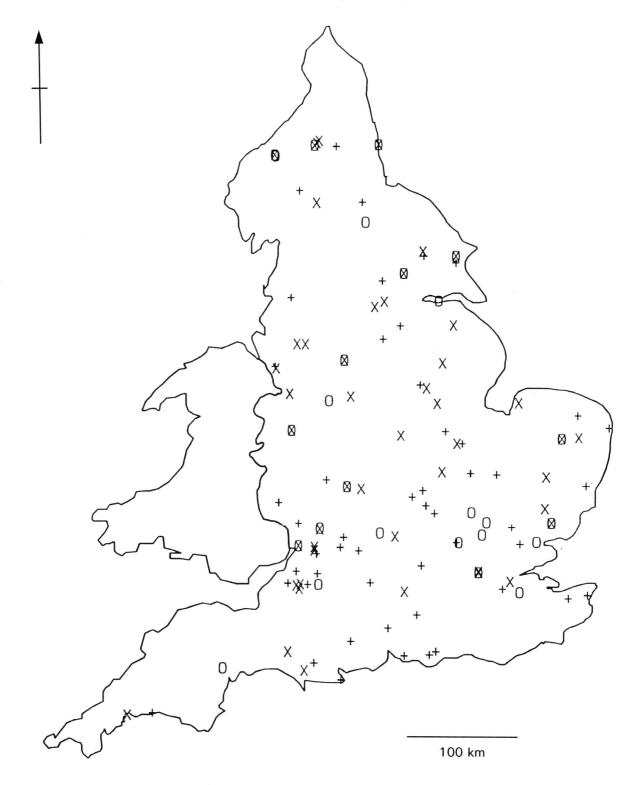

Fig 17.3 Distribution map of Roman copper alloy working finds in England: X = casting objects, 0 = wrought metalworking, + = non-specific metalworking

An example is enamelled vessels, which are thought to have been made in Roman Britain, but only because most types of them are more commonly found here than in continental Europe (Künzl 1995). A spectacular collection of nearly 1000 mould fragments from Castleford, Yorks had been used for casting flasks that were then enamelled (Bayley and Budd forthcoming), but the only known parallels for vessels of this type are metal objects from Nijmegen in the Netherlands, Istria in former Yugoslavia, and Spain. This is a warning against taking distribution maps at face value in trying to locate workshops, as they do not usually show negative evidence.

The Castleford finds lead back to the question of quantification, but from a rather different point of view. There are 15 different combinations of patterns on moulds for one shape of vessel, but only two of the examples noted above are of this form, neither of which have designs exactly paralleled on the moulds. The design on the third surviving vessel can be paralleled, but not its form.

This example demonstrates that present datasets are very partial ones. In more general terms, the gaps in our knowledge must not be used as a justification for further data-gathering at the expense of interpretation. It is possible to extrapolate from known facts with varying degrees of certainty. Hypotheses need to be formulated, and testing these models will give new impetus and direction to archaeological research.

Metals

In the Iron Age the main metals used were iron, some of which contained sufficient carbon that in modern terminology it is called steel, and bronze, by which I mean only the alloy of copper and tin. Bronze was deliberately made to a fairly constant recipe with an average of around 10% tin; there are hundreds of analyses that show this. Control over iron production was apparently less exact and parts of some blooms either accidentally or deliberately contained elevated carbon contents. It appears that this superior metal was recognised and selected for making tools where its properties would be advantageous; again there are hundreds of analyses, but far fewer detailed metallographic examinations that provide fuller information for iron objects.

Late in the Iron Age the range of metals in use began to expand. Torcs and coins were made of gold, silver, or more often mixtures of the two metals, sometimes with copper added too. Potin coins were cast from high-tin bronze and small numbers of lead objects began to be made.

For the Roman period there now are thousands of non-ferrous metal analyses, both qualitative and quantitative. Early analyses were undertaken to address basic questions about which metals or alloys were in use. They show that precious metals tended to be used alone rather than mixed, but that silver was often debased with copper or a copper alloy, whether in coinage or other objects. Tin on its own was occasionally used from the second century, while from the third century pewter (alloys of tin and lead in varying proportions) became relatively common. Lead was used in quantity for the first time; much of it for plumbing in buildings. The range of Roman copper alloys was far wider than in the Iron Age, with brass (an alloy of copper and zinc) appearing in the early mid first century AD, followed by leaded bronze before the end of the century; high-tin bronzes continued in use, but only for mirrors. Mixed copper alloys containing zinc, tin, and lead in varying amounts also appear, with increasing frequency, in later centuries. This trend continues into the early Saxon period; it is only from the eighth century that distinct alloys become dominant again.

A range of iron alloys continued in use. The number of analyses is relatively small so there is still uncertainty over the degree of control that Roman smiths exercised; certainly their combination of different iron alloys and use of heat treatment is rarely as sophisticated as that which developed in the post-Roman period when a far higher degree of craftsmanship is apparent, particularly in tools and weapons (eg Tylecote and Gilmour 1986).

The volume of analytical results, especially for copper alloys, means that it is now possible to pose, and answer, more complex questions than just identifying alloys. A large programme of analyses on Roman brooches (carried out at English Heritage's Ancient Monuments Laboratory) has shown correlations between typology, alloy composition, and date. This has allowed a reconsideration of likely areas of manufacture, which previously was based only on the distribution of finds; the example of the enamelled flasks quoted above has shown how inaccurate that can be. When compositional data is combined with information from metalworking finds such as moulds, it becomes possible to do more than speculate on the location and identification of the workshops that produced a particular type of object. As an example, a range of T-shaped brooches of first to second century date were thought to be made in south-west Britain. Analyses showed they were almost exclusively heavily leaded bronzes, confirming that they originated from a single metalworking tradition. One manufacturing site has now been identified at Compton Dando in the Mendips, with moulds for a range of different forms of this general type (Bayley 1985).

Another striking point to emerge from this analytical programme is the consistency of the metal used to make many types (Fig 17.4). Looking at Aucissa brooches, one of the brass types found in Britain in the mid first century AD, the cluster of analytical data is tight (Bayley 1990, table 1) (Fig 17.5). Many of these brooches were probably made in Gaul, where they are common in the half century or so before they appear in Britain. Recent analyses of visually identical objects from mid first century contexts in Israel, however, show that they have compositions within the same narrow range (Matthew Ponting personal communication). With data of this

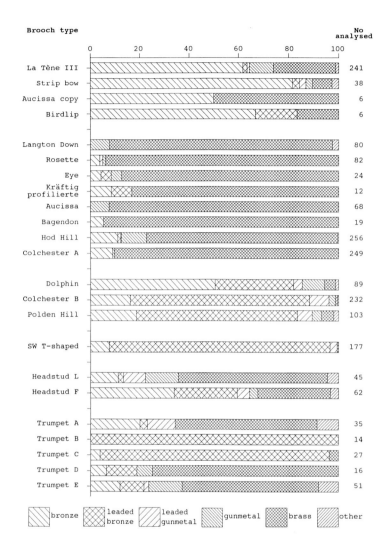

Fig 17.4 Histogram showing that many early Roman brooches have a preferred alloy composition

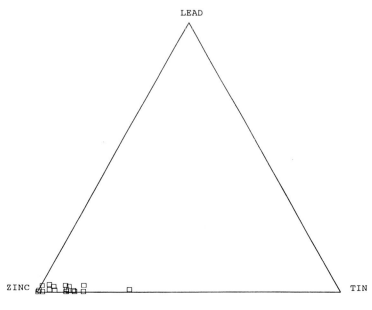

Fig 17.5 Ternary diagram showing the tight compositional cluster for British Aucissa brooches

type one can question whether the brooches were all made in only one or a small number of workshops, or whether they could have been manufactured more widely but from metal stock from a single source.

This degree of compositional consistency must lead one to question how this degree of control was exercised. Was it official or military, or just due to a merchant with a monopoly? In the early Roman period in Britain it is possible that there was centralised control or distribution of a suddenly enlarged, and probably largely imported, metal stock. But this is difficult to reconcile with the widely dispersed evidence for copper alloy working outlined above (cf Fig 17.3); this is the sort of issue where metals and metalworking have to be considered together, for to ignore part of the evidence can lead to fallacious conclusions.

Most of the existing interpretation of Roman and later compositional data has been at an alloy level; the extra information that trace element patterns and isotope ratios might provide has been discounted so far, mainly because of the belief that recycling was endemic by this period and so no patterning can be expected. If the early Roman period is one where there was an upsurge in the production of new metal, however, there must be a window of opportunity for using data of this type – provided that we can identify the new metal. The increasing incidence of mixed alloys through the Roman period and into the early Saxon period suggests increased levels of recycling of copper alloys. From about the eighth century, however, there appears to be a further influx of new metal, with brass again predominant; this represents a further period where trace element and/or isotope studies could be used to test hypotheses about metal sources.

When the question of metal usage over the whole of the first millennium is considered, there are both quantitative and qualitative changes that can be detected. It is generally accepted that in the late Iron Age there was some increase in the amount of metal in circulation, and that there were further increases after the Roman conquest. These increases were possible because of a number of factors, including technological change, trade, and craft specialisation – though whether they were the motor that drove the development, or the result of it, is less clear. It has already been argued that quantification of metalworking operations is desirable, and the same can be said for the volume of metal in circulation. The two are related and, if taken together, should help to clarify the relative importance of the factors facilitating or driving the upsurge in metal usage. The picture is less clear in the post-Roman period, though the evidence for recycling non-ferrous metals (above) suggests that little new metal was added to that in circulation until at least the middle Saxon period. The volume of ferrous metals probably also dropped.

The qualitative changes are more subtle and are only detectable by analysis, with alloys such as brass being common at one period and almost absent at others. The detail is less good for the post-Roman period as the total number of analyses are probably counted in hundreds rather than thousands. It could be that these changes in alloy usage are coincidences, but intuitively it is easier to believe that they are causally related to changes in socioeconomic conditions. The association of political upheaval with debasement of currency is generally accepted, but changes in the metals used for other objects also carry with them economic indicators, even if they cannot be as readily recognised. Changes in metal usage imply changes in the metal supply to a particular area. Reasons for these changes may not be obvious, but if they can be identified they have the potential to give us new insights into the economy of Roman and post-Roman Britain.

Metal analyses can contribute an added dimension to the conventional study of artefacts. Ideally finds researchers would like to know where objects were made, how they got to their findspot, and what they were used for. Metal analyses may not yet be able to provide specific answers to all these questions, but it is now possible to say that a group of objects were all made from the same basic metal, or from quite different metals – and so are probably from single or multiple sources.

As datasets of metal analyses increase in size, the sophistication of the social and economic questions they have the potential to answer will also increase. Rather than undertake more 'random' analyses, however, it is preferable to ask questions of our existing datasets and, if they are not yet answerable, make new analyses specifically to answer them. One reason that the potential of existing analyses is not fully realised is perhaps because the size of the datasets and the range of objects analysed is not well known; indeed many of the results are as yet unpublished. The analysts' apparent disinclination or lack of opportunity to ask socioeconomic questions of their data suggests that this is another area where a collaborative approach involving archaeologists, and historians too, is likely to maximise returns from past and future metal analyses.

Conclusions

This brief survey has outlined how far we have come, as well as pointing out some of the many possibilities where archaeometallurgy can contribute to answering wider archaeological questions.

I believe archaeometallurgists should in the short to medium term concentrate less on the details of metalworking processes but should instead learn to deal collaboratively with whole assemblages, and devise better ways to quantify the scale of metalworking operations; replication experiments may be one way to tackle the latter problem. They must, however, still be aware of new scientific techniques that may, in the longer term, prove able to answer presently intractable problems. In studying metals I believe more analytical data is needed, but specific questions must be posed before analyses are undertaken.

In order to maximise the information gain and increase knowledge, metallurgists and archaeologists must learn to work in even closer partnership than they now do. They must broaden their horizons, try to understand the conceptual frameworks in which both disciplines operate, and raise their expectations. The result should be that more potentially answerable questions are asked, and that means are found to address them.

Acknowledgements

I would like to thank David Starley and Roger Doonan for their comments on an earlier draft of this paper, and my father, Michael Bayley, for drawing Figure 17.1.

References

Bayley, J, 1984 Roman brass-making in Britain, *Hist Metall*, **18**, 42–3

—, 1985 Interim report on some clay moulds and associated finds from Compton Dando, Somerset, *Anc Mon Lab Rep* **4639**

—, 1990 The production of brass in antiquity with particular reference to Roman Britain, in *2000 years of zinc and brass* (ed P T Craddock), Brit Mus Occas Pap, **50**, 7–27, London

—, 1991a Archaeological evidence for parting, in *Archaeometry '90* (eds E Pernika and G A Wagner), 19–28, Basel

—, 1991b Analytical results for metal and glass-working crucibles from Frere's excavations at Verulamium, Herts, *Anc Mon Lab Rep* **68/91**

—, 1992 *Non-ferrous metalworking at 16–22 Coppergate*, The Archaeology of York, **17/7**, London

Bayley, J, and Budd, P, forthcoming The clay moulds, in *Excavations of Roman Castleford: 1974–85, volume 1: the finds* (ed H E M Cool)

Cleere, H, 1982 Industry in the Romano-British countryside, in *The Romano-British countryside* (ed D Miles), BAR, **103**, 123–35, Oxford

Crew, P, 1991 The experimental production of prehistoric bar iron, *Hist Metall*, **25**, 21–36

Frere, S S, 1972 *Verulamium excavations*, vol I, London

Lamm, K, 1980 Early medieval metalworking on Helgö in central Sweden, in *Aspects of early metallurgy* (ed W A Oddy), Brit Mus Occas Pap, **17**, 97–116, London

Lins, P A, and Oddy, W A, 1975 The origins of mercury gilding, *J Archaeol Sci*, **2**, 365–74

Künzl, E, 1995 Grossformatige Emailobjekte der römische Kaiserzeit, in *Acta of the 12th International Congress on Ancient Bronzes, Nijmegen 1992* (eds S T A M Mols, A M Gerhartl-Witteveen, H Kars, A Koster, W J T Peters, and W J H Willems), ROB Nederlandse Archeologische Rapporten, **18**, 39–49, Amersfoort

Notton, J H F, 1974 Ancient Egyptian gold refining: a reproduction of early techniques, *Gold Bull*, **7**, 50–56

Tylecote, R F, 1962 *Metallurgy in archaeology*, London

—, 1986 *The prehistory of metallurgy in the British Isles*, London

Tylecote, R F, and Gilmour, B J J, 1986 *The metallography of early ferrous edge tools and edged weapons*, BAR, **155**, Oxford

18 Medieval and later: composing an agenda

by Grenville Astill

Abstract

Most of the papers in session four of the Science in Archaeology conference contribute to general, socioeconomic questions that cut across the traditional boundaries of research, and so have yet to be adequately confronted. In order for these issues to be addressed, it is important to accept that we have to work with fragmentary primary data, and so a priority must be to develop appropriate methodologies. The medieval and post-medieval periods are critical in this methodological process because the existence of independent sources of information means that techniques can be formulated, refined, and validated.

Introduction

Any agenda for a better integration of archaeological and scientific methodologies should have at its heart a set of problems of mutual concern; I shall identify some of those that seem most pressing. In doing so I have tried to avoid falling into the trap of setting a specifically archaeological programme where scientific data would play a supporting role, much in the way that historic-period archaeology used to be regarded as the hand-maiden of history. Instead I have isolated specific themes that cut across the traditional boundaries of archaeological research.

Much of what I outline is dependent on the acquisition of more refined chronologies, and the application of 'low-technology' techniques to the point where the results might be regarded as convincing (Tite 1991). The existing archaeological database has a significant scientific component but is unsystematic and essentially anecdotal. I am still puzzled by the way that particular scientific techniques are employed only for specific periods whereas they potentially have a general application. And historic periods often miss out on the full range of scientific support.

One of the points I want to make in this review is that a major benefit of working in the historic periods is that independent information exists, which could be used to check, refine, and validate existing scientific methodologies. It is important to discriminate between this approach and one which is driven by other disciplines, which has happened all too frequently in the past. Neither archaeological nor scientific data duplicate information that already exists – they give us independent and different evidence about past societies. The consistent use of appropriate techniques over the major

periods would also allow comparisons to be made, and changes to be charted, over long periods of time, which is what we are always being told archaeology is good at doing. I am also puzzled by the lack of consistency in the questions being asked of different data sets. For example, why are issues of nutrition, diet, disease, growth, and life expectancy not more often approached in a consistent way for both the animal and human populations?

My themes have been chosen not only because they have a relevance for most of the millennium between 700 and 1700, but also because they have the potential for contributing to more traditional archaeological problems such as the chronology, character, and pace of social and economic change. Archaeologists often do not realise that many basic issues for this period have generated much debate, but are still unresolved. If one had to summarise the most distinctive, one might choose the development of complex national states, combined with an institutionalised religion, and the phenomenon of industrialisation, associated with increasingly aggressive trading societies, which found themselves on the threshold of colonisation. The wealth necessary to support such an infrastructure was based on a period of unprecedented urbanisation and of intense social stratification, which led to a fundamental change in the basis of economic organisation, a transition from feudalism to capitalism. But this depiction is very much a 'view from above', and it is perhaps more important to consider how such complex societies were supported in terms of production and the population, including the latter's attitudes and mentalities.

Much of what I discuss starts with the period from the fourteenth to the sixteenth centuries. This is not just because it is a 'bridge' between two artificially defined periods, the medieval and post-medieval, but because we know from historical data that it is a period of profound economic, social, and demographic change, the consequences and causes of which are still debated. It is therefore a time when change should be more easily identified and perhaps explained, and thus it has a relevance to all periods of the past (Gaimster and Stamper 1997). I have chosen to direct attention to rural issues: in doing so I am conscious that urban matters will seem neglected, although the urban dimension to the other themes, of population, buildings, and industry cannot be overestimated.

One of the underlying issues in this review is the potentially productive tension between the different geographical levels of explanation. On the one hand, we have the more established approach of seeking explanation for change through country-wide, even continental-wide, social and economic explanations, and we are particularly aware of the continental influence from increased trading and cultural transfers during the sixteenth and seventeenth centuries. On the other hand, there is the more recent attempt to see the locality or region as the essential crucible of change: this emphasises the importance of endogenous events and allows us to see the impact of communities and individuals on their own mental and physical environment.

Rural issues

The best known attempts to cut across traditional boundaries are concerned with the reconstruction of the rural landscape. When I reviewed the state of research on medieval rural settlement studies in 1993, I argued that, as the study was so influenced, if not dominated, by ideas from other disciplines, it was time to give the environmentalists a turn in order to concentrate on the study of land use rather than settlement (Astill 1993). I was, of course, naive in my proposals because I had not realised how difficult it would be to achieve a satisfactory cooperation; this is because most of our archaeological ideas and data relate to arable core areas, which do not often attract environmentalists.

Our experiences on the East Brittany Survey were also salutary. This survey was designed to elucidate (among other things) changes in land use over the last two millennia in a region of neutral to weakly acid soils, currently being farmed intensively, with few areas where there was good preservation of environmental material: it was, in other words, similar to large areas of cereal-growing Europe. There was, however, good documentary evidence for land use in the ninth century AD and from the fifteenth to twentieth century, and some of it could be fairly precisely localised. Yet the environmental evidence was not sufficiently intrinsically interesting to attract palynologists, because the pollen preservation was too variable and too much needed to be dated scientifically.

So we did not pursue environmental analyses. Instead, we exploited the archive data, and the extremely detailed land use information on the early nineteenth-century *cadastres*, together with the fieldwalking and excavation record to produce a surprisingly detailed picture of the continuity and change of land use over 200km^2 between the thirteenth and the nineteenth centuries. It was a picture that could not have been produced without the interaction between the two data sets (Davies and Astill 1994, 266–9; Astill and Davies 1997, 10–32). But the problem remains: when are we going to get to grips with poor pollen preservation? If we do not, we will never have an extensive environmental record for intensively cultivated, long-used lands. Can a methodology be devised to cope with poor zonation and fragmentary

remains? How sensitive is pollen analysis to relatively short phases of different land use? Can the deficiencies of the pollen sequences be offset by a combined sedimentological, micromorphological, and palynological approach? Could the results be compared with, or verified by, the archive land use data? The need to address the preservation problems was signalled in a review over ten years ago but, as far as I am aware, little methodological progress has been made (Balaam and Scaife 1987).

A bias against an extensive botanical record for the historic periods thus continues to exist. Most information comes from macrofossils, especially carbonised cereals, which really give us a local picture, but the wider view is also necessary (Carruthers 1993). One possible way forward is illustrated in the Ystad project in southern Sweden, where microfossil evidence, a liberal use of scientific dating, archaeological fieldwork and prospection, and detailed land use maps (from the seventeenth century, none of which cover the whole area) have been brought together to chart land use and settlement from the mesolithic to the twentieth century.

While one could question particular aspects of the strategy, what is impressive is the breadth of approach, the determination to treat each period as consistently as possible, while at the same time bringing out the quality of data sets particular to some periods. The willingness to exploit each data set to the full, and to extrapolate from limited information, is justified and supported by reference to other information. What comes over is the critical importance of the post-medieval changes, not only for the appearance and farming regimes of the contemporary landscape, but more importantly for validating methodologies for earlier periods (Berglund 1991).

Nucleation

What problems could be addressed if we were to try an integrated approach to land use and settlement? We might be able to say something about the relationship between the two, land use and settlement, which we have signally failed to do so far in a satisfying way. Settlement studies are still dominated by the quest for the origin and date of nucleation. Explanations for nucleation remain at a rudimentary level. So, it is argued, nucleation was the result of external stimuli, such as the growing demands of a centralised state, or urbanisation, or increasing aristocratic control of rural society. Or, the cause was internal pressures, where the intensification of cereal production had failed to match population growth, and any future increase in productivity or rationalisation of resources could only be achieved by a radical reordering of settlements and fields: the development of the mature forms of the open field system is usually associated with village creation

(Lewis *et al* 1997, 10–30 for a recent summary). The fact that nucleation occurs from the ninth to the twelfth centuries at least would suggest that it was a complex and drawn-out process that cannot be laid solely at the door of any of the above, more short-term, explanations.

Intensification must have been achieved at a community level. Nucleation may have been only one of many solutions that were available to a rural community in the face of increasing scarcity. The decision to go for a reallotment of resources, which nucleation implies, was influenced by the internal dynamics of agricultural communities, their perception of what solutions were available, and their relative effectiveness. A discussion, in terms of whether lords or peasants were the agents of change, has already started (Dyer 1985; Harvey 1989). To refocus the problem at a community, or even family, level means we could chart the fluctuating land use–settlement relationships from an archaeological point of view, which would be of relevance for the entire historic period, get us away from villages, and allow us to consider the more theoretical issue of collective agency.

Regions and specialisation

When and how the country developed distinctive regional characteristics is a related issue. Did land use strategies determine the variables that made a region distinctive, whether they be tenure, settlement pattern, town distribution and density, the relative proportion of arable/pastoral/industrial land use or the production of specialised commodities?

Marginal lands have now been rehabilitated as regions with distinctive economies that operated independently of, and faired better in the later Middle Ages than, the core, cereal producing areas (Bailey 1989; Dyer 1989). Their rehabilitation is, however, largely based on documentary evidence, and the impact of environmental and archaeological data would almost certainly change our perceptions of the distinctiveness of regions. One example concerns the 'multiple estate', the documentary model that dominates our view of how land was organised between the seventh and tenth centuries.

One aspect of the multiple estate that has attracted attention is its composition of federated areas, which grew specialised products most suited to the prevailing conditions, and which were coordinated from a central place. The sparse macrobotanic record does not always support this model of specialisation (Hinton 1994, 38), and raises the possibility that the charters merely specified as rent one of the many products that were produced, thus giving a spurious impression of agricultural specialisation. It is crucial to pursue this theme because it affects our perception of how the early medieval countryside was organised. Yet, from at least the twelfth century it appears that most regions of England were geared to cereal production and that the conditions (of a high population regime and an active market) were unsuitable for specialisation. While there was clearly scope for diversification in cereal production, our information is essentially archival and so far little independent information exists.

When does increasing specialisation start to occur? An appropriate historical context would be from the later fourteenth century, after the country had suffered a dramatic reduction in population. The shift from arable to pastoral farming in the former arable core areas can be seen as a response to the changed demographic conditions, and also the protein element of the medieval diet was increasing, all of which favoured pastoral farming, but of a type that was geared to producing meat and not multi-purpose animals (sheep being the exception). In these circumstances particular types of grain may have been confined to those areas most suited for their growth. Given the premium on labour-saving agricultural strategies, some regions may well have chosen to develop industrial products.

Specialisation and technological innovation

The interaction between specialised production and technological innovation should also concern us. Research on agricultural technologies has changed direction. Attention has shifted from 'agricultural revolutions' that were achieved on the back of inventions to a more gradualist view whereby significant changes in agricultural productivity were achieved by small-scale, incremental change; innovatory practices could occur in 'packages' or 'complexes' whereby pre-existing techniques were brought together in a new combination which was suited to contemporary needs (eg a greater emphasis on either labour-saving or labour-using techniques).

Physical evidence has made little impact on this area so far. Discussions have centred on which cereals were grown, sowing rates, weed control, rotations, inhoking (the temporary enclosure of fallow land for cultivation), and folding as examples of small-scale, but significant, changes. But there is little on the introduction of new types of cereal or indeed the prevalence or control of diseases, or changes in the processing or storage of grains (Astill and Langdon 1997).

The same state of research is true of animal management. What are the archaeological correlates of an animal husbandry that changes to predominantly meat production? Is there a change in breeding patterns? Is there an attempt to alter conformation by selective breeding? Our best information seems to be for sheep, based on the survival of different types of wool staples from urban deposits (Ryder 1983; Walton 1991) When do we start to see the development of specific breeds?

Did the process of enclosure affect animal management, and how long did it take for a particular technique to have an impact? The kind of examples I have given here are normally associated with the later seventeenth and eighteenth centuries, but some of the changes have been found in sixteenth-century faunal assemblages, suggesting that there had been some earlier manipulation of the stock (Albarella and Davis 1994; Dobney *et al* [1996]).

If we are back-dating post-medieval changes, we have to ask what is happening in the medieval period? Why do changes suddenly occur in the sixteenth century without any early signs? Have we telescoped the evidence? Attempts were made at selective breeding throughout the Middle Ages, but there is little sign of change. Would we see the start of the process if we paid more attention to non-metric traits or genetic links, or indeed evidence of disease and its control, or evidence for animal housing. Periodically the animal population was heavily depleted, especially during the early fourteenth century – we know very little about the rates of recovery or the survival of diseases, or indeed the extent to which disease was tolerated.

Population

Medieval population is traditionally viewed from above. The overriding concerns are with macrodemographic developments, especially the size of the population, and their effects on the country's economy. It is useful to start here, however, and again to consider the fourteenth to sixteenth centuries. Using what is now regarded as a conservative estimate, the population probably fell from five or six million to about two and a half million. Recent studies would revise upwards the orthodox estimate of a reduction in population of between a third and a half to well over a half (Bolton 1996, 28). We are fairly sure that the series of epidemics that occurred, especially in 1348, 1360–2, and 1369–75, was largely responsible for this demographic plunge. But why did it take almost two hundred years for the population to recover? What caused this low-level stability, which perhaps only started to end in the 1520s?

England's experience was different from that of other parts of Europe, where the recovery happened at a faster rate. Most explanations use mortality-driven models, such as continuing outbreaks of plague and bad harvests, and are therefore essentially exogenous. But what kept fertility down; and are there other, perhaps endogenous, factors that caused such a pattern (eg Harvey 1993, 114)? Some scholars are experimenting with socioeconomic explanations, in particular the changes in the way society and work was organised. So the weakening of the lord–tenant relationship, the growth in the system of service, the increasing independent economic

activity of women, and greater mobility would all potentially contribute to keeping nuptiality down, as would the practice of postponing marriage until people felt economically secure (see Smith 1988 for the above). But what was the relationship between fertility and levels of real income? We also need to consider what it was about pre-Black Death society that maintained a high population – what was demographically positive about the servile relationship, for example, or was there a relatively disease-free environment?

There are, however, also signs of shorter-term fluctuations within what are generally regarded as major periods of demographic expansion or contraction. The mid- to late-twelfth century may have been a period of population decline, for example (Smith 1988, 196). In addition, we have to remember that there are significant regional differences, especially in terms of when the maximum population was reached, and when the population started to recover in the later Middle Ages. These variations are sufficient to argue that blanket, institutional, or socioeconomic, explanations do not sufficiently explain these population changes.

We could aim for a greater input from archaeological and scientific data. We could think in terms of the 'quality' of the population in terms of its productive capabilities and its reproductive efficiency (Smith 1988, 188). In other words, we would need to consider the population not in terms of crude numbers, but to confront such issues as health and nutrition and how these were related to living conditions. Again, it would be necessary to cut across traditional areas of study and to construct a research agenda that incorporates a 'bio-cultural' approach (Roberts and Manchester 1995, 10–14, 196–7).

The revival of interest in medical history, for example, is a case where archaeology has made relatively little impact. But clearly the potential is there, most obviously from the analysis of skeletal material; but it does, however, require scientific programmes to date burial sequences. The critical importance of the post-medieval material in helping to improve and validate existing methodologies is illustrated by the Spitalfields and Barton on Humber projects (Molleson and Cox 1993; Reeve and Adams 1993).

Diet

Dietary historians tell us that major changes took place in the late medieval period (Dyer 1989, 55–71, 151–60). For the majority of the population there was an increased consumption of wheat (as opposed to other grains), of ale, and also of animal protein. There were important side effects: cooking methods changed; baking and roasting were preferred to boiling, reflecting the increased consumption of wheat and younger animals.

The oven became a common feature in houses. Fresh meat and fish were preferred, leading to a decline in the consumption of bacon and preserved fish. Ale consumption could only be satisfied by specialised ale houses. These trends are regarded as generally representing an improvement in peasant diet, in the sense that the cereal-dominated diet, supplemented by some dairy products and vegetables, was 'balanced' by a greater consumption of animal protein. Peasant diet was still, however, dominated by geographical and seasonal variations in a way that the aristocracy's was not. Noble diet did not change so radically: there was still a limited consumption of dairy products and fruit and vegetables. Medieval dietary theory distrusted green stuff.

What effect did this dietary shift have on the demography? Could it have affected resistance to disease, stature, life expectancy, or even fertility? If this were the case, would it have been socially selective with peasants becoming more fecund than nobles. The work needs to be extended into the sixteenth and seventeenth centuries and beyond, for there is – at present very slight – evidence for a deterioration in stature and an increase in disease (see Mays, this volume). Related issues such as hygiene and pollution need to be investigated (Waldron 1989). At present most of our information about quality of water and living conditions comes from sites with good preservation of fish bones, diatoms and insect fauna – which means organic urban deposits (Addyman 1989; Kenward and Allison 1994). As with the pollen data, can we make headway with the analysis of (normal) fragmented remains and tackle non-urban environments? Otherwise we cannot really discuss biocultural differences between urban and rural environments (but see Brothwell 1994; Mays, this volume).

Disease

We also need to consider the incidence and nature of disease (Manchester 1987; 1992). The challenge is to explain why diseases appear at particular times and decline at others: what conditions in Late Saxon England fostered rheumatoid arthritis and why did leprosy apparently disappear by the sixteenth century; and was this related to the increase of tuberculosis (Manchester and Roberts 1989; Rogers 1980)? Tuberculosis also reminds us of the importance of investigating human–animal relations, and the extent to which some diseases spread because of the relationship. We also need to acknowledge that there was a social dimension to some diseases, especially if the diseases were related to diet. The occupational disease DISH (diffuse idiopathic skeletal hyperostosis) is one such possibility (Waldron 1985).

A further social dimension would be to consider to what extent disease was tolerated or indeed ignored.

At present the best evidence we have concerns leprosy, but we need to broaden our enquiry and start designing research projects to recognise changing attitudes to disability, age, ethnicity, and gender, and the extent to which such attitudes were socially and/or biologically determined. Did any of these characteristics involve a predisposition to disease? This may seem a long way from osteological evidence, but I have found the only people so far to raise such issues as attitudes to disability have been palaeopathologists.

Such issues are relevant to all periods. We know, for example, that there was another long period of demographic stability in the seventeenth century, and this should be susceptible to such an enquiry as long as we realise the potential of the archaeological and scientific contributions. And when we have tapped the potential of working in periods with alternative sources of data, we might tackle another big problem, and that is the shape of the demographic profile between the third century AD, with its estimated population of five million, and Domesday, with an (?under-) estimated population of about two and a half million. I have chosen these examples deliberately because they all start off with the problem of numbers, but it is likely that they cannot be solved by blanket, country-wide, demographic explanations.

Buildings

The study of buildings has recently made a number of methodological breakthroughs, and this has brought it into the mainstream of archaeological enquiry. The study of vernacular buildings is now well established and structural surveys combined with dendrochronology have set new standards of recording and interpretation, for example in Kent or the east midlands (Pearson 1994). One of the most important effects of this work has been to make obsolescent the idea of a 'vernacular threshold' (Wrathmell 1989).

The demonstration that there was no significant difference between excavated evidence of buildings and the earliest standing structures made it unnecessary to argue for a missing link in building development. Indeed recent dendrochronological programmes are increasing our stock of medieval vernacular buildings and confirming the high standard of late medieval building techniques. Another important change in perspective has been to study buildings not only in terms of their structure, but also to try to place them in the context of their physical surroundings, and more importantly, of the people who lived in them. This approach tries to incorporate the study of buildings into a methodology that attempts to reconstruct regional mentalities and socioeconomic structure (Johnson 1993a). Research into regional 'traditions' has for long been regarded as a priority, but we need a refined chronology for the currency of distinctive constructional features, and the date of major alterations.

Such a dating programme also needs to include building materials, especially some of the most common; for example, characterising and dating brickwork, various sandstones, and, of course, mortars are important. The critical importance of reconstructing sources for stone, technologies of extraction, and methods of dissemination should be obvious (Parsons 1990; Peacock, this volume). The question remains, however, when do these existing and future techniques fail to be useful? Why are these techniques so rarely applied to late medieval or post-medieval buildings? In a sense the answer may be that our interest in technologies has traditionally centred on production sites rather than on consumption sites. Why cannot industrial technologies be investigated more often through the fittings of buildings, especially as the survival of organic materials is often fairly high? This would form an essential background to a consideration of patterns of consumption and how these vary from house to house. It would be a way of making our material culture work for us in a way that does not often happen today.

Most medieval and post-medieval excavation reports fail to exploit the small finds data sufficiently, particularly in relation to the structural evidence – the information lies inert in the catalogues, untouched by the intellectual effort of synthesis. It is also curious that for the last decade there has been growing research by European and North American social and economic historians into material culture because it is a way of investigating consumption patterns, lifestyle, and standards of living (Schuurman and Walsh 1994a). As far as I am aware, this research only exploits the information in probate inventories and rarely acknowledges, let alone uses, the archaeological material. This leads to curious statements, such as 'while we know quite a lot about the material culture in England around 1700, we know almost nothing about the second half of the eighteenth century' (Schuurman and Walsh 1994b, 16).

Dendrochronological dating programmes are also producing significant secondary information about, for example, woodland management and the identification of 'reduced felling or no-building' periods, which would considerably extend building history in this country (Baillie 1995, 122–8). The use of dendrochronology to identify the Little Ice Age of the sixteenth to seventeenth centuries or the warming of the later Saxon period could well put the climate debate on a surer and more sophisticated footing.

Alongside an essentially contextual approach to building data, we have to take account of extra-regional changes. Considering we are still discussing (40 years

on) whether Hoskins' theory of a Great Rebuilding helps or hinders the interpretation of sixteenth- and seventeenth-century history, it is perhaps surprising that we now have doubled our Great Rebuildings. The first has been developed to describe the spate of rebuilding churches in stone between the mid-tenth and early twelfth centuries (Morris 1989, 165–7). The rebuilding appears to have taken place in most parts of the country and, what is more, to a remarkably consistent plan and style. How were particular architectural ideas disseminated and why were so many communities receptive to such a change (Gem 1988)?

The departure from the timber-building tradition clearly raises important questions about where the masons came from, how they were trained, and where they obtained their raw materials at a time when a substantial number of cathedrals and castles were also being constructed. With the second, Hoskins', Great Rebuilding, the debate has focused on the geographical extent and timing of this reconstruction of vernacular buildings, and the extent to which this is directly related to the macroeconomic and social changes of 'Tawney's century'. But the questions about the dissemination and the acceptability of such a consistent architectural change still need to be pursued (Johnson 1993b).

Industry

A further theme worth pursuing concerns the organisation, characterisation, and social context of industrial processes. It is worth remembering, however, that the archaeological impact has been negligible on the study of the largest medieval and post-medieval industry: the textile industry, especially woollen cloth production. Yet the increasing recovery of textile fragments from organic (usually urban) deposits is making a major contribution to our knowledge about textile production. It is now possible to suggest periods when textile making changed – for example, in the eleventh and fourteenth centuries – which caused important implications for weaving technology (Crowfoot et al 1992, 15–25; Walton 1991). It is another example of the value of looking at areas of consumption rather than production.

But I wish to concentrate on the organisation of metalworking. In terms of basic identification, how close are we to characterising the sources of metal ores, especially of iron, and would it be possible to detect a high degree of recycling? We also need to know more about the intermediate processes between smelting and smithing. How and where were the smelted blooms worked to produce billets, the form in which iron was received by the smith? What particularities of the process would make it archaeologically visible? It would also be instructive to know what are the archaeological correlates of the apparent shift in the mid-thirteenth century from smelting tin ore twice to smelting it once (Greeves 1981). One of the characteristics of eleventh- to twelfth-century urban metalworking sites is that a variety of metals were worked together. What advantages were gained from the interaction of different metalworking technologies, and why and under what circumstances did metalworking move apart or become separated after the twelfth century (Bayley 1992; Ottaway 1992)?

Demand

It is difficult to discuss the organisation of industries without some sense of demand for the products. Clearly some assessment of changes in the units of production would be useful. Evidence for a high level of demand for iron is contained in the orders for military equipment, which exist from the thirteenth century onwards. Could such commissions be met by a particularly intense session of iron production using existing estate arrangements (Hinton 1990, 155–6)? There is clearly a role for experimental archaeology here, as indeed there is in trying to replicate and explain scientifically those procedures discussed and identified as troublesome by early commentators on metalworking. Sporadic demand may have been met within a part-time arrangement where metalworking could be accommodated within an agricultural regime. The environmental impact of metal extraction in particular could be great but may have been limited by its disturbance to farmland: this was a particular danger in the case of working alluvial tin deposits (Austin *et al* 1989).

There is also the question of fuel supplies. Most metalworking is assumed to have been dependent on coppiced woodland; again the units of production may have been kept small and worked to order so that fuel supplies were not over exploited. Furnaces may even have been located near different wood stands and used according to which stand had reached cutting stage in the coppicing cycle.

The increased production of iron using larger furnaces in areas such as the Weald from the sixteenth century must have been underpinned by adequate wood supplies. Is there evidence for more intensive coppicing and more land being converted to woods? How was the competition for fuel between the iron and glass industries, with their different demands on woodland, reconciled? Patterns of landholding are clearly crucial here, and this type of production may well have been concentrated in the hands of ironmasters who owned or who had leased extensive tracts of woodland (Crossley 1995).

Indeed it is important to consider the social specificity of metalworking and the extent to which the distribution of metals was controlled. The vast majority of metal-, glass-, and enamel-working areas found in middle and later Saxon England are found either on high-status sites (both secular and ecclesiastical) or within towns. The origin of urban industrial production may be related to a strong aristocratic presence in towns, which historians have now established (Fleming 1993). The aristocratic connection does not seem to go beyond the early twelfth century, when there is some sign of industrial contraction in towns and the absence of specialised production areas on high-status sites. The increase in the level of trade through the development of the market from the later twelfth century did not necessarily mean that industry responded by changing its organisation or level of production.

To take one example, it is extremely difficult to find evidence of medieval smithies in the archaeological record, partly because the traditional criteria used to identify such sites – such as industrial residues or iron-working tools or blanks – occur in such small quantities that this slight evidence has to be corroborated with clear structural evidence. This situation flies in the face of the common assumption that the blacksmith was one of the most frequently documented and revered members of the rural community. Clear evidence for village smithies does not occur in the archaeological record until the later fourteenth century. Was ironsmithing so unspecialised as to leave no trace until this time? This would certainly match the marked lack of specialised buildings excavated from village sites. Or do we need to rethink our criteria for identifying such sites? It is noticeable, however, that the only clear evidence for smithing sites occurs on castle, manor, and monastic sites, which raises the possibility that the working of iron ignored the general increase in marketing activity and was essentially an aristocratic monopoly (Astill 1995).

The adoption of waterpower for industry is little understood archaeologically, but the documentary evidence suggests that it was pioneered by monastic orders, largely for fulling, from the late twelfth century, although historians argue that demand for large quantities of cloth or metal products was so low that waterpower was only used for the processing of cereals (Holt 1988, 152–8). We may have to rethink the availability of iron at this time. The massive building programmes may have taken the lion's share, and caused a scarcity elsewhere, which may explain the occurrence of Roman and early Anglo-Saxon ironwork in eleventh- and twelfth-century hoards of scrap iron. Aristocratic control of metalworking is again evident in the sixteenth and seventeenth centuries, underpinned by monopolies granted to some families (Crossley 1990, 180–92).

The necessity to separate demand for a particular commodity from the evidence for a general increase in marketing activity should remind us that the nature of technological change is not necessarily geared to macroeconomic laws. Concepts of industrial technologies still seem to be dominated by a mentality of inventions. In some instances, this does appear to be the case, such as the blast furnace (in the late fifteenth century) or the more efficient form of glass furnace (in the mid-sixteenth century), both brought to this country by French immigrants. But, whereas we know the intrinsic importance of the development of the blast furnace, for example, the speed with which this method of iron-working was adopted in England was hardly rapid and was often dependent on the extent to which this technique of extracting iron could be grafted on to the existing methods (Crossley 1990, 156–62, 228–32). As with agricultural technologies, industrial change may have been achieved by small-scale, incremental change rather than by the introduction of inventions.

One of the characteristics of medieval and post-medieval industry is continuity of location, and a governing influence on the way technology developed may well have been the 'inherited landscape' (Clark 1995). In other words, the majority of innovations in industrial development may well have arisen as a result of adaptations rather than inventions. This would militate against any concept of a general 'transformation' of industry in the post-medieval period and would emphasise the importance of particular characteristics of 'place', which could be adapted to the needs of many different industrial processes.

Conclusion

There are a lot of questions here, and some no doubt will be regarded as impossible to answer – but only perhaps if we continue to develop our individual methodologies and theories in isolation. We also need to incorporate the historic periods into long-term thematic enquiries. But above all we must exploit, and not be scared by, the benefits of working on independently documented periods where we know that there was so much social and economic change.

References

Addyman, P, 1989 The archaeology of public health at York, England, *World Archaeol*, **21**, 244–64

Albarella, U, and Davis, S, 1994 Mammals and birds from Launceston Castle, Cornwall: decline in status and the rise of agriculture, *Circaea*, **12**, 1–156

Astill, G, 1993 The archaeology of the medieval countryside: a forty-year perspective from Britain, in *The study of medieval archaeology* (eds H Andersson and J Wienberg), Lund Studies in Medieval Archaeology, **13**, Stockholm

—, 1995 Medieval smithing in England: a review, in Magnusson 1995, 183–93

Astill, G, and Davies, W, 1997 *A Breton landscape*, London

Astill, G, and Langdon, J (eds), 1997 *Medieval farming and technology: the impact of agricultural change in northwest Europe*, Leiden

Aston, M, Austin, D, and Dyer, C (eds), 1989 *The rural settlements of medieval England*, Oxford

Austin, D, Gerrard, G, and Greeves, T, 1989 Tin and agriculture in the Middle Ages and beyond: landscape archaeology in St Neots parish, Cornwall, *Cornish Archaeol*, **28**, 5–251

Bailey, M, 1989 The concept of the margin in the medieval English economy, *Econ Hist Rev*, **42**, 1–17

Bayley, J, 1992 *Anglo-Scandinavian non-ferrous metalworking from 16–22 Coppergate*, Archaeol of York, **17/7**, London

Baillie, M, 1995 *A slice through time: dendrochronology and precision dating*, London

Balaam, N, and Scaife, R, 1987 Archaeological pollen analysis, in *Research priorities in archaeological science* (ed P Mellars), 7–10, London

Berglund, B (ed), 1991 *The cultural landscape during 6000 years in southern Sweden: the Ystad Project*, Ecological Bulletins, **41**, Copenhagen

Bolton, J, 1996 'The world upside down': plague as an agent of economic and social change, in *The Black Death in England* (eds M Ormrod and P Lindley), 17–78, Stamford

Brothwell, D, 1994 On the possibility of urban–rural contrasts in human population palaeobiology, in Hall and Kenward 1994, 129–36

Carruthers, W, 1993 A review of archaeobotanic research priorities, *Anc Mon Lab Rep*, **16/93**

Clark, C, 1995 Ticking boxes or telling stories?: the archaeology of the industrial landscape, in *Managing the industrial heritage* (eds M Palmer and P Neaverson), Leicester Archaeol Monogr, **2**, 45–8, Leicester

Crossley, D, 1990 *Post-medieval archaeology in Britain*, Leicester

—, 1995 The supply of charcoal to the blast furnace in Britain, in Magnusson, 367–74

Crowfoot, E, Pritchard, F, and Staniland, K, 1992 *Textiles and clothing* c 1150–c 1450, Medieval Finds Excav London, **4**, London

Davies, W, and Astill, G, 1994 *The east Brittany survey: fieldwork and field data*, Aldershot

Dobney, K, Jacques, D, and Irving, B, [1996] *Of butchers and breeds: report on the vertebrate remains from various sites in the city of Lincoln*, Lincoln Archaeol Stud, **5**, Lincoln

Dyer, C, 1985 Power and conflict in the medieval English village, in *Medieval villages: a review of current work* (ed D Hooke), 27–32, Oxford

—, 1989 'The retreat from marginal land': the growth and decline of medieval rural settlements, in Aston *et al* 1989, 45–58

Fleming, R, 1993 Rural elites and urban communities in late Saxon England, *Past Present*, **141**, 3–37

Gaimster, D, and Stamper, P, 1997 *The age of transition: the archaeology of English culture 1400–1600*, Oxford

Gem, R, 1988 The English parish church in the eleventh and early twelfth centuries: a great rebuilding?, in *Minsters and parish churches: the local church in transition, 950–1200* (ed J Blair), 21–30, Oxford

Greeves, T, 1981 The archaeological potential of the Devon tin industry, in *Medieval industry* (ed D Crossley), CBA Res Rep, **40**, 85–95, London

Hall, A R, and Kenward, H K (eds), 1994 *Urban–rural connexions: perspectives from environmental archaeology*, Symposia of the Association for Environmental Archaeology 12, Oxbow Monogr, **47**, Oxford

Harvey, B, 1993 *Living and dying in England, 1100–1540: the monastic experience*, Oxford

Harvey, P, 1989 Initiative and authority in settlement change, in Aston *et al* 1989, 31–44

Hinton, D, 1990 *Archaeology, economics, and society: England from the fifth to the fifteenth century*, London

—, 1994 The archaeology of eighth- to eleventh-century Wessex, in *The medieval landscape of Wessex* (eds M Aston and C Lewis), Oxbow Monogr, **46**, 33–46, Oxford

Holt, R, 1988 *The mills of medieval England*, Oxford

Johnson, M, 1993a *Housing culture: traditional architecture in an English landscape*, London

—, 1993b Rethinking the Great Rebuilding, *Oxford J Archaeol*, **12**, 117–25

Kenward, H, and Allison, E, 1994, Rural origins of the urban insect fauna, in Hall and Kenward 1994, 55–77

Lewis, C, Mitchell-Fox, P, and Dyer, C, 1997 *Village, hamlet, and field: changing medieval settlements in central England*, Manchester

Magnusson, G (ed), 1995 *The importance of ironmaking, technical innovation, and social change*, Jernkontorets Bergshistoriska Utskott, **H58**, Stockholm

Manchester, K, 1987 Skeletal evidence for health and disease, in *Death, decay, and reconstruction* (eds A Boddington, A Garland, and R Janaway), 163–79, Manchester

—, 1992, The palaeopathology of urban infections, in *Death in towns* (ed S Bassett), 8–15, Leicester

Manchester, K, and Roberts, C, 1989 The palaeopathology of leprosy in Britain: a review, *World Archaeol*, **21**, 265–72

Molleson, T, and Cox, M, 1993 *The Spitalfields project, volume 2: the anthropology – the middling sort*, CBA Res Rep, **86**, York

Morris, R, 1989 *Churches in the landscape*, London

Ottaway, P, 1992 *Anglo-Scandinavian ironwork from 16–22 Coppergate*, Archaeol of York, **17/6**, London

Parsons, D, 1990, Review and prospect: the stone industry in Roman, Anglo-Saxon and Medieval England, in *Stone quarrying and building in England, AD 43–1525* (ed D Parsons), 1–15, Chichester

Pearson, S, 1994 *The medieval houses of Kent: an historical analysis*, London

Reeve, J, and Adams, M, 1993 *The Spitalfields project, volume 1: the archaeology – across the Styx*, CBA Res Rep, **85**, York

Roberts, C, and Manchester, K, 1995, *The archaeology of disease*, 2 edn, Stroud

Rogers, J, 1980 Arthroses in some Saxon and medieval populations, *Palaeopathology Association, Third European Meeting*, 235–7

Ryder, M, 1983 *Sheep and man*, London

Schuurman, A, and Walsh, L (eds), 1994a *Material culture: consumption, life-style, standard of living, 1500–1900*, Proceedings of the Eleventh International Economic History Congress, Milan

—, 1994b Introduction, in Schuurman and Walsh 1994a, 7–18

Smith, R, 1988 Human resources, in *The countryside of medieval England* (eds G Astill and A Grant), 188–212, Oxford

Tite, M, 1991 Archaeological science: past achievements and future prospects, *Archaeometry*, **33**, 139–52

Waldron, T, 1985 DISH at Merton Priory: evidence for a 'new' occupational disease, *Brit Med J*, **291**, 1762–3

—, 1989 The effects of urbanisation on health: the evidence from skeletal remains, in *Diet and craft in towns: the evidence of animal remains from the Roman to the post-medieval periods* (eds D Serjeantson and T Waldron), BAR, **199**, 55–74, Oxford

Walton, P, 1991 Textiles, in *English medieval industries* (eds J Blair and N Ramsay), 319–54, London

Wrathmell, S, 1989 Peasant houses, farmsteads and villages in north-east England, in Aston *et al* 1989, 247–68

19 Continuity and change: environmental archaeology in historic periods

by Martin Bell and Petra Dark

Abstract

Environmental archaeologists have tended to focus their attention on prehistory, but there is an increasing amount of environmental information relating to historic periods also. This is of special importance because it provides the opportunity to 'calibrate' the environmental evidence against other sources, such as texts, maps, and instrumental records. Comparison of environmental and historical sources relies on chronological precision, an aspect discussed in relation to dendrochronology and radiocarbon dating. A focus of particular attention recently has been the nature of environmental changes at the beginning and end of the Roman period, especially whether there was continuity in land use. The principal technique for identifying environmental continuity and change is pollen analysis of off-site sequences of deposits, and this provides the basis for discussion of post-Roman landscape continuity, and other aspects of historic-period environments, such as the origins of 'ancient woodland'. Other sources of environmental evidence for historic periods are also considered, in relation to fields, farming practice, and gardens, and recommendations made for future research.

Introduction

It is the contention of this paper that the environments of the historic period deserve just as much attention from environmental archaeologists as those of prehistory, indeed sometimes they may deserve more. Environmental work from historic periods may have been seen as of lower priority because we have other sources of landscape data. We will argue a converse proposition, that other sources, historical, cartographic, pictorial, and instrumental, provide particular opportunities to test and refine methodology, interpretation, and conceptual approaches in environmental archaeology.

The proposition will be argued from two perspectives, illustrating different aspects of the interdisciplinary relationships of archaeology. On the one hand there is the interface with the environmental sciences; it will be argued that an understanding of historic period landscapes and biotic communities provides essential time depth for studies of contemporary environments. On the other hand there is the more specifically historical dimension, where our focus is on issues of continuity and change. This interfaces strongly with both history, historical geography and environmental science. There is, none the less, a need for a specifically

archaeological agenda, which has not always been sufficiently sharply focused and requires particular attention to issues of dating precision, drawing on new approaches to dating outlined by Bayliss (this volume).

Questions of continuity and change have tended to be tackled from the perspectives of art history, place names, and settlement pattern studies. Palaeoenvironmental evidence provides the opportunity for a contrasting perspective, a way of testing interpretations derived from other sources. This can be particularly important because so much of the archaeological record tends to be site specific, resting on generalisation from the particular site to the wider settlement pattern. Off-site environmental sequences can provide us with evidence for land use that is independent of the vicissitudes of individual settlements. The failure of some settlements does not necessarily imply the abandonment of associated agricultural landscapes, whether they be those of Romano-British villas, deserted medieval villages, or crumbling post-medieval mansions.

An additional, much broader, argument for giving adequate emphasis to historic-period environments concerns the interface with other environmental sciences. There is a complementarity between the retrogressive approach of the landscape archaeologist and the essentially uniformitarian reasoning of much environmental science. In the retrogressive approach the starting point is the present landscape, successively earlier elements being stripped away to reveal its earlier character. In environmental science our knowledge of living plant and animal communities and environmental processes provides a basis for interpreting those of the past. Retrogression and uniformitarianism have the logical strength of acknowledging that our encounter with the past is inevitably conditioned by how we experience the present.

This is not to disregard the problematic nature of uniformitarian assumptions. For social questions it is often an inappropriate approach, so much recent archaeological work has served to emphasise the differences between past and present societies. In environmental terms also, current work tends to emphasize dynamism and the frequent absence of long-term stability inherent in a concept such as climatic climax. Many environments have also been so altered by human agency that analogues for environments of the past may no longer survive. Understanding of an environment requires a degree of time depth, for instance to indicate its relative stability, or the timescale of episodic changes which are influential in determining its character. As a generalization, knowledge of environments is most precise in the

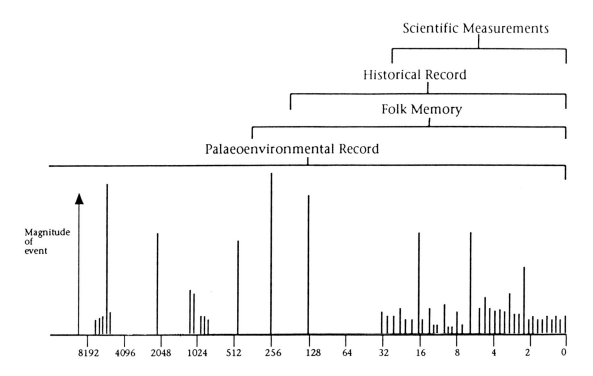

Fig 19.1 Hypothetical diagram to illustrate the relationship between different sources of environmental knowledge, event magnitude, and time, shown on the horizontal axis in years. The diagram highlights the significance of those recent periods for which various sources of knowledge overlap (after Bell 1992, fig 3.1)

present and tends to become increasingly patchy as one goes back in time (Fig 19.1) through the relatively brief period of instrumental records, oral history, and written history to prehistory.

It is argued that, in understanding long-term change, particular importance attaches to those recent periods in which a range of sources overlap. This is shown clearly by Keith Barber's palaeoclimatic sequences based on bog surface wetness curves, which are calibrated by early instrumental records. The top part of Bolton Fell Moss provides the evidence that validates the whole exercise in palaeoenvironmental reconstruction (eg Barber 1981; Barber *et al* 1994). Sadly, it is that part of the sequences which is most vulnerable to drainage, drying out, and loss.

Complementary datasets in historic periods also enable us to compare the physical and biological evidence for environmental change with written, pictorial, or oral sources relating to the perception of environmental change by human communities. This is a perspective little explored by archaeologists, but a brief mention of a few examples, which draw on both earth science and social perspectives, may serve to illustrate the potential. In terms of precisely defined and dated specific events there is the impact of volcanism on farming, which has been studied in such diverse contexts as Iceland (Thorarinsson 1979) and Papua New Guinea (Blong 1982). Flooding, another form of event, is illustrated by

the inundation of the Severn Estuary in AD 1606, where the physical and documentary evidence for its effects may be compared to evidence for perception of the event contained in a polemical tract (Anon 1607) and church brasses recording the depth of flooding (Boon 1980). Both rationalise the event as an unavoidable act of God and, in the case of the tract, the punishment of sinners. Comparable perspectives, with a similar religious message, are contained in accounts of the flooding of agricultural land in the Till Valley, Wiltshire in 1841 (Bell 1992; Cross 1967).

Obviously, we are not arguing that these historic-period analogies demonstrate *how* earlier environmental changes would have been perceived and have impacted on the lives of communities, including those of prehistory. Rather, it is argued that by drawing analogy from the broadest possible chronological spectrum we will be in a stronger position to develop multiple working hypotheses regarding the effects of environmental change on communities. These hypotheses can then be evaluated against the evidence of specific cases. This is one way of helping us to think beyond the limitations of our own experience. The need to try to develop this broader perspective is particularly clear in the case of infrequent and episodic environmental change, some types of which may lie outside the period of instrumental records or scientific observation. One has only to think of the extent to which the perception which palaeoenvironmentalists had of woodland stability and disturbance factors changed overnight as a result of the storm which hit southern England on 16 October 1987, felling 15 million trees (Ogley 1988).

Although historic-period rural environments have not received the attention of those in prehistory there is none the less a growing body of data and synthesis. Most of this is in edited volumes comprising articles on specific sources of evidence (eg plant remains or bones) or geographical areas, highlighting the difficulties of broader interdisciplinary synthesis. An attempt to erode the divide between the study of prehistoric and historic-period environments has been provided by Jones and Dimbleby (1981). The landscape of the Roman period has been recently discussed by Dark and Dark (1997). Much relevant material is also contained in syntheses relating to the Anglo-Saxon period (Rackham 1994) and to the medieval countryside (Astill and Grant 1988a; Aston et al 1989). Issues of continuity and change across these periods have previously been reviewed by Bell (1989; 1995) and by Dark (1996).

We will address these issues using examples from rural contexts. In doing so we must acknowledge the links that exist between rural and urban activities (Hall and Kenward 1994), which themselves can contribute to the study of continuity and change. In a number of towns Roman layers are separated from those of the medieval period by 'dark earths'. Investigation of these is central to establishing the degree of continuity that exists, the extent to which former urban areas may have been used for activities such as crop growing and waste disposal, and also the distinctive processes, such as reworking, which govern the formation of the archaeological record in urban contexts (Macphail 1994). More specifically urban biota, such as pests of stored grain, may help to evaluate the extent of continuity or discontinuity in crop growing, as Buckland (1997) has noted in reviewing the Coppergate evidence (Kenward and Hall 1995).

Much of the following discussion will be based on evidence from 'off-site' pollen sequences. This reflects the fact that pollen analysis is the most widely applicable tool for environmental reconstruction over long time scales: pollen grains from lake and mire deposits provide a continuous record of the surrounding vegetation, reflecting periods of change in land use through fluctuations in inputs of pollen of trees and herbaceous plants, including pollen of crops. Pollen grains are obviously not the only type of biological remains from off-site sequences, but they are usually by far the commonest, owing to their small size, widespread dispersal, and resistance to decay in waterlogged conditions.

The key aspect of such off-site sequences is that they have often accumulated undisturbed over periods of thousands of years. This is in contrast to pollen-bearing deposits from archaeological contexts such as ditches and wells, which may represent periods of only decades or centuries. On-site sequences, while of obvious value in enabling reconstruction of the environment of the site at specific periods, are therefore usually of lesser value for detecting long-term change in the surrounding landscape.

Pollen analysis and issues of continuity

Palynology of 'off-site' lake and peat deposits offers considerable opportunities for addressing questions of landscape continuity, because it can provide long sequences of vegetational change on a scale beyond that of the individual settlement. A major problem, however, is correlation of the environmental record with historical events, as recently discussed by Dumayne et al (1995) in the context of the Hadrianic and Antonine Walls. Despite production of seven pollen sequences from the area, supported by a total of 38 radiocarbon dates, at no site was it possible, on the basis of the radiocarbon evidence alone, to provide a confident association between woodland clearance and Wall construction. At Fozy Moss, however, Dumayne et al felt able to use the palaeoecological and archaeological evidence, including an erosion episode possibly related to construction of Hadrian's Wall, 'to constrain the radiocarbon record', arguing that a major and apparently rapid phase of woodland clearance did indeed reflect this event.

Recent research by one of the present authors (PD) has been aimed specifically at overcoming this problem, by detecting 'markers' from the construction of Hadrian's Wall and the Stanegate road (including particles of building materials) in the sediments of adjacent lakes. This provides a direct stratigraphic link between the pollen record and the Wall and road, overcoming a reliance solely on radiocarbon dating for correlation.

In addition to questions of chronological control, we must also consider the degree of temporal resolution provided by pollen sequences. What is the period of time represented by each sample, and what is the interval between samples? In many cases the sampling interval will be too wide to enable comparison with specific historical records, even without the additional problems of radiocarbon dating (see below). The quest for continuity is especially reliant on high resolution analyses, yet many pollen diagrams have samples at intervals of approximately one hundred years (often longer), so that short-term changes would not be detected.

For example, the well-known pollen sequence from Tregaron Bog, Dyfed (Turner 1964), has only two samples from the probable Roman-period deposits. Yet the

Iron Age part of this sequence provides one of the earliest examples of high resolution pollen analysis. Turner took contiguous samples 1/4in apart (each sample representing approximately two years) to investigate in detail the vegetational changes associated with an Iron Age 'small temporary clearance'. The potential for such detailed sampling has only in fairly recent times been extended to historic periods, as at Bolton Fell Moss in Cumbria (Barber 1981), Fozy Moss in Northumberland (Dumayne and Barber 1994), and Fairsnape Fell in Lancashire (Mackay and Tallis 1994).

The question of environmental change at the end of the Roman period illustrates further problems. Woodland regeneration phases that seem – often on the basis of poorly dated, or even undated, pollen diagrams – to correspond to approximately the 'right' part of the sequence have sometimes been ascribed, often by non-archaeologists, to the end of the Roman period (eg Moore 1968). Before radiocarbon dates were widely available this reflected a need to find 'palynological markers' to enable comparison between sites. For the first half of the Holocene the spread of arboreal taxa, and then the early Neolithic elm decline, provided the basis for such comparisons. For the post-Neolithic deposits correlation was more difficult, and the assumed regeneration of woodland in the post-Roman period appeared to provide a further fixed point.

Even today, where most sequences have at least some radiocarbon dates, the problem of 'hard water error' means that lake sediments in areas of carbonate-rich bedrock may not be suitable for radiocarbon dating, so that high quality data may lack an accurate chronology. Diss Mere, Norfolk provides an example (Peglar 1993a; Peglar et al 1989). In environmental terms this sequence is of great importance, particularly for the mid Holocene, where the annually laminated sediments have enabled a detailed analysis of the Neolithic elm decline (Peglar 1993b). The later sediments are unfortunately both unlaminated and highly calcareous, and have not been radiocarbon dated. This part of the sequence has been used to reconstruct a detailed correlation between the palynological and cultural sequences, but one that must remain tentative in the absence of independent chronological control.

This illustrates the frustrating problem that despite the increasing availability of detailed pollen sequences, their interpretation in cultural terms must often be based on, at best, tenuous chronological linkages. This means that assumptions are often made about key hypotheses, in this case that the end of Roman Britain led to widespread abandonment of agricultural land, which we ought to be able to test. Archaeologically, the period around AD 410 deserves a similar level of attention to the elm decline – although there are currently no known

sites in Britain where laminated sediments could provide the opportunity for such detailed analysis as was possible for the elm decline at Diss – but there has been little palynological work concentrating on this period. This state of affairs makes the point that where specifically archaeological hypotheses need to be tested, we may not be able simply to rely on long palaeoecological sequences provided by botanists and geographers, who not unnaturally may have significantly different research agendas.

Where issues of continuity and change have been addressed in a way that enables our expectations and theories to be tested, a complex picture may emerge. One of the first attempts to adopt such an approach was Turner's (1979) use of a series of radiocarbon-dated pollen diagrams to reconstruct the Roman-period environment of north-east England. She argued that some sites showed regeneration at various dates in the centuries after Roman withdrawal, but with continuity 'well into the sixth century AD'. The validity of the suggested chronologies for some of these regeneration episodes have recently been questioned (Dark 1996; Dark and Dark 1996), however, suggesting that the evidence for post-Roman continuity in this area is not secure.

In a slightly more recent review of the evidence for the environment of the Iron Age to Anglo-Saxon periods for Britain overall, Turner (1981) was able to draw on few additional sequences to those from the north-east, and those discussed remained biased to the northern half of Britain. These, she argued, indicated that 'during Anglo-Saxon times considerable tracts of land were falling waste and forest re-establishing itself with the Iron Age level of farming being continued in only a few places' (Turner 1981, 72).

Recent archaeological overviews of the environmental context of the end of Roman Britain have continued to draw largely on the pollen sequences discussed in Turner's synthesis (eg Jones 1996), despite the wealth of new palynological data covering the end of Roman Britain. Once again, this highlights the problem created by a necessary reliance by archaeologists on palynological data which has often been produced for other than archaeological purposes. Pollen sequences from lakes and peat deposits often represent vegetation change over thousands of years, and the attention of the analyst tends to focus on prehistoric environments. Historic-period changes often receive little specific comment, at least in relation to cultural history.

A recent attempt to 'open up' the potential of all this new data has involved syntheses of all well dated off-site pollen sequences spanning the Iron Age and Roman periods in the area south of the Antonine Wall (Dark and Dark 1997), and also an examination of the effects of Roman withdrawal from Britain on the environment by analysis of all sequences covering the period AD

400–800 (Dark 1996). In relation to the question of post-Roman landscape continuity (Fig 19.2), of 51 sites with deposits spanning the period AD 400–800, 24 showed signs of reduced intensity of land use, with over half of these being concentrated in the area of the Hadrianic frontier. Continuity, or an increase of activity,

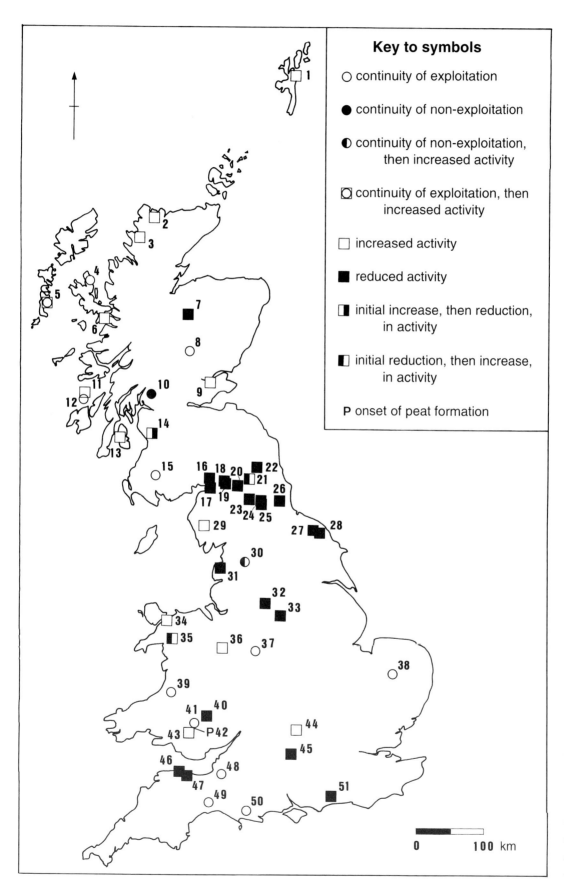

Key to symbols

○ continuity of exploitation

● continuity of non-exploitation

◐ continuity of non-exploitation, then increased activity

◙ continuity of exploitation, then increased activity

☐ increased activity

■ reduced activity

◨ initial increase, then reduction, in activity

◧ initial reduction, then increase, in activity

P onset of peat formation

Fig 19.2 Locations of pollen sequences with evidence for environmental continuity and change in the period AD 400–800 (after Dark 1996, fig 1)

is evident at most Scottish sites, and in Wales, and at about half the sites in England south of the Wall. Overall, sites that do show reduced activity tend to be at higher altitudes than those showing continuity or increased activity, although this is far from always the case. Clearly, woodland regeneration was not a universal result of Roman withdrawal, but it is notable that all sites within 20km of Hadrian's Wall show a reduction in intensity of land use at the end of the Roman period. This area saw one of the most dramatic increases in clearance during the Roman occupation (Dark and Dark 1997, 30–35), presumably at least partly as a result of pressure on agricultural systems to supply the army, and it is possible that once the army withdrew the reduced demand for produce led to some abandonment of land (Dark and Dark 1996).

It is unfortunate that there is a bias in the distribution of pollen evidence to those areas of Britain that were apparently least Romanised, owing to the greater abundance of lakes and peat bogs in the north and west than in the south and east. It is hoped that the recent increase in efforts by palynologists to examine sites in the south will help to overcome this imbalance over the next few years. Recent results from this area have included analysis of a near-complete Holocene sequence from Sidlings Copse, Oxfordshire (Fig 19.3; Day 1991; 1993b; Preece and Day 1994). This site is of significance for the Roman and later periods because of its location in the centre of the production area of Oxfordshire Ware pottery (Young 1977), and because the medieval and later parts of the sequence have been compared with textual and cartographic evidence of the changing extent of woodland in the medieval Royal Forest of Shotover and Stowood (Day 1990).

Woodland history is another area where the search for continuity has provided an area of mutual interest both for archaeologists and palaeoecologists. It is a subject where reliable evidence is particularly sparse, and could again benefit from a targeted approach to the collection of new data.

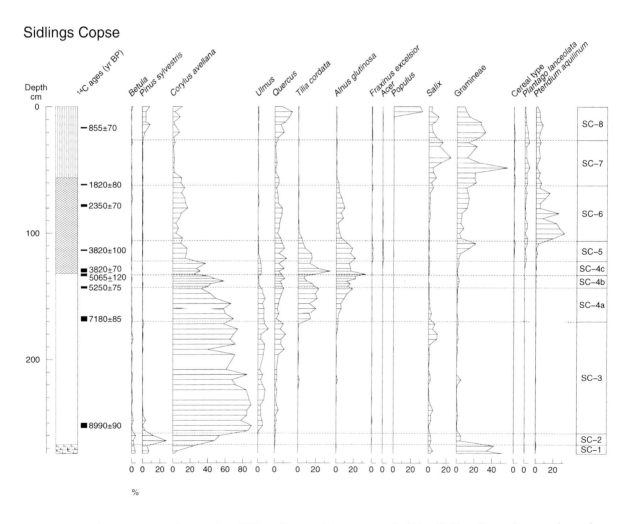

Fig 19.3 Summary pollen percentage diagram from Sidlings Copse: pollen sum is total of identifiable pollen and spores of vascular plants, excluding aquatics; lithology symbols follow Troels-Smith (1955), but tufa is left blank; radiocarbon dates are in uncalibrated radiocarbon years BP using a half life of 5568 years and are quoted at one sigma levels (pollen data summarized from Day 1991 with additional radiocarbon dates from Preece and Day 1994)

Ancient woodland

The realisation of the significance of ancient woodland in landscape history has come largely from the work of Oliver Rackham (1976; 1980; 1990), especially his detailed investigations into the history of individual sites based on the study of a combination of textual sources, maps, earthwork survey, and floral composition. Woods that can be shown to be at least centuries old, on the basis of textual and cartographic sources, often contain a distinctive set of plants that is not found on recent 'secondary' woodland (on sites that had previously been open land). These plants have been termed 'ancient woodland indicators' (AWIs), and have been extensively used both in studies of woodland history and in the development of nature conservation strategies (Peterken 1974; 1981; Peterken and Game 1984; Rackham 1980).

A problem with many studies of woodland rich in AWIs is that it tends to be assumed that the presence of these plants is evidence for a link with the original early Holocene woodland cover (Rackham's 'wildwood'), but there is almost never any direct evidence to support this. The only way that a site can be shown to have been continuously wooded over this period is by pollen analysis of a sequence of deposits from within the wood. Unfortunately, suitable deposits are rarely found in woods, so that opportunities for testing the assumptions behind the use of AWIs are few.

The first 'ancient woodland' pollen diagram was from Epping Forest, Essex (Baker *et al* 1978). This was argued to indicate woodland continuity throughout the 4000 years covered by the sequence. Unfortunately, however, there are a number of problems with this interpretation. Perhaps the most obvious is the authors' own description of how the original lime woodland came to be replaced by beech: 'lime clearance in Epping Forest by Saxon settlers was, for all its severity, a temporary phenomenon, the cleared areas being later abandoned as oak and beech invaded them' (Baker *et al* 1978, 665). Whether temporary or not, this clearance means that the woodland resulting from beech and oak invasion was secondary! Closer inspection of the pollen diagram once again reveals the problem of temporal resolution: the wide sampling interval means that it would simply not be possible to detect even relatively long periods of open land from the sequence – samples are spaced at approximately 600 year intervals for the Neolithic to Anglo-Saxon deposits! The presence of a probably Iron Age hillfort (Ambresbury Banks) only 700 m from the site suggests the possibility of substantial clearance in the Iron Age as well as the already noted Anglo-Saxon episode.

The most recent attempt to address the issue of the significance of ancient woodland and ancient woodland indicators has been based on the pollen sequence from Sidlings Copse, in Oxfordshire (Day 1993b). The site has a rich assemblage of 43 plants which have been suggested to be indicative of ancient/primary woodland in lowland England. On this basis it would conventionally be argued to provide a classic example of a site with continuity of woodland cover throughout the Holocene. However, pollen analysis of deposits from the site (Fig 19.3) shows that major woodland clearance began in the early Bronze Age, and all local woodland was finally removed in the late Roman or early Anglo-Saxon period. The woodland now on the site, with its diverse assemblage of AWIs, is the result of regeneration in the early medieval period. A possible reason for this regeneration is that changes in land use may have been initiated when the area was designated a legal Royal Forest (Day 1990).

The rapidity with which woodland can regenerate on abandoned open land (in a matter of decades) means that woodland continuity on a site would be difficult to prove without high resolution pollen analysis of a complete Holocene sequence. There is no pollen sequence from a British wood that shows continuity with the original woodland cover (see reviews of the evidence in Day 1993a and 1993b). Discontinuity is more easily detected, both palynologically and archaeologically. Several areas of medieval woodland have been shown to contain archaeological sites that are unlikely to have been constructed in woodland. An example is Wychwood Forest, Oxfordshire (Schumer 1984), where the medieval woodland apparently overlay a number of Roman villas, indicating that at least part of it must have been secondary in origin.

There is scope for much more archaeological and palynological research to test the assumption of woodland survival throughout the Holocene. Practical problems of archaeological fieldwork in densely wooded areas, combined with the rarity of long sequences of organic deposits in woodland, make this difficult, but the available data are so minimal that concerted research into this issue would almost certainly provide valuable new information.

Farming practice and fields

Turning to the evidence of agriculture from on-site sources and fields, macroscopic plant remains from archaeological sites provide some evidence of continuity in the growing of individual crops. For example at Barton Court Farm, Oxfordshire, *Camelina alyssum*, an unusual weed of flax, occurs in both Romano-British and Anglo-Saxon contexts (Robinson and Wilson 1987). Spelt was replaced as the main crop in the post-Roman period, but there are interesting instances of its continued occurrence on Anglo-Saxon and early medieval sites, eg around Chelmsford, Essex (Murphy 1987), and at Cefn Graeanog, Gwynedd (Kelly 1982).

Murphy (1994) has highlighted examples where this cannot just be a result of contamination from earlier contexts. He does, however, identify the additional possibility that some plants may have hung on as weedy contaminants of main crops, rather than as cultivars.

In the study of fields themselves, air photography, field survey, and comparison with historical and cartographic sources have dominated the recent research agenda (Hall 1993). There has, in recent years, been much less emphasis on excavation, dating, and soil analytical approaches in relation to later periods. The field systems of the period between the end of Roman Britain and the appearance of open fields, perhaps in the tenth century AD in Wessex (Costen 1994; Hooke 1994), remain very poorly understood. Here the excavation of fields with environmental evidence could make an important contribution. There is a case for focusing on lynchets and other colluvial deposits, particularly around sub-Roman, Anglo-Saxon, and other early medieval sites.

Fig 19.4 A lynchet at Bishopstone, Sussex, which accumulated between the Bronze Age and the Romano-British period, and in the Anglo-Saxon period provided a terrace for building construction (photo: Brenda Westley)

Some rather limited attempts have been made to do this. At Bishopstone, Sussex a section across a prehistoric and Romano-British field of 'Celtic' type (Fig 19.4) showed that it went out of use in the post-Roman period and the flat lynchets served as platforms for Anglo-Saxon buildings (Bell 1977). At Chalton, Hampshire a colluvial sediment sequence (Fig 19.5) adjacent to the medieval village produced evidence of later Saxon and medieval agriculture and its destructive effects on earlier archaeology (Bell 1983; 1989). Unfortunately, the Chalton data did not provide evidence that could be correlated with an earlier Anglo-Saxon settlement 1.3km away on Church Down (Champion 1977). Air photographic and field survey evidence showed that this settlement had been established on a hilltop which previously, in Romano-British times, had been surrounded by fields but with an unenclosed top, which was assumed to be pasture (Cunliffe 1973).

Colluvial deposits do have the capacity to provide land-use histories relevant, for instance, to what is frequently a long blank period between the Roman and medieval periods. It must be acknowledged, however, that the dating of colluvium, whether by artefacts or by radiocarbon, will seldom be sufficiently precise for confident correlation with individual historical events. Thus the investigation of colluvial deposits is likely to be most effective as part of wider landscape investigations integrating evidence from a range of spatial scales and chronological resolutions and including off-site palynological sequences which may potentially be more closely datable.

Boundaries and hedges are of particular relevance to studies of continuity and change, as shown for instance by the survival of pre-Roman boundaries in East Anglia (Williamson 1988) and, controversially, evidence from hedgerow dating for boundary continuity elsewhere (Pollard *et al* 1974). Environmental archaeologists have long been aware of the importance of identifying hedges (eg Groenman-van Waateringe 1978, 140; Robinson 1978). So far, however, there has been limited success in the identification of hedges using palaeoenvironmental evidence. This is another topic that might benefit from targeted research.

Analytical approaches also have a contribution to make in evaluating the hypothesis of soil exhaustion as an explanation for historically recorded declining yields, for example during the thirteenth and fourteenth centuries (Astill and Grant 1988b). Dodgshon (1994) has tackled this problem in the context of traditional highland farming in Scotland. The opportunities afforded by a combination of analytical and ethnohistorical perspectives are shown both by that study and by Davidson and Simpson's (1994) work on soils and landscape history in the Northern Isles of Scotland. Such studies seem to have received less emphasis in England, perhaps because the potential of the recent ethnohistorical record has not been as fully explored as in Scotland (Fenton 1976) and Ireland (Mitchell 1986).

The need for analytical data relating to past fields emerges particularly clearly when we try to model change through time. An example is a recent attempt at computer modelling of long-term soil erosion on chalk (Favis-Mortlock *et al* 1997). However questionable some of the assumptions made by this modelling exercise may be, it does help to focus much more clearly on the gaps in present knowledge. By modelling we can establish which parameters are of particular importance in determining outcomes and thus the types of analytical evidence we require to increase the reliability of future modelling exercises.

Fig 19.5 Colluvial valley sediments at Chalton village, Hampshire: this sequence demonstrated agricultural activity in the area of the existing village since the Bronze Age and a period of much more intensive activity marked by the incorporation of abundant pottery in fields from the late Saxon period (photo: Brenda Westley)

Gardens

Gardens deserve special emphasis in view of their increasing prominence, both academically (see also Johnson, this volume) and in the brief of heritage organisations. Pollen, macrofossils, and soil micromorphology have a part to play in elucidating garden histories (Murphy and Scaife 1991), as they did in the recent reconstruction of the King's Privy Garden at Hampton Court (Thurley 1996). The work of Kerkham and Briggs (1991) shows what can be achieved through the successful synthesis of fieldwork, literature, and art. In future, palaeoenvironmental studies have a contribution to make to such syntheses. Potential may exist where lakes, ponds, and ornamental canals contain sediment sequences that have escaped cleaning.

Evidence from gardens for landscape changes even over recent centuries could prove useful in several ways: such evidence provides data for comparison with other sources, eg texts and art. Since the character of the surrounding landscape may be well known for a period of centuries even down to individual tree plantations, exotic introductions, etc, such issues could contribute to issues of pollen recruitment and interpretation.

On a more philosophical plane the interdisciplinary synthesis involved in garden archaeology may serve as a medium that could help to stimulate a more perceptually aware approach to past environments. It is a context in which the landscape and environmental evidence may be interpreted in the light of, for example, eighteenth-century tracts on the philosophy of the picturesque (eg Price 1794) and work on the iconography of landscape from human geography (Cosgrove and Daniels 1988). Studies of relatively recent records of this kind may help to broaden the interpretation of environmental sequences from earlier periods which lack historical sources. This may help environmental archaeologists to think not just about how landscapes were, in some abstract reality, but about how they may have been perceived.

Landscape projects

The next generation of landscape projects would benefit from particular emphasis on the selection of sites where it is possible to obtain long palaeoenvironmental sequences within the context of a retrogressive landscape analysis. There are some excellent European studies that link palaeoenvironmental work to detailed archaeological landscape analysis, eg the Ystad Project, Sweden (Berglund 1991), Mikkelsen's (1986) pollen work at Borup, Denmark, building on the earlier fieldwork of Steensberg (1983), and the Kootwijk project in the Netherlands (Groenman-van Waateringe and Wijngaarden-Bakker 1987; Heidinga 1987).

In Britain pollen work has been highly influential in looking at issues of landscape continuity and change. This was discussed earlier in relation to the end of Roman Britain but applies equally to the medieval period. In Devon, for instance, there are several examples: Hound Tor (Austin and Walker 1985), Okehampton Park (Austin et al 1980), and Holne Moor (Maguire et al 1983). Smith (1979; 1980) made full use of limited environmental evidence in his retrogressive analysis of the Fisherwick landscape in the Midlands. Other English Heritage landscape projects have, in recent years, provided important environmental sequences, for example, Wharram Percy, Yorkshire (eg Bush 1981), Raunds, Northamptonshire (Campbell 1994), or Roadford, Devon (Vanessa Straker personal communication), although so far the environmental aspects of these projects have not been published. It would, however, probably be fair to say that in none of these cases was the choice of study area based on the established presence of a really high-quality palaeoenvironmental sequence.

There is a case to be made for instigating future surveys in areas of lowland agricultural landscape with the best environmental sequences. Examples of the types of site that might repay further work are the peat sequences identified by Waton (1982) on the edges of the chalk. All have surviving records for at least the last two millennia but only one, Rimsmoor in Dorset, has any degree of chronological precision. One of the most promising may be Amberley Wild Brooks in Sussex, just 4km from the substantial Bignor Roman villa. Here Waton identified possible Roman regeneration and renewed clearance with a calibrated date centring on the seventh century AD. Existing chronological resolution is, however, low with just two dates in two millennia.

In selecting sites we might look, for instance, at pollen diagrams constructed for other purposes and consider whether there are instances in which a specifically targeted dating programme might create a valuable sequence for the historic period. For example, were it to become possible to date the deposits from Diss Mere, Norfolk (discussed earlier), they might provide a way of investigating the continuity in the orientation of land boundaries which Williamson (1988) has recognised in the adjacent landscape. Specifically, it would be possible to test his hypothesis that Romano-British farms on the clay districts were abandoned, but continued grazing led to the survival of field systems (Murphy 1994; Williamson 1988). In fact, the existence of coaxial field systems was one piece of evidence used to suggest that the main clearance reconstructed from the pollen sequence was Iron Age (Peglar et al 1989). Since there is no independent dating evidence, the dangers of circular reasoning are evident. The only currently available long pollen sequence for East Anglia with radiocarbon dates from post-Roman deposits is from Hockham Mere (Bennett 1983; Sims 1978), although here regional vegetational changes after the tenth century AD are obscured by infilling of the lake and colonisation of the deposits by wetland plant communities. Further detailed, and well dated, sequences from this area would be a valuable complement to the significant body of archaeological site-based data assembled by Murphy (1994). Such sequences would additionally provide an opportunity to investigate evidence of settlement nucleation and the dates when new crop introductions, such as hemp and flax, became important. The introduction of these crops and medieval agricultural intensification has been investigated by Pat Wiltshire (personal communication) in the context of a palaeochannel sequence at Market Lavington, Wiltshire, a study which is complemented by a specifically designed precision-dating strategy using the approaches outlined by Bayliss (this volume).

In a wetland context comparable issues to those raised by the co-axial field systems of East Anglia exist in the Severn Estuary Levels. At Rumney Great Wharf, east of Cardiff, there is evidence that an existing pattern of landscape drainage was first established in the Romano-British period (Allen and Fulford 1986; Fulford *et al* 1994). The question is, does that imply continuity of land use through the dark ages and beyond (Rippon 1996)? The issue could be addressed using environmental evidence if suitable deposits spanning the Roman to early medieval periods can be found.

Dating and dendrochronology

Correlations of environmental data with historical events have often been made on the basis of single radiocarbon dates and without explicit discussion of calibration issues and the range of other factors affecting dating precision. Pilcher (1993, 28), in a review of radiocarbon dating in palynology, concludes that 'attempts to interpret time differences or real ages closer than 500 years by conventional dates are simply not valid'. Issues of interpretation are also addressed by Baillie (1991) who describes phenomena which he calls 'suck in', by which age estimates with large ranges are assigned to known events , and 'smear', where wide age ranges can spread synchronous events through time.

Where key issues of historical correlation are being addressed there is a clear case for larger numbers of dates than has tended to be the norm in this period; compare, for instance, the number of dates (where there are any) in most early medieval sequences with the dating programmes implemented in the Mesolithic and Neolithic periods. The early historic periods will often

also require higher precision on smaller AMS samples. Methods for estimating the confidence limits of age determinations in palynology have been put forward by Bennett (1994) who regards these of particular importance in studies where palynology is concerned with the explicit testing of hypotheses. Estimation of the number of dates needed in order to achieve a required level of precision may be obtained from simulation modelling. Bayliss (this volume) concludes that mathematical modelling can as much as double the precision of dating.

Dendrochronology alone may provide the precision we require in order to address some questions. Detailed sequences linking dendrochronology, pollen, and woodland history exist in prehistoric contexts, particularly from Alpine lake settlements (eg Billamboz 1995). Historic period examples are fewer but include a medieval settlement at Charavines-Collective, France, associated with a dendrochronologically dated felling sequence of local woodland and major agricultural clearance between AD 1003 and 1040 (Coles and Coles 1996, 80). In the British Isles tree-ring sequences from buildings and bogs have identified periods of regeneration and intensive woodland exploitation, and in Ireland that has led to the identification of episodes of remarkable social change (Baillie 1995). Examples include the later Iron Age, when such major works as the Corlea trackway and Black Pig's Dyke were constructed within less than a decade, as part of a period of 'massive building enterprises' between 150 BC and 95 BC (Baillie 1995, 66). Another Irish example is the period of particular building activity which occurred in the Early Christian period (Baillie 1995). The Iron Age episode was quite unexpected, at least in terms of its sharp chronological focus. The Early Christian episode supported existing evidence regarding the cultural flowering in this period, which was based on material culture, historical sources, and palaeoenvironmental evidence for agricultural intensification (eg Mitchell 1986).

Conclusions and recommendations

The importance of chronological precision has been highlighted as of special importance where we seek to compare palaeoenvironmental sources and historical records. It is highly desirable that specific studies attempt to quantify the degree of chronological resolution which they feel has been achieved given sampling intervals, the spacing of dated horizons, and the uncertainties of the dating method used. This is of particular importance in historic periods, in which interdisciplinary synthesis is often carried out by those from different academic disciplines.

The emphasis here has very much been on the capacity of pollen analysis to contribute to our understanding of continuity and change. Palynology offers the greatest scope in situations where chronological precision can be improved, where sequences can be obtained relating to various spatial scales, on-site as well as off-site, within an area; also in situations where comparison is possible with other sources such as macrofossils or colluvial sequences providing a complementary perspective on the more specifically agricultural parts of a landscape.

The concentrated periods of activity that have been identified in Iron Age and early medieval Ireland, as a result of dendrochronological precision, serve to emphasise our limited knowledge of what was going on at the same time elsewhere in the British Isles. This is particularly the case in Wales, the West Country or North West England, where comparison with the Irish evidence would be of special interest. Regional research agendas need to be evolved to tackle issues of this kind and may now achieve a more tangible significance given the context of greater political emphasis on regionality and the possibility of political change in Wales and Scotland.

We need to consider whether the environmental evidence relating to the early medieval period is less well preserved in mainland Britain than in Ireland, or have we not invested the resources in order to find it? The two successive versions of the published research agenda for English Heritage (English Heritage 1991; 1997) emphasise the importance of issues of continuity and change. Yet, although substantial investment has been directed towards these issues, English Heritage (1997, 43) acknowledges that projects have tended to focus on site-based studies and have not always yielded anticipated academic advances. It has been suggested above, in the context of landscape projects, that one reason for this may be a lack of emphasis on environmental potential in the initial selection of landscapes for major projects.

We have argued that the environments of the historic periods deserve particular attention because they provide the opportunity for comparison between multiple sources of evidence such as palaeoenvironmental, written, artistic, and cartographic, etc. Comparisons between sources provide the opportunity to challenge existing orthodoxy. The pollen evidence reviewed challenges some assumptions about the extent of post-Roman woodland regeneration and the significance of ancient woodland indicators. Comparison of a range of sources relating, for example, to a specific flooding event or to a garden layout has the potential to broaden our understanding of the range of ways in which particular landscapes and events may have been encountered beyond purely utilitarian and economic dimensions. It is proposed that this may play a part in cultivating a broader approach to past environments, not just in the historic period, but in prehistory. This would be more in tune with the phenomenological and perceptual emphasis of current landscape work by prehistorians (eg Barrett 1994; Gosden 1994; Tilley 1994).

It is suggested that a broader approach to the environmental archaeology of landscapes may be achieved using the richness of different sources available in historic periods. A complementary reason for concentrating on the last millennium is that this is of particular relevance to extending the timescale of environmental knowledge beyond the period of instrumental records. This period of overlap between instrumental sources, historical records, and palaeoenvironmental evidence can facilitate calibration of palaeoenvironmental records. In that sense the perceptual and the instrumental come together as different forms of knowledge about specific environmental changes.

Beyond the philosophical and academic reasons for giving particular emphasis to the environmental archaeology of the last two millennia, there are practical concerns of planning issues and conservation, which give urgency to such studies because it is the more recent parts of the palaeoenvironmental record that are most under threat from development pressures.

Decisions about planning and conservation matters are inevitably based on imperfect data. Palaeoenvironmental evidence can provide clues to missing archaeology. Edwards (this volume) has noted the predictive potential of palynology in the Mesolithic of the Hebrides. Such potential also exists in historic periods such as the sub-Roman period in Wales and the west. Environmental evidence provides a way of testing the reality of gaps in the archaeological record.

There is a strong case for environmental archaeologists becoming more actively engaged in the development of nature conservation strategies. Management plans for nature reserves are often based on very short-term data. There is frequently limited information about historic and prehistoric environmental changes, which would provide a longer time perspective. Effective management often demands knowledge of environmental change on a variety of timescales. Research input to nature conservation strategies could become a major area of activity for environmental archaeologists in coming years. A particular pressing case might concern ancient woodland and the criteria used in its identification.

Bog sequences with evidence of medieval vegetation change have received much less attention than those of prehistory. Paradoxically, suitable surviving sites are far fewer than for prehistory and continue to diminish, the upper levels of bogs having often been cut away. In Somerset, for example, only the Meare Heath pollen diagram (Beckett and Hibbert 1978; 1979) extends into the early medieval period. Elsewhere later layers have been cut away, oxidized, or peat growth ceased as a result of marine incursion. In developing landscape conservation strategies for Somerset, and other wetlands (Cox *et al* 1995), any areas where bog growth continued into recent times should have a high priority. Before resources were put into their conservation, such areas would need to be evaluated in terms of the quality of pollen preservation and the degree of chronological precision that the surviving evidence could provide. We have already noted that it is these upper layers which offer particular opportunities for comparison with historical and instrumental data. Furthermore, it is these upper levels which will often be of particular significance in understanding the origins of distinctive landscape types in many parts of Britain and may provide an academic foundation for assessment of their conservation value.

Acknowledgements

We are grateful to Professor Kevin Edwards, Dr Pat Wiltshire, and Peter Murphy for information. Dr Ken Dark, Peter Murphy, and an English Heritage referee are also thanked for their comments on an earlier version of this paper.

References

Allen, J R L, and Fulford, M G, 1986 The Wentlooge Level: A Romano-British saltmarsh reclamation in Southeast Wales, *Britannia*, **17**, 91–117

Anonymous, 1607 *Lamentable news out of Monmouthshire in Wales*, London

Astill, G, and Grant, A, 1988a *The countryside of medieval England*, Oxford

—, 1988b The medieval countryside: efficiency, progress, and change, in Astill and Grant (eds) 1988a, 213–34

Aston, M, Austin, D and Dyer, C, 1989 *The rural settlements of medieval England*, Oxford

Austin, D, Daggett, R H and Walker, M J C, 1980 Farms and fields in Okehampton park, Devon: the problems of studying medieval landscapes, *Landscape Hist*, **2**, 39–58

Austin, D, and Walker, M J C, 1985 A new landscape context for Houndtor, Devon, *Medieval Archaeol*, **29**, 147–52

Baillie, M G L, 1991 Suck-in and smear: two related chronological problems for the 1990s, *J Theor Archaeol*, **2**, 12–16

—, 1995 *A slice through time: dendrochronology and precision dating*, London

Baker, C A, Moxey, P A and Oxford, P M 1978 Woodland continuity and change in Epping Forest, *Fld Stud*, **4**, 645–69

Barber, K E, 1981 *Peat stratigraphy and climatic change*, Rotterdam

Barber, K E, Chambers, F M, Maddy, D, Stoneman, R and Brew, J S, 1994 A sensitive high-resolution record of late Holocene climatic change from a raised bog in northern England, *The Holocene* **4**, 198–205

Barrett, J, 1994 *Fragments from antiquity*, Oxford

Beckett, S C, and Hibbert, F A, 1978 The influence of man on the vegetation of the Somerset Levels: a summary, *Somerset Levels Pap*, **4**, 86–90

—, 1979 Vegetational change and the influence of prehistoric man in the Somerset Levels, *New Phytol*, **83**, 577–600

Bell, M, 1977 *Excavations at Bishopstone*, Sussex Archaeological Collections, **115**

—, 1983 Valley sediments as evidence of prehistoric land-use on the South Downs, *Proc Prehist Soc*, **49**, 119–50

—, 1989 Environmental archaeology as an index of continuity and change in the medieval landscape, in Aston *et al* (eds) 1989, 269–86

—, 1992 The prehistory of soil erosion, in *Past and present soil erosion* (eds M Bell and J Boardman), Oxbow Monogr, **22**, 21–36, Oxford

—, 1995 People and nature in the Celtic world, in *The Celtic world* (ed M Green), 145–58, London

Bennett, K D, 1983 Devensian late-glacial and Flandrian vegetational history at Hockham Mere, Norfolk, England, I: pollen percentages and concentrations, *New Phytol*, **95**, 457–87

—, 1994 Confidence intervals for age estimates and deposition times in late-Quaternary sediment sequences, *The Holocene*, **4**, 337–48

Berglund, B, (ed) 1991 The cultural landscape during 6000 years in southern Sweden: the Ystad project, Ecological Bulletins, **41**, Copenhagen

Billamboz, A, 1995 Proxyseries dendrochronologiques et occupation Néolithique des bords du lac de Constance, *Palynosciences*, **3**, 69–81

Blong, R J, 1982 *The time of darkness*, Canberra

Boon, G C, 1980 Caerleon and the Gwent Levels in early historic times, in *Archaeology and coastal change* (ed F H Thompson), 24–36, London

Brown, A E (ed), 1991 *Garden archaeology*, CBA Res Rep, **78**, London

Buckland, P 1997 Review of *Biological evidence from 16–22 Coppergate. Archaeology of York: the environment 14/7* (H K Kenward and A R Hall), 1995, York, in *J Archaeol Sci*, 24, 962–3

Bush, M, 1981 Report on the palynology of the samples from the ponds at Wharram Percy, unpubl rep, Dept Geography, Hull Univ

Campbell, G, 1994 The preliminary archaeobotanical results from Anglo-Saxon West Cotton and Raunds, in Rackham 1994, 65–82

Champion, T, 1977 Chalton, *Curr Archaeol*, **59**, 364–9

Coles, J, and Coles, B, 1996 *Enlarging the past*, Soc Antiq Scotl Monogr Ser, **11**, Edinburgh

Cosgrove, D and Daniels, S, 1988 *The iconography of landscape*, Cambridge

Costen, M, 1994 Settlement in Wessex in the tenth century: the charter evidence, in *The medieval landscape of Wessex* (eds M Aston and C Lewis), Oxbow Monogr, **46**, 97–114, Oxford

Cox, M, Straker, V, and Taylor, D, 1995 *Wetlands: archaeology and nature conservation*, London

Cross, A E, 1967 The great Till flood of 1841, *Weather*, **22**, 430–3

Cunliffe, B W, 1973 Chalton, Hampshire: the evolution of a landscape, *Antiq J*, **53**, 173–90

Dark, K R, and Dark, S P, 1996 New archaeological and palynological evidence for a sub-Roman reoccupation of Hadrian's Wall, *Archaeol Aeliana*, 5 ser, **24**, 57–72.

—, 1997 *The landscape of Roman Britain*, Stroud

Dark, SP, 1996 Palaeoecological evidence for landscape continuity and change in Britain ca AD 400–800, in *External contacts and the economy of late Roman and post-Roman Britain* (ed K R Dark), 23–51, Woodbridge

Davidson, D A, and Simpson, I A, 1994 Soils and landscape history: case studies from the Northern Isles of Scotland, in Foster and Smout (eds) 1994, 66–74

Day, S P, 1990 History and palaeoecology of woodlands in the Oxford region, unpubl DPhil thesis, Univ Oxford

—, 1991 Post-glacial vegetational history of the Oxford region, *New Phytol*, **119**, 445–70

—, 1993a Origins of medieval woodland, in *Ancient Woodlands: their Archaeology and Ecology* (eds P Beswick and ID Rotherham), 12–25, Sheffield

—, 1993b Woodland origin and 'ancient woodland indicators': a case-study from Sidlings Copse, Oxfordshire, UK, *The Holocene*, **3**, 45–53

Dodgshon, R A, 1994 Budgeting for survival: nutrient flow and traditional Highland farming, in Foster and Smout (eds) 1994, 83–93

Dumayne, L, and Barber, K E 1994 The impact of the Romans on the environment of northern England: pollen data from three sites close to Hadrian's Wall, *The Holocene*, **4**, 165–73

Dumayne, L, Stoneman, R, Barber, K, and Harkness, D, 1995 Problems associated with correlating calibrated radiocarbon-dated pollen diagrams with historical events, *The Holocene*, **5**, 118–23

English Heritage, 1991 *Exploring our past: strategies for the archaeology of England*, London

—, 1997 *Archaeology Division draft research agenda*, London

Favis-Mortlock, D, Boardman, J, and Bell, M, 1997 Modelling longterm anthropogenic erosion of a loess cover: South Downs, UK, *The Holocene*, **7**, 79–89

Fenton, A, 1976 *Scottish country life*, Edinburgh

Foster, S, and Smout, T C (eds), 1994 *The history of soils and field systems*, Aberdeen

Fulford, M G, Allen, J R L, and Rippon, S J, 1994 The settlement and drainage of the Wentlooge Level, Gwent: excavation and survey at Rumney Great Wharf 1992, *Britannia*, **25**, 175–211

Gosden, C, 1994 *Social being and time*, Oxford

Groenman-van Waateringe, W, 1978 The impact of Neolithic man on the landscape in the Netherlands, in Limbrey and Evans 1978, 135–46

Groenman-van Waateringe, W, and van Wijngaarden-Baaker, L H, 1987 *Farm life in a Carolingian village*, Assen

Hall, A R, and Kenward, H K, 1994 *Urban-rural connexions: perspectives from environmental archaeology*, Oxbow Monogr, **47**, Oxford

Hall, D, 1993 *The open fields of Northamptonshire: the case for the preservation of ridge and furrow*, Northampton

Heidinga, H A, 1987 *Medieval settlement and economy north of the Lower Rhine: archaeology and history of Kootwijk and the Veluwe (the Netherlands)*, Assen

Hooke, D, 1994 The administrative and settlement framework of early medieval Wessex, in *The medieval landscape of Wessex* (eds M Aston and C Lewis), Oxbow Monogr, **46**, 83–96, Oxford

Jones, M, and Dimbleby, G W (eds), 1981 *The environment of man: the Iron Age to the Anglo-Saxon period*, BAR, **87**, Oxford

Jones, M E 1996 *The end of Roman Britain*, Ithaca and London

Kelly, R, 1982 The excavation of a medieval farmhouse at Cefn Graeanog, Clynnog, Gwynedd, *Bull Board Celtic Stud*, **29**, 859–908

Kenward, H K, and Hall, A R, 1995 *Biological evidence from 16–22 Coppergate*, Archaeology of York, **14/7**, York

Kerkham, C, and Briggs, C S, 1991 A review of the archaeological potential of the Hafod landscape, Cardiganshire, in Brown 1991, 160–74

Limbrey, S, and Evans, J G (eds), 1978 *The effect of man on the landscape: the lowland zone*, CBA Res Rep, **21**, London

Mackay, A W, and Tallis, J H, 1994 The recent vegetational history of the Forest of Bowland, Lancashire, UK, *New Phytol*, **128**, 571–84

Macphail, R I, 1994 The reworking of urban stratigraphy by human and natural processes, in Hall and Kenward 1994, 13–43

Maguire, D, Ralph, N, and Fleming, A, 1983 Early land use on Dartmoor- palaeobotanical and pedological investigations on Holne Moor, in *Integrating the subsistence economy* (ed M Jones), BAR, Int Ser, **181**, 57–106, Oxford

Mikkelsen, V M, 1986 *Borup man and vegetation*, The Royal Danish Academy of Sciences and Letters' Commission for Research on the History of Agricultural Implements and Field Structures, **4**, Copenhagen

Mitchell, F, 1986 *The Shell guide to reading the Irish landscape*, Dublin

Moore, P D, 1968 Human influence upon vegetational history in north Cardiganshire, *Nature*, **217**, 1006–7

Murphy, P, 1987 Plant macrofossils from two sections through river valley sediments on the Chelmsford by-pass, Essex, Anc Mon Lab Rep, **120/87**, 1–13

—, 1994 The Anglo-Saxon economy: some results from sites in East Anglia and Essex, in Rackham 1994, 23–39

Murphy, P, and Scaife, R G, 1991 The environmental archaeology of gardens, in Brown 1991, 83–99

Ogley, B, 1988 *In the wake of the hurricane*, Westerham

Peglar, S M, 1993a The development of the cultural landscape around Diss Mere, Norfolk, UK, during the past 7000 years, *Rev Palaeobot and Palynol*, **76**, 1–47

—, 1993b The mid-Holocene *Ulmus* decline at Diss Mere, Norfolk, UK: a year-by-year pollen stratigraphy from annual laminations, *The Holocene*, **3**, 1–13

Peglar, S M, Fritz, S C, and Birks, H J B, 1989 Vegetation and land-use history at Diss, Norfolk, UK, *J Ecol*, **77**, 203–22

Peterken, G F, 1974 A method for assessing woodland flora for conservation using indicator species, *Biol Conservation*, **6**, 239–45

—, 1981 *Woodland conservation and management*, London

Peterken, G F, and Game, M, 1984 Historical factors affecting the number and distribution of vascular plant species in the woodlands of central Lincolnshire, *J Ecol*, **72**, 155–82

Pilcher, J R, 1993 Radiocarbon dating and the palynologist: a realistic approach to precision and accuracy, in *Climate change and human impact on the landscape* (ed F M Chambers), 23–32, London

Pollard, E, Hooper, M D, and Moore, N W, 1974 *Hedges*, London

Preece, R C, and Day, S P, 1994 Comparison of post-glacial molluscan and vegetational successions from a radiocarbon-dated tufa sequence in Oxfordshire, *J Biogeogr*, **21**, 463–78

Price, U, 1794 *An essay on the picturesque*, London

Rackham, O, 1976 *Trees and woodland in the British landscape*, London

—, 1980 *Ancient woodland*, London

—, 1990 *Trees and woodland in the British landscape*, rev edn, London

Rackham, J, (ed) 1994 *Environment and economy in Anglo-Saxon England*, CBA Res Rep, **89**, York

Rippon, S, 1996 *Gwent Levels: the evolution of a wetland landscape*, CBA Res Rep, **105**, York

Robinson, M, 1978 The problem of hedges enclosing Roman and earlier fields, in *Early land allotment* (eds HC Bowen and PJ Fowler), BAR, **48**, 155–8, Oxford

Robinson, M and Wilson, B, 1987 A survey of the environmental archaeology in the south Midlands, in *Environmental archaeology: a regional review, vol II* (ed H C M Keeley), DAMHB Occas Pap, **1**, 16–100, London

Schumer, B, 1984 *The evolution of Wychwood to 1400: pioneers, frontiers, and forests*, Univ Leicester, Dept English Local History, Occas Pap, 3 ser, **6**, Leicester

Sims, R E, 1978 Man and vegetation in Norfolk, in Limbrey and Evans 1978, 57–62

Smith, C 1979 *Fisherwick: the reconstruction of an Iron Age landscape*, BAR, **61**, Oxford

—, 1980 The historical development of the landscape in the parishes of Alrewas, Fisherwick and Whittington: a retrogressive analysis, *S Staffordshire Archaeol Hist Soc Trans*, **20**, 1–14

Steensberg, A, 1983 *Borup AD 700–1400: a deserted settlement and its fields*, Copenhagen

Thorarinsson, S, 1979 On the damage caused by volcanic eruptions with special reference to tephra and gases, in *Volcanic activity and human ecology* (eds P D Sheets and D K Grayson), 125–59, New York

Thurley, S, 1996 *The King's Privy Garden at Hampton Court Palace 1689–1995*, London

Tilley, C, 1994 *A phenomenology of landscape*, Oxford

Troels-Smith, J, 1955 Karakterisering af løse jordata, *Danmarks Geologiske Undersøgelse*, Raekke IV, **3**, 1–73

Turner, J, 1964 The anthropogenic factor in vegetational history I: Tregaron and Whixall mosses, *New Phytol*, **63**, 73–90

—, 1979 The environment of northeast England during Roman times as shown by pollen analysis, *J Archaeol Sci*, **6**, 285–90

—, 1981 The vegetation, in Jones and Dimbleby 1981, 67–73

Waton, P V, 1982 Man's impact on the chalklands: some new pollen evidence, in *Archaeological aspects of woodland ecology* (eds M Bell and S Limbrey), BAR, Int Ser, **146**, 75–92, Oxford

Williamson, T, 1988 Settlement chronology and regional landscapes: the evidence from the claylands of East Anglia and Essex, in *Anglo-Saxon settlements* (ed D Hooke), 153–75, Oxford

Young, C J, 1977 *The Roman pottery industry of the Oxford region*, BAR, **43**, Oxford

20 The archaeological study of medieval English human populations, AD 1066–1540

by Simon Mays

Abstract

Our most direct source of evidence concerning earlier human populations is the remains of the people themselves, yet a browse through some of the general archaeological textbooks used in British universities reveals that few devote much space to the discussion of results of scientific work on human remains. This is symptomatic of the way in which the study of human bones has become marginalised in British archaeology since the 1960s. There are a variety of reasons for this rather sorry state of affairs, but in recent years things have started to improve, as human bone specialists become more attuned to the needs of the archaeological mainstream, and increasingly orientate their work towards issues of general rather than purely specialist interest. This paper attempts to illustrate this point for the medieval period in England using recent scientific work that has been carried out on human remains. It begins with a brief resume of the history of human osteoarchaeology in Britain. There then follows a consideration of the nature of the bone evidence we have from the medieval period, and what we have learnt from it so far. In the light of this, possible future directions for archaeological work on medieval populations are discussed.

Human osteoarchaeology in Britain

Until the 1960s, major changes in material culture in British archaeology were generally explained with reference to invading or immigrant peoples. Within this paradigm, studies of human remains played a central part, as skulls were measured in an effort to find evidence for ancient migrations. With the abandonment of this traditional framework, the study of human skeletal remains tended to drift into something of a backwater as far as archaeology was concerned. There were changes in the character of research in human remains, as more practitioners came to it from a medical rather than from a physical anthropology background. This led to an increasing emphasis on palaeopathology, the study of disease in ancient bones. A corollary of this was that much osteological work was driven by medico-historical rather than by archaeological questions, an approach that increased the isolation of human osteology from mainstream archaeology in Britain.

This approach has had mutually disadvantageous effects. Many mainstream archaeologists were unaware of the potential of human remains for addressing questions of general rather than of specialist interest; the same appeared to be true of many bone specialists. Then, as now, much human bone work took the form of osteological reports for site monographs. Many human bone reports were, however, rather stereotyped and were primarily directed at a specialist audience, making it difficult to integrate them with the rest of the site report. As a result, bone reports tended to be consigned to appendices or microfiche.

The lack of impact made on archaeology by scientific analyses of human remains is evident when consulting standard university textbooks: few contain much in the way of discussion of results of osteological work. Many undergraduate courses in archaeology included little on the study of human skeletal remains, a situation that would have been unthinkable for other classes of evidence, such as pottery or metalwork.

This rather sorry state of affairs is starting to change. A 'biocultural approach' has increasingly been adopted by British workers in recent years. This originated in the 1960s and 1970s in the US as part of the 'New Archaeology', which took the view that man adapted to his environment by a combination of biological and cultural adaptation (eg Binford 1962). This perspective facilitated the integration of osteological and artefactual data in order to present a more complete picture of the human past. It was seized upon by US physical anthropologists tired of seeing their work consigned to appendices of site reports (discussion in Buikstra 1977).

The biocultural approach adopted in recent years by British human bone specialists is less rigidly bound to the notion of adaptiveness as an explanation for patterns observed than were the early efforts of the American New Archaeologists. Indeed, a perusal of some recent British publications claiming a biocultural approach would seem to indicate that the only common factor is a realisation that skeletal data need to be integrated with other evidence, and that the focus should be on the study of patterns at a population level rather than on the study of individual cases. Cynics might say workers such as Thurnam were taking exactly this sort of approach more than 100 years ago in their studies using skull form to investigate migrations. The reinstatement of this type of approach in osteoarchaeology, however, is belated and to be welcomed.

On a practical level, trends towards improvements in integration between human bone work and mainstream archaeology are also evident. Ten years ago, many human bone specialists worked in isolation, a situation that led to the discipline being characterised as a 'cottage industry' (Roberts 1986). In recent years this has changed, as more bone specialists are located in university departments and archaeological units, so that the work is carried out in an academic environment and is not starved of other archaeological input. Another healthy sign is the establishment of postgraduate courses at some British universities teaching human osteology from an explicitly archaeological viewpoint.

The burial evidence for the medieval period

Almost 30,000 medieval burials have been recovered from archaeological excavations in England (Mays nd). These burials come from about 200 sites, ranging from chance finds of single skeletons to systematic excavations of cemeteries yielding hundreds or even thousands of interments. If a large assemblage is taken as one containing 100 burials or more, about 50 such are known. Only a fairly small sub-set of these have been the subject of adequate published reports, however (Table 20.1).

Many of the sites listed in Table 20.1 are religious foundations, with burials of brethren and lay benefactors,

and in addition, most are urban. These imbalances in the data will be redressed to some extent when large rural lay sites, such as Wharram Percy, Kellington, and the collection from the small town of Barton-on-Humber, are published.

At many medieval sites, the burials can only be dated to within rather broad limits, and it is often impossible to split assemblages by phase. For example, many friaries were founded in the thirteenth century and were used for burial until the dissolution in about 1540; in most instances it is not possible to date burials more closely. It is rarely possible to split medieval skeletal assemblages into pre- and post-Black Death burials. The depletion of population in England in the mid fourteenth century as a consequence of the Black Death resulted in better living conditions for most of those who survived, as labour became scarcer and wages rose (Hatcher 1994). One aspect of this was the improvement in diet of the poor (Dyer 1989; Hatcher 1994). In theory, scientific study of human skeletal remains would be well-suited to the study of this phenomenon; little has yet been done in this direction, however, mainly owing to problems over dating.

Table 20.1 Some large medieval English assemblages with published (or at least readily available) bone reports

site	no of burials	reference
Carlisle Blackfriars	214	Henderson (1990)
Chelmsford Blackfriars	138	Bayley (1975)
Gloucester Blackfriars	129	Wiggins et al (1993)
Guildford Blackfriars	113	Henderson (1984)
Hartlepool Greyfriars	150	Birkett and Marlow (1986)
Ipswich Blackfriars	250	Mays (1991)
Lincoln, St Marks Church	299	Dawes (1986)
London, Stratford Langthorne Priory	c 500	Stuart-Macadam (1986)[1]
London, Merton Priory	c 230	Waldron (1985a)[2]
London, St Nicholas Shambles	234	White (1988)
Raunds	363	Powell (1996)[3]
Rivenhall Church	229	O'Connor (1993)[3]
Stonar Church	147	Eley and Bayley (1975)
Taunton Priory	162	Rogers (1985)
Trowbridge Castle	293	Jenkins and Rogers (1993)[3]
York Fishergate, Gilbertine Priory	271	Stroud and Kemp (1993)
York, Jewbury	476	Stroud et al (1994)
York, St Helen-on-the-Walls	1041	Dawes (1980)

[1] report on 104 burials
[2] report on 74 burials
[3] includes some pre-conquest burials

note: when results from individual sites are discussed in the text, the data come from the works cited in this table unless otherwise stated

What have the bones told us?

The study of human skeletal remains can provide a variety of information of value both to a specialist and to a more general archaeological audience. This paper concentrates on the latter. The discussion below considers the contribution of studies of medieval human remains to a number of themes of mainstream archaeological interest.

Burial practices

Until fairly recently, the archaeological study of mortuary practices in medieval cemeteries had been comparatively neglected, but lately, improved excavation and field recording protocols have shown that Christian burials, although of course generally lacking grave goods, are far from blandly uniform. They show a surprising range of variation in grave structure, burial type, body position, and other features, and recently the study of Christian mortuary practices has been something of a growth area (eg Boddington 1996; Daniell 1997, 118–19, 145–174).

In cemetery excavations, detailed recording of body position of burials is now routine. In most medieval cemeteries, the usual practice is burial of a supine corpse with the arms placed by the sides or over the pelvic area. Which arm position is favoured does not seem to show any regular geographical or chronological pattern (Heighway nd), but on a local level some patterning has been observed. For example, most cemeteries in the York area favour a hands-across-the-pelvis position. The exception is Jewbury, where the normal posture was with the arms by the sides. This was interpreted as a distinctive Jewish burial practice, along with the avoidance of intercutting of graves (Lilley *et al* 1994).

At Ipswich Blackfriars, the body posture of the inhumations seemed to show a relationship with gender (Table 20.2). At this site, nearly all interments with hands placed on the chest are males, indeed no certain females are found in this position. It is unclear why this posture should be (?exclusively) associated with males while at the same time being the burial posture for only a minority of men. At the Ipswich Blackfriars, no cemetery for the exclusive use of brethren was located, and it is tempting to speculate that these 'praying position' burials are interments of friars.

At some sites there is evidence for discrete spatial clustering of infant burials. At Wharram Percy, infants were found to be concentrated in the portion of the churchyard immediately to the north of the church (Table 20.3). About two-thirds of infants who died before their first birthday were buried in the north churchyard, compared with only about one third of children older than two years. A transition in preference for burial location seems to occur between one and two years old. One obvious explanation might be that baptism of infants generally occurred at this age: the north side of the church is the traditional area for, among others, burials of the unbaptised (Grauer 1991, 70; Harding 1996).

In medieval times, baptism was an important sacrament: the infant, born from the carnal lust of his parents, and inheriting the sin of Adam and Eve, needed to be cleansed of the sin of his conception and heritage. Proper baptism was undertaken one week after birth (Shahar 1990, 46); if the newborn infant's life appeared in danger, however, then it was baptised immediately. In the absence of a priest any lay person could perform a baptism, and indeed were obliged to do so as a Christian duty. Furthermore, if during delivery it appeared that the child might be stillborn, midwives were permitted to baptise any limb that emerged (Shahar 1990, 49).

Given the importance of baptism in the medieval mind, it seems inconceivable that it could be routinely delayed for one to two years, and hence, because of the

Table 20.2 Arm position in adult burials from Ipswich Blackfriars

	males	*females*
on chest	21[*]	3[#]
across pelvic area	16[*]	5[*]
by sides	66[+]	44[*]

[*] includes one case in which sex could not be determined with certainty

[+] includes two cases in which sex could not be determined with certainty

[#] includes three cases in which sex could not be determined with certainty

Table 20.3 Age structure of burials to the immediate north of the church (NA) compared with those from other areas at Wharram Percy

	location			
age (years)	*NA*		*other*	
perinatal	44	(67%)	22	(33%)
0–0.9	21	(60%)	14	(40%)
1–1.9	15	(50%)	15	(50%)
2–2.9	8	(38%)	13	(62%)
3–4.9	12	(38%)	20	(62%)
5–18	47	(33%)	96	(67%)
adults (18+)	70	(19%)	290	(81%)

high infant mortality, denied to so many infants. Perhaps some other life transition occurred during this period which was given recognition in burial treatment at Wharram Percy. Table 20.3 also shows that more children (aged 2–18) were interred in the north churchyard than adults. Perhaps the transition to adulthood was also to some extent being given recognition in burial location at Wharram Percy, although the small numbers of adolescent burials means that the precise age at which this transition occurred cannot be established.

Monastic life

Given the large proportion of medieval burials that come from religious houses, an important area of potential is the study of monastic life.

Diffuse idiopathic skeletal hyperostosis (DISH) is a condition in which there is new bone formation, particularly at ligament and tendon insertions. It is generally a disease of older people, being rare before 40 years of age, and it is more common in men. Its most striking manifestation in skeletal remains is in the thoracic spine, where large, flowing ossifications may unite several vertebrae. The causes of DISH are not fully understood, but there does seem to be an association with obesity and late-onset diabetes (Julkunen et al 1971). Rogers et al (1985) looked at a large number of skeletons of various dates and found DISH in about 2.3%. Many of those with DISH came from the upper social classes with higher standards of living and nutrition than most. Waldron (1985b) found a high prevalence of DISH (8.6%) among burials from the canons' cemetery at Merton Priory. He felt that this might be associated with obesity among the brethren, a possibility perhaps supported by documentary accounts of over-enthusiastic consumption of food and drink by medieval monks and friars.

The association between DISH and high status/religious sites was also evident at Ipswich. At the Blackfriars site, DISH was present in 9 (13%) of the 67 adults for which the condition could be scored; all except one were males. The frequency of DISH in the over 40s today was reported as 2.8% by Julkunen et al (1971). As well as being higher than in a recent population, the frequency of DISH at the Ipswich Blackfriars was also greater than in a nearby non-monastic burial ground of tenth–eleventh century date. Here none of the 51 adults who could be scored for DISH showed the disease (Mays 1991, 41). If Waldron was correct to emphasise the association with obesity, then the Ipswich results would seem to suggest a lifestyle difference between those at the lay and those at the monastic site, implying over-nutrition and obesity among those buried at the friary. At the Blackfriars site, as at many other friary sites, it was impossible to determine in individual cases whether a burial was of a friar or of a lay person. It is unclear whether the Ipswich pattern is connected with monastic lifestyles or whether it simply reflects high living among the monied benefactors who elected to be buried at the friary.

A friary where burials of brethren could be distinguished from those of lay benefactors is that of the Gilbertines at Fishergate, York. To the east of the conventual church lay a burial area that, except for a few burials around the periphery, contained only adult males. For this reason it was interpreted as the burial ground for members of the priory (Stroud and Kemp 1993, 136). By contrast, most other areas of the site, such as the church nave, contained burials of men, women, and children, and so were thought to be for lay burial. There was no significant difference in the prevalence of DISH between lay and monastic burials here, but there was other evidence, in the form of bone carbon stable isotope ratios, for dietary differences between the two groups.

Carbon stable isotope values are conventionally measured in delta units (‰), values for biological samples are generally less than zero. In terrestrial ecosystems there are differences in carbon stable isotope ratios according to the photosynthetic pathway of the plant. Plants using the C3 pathway (most temperate zone vegetation) have more negative delta values than C4 plants (some tropical and sub-tropical species). There are also differences between marine and terrestrial organisms, the former having less negative values than the latter. These differences are transmitted to animal and human tissues via the foods eaten, so bone stable isotope ratios have the potential to inform us about ancient diets. Prior to their importation from abroad, there were no C4 foods in northern Europe, so most European work on carbon stable isotopes has been directed at the study the relative marine contribution to ancient diets. The carbon stable isotope results for the Fishergate site are shown in Figure 20.1.

The bone collagen delta value expected from an individual on a purely terrestrial diet is about -21.5‰, that corresponding to an entirely marine diet is about -12‰ (Mays 1997a). Although precise quantification of dietary components from stable isotope data is problematic, the Fishergate figures indicate (as might be expected) a predominantly terrestrial diet, but one in which a significant part (perhaps about one fifth to one third) of the protein component was supplied by marine foods. As well as attesting to the importance of fish in diets in medieval York, the stable isotope data also indicate a dietary difference between lay and monastic burials: the less negative delta value of the monastic individuals indicates that marine foods made up a greater proportion of their diets.

The dietary rules of many medieval religious houses proscribed the consumption of meat, but fish could be

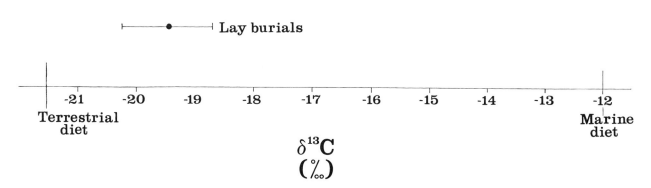

Fig 20.1 Carbon stable isotope data from the burials from the York Fishergate site (drawn from figures in Mays 1997a)

substituted. Documentary evidence indicates considerable consumption of fish by religious communities, and sea fish were generally preferred to fresh-water varieties (Bond 1988). Little in the way of food remains was found at the priory, but the study of what was recovered enabled O'Connor (1991) to infer that fish, particularly herring, formed a substantial minority of the diet. Stroud and Kemp (1993) found that the dental caries rate was lower among those in the eastern cemetery. This may reflect the cariostatic effects of heavy seafood consumption or it may be associated with some additional, unsuspected dietary difference between monastic and layfolk.

The monastic burials at the Fishergate site all came from the first two centuries of the priory's existence. The stable isotope evidence would seem to indicate that religious edicts were exerting an influence over eating habits, at least during the earlier years of the priory, and the lack of a raised level of DISH in this population may indicate that the brethren there had not (yet?) succumbed to the sin of gluttony.

Towns and their hinterlands

Human remains have great potential to contribute to this theme, but the extent to which this has been realised is limited by the availability of material. The only region in which medieval data are available both for urban sites, and for rural settlements in their environs, is the York area. Table 20.1 shows that York itself is rich in medieval remains, and some results from the large assemblage from the deserted medieval village of Wharram Percy, which lies in its general hinterland, are also available. Further unpublished large rural assemblages from Kellington and Barton-on-Humber will add to the picture in future. The following discussion is based on work that has been done on sites in the York area. Environment, diet, public health, and migration patterns have been investigated.

Environment

Lewis *et al* (1995) investigated airborne pollution and its effects on human health. They looked at Wharram Percy and the urban group from St Helen-on-the-Walls, Aldwark, a church that served a poor parish in York with much craft and small scale industrial activity. They studied maxillary sinusitis in these skeletons and found a higher level in the urban sample. Air pollution has been associated with rises in respiratory tract infections, including sinusitis, so Lewis *et al* (1995) suggest that increased air pollution, as a result of industrial activities in the urban environment, may have been a cause of the pattern they observed.

Diet

In addition to the work directed at investigating monastic diet, carbon stable isotopes have been used to investigate possible dietary differences between urban York and rural Wharram Percy. York was a major trading centre in the medieval period, Wharram Percy was a fairly small and remote upland settlement. One might expect that the wealthy townsfolk buried at the Fishergate site had greater access to foods of non-local origin, such as sea foods, than did their contemporaries at Wharram Percy. This expectation was not supported by the stable isotope data: the mean value for Wharram Percy (-19.70‰) was similar to that among the layfolk from Fishergate. Neither were there apparent differences in the rate of dental caries, about two thirds of adult individuals being affected at each site. The work that has thus far been done reveals no evidence of a dietary difference between the two sites in the medieval period.

Public health

Porotic hyperostosis is a condition manifest in skeletal remains as pitting of the skull, particularly the roofs of the orbits. It represents an overgrowth of the diploe, apparently in response to anaemia (Stuart-Macadam 1987; 1989), in the majority of populations iron-deficiency anaemia. Iron-deficiency anaemia is rarely the result of lack of iron in the diet, it generally results from disease, particularly gastro-intestinal parasites or infections: diarrhoea causes food to pass through the gut too quickly for nutrients and minerals such as iron to be absorbed, and parasite infestations may lead to anaemia through chronic blood loss (Kent and Dunn 1996; Kent *et al* 1994; Stuart-Macadam 1992).

A higher rate of porotic hyperostosis is evident in the York St Helen's group than at Wharram Percy (Table 20.4). Large numbers of people living in close proximity favour the spread of disease. As well as offering increased opportunities for disease transmission between persons, sanitation and hygiene also tend to be poorer, mainly due to contamination of water supplies. These sorts of crowded, unhygienic conditions characterised many medieval cities, and written sources show that York was no exception (Grauer 1993). The high rate of porotic hyperostosis at St Helen-on-the-Walls, situated in one of the poorest parishes, may reflect this. The lower rate at Wharram Percy may testify to the lesser sanitation problems posed in a rural parish with a lower population density.

The conditions in medieval cities would doubtless have been conducive to the spread of most infectious diseases. An important way in which infectious disease manifests itself on the skeleton is via periostitis, the subperiosteal deposition of fresh bone on existing bone surfaces. Frequencies of periostitis are higher at York than at Wharram Percy (Table 20.5). This suggests a greater pathogen load in the urban environment. More of the St Helen's urban people were probably suffering from infectious disease for more of their lives than were those from Wharram Percy.

It takes time for infectious disease to produce skeletal changes, so it is only the longer-lasting conditions that have the potential to leave traces on the bones. A group such as that from Wharram Percy, which shows relatively little in the way of bone infections, may do so because few had enough resistance to infectious disease

to survive long enough once they did contract it for it to affect the skeleton. Perhaps those at Wharram Percy did not have the long-term exposure from birth to a large variety of pathogens that city dwellers did, so that when infectious disease did strike it generally killed quickly, before bone changes could occur. The high rate of bone changes in the York group, as well as indicating a greater disease load, may also be a testament to these people's resistance to disease, many recovering or at least surviving for extended periods before succumbing.

Another aspect of the bone evidence perhaps supports this idea. Of the periosteal lesions in the York group, the majority (68%) were remodelled, indicating that the individual was rallying or had rallied from the disease that caused them (Grauer 1993). At Wharram Percy, remodelled lesions are a minority (40%).

Migrants

A potential problem when comparing urban and rural sites is that we do not know what proportion of their lives people spent in the parish in which they were buried. In the medieval period, urban centres were maintained by immigration from surrounding rural areas (Russell 1948), so some of those buried at urban cemeteries may have spent some part of their lives in a rural rather than an urban environment. This means that there may in many cases be a blurring of distinctions in terms of pathologies, etc, between urban and rural assemblages, and it also reminds us to treat comparisons between sites with caution.

Goldberg (1986) has shown from a study of documentary evidence from northern England, that in the medieval period the populations of many urban centres showed a sex imbalance in favour of females. For example in Hull the sex ratio was 0.86 and at York 0.91. She connects this with female-led migration into urban centres from surrounding rural areas. Migrant female labour was absorbed into domestic service and craft industries such as weaving. Many of these migrants probably settled in the poorer areas of cities.

In York, rental evidence points towards a high incidence of single women living in cheap tenements in poor districts such as Aldwark (Goldberg 1986). In the

Table 20.4 Porotic hyperostosis

	frequency of porotic hyperostosis
Wharram Percy	125/502 (25%)
York, St Helen-on-the-Walls[*]	267/460 (58%)

[*] St Helen's data are from Grauer (1993)

Table 20.5 Periostitis

	frequency of periostitis
Wharram Percy	59/687 (9%)
York, St Helen-on-the-Walls[*]	144/661 (22%)

[*] St Helen's data are from Grauer (1993)

skeletal assemblage from the cemetery of the church of St Helen-on-the-Walls, Aldwark, there were 394 adult females and 338 adult males, a statistically significant sex imbalance in favour of females. Although we should be wary of making simplistic connections between historical and archaeological data, one cannot help but wonder whether the excess of females at St Helen's is a reflection of female-led migrations into the parish from rural settlements in the York area.

At Wharram Percy there are 215 males and 136 females, giving a sex ratio of 1.58 in favour of males. Wharram Percy lies about 20 miles from York, and Russell (1948) offers historical evidence pertaining to York that many probably migrated this sort of distance to become resident in the city. Perhaps at Wharram Percy we are seeing the other side of the coin as far as migration patterns are concerned, as female-led emigration left a rural sex ratio dominated by males.

Cranial measurements are collected on a routine basis when skeletons are examined for the purpose of preparing bone reports for site monographs, so such data are abundant for the medieval period. There is a huge literature on the causes of cranial variation, including the contributions of genetic factors, diet, nutrition, and climate (discussion in Mays 1998, 77–86). Despite this abundance of data, and background information to help us interpret it, little progress has been made recently on craniometric studies in Britain. Few bone reports show any real analysis of the craniometric data they generate, and fewer still show data collection strategies and analyses properly directed at archaeological problems. However, there have been some useful multivariate studies of medieval crania in the last 20 years. For example Dawes (1980) studied data from various populations from York and the surrounding area. Interestingly, in view of the above discussion, she found a particularly close affinity between Wharram Percy crania and those from St Helen's.

In a more recent multivariate study, also from York, Williamson (1994) examined the material from Jewbury. He found that the cranial form of the Jewish burials was distinct from another York population (St Helen's), although differences were quite small. Distinction in terms of cranial form is congruent with the notion that this population was culturally, and to some extent biologically, isolated from the rest of the city's inhabitants.

Demography

Infant burials are often only found in rather small numbers in medieval cemetery sites (Table 20.6). What sort of proportion of infants might we expect to find in a medieval skeletal assemblage if the sample accurately reflected mortality patterns? Documentary data on infant mortality in the medieval period are almost non-existent, but we can perhaps make estimates by projecting back from post-medieval data. At Colyton, Devon, Wrigley (1968) infers that about 12–20% of infants died in their first year during the period 1538–1837. The corresponding estimate for Wrangle, Lincolnshire, in the period 1597–1642 is 24%, that for the urban parish of St Michael le Belfry, London, in 1571–86 is 23.5% (ibid). Of course, documentary data of this sort have their own problems and biasses, some of which lead to over- and some to under-enumeration of infant deaths. Nevertheless, they do give an approximate idea of the kinds of figures we might expect in medieval times. From this it would seem that only Stonar, Raunds, and Wharram Percy approach the levels of infant mortality we might expect to see.

It is often argued that infant bones preserve more poorly than those of older children and adults. This may be true under soil conditions that are marginal for bone preservation (Gordon and Buikstra 1981), but personal observation of the state of infant bones suggests that this does not hold true for most sites, where bone survival is generally reasonable, and this subjective impression is

Table 20.6 Proportions of infants at various sites

site	proportion of infants		
Chelmsford Blackfriars	1%	(1/138)	(under 1 year)
Ipswich Blackfriars	2%	(5/250)	(under 2 years)
Jewbury	3%	(13/471)	(under 1 year)
York, St Helen-on-the-Walls	3%	(33/1041)	(under 2.5 years)
Rivenhall	4%	(9/229)	(under 1 year)
St Nicholas Shambles, London	5%	(12/234)	(under 2 years)
St Marks, Lincoln	8%	(23/299)	(under 2.5 years)
Gloucester Blackfriars	8%	(10/129)	(under 2 years)
Stonar	18%	(26/147)	(under 1.5 years)
Wharram Percy	19%	(131/687)	(under 2 years)
Raunds	20%	(73/363)	(under 1 year)

supported by recent work that involved checking burial records against excavated interments (Saunders 1992). Saunders suggests that most losses of small infant bones are due to poor recovery rather than to preservation factors, and in addition more shallow infant graves may be lost by erosion or machining of a site prior to excavation than the (presumably) deeper adult burials. It seems unlikely, however, that these factors can account for the very low numbers of infants at many medieval sites, nor can they account for the differences between sites seen in Table 20.6.

At monastic sites, the payment necessary to secure a burial plot may have meant that infants were simply not selected for burial there, they went into the local parish churchyard, most of which are still in use today and so have never been excavated. It must be admitted, however, that urban churchyards that have been excavated, such as St Nicholas Shambles and St Helen-on-the-Walls, were found to contain few infants. Reasons for this are not clear. It might be suggested that at these sites infant burials were localised in some part of the churchyard that lay beyond the excavated area. At some churchyards, such as Rivenhall, Wharram Percy, and Raunds, spatial clustering of infant burials has been found. These sites, however, indicate that such clusters, when they occur, tend to be located close to the church walls; these areas were indeed excavated at St Nicholas Shambles and at St Helen-on-the-Walls, but few infants were found. Some (eg Daniell 1997, 127–8; Grauer 1993) have argued that unbaptised infants may have been excluded from burial grounds. This is not, however, a likely explanation for the patterns observed in Table 20.6: as we have seen, baptism was normally carried out promptly, particularly if the infant's life was thought to be in danger, and in any event, it is not just the newborn that are missing, for older infants, too, are absent. Furthermore, it is unclear why, if Table 20.6 is anything to go by, infants seem to have regularly been denied burial in urban churchyards whereas this does not appear to be the case (or at least not nearly to the same extent) in rural ones.

Turning to the other end of the demographic scale, to adult age at death, we are immediately faced with problems in analysing this from cemetery data. The greatest difficulty is problems in determining accurately age at death from skeletal material in the adult, and it is only recently that the extent of the problems with many of the routinely used methods of ageing has been generally appreciated, mainly as a result of work on the Spitalfields collection of known-age-at-death material (Aiello and Molleson 1993; Molleson and Cox 1993). The sheer variety of techniques used by different writers to estimate adult age also makes inter-site comparisons difficult. The most reliable adult ageing technique for

archaeological material is dental wear, particularly when rate of wear can be calibrated using the juvenile portion of the assemblage. This was the technique used at Wharram Percy. The results are shown in Table 20.7.

Table 20.7 suggests that at Wharram Percy a medieval peasant on the threshold of adulthood had about a four in ten chance of living to beyond 50 years old. There are, however, a number of possible biassing factors that need to be taken into account before this interpretation can be accepted. If one accepts the evidence discussed above, that emigration to cities such as York was an important factor at Wharram Percy, then the effect of this needs to be considered. The key point here is the age at which migrants tended to leave. For example, if most left in middle age, this would have the effect of skewing the Wharram Percy adult age at death distribution towards the younger age groups, whereas if most left in late adolescence this would have little effect, as those that remained could either die young or live to grow old. Logically, one might expect most migrants to leave in late adolescence or early adulthood, and this is to some extent supported by Goldberg's documentary data for migrants into York, but in the last analysis this question must remain unresolved. We also need to remember that the Wharram Percy burials, like most assemblages from archaeological sites, cover a period of several centuries, so that at best they will represent longevity data averaged over a very long period.

Table 20.7 Age distribution of Wharram Percy adult burials

estimated age	number	percent
18–29	65	21
30–49	116	39
50+	119	40

As with the infant mortality data, it is worth comparing osteologically derived patterns of adult ages at death, with those estimated from documentary evidence. Two studies are used here, that of Russell (1937), which uses data from Inquisitions Post Mortem relating to the period 1250–1348, and Thrupp's (1962) study of London Merchants who died during the period 1448–1520 (Table 20.8). Given the vagaries of the sources and the differences between the samples in social and chronological terms, the nearly identical results of the two historical studies are surprising indeed. The distributions are also not too dissimilar to that from Wharram Percy, although the former are in general a little older, with more dying in the 50+ age group. Although, due to likely shortcomings in both the historical and archaeological data, we should probably draw comparisons only in the most general terms: the differences observed between the Wharram Percy and the historical results are understandable in the light of differences between the data sets. For example, the Wharram Percy peasants were among the poorest members of what was a highly stratified society, whereas the documentary data refer to wealthy landowners and merchants. One might therefore expect the longevity of the Wharram Percy peasants to be less. Furthermore, the documentary data exclude the great plague years of the mid fourteenth century, whereas the osteological data cover the entire medieval period, plagues and all. This would tend to skew the documentary data towards the older ages.

Continuity and Change

Processes of change are an important focus for studies using human remains just as they are for archaeology as a whole. The following examples show how continuity and change in medieval and later human populations have been investigated.

Moore *et al* (1968) analysed the form of the mandible in British populations from approximately 3000 BC to recent times. They found a reduction in mandible size over time, particularly in the areas most associated with the attachment of powerful chewing muscles (Fig 20.2). The greater part of this reduction occurred between the medieval period and the seven-

Table 20.8 Age distribution in Russell's (1937) and Thrupp's (1962) demographic studies

	Russell		Thrupp	
age	number	percent	number	percent
22–29*	58	10	10	10
30–49	232	40	39	40
50+	292	50	48	50

*21–29 in Russell's case

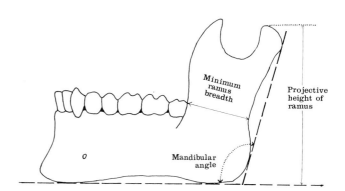

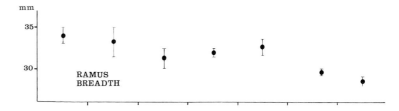

Fig 20.2 Three mandibular measurements, showing trends in British material from the Neolithic to the nineteenth century AD (after Moore et al 1968, figs 1, 3, and 4): the reduction in ramus dimensions is indicative of a reduction in the chewing muscles associated with this part of the jaw; the increase in the mandibular angle is probably partly associated with the reduction in the mandibular ramus, but also reflects a reduction in the development of the angular region itself, where the powerful masseter muscle attaches

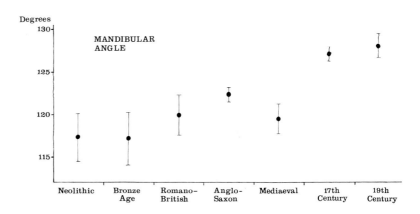

teenth century. The tougher the diet, the greater the bite forces required. This leads to greater development of the jaw muscles and hence to greater development of the bones of the facial skeleton to which they attach. Moore *et al* (1968) associated the reduction in mandibular development with a transition to a softer diet in post-medieval times, a change for which there is also documentary evidence. By the seventeenth century it is likely that urban groups were generally consuming bread made from finely milled flour, in contrast to the coarse bran and rye breads that formed the staples in earlier periods. Consistent with this conclusion there is also a decrease in the rate of dental wear in post-medieval populations (Brothwell 1963; Moore and Corbett 1978).

The post-medieval material examined by Moore *et al* (1968) was all from urban sites, so it is unclear whether the changes they observed also occurred at the same time in rural populations. Preliminary data from Wharram Percy suggest that they may not have done. Although the bulk of the burials from Wharram Percy are of medieval date, there are also some from the post-medieval period. The post-medieval (seventeenth to early nineteenth century) mandibles were similar in form to those from the medieval burials at the site, and there was also no evidence from the teeth for any reduction in the rate of dental wear. It would seem likely that at this rural settlement the old medieval 'foodways' continued long into the post-medieval period.

At urban sites, an increase in the rate of caries has been observed in the post-medieval period, coinciding with the increasing importation of cane sugar (Brothwell 1959; Moore and Corbett 1978; Whittaker and Molleson 1996). This too was not evident at Wharram Percy, the rate of caries among post-medieval burials was similar to that in earlier times. At Barton-on-Humber, too, prevalences of dental diseases did not show the increase found in urban environments (Juliet Rogers, personal communication 1997). Lack of dietary change over time at Wharram Percy was also evident from the stable isotope data: seventeenth–nineteenth century burials showed similar isotope ratios to their medieval forebears.

Changing patterns of infectious disease during the medieval period are another important area of work. The historical and archaeological evidence for the rise and fall of leprosy is a case in point.

Osteoarchaeology provides us with the first good evidence of leprosy in Britain, in the sixth century AD (Wells 1962). Written sources suggest that the disease increased in frequency, to peak in about the twelfth–thirteenth century, declining thereafter, to become rare by the fifteenth century (Clay 1909; Manchester and Roberts 1989). Although sporadic cases of leprosy are found from some medieval cemetery sites (eg Wharram Percy, Stonar Church, Ipswich Blackfriars), they are few due to the medieval practice of incarcerating sufferers in leprosy hospitals, within whose confines they were normally buried. Recently, some leper hospital cemeteries have been excavated in Britain, the largest of which is that of St James and St Mary Magdalene, Chichester. A full report on the bones from this site has yet to appear, but an account of some of the findings from 350 skeletons from the site has been published (Lee and Magilton 1989). The burials date from the twelfth to the seventeenth century. Skeletal evidence from this site testifies to the decline of the disease through the medieval period. In the earliest part of the cemetery, area one, 54% of the burials showed skeletal signs of leprosy, compared with 17% in area two, and 16% in area three, the latest part (Lee and Magilton 1989).

Reasons for the decline of leprosy are not well understood. The segregation of sufferers in leprosy hospitals is unlikely to have helped much: during the early period of infection there are few overt signs of the disease, so these highly infectious individuals would have avoided detection (Lee and Magilton 1989). One hypothesis, suggested by Richards (1960) as a possible explanation for the decrease in frequency of the disease in late medieval Denmark, and later espoused by Manchester (1984; 1991) to explain its concomitant decline in England, is that the decline is related to the rise of tuberculosis. The increase in the prevalence of tuberculosis is thought to be connected with increasing urbanisation favouring person to person transmission of the pulmonary form of the disease, so that by the mid seventeenth century in London it was implicated in 20% of all deaths in non-plague years (Manchester 1991). There is some cross-immunity between *Mycobacterium leprae* and *Mycobacterium tuberculosis*. The latter is more virulent and tends to be contracted earlier in life, so with increased aggregation of population, favouring transmission of tuberculosis, leprosy may tend to be driven out.

If this theory is correct we might expect to see more tuberculosis in urban cemeteries, and more and later leprosy in rural ones. Owing to the segregation of lepers it is difficult to look at the leprosy side of this equation archaeologically, although there is historical evidence from the post-medieval period that the disease hung on for much longer in remote, rural areas (Hart 1989). Medieval documentary evidence for tuberculosis is very sparse and highly problematic. Perhaps the most reliable is that relating to the monks from the Benedictine priory at Christ Church, Canterbury in the fifteenth century (Hatcher 1986). In an analysis of a small dataset relating to causes of death in these monks, Hatcher found that in 31% of instances death was attributed to tuberculosis. By contrast, skeletal cases of tuberculosis are only found in quite small numbers at most cemetery sites. This is due, at least in part, to the fact that only a minority of sufferers show skeletal lesions – about 5–7% according to Steinbock (1976).

This low prevalence in the skeletal record makes it difficult to make inferences from archaeological data, but what evidence we do have gives little sign of an increased prevalence of tuberculosis in urban assemblages. For example it was diagnosed in 1.3% (3/229) of medieval adult skeletons from the York Fishergate site, compared with 2.2% (8/360) at Wharram Percy. A possible complicating factor is that those in rural communities may have suffered more from the form contracted from cattle (*Mycobacterium bovis*), and urban populations more from the human form (*Mycobacterium tuberculosis*). The human form is acquired via the respiratory tract from inhalation of droplets infected by bacilli. The bovine form may be acquired from infected cattle via droplet infection or by consumption of infected meat or milk. Some aspects of living conditions may have encouraged the spread of tuberculosis at Wharram Percy, particularly the fact that peasant long-houses were shared by human and bovine inhabitants. This arrangement would favour the transmission of the disease to man via inhaled droplet infection from cattle. Whether it was indeed the bovine form that was the more common at Wharram Percy remains unresolved as it is difficult to distinguish the two forms osteologically.

Palaeopathology also makes a contribution to the study of the rise of new diseases in the medieval period. Perhaps the best known example concerns the rise of syphilis in Europe. The debate, which has focused on whether the disease was brought back by Columbus and his men or was present in Europe prior to this, is well known and has been adequately covered elsewhere (Baker and Armelagos 1988; papers in Dutour *et al* 1994). Suffice to say that documentary sources, although quite voluminous, have failed to resolve the issue, but a number of finds of pathological skeletons do indicate that some form of treponemal disease was present in Europe before 1493. Due to difficulties in distinguishing in dry bones other treponemal diseases (treponarid [endemic syphilis] in the European context) from the venereal disease, which has traditionally been the subject of the debate, some might still maintain that all pre-Columbian skeletal cases of treponemal disease are of treponarid, and venereal syphilis was imported from the Americas in the late fifteenth century. However, as more skeletal examples of pre-Columbian date with advanced cranial vault changes, which are characteristic of venereal syphilis but less so of treponarid, turn up (including a number of important specimens from Britain; Roberts 1994), this argument becomes increasingly tenuous.

Skeletal remains have increasingly allowed studies of aspects of earlier human populations, which have traditionally been investigated using historical evidence, to be extended back into the more remote past before the first reliable written records. One such aspect is child growth.

The first large-scale study of the height of living children was conducted about 150 years ago. These and subsequent data show that there has been a trend for an increase in height in children, and to a lesser extent in adults, in the developed world. Most of this increase has occurred during the last 100 years, and in most instances it is now slowing or stopping (Tanner 1989). In archaeological material, stature can be studied from bone lengths. Plotting this against age, which can accurately be inferred from dental calcification, allows the relationship between age and standing height to be estimated. Analysis of skeletal remains therefore enables the study of human growth to be extended back into the more remote past, before the first height surveys of living children.

I studied growth in children at medieval Wharram Percy in this way (for further details of methodology see Mays 1998, 67–70), and compared them with recent data (Tanner *et al* 1966) and with data from early nineteenth-century British children (Tanner 1981). Although there are potential problems to be born in mind when comparing archaeological data with those from living subjects (Mays, 1998, 67), some interesting comparisons can be drawn (Fig 20.3). There is a striking difference between the medieval and the modern data, for example at age ten the mean Wharram Percy stature (117cm) is fully 20cm shorter than the modern figure. The differences between the medieval and the nineteenth-century data are less pronounced, but the medieval children do seem to be somewhat shorter, lagging behind in growth by about one to two years at most ages.

Growth in children is strongly dependent on nutrition and disease experience (Eveleth and Tanner 1990), so much so that height has been used as a proxy for health when making comparisons on a population level (Tanner 1989, 163). The Wharram Percy results suggest, not surprisingly, that the medieval children had poorer nutrition and a greater disease load than did the modern sample. If the present figures are anything to go by, the health of the Wharram Percy children may have been less good even than that of the urban poor during the industrial revolution.

The future

On a general note, it is to be hoped that the reintegration of human osteology with mainstream archaeology continues. Now, as in the past, much human bone work is conducted on a site-by-site basis, the published

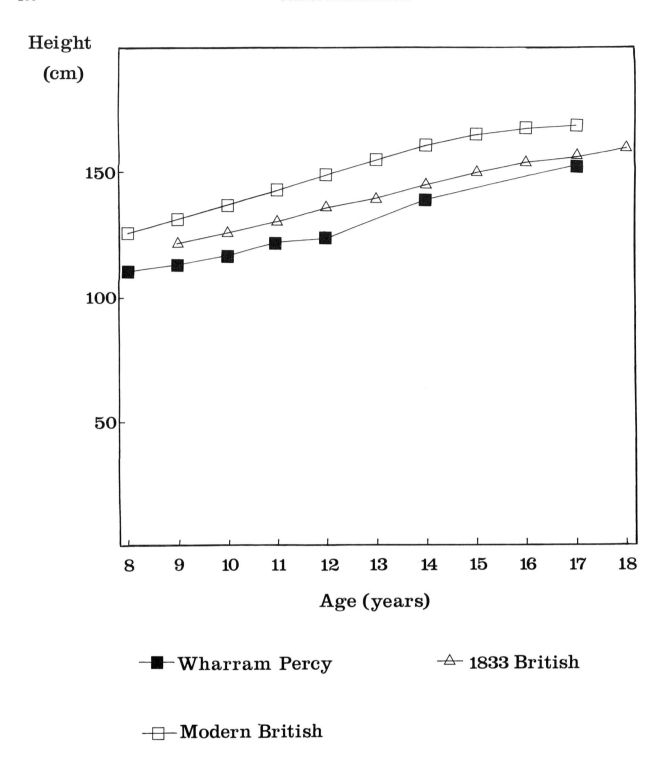

Fig 20.3 Stature plotted against age for the Wharram Percy children: figures for recent and nineteenth-century British children are included for comparison; stature figures are mid-sex means (see text for data sources)

output being bone reports published as specialist contributions to excavation monographs. Although findings from specialist studies of human remains do now tend to be given greater prominence in the main text in the excavation monograph, further progress in this direction is still needed. At present many bone reports are still rather stereotyped in the data collected, the way the data are presented and the analyses to which

they are subjected. To facilitate the fuller integration of results from scientific analyses of skeletal material into the main text of site monographs, we need to continue to move away from this stereotyped approach to site-based bone work, towards one more orientated towards the resolution of archaeological problems relevant to the interpretation of the site and the region in which it is situated.

In archaeology in general, although site-based work continues to be important, an additional emphasis on broader synthetic work does seem to be emerging. It is important that osteological work should also be undertaken on a synthetic as well as a site-based level. Works of synthesis should be directed at understanding specific and pressing archaeological problems (perhaps, in the context of medieval populations, directed at further understanding of some of the themes discussed here). An analysis of published journal articles (Mays 1997b) has indicated that this sort of osteological work is much more frequently carried out in other parts of the world, particularly in North America, than it is in Britain. This situation clearly has to do with differences in the historical development of osteoarchaeology, particularly the close ties between anthropology and archaeology in North America. However the recent moves towards reintegration of osteological work with the archaeological mainstream in Britain have created an academic environment more conducive to this kind of study.

The integration of osteological data with other sources of evidence is clearly important in works of synthesis, just as it is at the site-based level. Much of the work on medieval human remains described above has drawn on historical evidence, but by contrast, human osteologists have drawn rather less on work done on other classes of archaeological remains. Despite the fact that the preparation of most excavation reports involves collaboration, at least to some degree, between archaeologists with a wide range of specialisms, there have been few broader, synthetic projects aimed at mainstream archaeological problems that have involved collaboration between human bone specialists and archaeologists with other areas of expertise. Some of the research areas discussed in this paper might lend themselves to such an approach. For example, animal and plant remains clearly have the potential to complement information obtained about diet from human bones, and relationships between towns and their hinterlands might also be usefully studied using an integrated approach in which human osteological and other data are combined in regions where both exist.

There are some new theoretical directions in archaeology to which osteological data may make a significant contribution. The recent growth in interest in the archaeology of gender is a case in point: the reliability with which we can determine sex, in adult skeletons at least, makes human skeletal studies potentially important here. We saw this at one level in the comparison of York with Wharram Percy, where sex ratios were used to help argue for evidence of female-led migration from village to city. At a more detailed level the prospects seem to be mixed. Comparing frequencies of diseases between males and females is a routine part of most recent bone reports, yet few convincing differences have been found. This may mean that, contrary to the prior expectations of some, health and living conditions varied little according to gender, other factors, such as whether one dwelt in an urban or rural area, were much more important. On the other hand, it may be that gender differences did exist but were too small to be regularly apparent as differences in frequencies of pathological lesions. Perhaps a more subtle approach to the study of gender differences than simply counting pathologies in needed. Work in the USA, looking at normal rather than pathological skeletal variation (specifically biomechanical properties of long bones), has shown evidence for gender related activity patterns congruent with those inferred from other sources (eg Bridges 1989; Fresia et al 1990). Work has begun to be carried out looking at skeletal variation from this perspective in Britain, both on medieval groups, and on later assemblages where activity patterns and occupation are documented.

Progress in the study of medieval human populations depends not only on the academic outlook of its practitioners, but also of what assemblages and techniques are available. For some important questions, such as the impact of the Black Death on human populations, sufficient adequately dated material is not yet available to address them. Perhaps the application of radiocarbon dating to large medieval assemblages will help here. In order to expand on some of the themes outlined above, additional material is needed, for example more rural assemblages from different areas of the country are needed to help address general questions concerned with relationships between towns and their hinterlands.

We also need to be cognisant of methodological developments that might usefully be applied to medieval population studies. In some instances these developments take the form of testing the reliability of existing methodologies. For example, regarding the reliability of adult ageing techniques, recent work has helped to show which, out of the barrage of techniques that have been used, are reliable and which are not. These sorts of developments allow us to review critically previous work and interpretations. Other developments consist of the introduction of techniques that have hitherto made little impact in medieval archaeology. Stable isotope work, while better known to prehistorians, has only now begun to be applied to investigate problems in medieval population studies. Looking further ahead, analysis of ancient DNA may also offer some assistance, for example it may be possible to sex juvenile skeletons reliably and so facilitate the study of male/female differences in growth and development, and it may also be useful in the future as an aid to diagnosis of infectious disease in skeletal remains.

References

Aiello, L, and Molleson, T, 1993 Are microscopic ageing techniques more accurate than macroscopic ageing techniques? *J Archaeol Sci*, **20**, 689–704

Baker, B J, and Armelagos, G J, 1988 The origin and antiquity of syphilis, *Curr Anthropol*, **29**, 703–37

Bayley, J, 1975 Chelmsford Dominican Priory human bone report, *Anc Mon Lab Rep*, **1890**, London

Binford, L R, 1962 Archaeology as anthropology, *Amer Antiquity*, **28**, 217–25

Birkett, D A, and Marlow, M, 1986 The human burials, in The excavation of the church of the Franciscans, Hartlepool, Cleveland (R Daniels), *Archaeol J*, **143**, 291–9

Boddington, A, 1996 *Raunds Furnells, the Anglo-Saxon church and churchyard*, English Heritage Archaeol Rep, 7, London

Bond, C J, 1988 Monastic fisheries, in *Medieval fish, fisheries, and fishponds in England* (ed M Aston), BAR, **182(i)**, 69–112, Oxford

Bridges, P S, 1989 Changes in activity with the shift to agriculture in the southeastern United States, *Curr Anthropol*, **30**, 385–94

Brothwell, D R, 1959 Teeth in earlier human populations, *Proc Nutrition Soc*, **18**, 59–65

—, 1963 *Digging up bones*, Oxford

Buikstra, J E, 1977 Biocultural dimensions of archaeological study: a regional perspective, in *Biocultural adaptation in prehistoric America* (ed R L Blakely), Southern Anthropol Soc Proc, **11**, 67–84, Athens GA

Clay, R M, 1909 *The medieval hospitals of England*, London

Daniell, C, 1997 *Death and burial in medieval England*, London

Dawes, J, 1980 The human bones, in *The cemetery of St Helen-on-the-Walls, Aldwark* (J Dawes and J Magilton), The Archaeology of York, **12/1**, 19–120, London

—, 1986 Human Bones From St Mark's, in *St Mark's Church Cemetery* (eds B J Gilmour and D A Stoder), The Archaeology of Lincoln, **XIII-1**, 33–5, London

Dutour, O, Palfi, G, Berato, J, and Brun, J-P (eds), 1994 *L'origine de la syphilis en Europe, avant ou apres 1493?*, Toulon

Dyer, C, 1989 *Standards of living in the later Middle Ages*, Cambridge

Eley, J, and Bayley, J, 1975 Stonar human bones, *Anc Mon Lab Rep*, **1903**, London

Eveleth, P B, and Tanner, J M, 1990 *Worldwide variation in human growth*, 2 edn, Cambridge

Fresia, A E, Ruff, C B, and Larsen, C S, 1990 Temporal decline in bilateral asymmetry of the upper limb on the Georgia Coast, in *The archaeology of the mission Santa Catalina de Guale: 2 Biocultural interpretations of a population in transition* (ed C S Larsen), Anthropol Pap Amer Mus Nat Hist, **68**, 121–32, New York

Goldberg, P J P, 1986 Female labour, service, and marriage in the late medieval urban north, *Northern Hist*, **22**, 18–38

Gordon, C G, and Buikstra, J E, 1981 Soil pH, bone preservation, and sampling bias at mortuary sites, *Amer Antiquity*, **46**, 566–71

Grauer, A L, 1991 Patterns of life and death, in *Health in past societies* (eds H Bush and M Zvelebil) BAR, Int Ser, **567**, 67–80, Oxford

—, 1993 Patterns of anaemia and infection from medieval York, England, *Amer J Phys Anthropol*, **91**, 203–13

Harding, C, 1996 Wharram Percy (North Yorkshire): topography and development of the churchyard, in *Archeologie du cimetiere Chretien* (eds H Galinie and E Zadora-Rio), Actes du 2[e] colloque ARCHEA, 183–91, Tours

Hart, J, 1989 Leprosy in Cornwall and Devon: problems and perspectives, in *From Cornwall to Caithness, some aspects of British field archaeology* (eds M Bowden, D Mackay, and P Topping), BAR, **209**, 261–9, Oxford

Hatcher, J, 1986 Mortality in the fifteenth century: some new evidence, *Econ Hist Rev*, **39**, 19–38

—, 1994 England in the aftermath of the Black Death, *Past Present*, **144**, 3–35

Heighway, C, nd Report on attributes of burials from Wharram Percy church, unpubl ms

Henderson, J, 1984 The human remains, in *Excavations on the site of the Dominican Friary at Guildford in 1974 and 1978* (ed R Poulton), Res Vol Surrey Archaeol Soc, **9**, 58–71

—, 1990 The human skeletal remains, in *A Roman, Anglian, and medieval site at Blackfriars Street, Carlisle* (ed M R McCarthy), Cumberland and Westmorland Antiq Archaeol Soc Res Ser, **4**, 330–55, Kendal

Jenkins, V, and Rogers, J, 1993 The human bone, in *Excavations in the town centre of Trowbridge, Wiltshire, 1977 and 1986–88* (eds A H Graham and S Davies), Wessex Archaeol Rep, **2**, 120–27, Salisbury

Julkunen, H, Heinonen, O P, and Pyorala, K, 1971 Hyperostosis of the spine in an adult population, *Annals of the Rheumatic Diseases*, **30**, 605–12

Kent, S, and Dunn, D, 1996 Anaemia and the transition of nomadic hunter-gatherers to a sedentary lifestyle: follow-up study of a Kalahari community, *Amer J Phys Anthropol*, **99**, 455–72

Kent, S, Weinberg, E D, and Stuart-Macadam, P, 1994 The etiology of anaemia of chronic disease and infection, *J Clinical Epidemiol*, **47**, 23–33

Lee, F, and Magilton, J, 1989 The cemetery of the hospital of St James and St Mary Magdalene, Chichester – a case study, *World Archaeol*, **21**, 273–82

Lewis, M E, Roberts, C A, and Manchester, K, 1995 Comparative study of the prevalence of maxillary sinusitis in later medieval urban and rural populations in northern England, *Amer J Phys Anthropol*, **98**, 497–506

Lilley, J M, Stroud, G, Brothwell, D R, and Williamson, M H, 1994 *The Jewish burial ground at Jewbury*, The Archaeology of York, **12/3**, York

Manchester, K, 1984 Tuberculosis and leprosy in antiquity: an interpretation, *Medical Hist*, **28**, 162–73

—, 1991 Tuberculosis and leprosy: evidence for interaction of disease, in *Human palaeopathology, current syntheses and future options* (eds D J Ortner and A C Aufderheide), 23–35, Washington DC

Manchester, K, and Roberts, C, 1989 The palaeopathology of leprosy in Britain: a review, *World Archaeol*, **21**, 265–72

Mays, S, 1991 The medieval burials from the Blackfriars Friary, School Street, Ipswich, Suffolk (excavated 1983–85), *Anc Mon Lab Rep*, **16/91**, London

—, 1997a Carbon stable isotope ratios in medieval and later human skeletons from northern England, *J Archaeol Sci*, **24**, 561–7

—, 1997b A perspective on human osteoarchaeology in Britain, *Int J Osteoarchaeol*, **7**, 600–604

—, 1998 *The archaeology of human bones*, London

—, nd A computer database of sites yielding human bone in England, Ancient Monuments Laboratory, London

Molleson, T, and Cox, M, 1993 *The Spitalfields project, volume 2: the anthropology – the middling sort*, CBA Res Rep, **86**, York

Moore, W J, and Corbett, M E, 1978 Dental caries experience in man, in *Diet, nutrition, and dental caries* (ed N H Rowe), 3–19, Chicago

Moore, W J, Lavelle, C L B, and Spence, T F, 1968 Changes in the size and shape of the human mandible in Britain, *Brit Dental J*, **125**, 163 9

O'Connor, T P, 1991 *Bones from 46–54 Fishergate*, The Archaeology of York, **15/4**, York

—, 1993 The human skeletal material, in *Rivenhall: investigations of a Roman villa, church, and village, 1950–77, volume 2: specialist studies* (eds W Rodwell and K Rodwell), CBA Res Rep, **80**/Chelmsford Archaeol Trust Rep, **4.2**, 96–102, York

Powell, F, 1996 The Human Remains, in *Raunds Furnells, the Anglo-Saxon church and churchyard* (A Boddington), English Heritage Archaeol Rep, **7**, 113–24, London

Richards, P, 1960 Leprosy in Scandinavia, *Centaurus*, 7, 101–33

Roberts, C, 1986 Palaeopathology: cottage industry or interacting discipline? in *Archaeology at the interface* (eds J L Bintliff and C F Gaffney), BAR, Int Ser, **300**, 110–28, Oxford

—, 1994 Treponematosis in Gloucester, England: a theoretical and practical approach to the pre-Columbian theory, in *L'origine de la syphilis en Europe, avant ou apres 1493?* (eds O Dutour, G Palfi, J Berato, and J-P Brun), 101–8, Toulon

Rogers, J, 1985 Skeletons from the lay cemetery at Taunton Priory, in *The archaeology of Taunton: excavations and fieldwork to 1980* (ed P Leach), Western Archaeol Trust Excav Monogr, **8**, 194–9

Rogers, J, Watt, I, and Dieppe, P, 1985 Palaeopathology of spinal osteophytosis, vertebral ankylosis, ankylosing spondylitis, and vertebral hyperostosis, *Annals of the Rheumatic Diseases*, **44**, 113–20

Russell, J C, 1937 Length of life in England 1250–1348, *Human Biol*, **9**, 528–41

—, 1948 *British medieval population*, Albuquerque

Saunders, S R, 1992 Subadult skeletons and growth related studies, in *Skeletal biology of past peoples: research methods* (eds S R Saunders and M A Katzenberg), 1–20, Chichester

Shahar, S, 1990 *Childhood in the Middle Ages*, London

Steinbock, R T 1976 *Palaeopathological diagnosis and interpretation*, Springfield

Stroud, G, and Kemp, R L, 1993 *Cemeteries of St Andrew, Fishergate*, The Archaeology of York, **12/2**, York

Stroud, G, Brothwell, D R, Browne, S, Watson, P, and Dobney, K, 1994 The population, in *The Jewish burial ground at Jewbury* (J M Lilley, G Stroud, D R Brothwell, and M H Williamson), The Archaeology of York, **12/3**, 424–521, York

Stuart-Macadam, P, 1986 Health and disease in the monks of Stratford Langthorne Abbey, *Essex J*, **21**, 67–71

—, 1987 Porotic hyperostosis: new evidence to support the anaemia theory, *Amer J Phys Anthropol*, **74**, 521–6

—, 1989 Nutritional deficiency disease: a survey of scurvy, rickets and iron deficiency anaemia, in *Reconstruction of life from the skeleton* (eds M Y Iscan and K A R Kennedy), 201–22, New York

—, 1992 Porotic hyperostosis: a new perspective, *Amer J Phys Anthropol*, **87**, 39–47

Tanner, J M, 1981 *A history of the study of human growth*, Cambridge

—, 1989 *Foetus into man*, 2 edn, Ware

Tanner, J M, Whitehouse, R H, and Takaishi, M, 1966 Standards from birth to maturity for height, weight, height velocity, and weight velocity: British children 1965, *Archives of Disease in Childhood*, **41**, 454–71, 613–35

Thrupp, S L, 1962 *The merchant class of medieval London*, Ann Arbor

Waldron, T, 1985a A report on the human bones from Merton Priory, *Anc Mon Lab Rep*, **4483**, London

—, 1985b DISH at Merton Priory: evidence for a 'new' occupational disease? *Brit Medical J*, **291**, 1762–3

Wells, C, 1962 A Possible case of leprosy from a Saxon cemetry at Beckford, *Med Hist*, **6**, 383–6

White, W, 1988 *The cemetery of St Nicholas Shambles*, London

Whittaker, D K, and Molleson, T, 1996 Caries prevalence in the dentition of a late eighteenth-century population, *Archives Oral Biol*, **41**, 55–61

Wiggins, R, Boylston, A, and Roberts, C, 1993 Report on the human skeletal remains from Blackfriars, Gloucester, on file at the Calvin Wells Library, Univ Bradford

Williamson, M H, 1994 Multivariate Studies, in *The Jewish burial ground at Jewbury* (J M Lilley, G Stroud, D R Brothwell, and M H Williamson), The Archaeology of York, **12/3**, 450–55, York

Wrigley, E A 1968 Mortality in pre-industrial England: the example of Colyton, Devon, over three centuries, *Daedalus*, **97**, 546–80

21 On science, buildings archaeology, and new agendas

by Matthew H Johnson

Abstract

This paper reviews what I consider to be the 'big questions' in buildings archaeology. I urge that science-based techniques take their place alongside a broad array of techniques within a more holistic and contextual approach to buildings. Such an approach stresses that we must explain buildings in terms of the people who built and lived in them. We must therefore deal in a more wide-ranging way with the landscape context, the social structure, and the mentalities of these builders and users.

Introduction

First, a confession. I do not believe there is such a thing as 'science in archaeology'. We are all archaeologists; we are all interested in the material remains of the past. Further, we are all scientists; we all study empirical material, and while debates rage on other interpretive issues I do not know of anybody who would deny that we should bring scholarly discipline and rigour, however defined, to our work. In this work, we often bring techniques and insights borrowed from other disciplines to answer interesting questions. Some of these techniques and insights have been used for so long that we have forgotten that we originally borrowed them from another discipline. A classic example is stratigraphy, borrowed from geology in the nineteenth century; other examples, such as typology or the use of documentary information, are not normally thought of as 'scientific', although they do involve the use of specialist skills.

An idea of a restricted domain of 'scientific' techniques that can be brought to bear on what is implied to be a 'non-scientific' archaeology exists only as a result of the historical accidents in intellectual and cultural life over the last few centuries that have led to the academic and social carving-up of a seamless domain of knowledge in a certain arbitrary way. Despite being arbitrary, it is nevertheless a very real carving-up, because it is very firmly embedded and enshrined in the academic, professional, and, particularly, the financial structures of our discipline. If we want to do archaeology in the real world, we have to live with this structuring of finance and knowledge, and we have to manipulate constructively the existing structures as best we can.

I am therefore going to adopt Tite's self-confessedly operational definition of science as not a discipline, but more a 'meeting ground for a series of collaborations between disciplines' (1991, 139) and to look pragmatically at a selection of techniques within the five areas he identifies: dating, artefact studies, 'man and his environment', remote sensing, and conservation.

Buildings archaeology

Now if there is no such thing as science in archaeology, there is also no such thing as 'buildings archaeology'. As an archaeologist, my interest, in common with Simon Mays (this volume), is in people, not in buildings. I am interested in cultural systems in the past, in the lives, actions, and thoughts of women and men. The study of buildings, like the study of any other class of artefact or ecofact, is only important insofar as it helps me towards that goal; it is a means to an end. Obviously buildings are a very important means to that end, and much of my previous work has argued that we have underestimated the potential value of buildings in telling us about people's social and cultural lives.

The confusion between means and ends that is embodied in the term 'buildings archaeology' is compounded by the statutory duties and functions that many of us, particularly those outside the strictly academic sphere, have to carry out. While our intellectual interest may be in past peoples, our duties of conservation, heritage management, and public presentation may lead us to put the buildings first. I can plausibly argue that it will not matter much in terms of our understanding of the past if this or that great monument is allowed to fall down. This does not mean that it should be allowed to happen. But we must nevertheless keep such a distinction in mind. In practice such a distinction is blurred; conservation funding enables us to tackle exciting research questions along the way, as I shall discuss below, and anyone who has worked in the field knows that new forms of public presentation go hand-in-hand with new insights in interpretation.

This problem of 'buildings versus the past' is exacerbated by the vast range and diversity of material to hand when we consider what is meant by buildings archaeology. The date range runs from Stonehenge to the present, and socially from the tiniest cottage to the grandest royal palace. Religious, domestic, and industrial buildings offer different potentials and problems. Finally, we should not forget that the divide between excavated and standing buildings is an artificial one – buildings archaeology must also include below-ground evidence.

The end result of this problematic view is that the value of buildings archaeology is not intrinsic; it is, rather, directly dependent on the questions we want to ask of it. One of the questions that is often asked of buildings archaeologists is: what age does a building have to be before we look at it? The answer is: any age. We may legitimately choose to devote little time to a very old building because it has no new information to offer us. A fifteenth-century peasant house in Essex is unlikely to yield information that will completely transform our knowledge of the region or the period. Conversely, some of the most exciting recent work has been on eighteenth- and nineteenth-century buildings, and specifically on the relationship between patterns of space and material life within industrial and domestic settings (Campion 1996, Shackel 1996). We may choose to examine a 1960s tower block because it can help us answer important questions of post-war social and economic history.

What, then, are the exciting research questions around which we should frame our research? What follows is a purely personal view, and has one important caveat. Intellectual enquiry moves forward through structured anarchy, through a diversity of views and debates between those views (Johnson forthcoming). Therefore, my first concrete recommendation, as a preface to what follows, is that *a formal set of priorities for science-based buildings archaeology should not be so inflexible as to inhibit a diversity of approaches and research agendas. The first question to be asked of any piece of work should not be 'does it fit in to our pre-conceived agenda?', but should be 'will this work be exciting, is the research design coherent, will it tell us new, exciting, wide-ranging things about the past?'*

Conversely, however, much science-based archaeology has been on an opportunistic basis (through the conservation of buildings with private or European Community finance, or dendrochronological dates) and one theme that is as important as the need for diversity is the need for more overall strategy.

My personal set of ideas about what directions buildings archaeology should take is underpinned by a second general point: the conviction that *science-based techniques have the potential to address wide-ranging national and international research questions of fundamental importance in understanding the medieval–modern transition in buildings archaeology and in archaeology and cultural history generally.* Two developments in the way we think about buildings have increased this potential for science in buildings archaeology, encapsulated in two buzz-words: context and form.

Context and form

The word context has been used in different ways (Hodder 1990). Part of a contextual approach is the conviction that buildings tell us not just about economic history, but about social and cultural life as well; and that further, they reflect the values and mentalities of past peoples and should be interpreted in those terms,

not by use of concepts derived from the present, such as the glib use of 'fashion', 'status', or 'conspicuous consumption'. These points are familiar enough, but I would go further.

One of the most frustrating aspects of working in medieval and post-medieval archaeology is the way thinking in the discipline is permeated with *a priori* distinctions between domestic and agrarian, industrial and religious life, distinctions which tell us far more about twentieth-century patterns of life and thought than they do about the past. If we want to utilise the real potential of science-based techniques we have to look beyond artificial categories, towards the realities of people's daily lives in the past.

In 1624, a woman walks out of the back door of a Norfolk farmhouse. She pauses to tell her daughter to get back inside, and glances with narrow eyes at the widow next door, whom she suspects of witchcraft. She has recently installed witchcraft precautions around the doors and windows of the house. Pausing to throw some scraps to the pigs snuffling around in a pen, she notes that her husband should spend less time in the alehouse consuming beer and tobacco and more time repairing the fence in the back yard; as the preacher said on Sunday, 'love thy neighbour, but keep thy fence in good repair'. A pity that some in the congregation are in uproar about the new altar rails and other fittings in the church. She takes a bucket of inedible scraps and disposes of them in a pit at the back of the garden. She gets back inside quickly, before the neighbours on the other side start to talk...

Is this sequence of actions about buildings archaeology, or about economic archaeology, or about social or cultural history? Clearly, it is all of these, and to draw dividing lines between specialisms is to inhibit the development of really exciting insights into the past. We must work hard to be contextual – to draw the insights of different specialisms together not as a cut-and-paste exercise, but to form a coherent and sympathetic picture of medieval and post-medieval life.

An interest in context goes hand-in-hand with an interest in form. The study of changing form is one of the traditional concerns of archaeology, most obviously in typology and technological studies. In the 1970s and 1980s buildings archaeology moved away from form for some excellent reasons: endless typologies of crucks, hood-mouldings, and decorative features seemed irrelevant to the big questions of socioeconomic history that archaeologists were trying to address. Many of these big questions were defined by documentary historians rather than by archaeologists, and were quantitative rather than formal ones: of rates of consumption, the great rebuilding, of rates of agricultural improvement. As a result, the study of changing form tended to take second place to quantitative measures. In its urge, therefore, to address wider questions archaeology tended to take second place to history.

These big questions have recently often been redefined in ways that make form important once again. For example, my work on the Great Rebuilding has stressed that we should look at the changing layout and appearance of the house as much as at rates of building activity (Johnson 1993). Or again, we should be interested not just in how much food was being produced and consumed by pre-industrial populations, but also at changing patterns of food preparation and the cultural messages embedded in the ceremony of the mealtime (Pennell forthcoming).

The return to context and form offers new and exciting opportunities for science-based archaeology. In the past, it has tended to be assumed that because certain techniques are science-based, the conclusions are most germane to 'hard' questions, such as those of subsistence, palaeoeconomy, and environment. These are all important and useful contributions that science-based archaeology has to make. One of the general points I want to stress, however, is that science-based techniques can do so much more. They can tell us also about the social and cultural life of past peoples. This opens up new opportunities for science-based archaeology, since it means that *science-based archaeology need no longer confine itself to 'hard' questions of technology and economy defined in the narrowest sense.*

Questioning documents

In some ways, social levels below those of the medieval and early modern elite are effectively protohistoric. There is copious documentary evidence of a variety of forms, but its use is problematic for reasons I have discussed elsewhere (Johnson 1996, 97–118). Science-based archaeology can act as a useful check on these forms of evidence. At all levels, from the greatest castle to the humblest cottage, one often encounters assumptions 'generally known' or 'accepted' that turn out to have very little evidence to support them one way or another. These questions can often be settled using science-based techniques.

It is worth explaining in detail why this is the case. Go to a history library and you will find no shortage of books on the life of the middling sort and the labouring poor in medieval and early modern England. When you look at the sources such books use, however, you will find that they are more often than not written by the landed or urban elite about people further down the social scale. Thus, for example, we 'know' about the house and household as a patriarchal political unit from seventeenth century political tracts and conduct books

written by the gentry or by clergy, but explicitly aimed at a socially middling readership (Brooks and Barry 1994). We do not, however, have a secure documentary handle on how people below the elite social level reacted to these exhortations; they may have followed them diligently, or in the words of one servant girl commenting on a learned sermon they may 'have been such a deale of bibble babble that I am weary to hear yt and I can then sitt downe in my seat and take a good napp' (quoted in Wrightson 1982, 219).

It is tempting to go on to talk about documents as technologies of power, but I have said enough I hope to demonstrate that Millett's views on the nature of documents in protohistoric periods (this volume) find resonance in vernacular, rural England. There are two wider points here. First, the question, 'did people blindly follow elite models laid down for them, or did they make their own history?' is a question with exciting theoretical as well as substantive implications. Second, it was this vernacular culture which was exported to various colonial contexts around the globe, to Virginia and New England in particular (Deetz 1977). So these questions also have an international and theoretical significance.

Science-based archaeology, therefore, *can work within the space between document and artefact to explore wide-ranging questions of interpretation at both national and international levels.*

I will now address a series of concrete suggestions with these general points in mind.

Geophysics and landscape

One of the most exciting developments in recent years has been in the study of the landscape context of buildings. Buildings both polite and vernacular were deliberately placed in certain settings. The setting presented a building and its occupants in certain ways: the great house framed by a formal garden, the position of the tenement relative to the road defining front and back space. Further, these settings were not simply dictated by the apparently trivial whimsy of fashion; work in garden and art history, in literature and in cultural geography has stressed that conceptions of landscape and nature are a microcosm of conceptions of society (Cosgrove 1993; Schama 1995; Williamson 1995).

I see great potential in geophysics for understanding this landscape setting in more detail, a potential that increases with every refinement in geophysics technology. Polite houses, in particular, had the landscapes and gardens around them redesigned regularly; such periodic remodelling of house and landscape, each generation of owners making its mark on the land, was part of the great owner's affirmation of elite identity (Airs 1995). Often, therefore, entire garden and landscape styles have been swept away, most obviously to make way for the great landscape gardens of the eighteenth century. Full excavation of elite gardens and landscapes is possible at flagship projects like Hampton Court, but in other contexts holds prohibitive costs. Before 1550, such elite landscapes often included extensive and rambling ranges of ancillary buildings, stables, and workshops, ranges again often swept away by later fashions (Howard 1986).

Entire phases of ancillary buildings and landscape design can therefore, I suggest, be revealed by geophysics techniques. Such data hold the key to exciting new avenues of research.

Take, for example, the formal landscape around Bodiam Castle, which was only recognised in the 1980s (Taylor *et al* 1990). Chris Taylor has collated this and numerous other examples of formal landscape settings around late medieval castles, directly contradicting many of the easy document-based assumptions of architectural and garden historians in which formal gardens and landscapes are unproblematic artefacts of 'the impact of the Renaissance'.

Phil Dixon and Pamela Marshall (1993, 410) have recently remarked that we think we know everything about a polite building such as a castle, but when we look at its fabric closely we find that this is not the case. I would make parallel remarks about the landscape context of such structures. Consider, for example, the extensive archaeological, historical, and literary discussions of the Pleasaunce, a fifteenth-century adjunct to Kenilworth Castle, one of the jewels in English Heritage's crown; we have documentary references to late medieval building and garden complexes there; but though there have been several small-scale excavations in the area it has never been subjected to a geophysical survey.

Geophysics may also give us an imperfect but interesting handle on questions of survival and the vernacular threshold. Is a late fifteenth-century house the first building on the site? What of its impermanent ancillary buildings? I have felt for a few years now that someone should collate at a national level examples of standing buildings that have also been excavated; if such intensive examples were combined with more extensive geophysical survey, a major question in architectural studies could be resolved.

Cultural history of technology

The development of conservation and materials technology studies over the last few years has been impressive. Though often concerned with conservation questions, I think it could answer some exciting research questions along the way.

These are related to the rediscovery of form mentioned above. For example, we have spent a great deal of time debating housebuilding rates, and more recently,

the meanings of different ground plans. But we actually know very little about the appearance of vernacular buildings, both external and internal. Were stone vernacular farmhouses ever painted, as they are in Teesdale or in Scotland? If so, how often was this the case? What colour were timber-framed houses painted? Where the timber frame was exposed, was it painted too, or treated with preservative in any way? Was pargetting painted as it is now, and if so what colour schemes were used?

What goes for the exterior also goes for the interior. What of the colour of internal spaces? Were internal timber framing and floor joists coloured? What of the fittings of the house? Evidence on these questions tends to be anecdotal, in Astill's terms (this volume), consisting of a string of isolated examples more often than not from houses at the upper levels of the social scale (for example Beard 1975). Science-based archaeology can examine these questions in a more systematic way.

These questions are important because colour, appearance, and fittings are so much more than just passive indicators of status and wealth or of levels of domestic comfort, however defined. Colour, appearance, and fittings were part of an everyday world that structured and conditioned people's lives and mentalities; people in turn made choices about how to build, decorate, and act within such settings, choices that reacted back and transformed their world. Such structuring is most visible in overt and implicit reading of religious space (Graves 1989), but must be looked at contextually, across different spheres.

For example, I would argue that the sixteenth- and seventeenth-century house was becoming a more colourful place just as the church was becoming less colourful. The domestic interior was therefore becoming not just more significant in terms of the investment of time and money being put into it, but was a more significant social and cultural arena in other senses. It formed part of the complex process of secularisation that was affecting all levels of society. Now historians often look at secularisation in a top-down way; they look at the impact of changes in formal doctrine upon the lower social orders. So archaeology can impinge on current debates over the nature of secularisation in post-medieval society, and give a bottom-up view of contemporary social changes, focusing as it does on everyday experiences of houses and churches rather than the textual ramblings of the literate elite.

How were pre-industrial buildings put together, and why do they stand up? These very traditional questions have a reputation for generating obscure articles on building techniques and timber-framing technology that few people ever read and fewer still understand. One of the insights of a contextual approach, however, is that technology is just as much social and cultural as it is practical, particularly within vernacular craft traditions; this insight is borrowed from historians of technology. Technological details therefore offer science-based archaeology a chance to contribute to some pressing debates over the social and cultural history of technology.

Again, this point is particularly valid for vernacular as opposed to polite buildings. Peter Smith (1975) drew some famous maps of the places of origin of Edward I's workmen for Welsh castles, and used these to suggest possible influences on Welsh vernacular architecture; but we still know very little about how building techniques were transmitted between polite and vernacular levels of building. Further, such evidence is again anecdotal rather than systematic. The study of materials technology has an obvious role to play here, for example in looking at the composition of plaster, and the origins and processing of the raw materials used for vernacular wall paintings. We need more discussion of the interplay between influence as defined by art historians and evidence of contact between regions and social levels seen archaeologically.

If technology is cultural, cruck forms can stop being boring and start being exciting. Richard Harris has explored the idea of a grammar of timber-framed architecture, looking at the translation of trees into buildings (1989). Tree-ring studies have a role to play here beyond questions of dating. The production of building timber was a process with many stages and bringing together many interests even before the first cruck of the house was raised. It involved issues of rights over woodland, and conflicts between use rights and ownership, the relative role of large estates and smaller interests in woodland management, and the organisation of large units of skilled labour.

There are important questions of regionalism to be addressed here. Again, regionalism and expression of regional identity has gone from being very boring to being very exciting – a matter of choice of affiliation, often in the face of powerful national forces of centralisation and class polarisation, as an increasing number of cultural historians are appreciating (Marshall 1996; Phythian-Adams 1987; 1993).

I argue that choice of regional over national style was partly a conscious or subconscious statement of local identity over national or class affiliation. Others have pointed instead to what they see as innate conservatism, and have pointed out that we actually know very little about the habits of vernacular carpenters and masons. Here is another topic to which science-based archaeology can contribute directly. It can look at the sources of bricks, stone, mortar, and thatch: how far away does this material come from? what is the sphere of trade and of movement for vernacular builders? what degree of academic as opposed to vernacular knowledge was required in their constitution?

Dating

There is still a huge amount of work to be done in dating buildings using science-based techniques. Many archaeologists and art historians still rely on untested rules of thumb in dating buildings (for example, do crown posts really get simpler through time?). Dendrochronology has a huge potential in this regard. It has a knock-on effect in facilitating innovative thinking – we can stop arguing about the date of buildings and move on to considering what they mean.

I do feel that dendrochronology has yet to fulfil its real potential in buildings archaeology. This cannot be assessed until the imminent publication of the Leverhulme project on crucks in the Midlands, but I do feel that programmes of dendrochronological dating should be more clearly focused on specific issues. More dendrochronological dates on their own do not get us closer to understanding architectural developments. They will not even get us closer to dating architectural trends without a clear and reasoned sampling procedure behind them; otherwise, we will never know whether we are looking at typical or exceptional buildings. (Not quite within the remit of this paper is a belief that questions of differential survival of buildings are depressing but crucial to the future of buildings archaeology, and a plea for more refined sampling procedures in buildings archaeology, related to the computerisation of databases such as County Lists of buildings).

The advantage of dendrochronology, of course, is its exactitude; but this does not mean that other techniques are useless in this period. Like many archaeologists I view with suspicion the easy assurances of architectural historians that they can date a building within 25 years, a suspicion that deepens the more vernacular the structure under discussion. We have become more conscious of the need to look more closely at the fabric of a building over the last 20 years or so, but have not fully grasped the implication that independent dating techniques are needed even with polite buildings that have building accounts and the like. Indeed, when I hear an architectural or documentary historian preface a remark with the phrase 'we know that...', I suspect that something highly contentious is about to be proffered.

At the other end of the social scale, we should not be afraid to admit that there are classes of building that we really cannot date within a few hundred years. Science-based archaeology in its various forms, usually thought of as only appropriate in prehistory, can be very useful with these classes of buildings.

'Archaeology' and buildings

My last theme is to draw together science-based insights from areas not normally considered to be relevant to the buildings archaeologist. One small example is witch bottles, buried under hearths in the sixteenth and seventeenth centuries (Merrifield 1978). What can be done with the traces of urine and hair that are often found within them?

More broadly, I am interested in the raw materials that are the stuff of environmental archaeology, and would like to redefine them in terms of activities around the house and household. Practices of butchery, of food preparation and consumption, and of rubbish disposal are all culturally variable; cultural historians have looked at all these areas and used them to explore changing attitudes to family and the individual at the level of the small-scale and the everyday. They rarely if ever use archaeological evidence in their accounts.

This is a shame, because there are some strange data, particularly on rural sites that have no documentary references. I am thinking of the burial of entire carcasses of dead animals in the middle of the courtyard at Wood Hall, for example. More broadly, American historical archaeologists have uncovered changing patterns of refuse disposal around excavated buildings – a shift from broadcast refuse to disposal in square pits – and interpreted these as indicative of a change from medieval to Georgian lifestyles, and have correlated this evidence to changing patterns of space inside the house (Deetz 1977). I have stood up several times at American conferences to suggest that things are far more complex than this, but their quiet response 'Well, tell us about archaeological studies of changing patterns of refuse disposal in the post-medieval English countryside' has left me struggling.

A good example of recent work in this area is the bone report by Umberto Albarella and Simon Davis at Launceston Castle (Albarella and Davis 1996). I was excited by this report in that it is one of the first uses of a late medieval and post-medieval faunal assemblage to address a continuing historical debate: that over the existence or otherwise of an agricultural revolution in the sixteenth and seventeenth centuries that overshadows the better-known later changes of the period 1750–1850. Albarella and Davis address this debate clearly, and come up with a convincing argument that economic historians would be well advised to read and digest.

How could this work be taken forward? The sequence of actions that leads to the deposition of sheep, cattle, and pig bones are full of cultural resonance. The choice of species to rear, and how to rear the species, is partly a matter of cultural preference, and is linked to questions of identity. No one who has cast a glance at William Hogarth's painting *The Roast Beef of Old England* could suggest otherwise. Butchery practices – how the animal is carved up – have been related by anthropologists in many different contexts to different conceptions of the social body – how society is carved up. The choice of hacking versus sawing has been related by American historical archaeologists to different approaches to portion control and food preparation in general; and the way mealtimes are organised and food prepared and distributed tells us exciting things about changing conceptions of family and household. Finally, rubbish disposal is more than an act of convenience. Albarella and Davis' material was dumped in what was by then a marginal area of town; the presence of vast piles of rotting refuse indicates an attitude about civic identity in Launceston (or the lack of it) beyond simply a decline in status, and in particular how the castle was viewed in the post-medieval period.

Recent work on early modern London has shown how changing ideas of the city affected changing consciousness of the smell and unsightliness of refuse, and thence to developing strategies of refuse disposal (Mullaney 1988). So, to work in the opposite direction, the work of faunal analysts examining material dumped in back yards in London tenements even as civic authorities were trying to clean up the front can tell us about private attitudes to space, to ideas of hygiene and of the body.

Conclusion

I would like to end with what I feel is going to be one of the major debates in late medieval and post-medieval archaeology over the next few years, though it is only beginning to surface implicitly. Many social historians, implicitly followed by many archaeologists working in the period, feel that continuity rather than change is the theme of life in the English countryside before 1600. While such a binary opposition is an oversimplification of the issues, I nevertheless disagree fundamentally with such a view. I feel that there was a fundamental transformation in patterns of household and community life from the later fourteenth century onwards, one that, following the tradition of Richard Tawney, was every bit as devastating as and closely related to the rise of urban capitalism.

This debate is related in part to debates over sources: some scholars point out a lack of evidence for change in the domestic interiors discussed in probate inventories; I would like to discuss the reasons for the presence of inventories in the first place.

The question of the differential survival of house forms is clearly important here. It is also related to debates over social change: those stressing continuity tend implicitly to favour a top-down model of social change, whereas following Giddens I see change arising out of interaction between individuals and groups.

Science-based archaeology will play a central role in resolving this debate. It will look at changing peasant diet; at the relative quantities of vegetables, meat, and bread; at the more precise dating of changing houses and thus at the pace of domestic change; and, as I have argued above, at the changing patterns of everyday life in general, within and beyond 'buildings archaeology'.

Debates over continuity versus change are at heart theoretical debates about how modern scholars should understand social and urban–rural diffusion: did change start in the towns and at upper social levels, and diffuse down, or was it more bottom-up? Did women and men renegotiate and respond actively to structures of authority and wider processes of change? These are big questions for the fourteenth to eighteenth centuries, but they relate to wider questions still: should we see human beings as passive dupes of fashion and of the whim of the upper classes, or are they actively involved in creating their own destinies?

In this sense, I want to reverse my starting point that new theoretical developments have made science-based archaeology especially pertinent. Science-based archaeology can go further still. It can transform our theoretical ideas, make us rethink the way we approach not just buildings archaeology but archaeology, history, and the human sciences generally. Science-based archaeology has nothing to lose but its chains. It has a world to win.

Acknowledgements

I thank Andrew Millard and Chris Caple for helping with the scientific background to this paper. The opinions expressed remain my responsibility.

References

Airs, M, 1995 *The Tudor and Jacobean country house: a building history*, 2 edn, Stroud

Albarella, U, and Davis, S J M, 1996 Mammals and birds from Launceston Castle, Cornwall: decline in status and the rise of agriculture, *Circaea*, **12**, 1–156

Brooks, C, and Barry, J, 1994 *The middling sort of people: culture, society, and politics in England, 1550–1800*, Basingstoke

Beard, G, 1975 *Decorative plasterwork in Great Britain*, London

Campion, G, 1996 People, process, and the poverty-pew: a functional analysis of mundane buildings in the Nottinghamshire framework-knitting industry, *Antiquity* **70**, 847–60

Cosgrove, D, 1993 *The Palladian landscape: geographical change and its cultural representation in 16th-century Italy*, Leicester

Deetz, J, 1977 *In small things forgotten: an archaeology of early American life*, New York

Dixon, P, and Marshall, P, 1993 The great tower in the 12th century: the case of Norham Castle, *Archaeol J*, **150**, 410–32

Graves, C P, 1989 Social space in the English parish church, *Economy and Society*, **18**, 297–322

Harris, R, 1989 The grammar of carpentry, *Vernacular Architect*, **20**, 1–8

Hodder, I, 1990 *Reading the past*, 2 edn, Cambridge

Howard, M, 1986 *The early Tudor country house: architecture and politics 1485–1550*, London

Johnson, M H, 1993 Rethinking the Great Rebuilding, *Oxford J Archaeol*, **12**, 117–25

—, 1996 *An archaeology of capitalism*, Oxford

—, forthcoming Vernacular architecture: the loss of innocence, *Vernacular Architect*, **28**

Marshall, J D, 1996 Communities, societies, regions, and local history: perceptions of locality in High and Low Furness, *Local Historian*, **26**, 36–47

Merrifield, R, 1978 *The archaeology of ritual and magic*, London

Mullaney, S, 1988 *The place of the stage*, Chicago

Pennell, S, forthcoming The material culture of food in early modern England, circa 1650–1750, in *The familiar past?* (eds S Tarlow and S West), London

Phythian-Adams, C, 1987 *Re-thinking English local history*, Leicester Univ Dept Local Hist Occas Pap, 4 ser, **1**, Leicester

Phythian-Adams, C ed, 1993 *Societies, cultures, and kinship, 1580–1850: cultural provinces and English local history*, Leicester

Schama, S, 1995 *Landscape and memory*, London

Shackel, P, 1996 *Culture change and the new technology: an archaeology of the early American industrial era*, New York

Smith, P, 1975 *Houses of the Welsh countryside*, London

Taylor, C C, Everson, P, and Wilson-North, R, 1990 Bodiam Castle, Sussex, *Medieval Archaeol*, **34**, 155–7

Tite, M S, 1991 Archaeological science: past achievements and future prospects, *Archaeometry*, **33**, 139–51

Williamson, T, 1995 *Polite landscapes: gardens and society in 18th-century England*, Stroud

Wrightson, K, 1982 *English society 1580–1680*, London

22 The archaeologist and evidence from field sampling for medieval and post-medieval technological innovation

by David Crossley

Abstract

A combination of archive and archaeological evidence has clarified outlines of change in the technologies of certain early industries in Britain and Europe. The paucity of descriptions of processes before the end of the seventeenth century places weight on the recording of structures and residues of industries, examples being the extraction of iron and non-ferrous metals, notably lead, and the production of glass. For most industries, samples from firm excavated contexts remain few, and the reduction in research and rescue excavation on industrial sites over the 1990s has resulted in little recent addition to the resource. Laboratory examination and characterisation of residues, however, have shown what can be gained from samples collected during field-walking and from minor evaluation works. There remain problems that justify laboratory effort: for example, the distinction between bloomery and finery residues in the iron industry, identification of slag-hearth waste in lead smelting, and problems over durability of glass and the sourcing of refractories used in glass production. With these and other residues a knowledge of how and why field deposits have been degraded over time is important in the planning of sampling strategies and the interpretation of the results.

Archaeological evidence for changes in technology

During the centuries between 1300 and 1750 there were significant changes in methods in traditional, rurally based industries. There was a need for reductions in labour costs during the late-medieval demographic decline; greater efficiency in the use of fuel was required in the competitive market for products of woodlands during the sixteenth and seventeenth centuries, and there were quantitative and qualitative developments of markets in the post-medieval centuries, which justified larger-scale methods of production, particularly those that resulted in improvements in quality. Three examples will be used here, from the iron, lead, and glass industries.

Iron

The changes in techniques are well known in outline: the ironworker adopted water power for the bloomery, in which ore was smelted to produce a bloom of wrought iron. This took place on the continent of Europe by the end of the thirteenth century, and in Britain during the fourteenth and fifteenth centuries. The indirect process,

smelting ore in the blast furnace and converting the cast high-carbon product to wrought iron in the finery forge, was developed in Sweden around 1300, in the southern Netherlands, Germany, and Italy in the fourteenth and fifteenth centuries, and was brought to England by French craftsmen at the end of the fifteenth century, replacing the powered bloomery over the ensuing two hundred years. Early in the eighteenth century the use of low sulphur coals or of coke allowed the industry to expand in size, away from the traditional sources of fuel derived from managed woodlands.

A series of excavations on British iron-smelting sites 1965, and the examinations of excavated materials that have followed, have clarified the nature of these changes. Three water-powered bloomeries have been excavated (reviewed in Crossley 1990, 154–6), at Rockley, Yorkshire, Muncaster Head, Cumbria, and Stoney Hazel, Cumbria. None gave a full picture of the ultimate development of the bloomery. In the case of Rockley (*c* 1500–*c* 1640) there was no satisfactory evidence for a water-powered forging hammer, the Muncaster site (seventeenth century) had been robbed and eroded, and at Stoney Hazel (early eighteenth century) only the smelting element of the site was excavated, leaving questions about the forge hammer and the reheating (string-hearth) parts of the works.

There have been numerous excavations on the sites of early blast furnaces, summarised by the writer elsewhere (Crossley 1990, 156–69). In total, this work presents an adequate picture of the technology of this phase of the industry from soon after its introduction, as shown by the furnace at Panningridge, Sussex, amply documented from its construction in 1542, through late sixteenth-century sites such as Batsford and Maynards Gate, Sussex, furnaces of the seventeenth century at Sharpley Pool, Worcestershire and at Tintern, Gwent, to the adaptation of a charcoal blast furnace to use coke at Rockley, Yorkshire (Crossley 1995). The finery forges, in which pig iron produced in the blast furnace was converted to wrought-iron bar, are known from the Wealden examples at Ardingly, Sussex, Blackwater Green, Sussex, and Chingley, Kent.

From this resource of published work, and the specialist reports which it contains, there now exists a body of knowledge of the character of products and residues which enables sites to be identified and techniques to be evaluated from sampling, often of surface scatters. The range of slags produced by bloomeries and blast furnaces is well established, and can be related to ores and products. In both the bloomery and the blast furnace, material of value comes from the end of a smelt, retained in the base of the furnace hearth, which can contain ore, metal, and slag, the slag on occasion showing impressions of the charcoal, the assemblage presenting a microcosm of smelting practice. A recent case is the examination of ore, slag, and metal from Rockley, which has indicated that bloomery slags had been added to the blast furnace charge, giving credence to a late eighteenth-century description of the operation of this furnace, whose archive source is now lost (Starley in Crossley 1995). This was the period when most iron-masters adopted coke as a fuel: the archaeological evidence for this change is generally a higher level of sulphur in coke-smelted iron than in the product of the charcoal blast furnace, but another approach is by ^{14}C dating, using samples of cast iron: the results of determinations using samples of cast iron from Rockley furnace are awaited, for publication in *Historical Metallurgy*.

A persistent problem is the difficulty of separating some kinds of bloomery wastes from those found at finery forges. Much of the slag from the bloomery is easily distinguishable, with hard black or grey-black surfaces showing evidence of viscous flow. Some cindery wastes from bloomeries can, however, resemble finery cinder, a problem that deserves further consideration. An incentive to do this is the realisation that powered bloomeries were adapted for use as finery forges: the bloom hearth could be rebuilt as a refining hearth, the string hearth, in which blooms were reheated, was essentially similar to a chafery hearth, and both processes required a forge hammer. Such continuity has been seen in the Weald, and distinguishing the process in use was a long-standing problem at Stoney Hazel before the excavations of the 1980s clarified the issue.

Lead

Among the non-ferrous metal industries, there were particularly radical changes in methods of smelting lead. Smelting in hill-top bole hearths, blown by natural draught, was succeeded by the more efficient water-powered ore hearth in the second half of the sixteenth century, the latter to be replaced by the coal-fired induced-draught reverberatory cupola during the eighteenth century. Changes in tin smelting are in some respects analogous, the water-powered blowing house being introduced at the end of the Middle Ages and being replaced by reverberatory induced draught furnaces in the eighteenth century (Greeves 1996; Smith 1996).

There are problems and rewards in distinguishing surface residues from lead smelting. Documentary evidence, largely from Derbyshire and the north Pennines, which provides a framework for the change from the medieval bole smelting hearth and secondary blackwork oven to the ore hearth and slag hearth (Kiernan 1988),

has been complemented by field research. Work at Totley has shown how surface evidence can distinguish the siting of the medieval bole, the smelting hearth, from that of the blackwork oven, which was used for re-smelting bole slags to increase overall yield (Kiernan and Van de Noort 1992). The pattern has been complicated by field and documentary research in other areas, notably in Teesdale (Pickin 1992), where there are variations in the siting and details of bole sites. There has been no excavation of boles, so the residues that have been recovered have been distinguished by location and by the visual characteristics of the slags, the boles being set on hill tops and scarp edges to make use of natural draught. Geochemical examination of soils in areas downwind from boles has also proved rewarding (Wild and Eastwood 1992).

The ore hearths and the secondary slag-smelting hearths, which written sources show were introduced in the second half of the sixteenth century, were built alongside streams, the bellows being operated by water wheels (Crossley and Kiernan 1992). Field survey has shown how siting was governed by a balance between the availabilities of ore, wood, and water, and the direction of markets for the product. The discovery of sites has been determined by the survival of slags. Where these have been dispersed, geochemical sampling of high-lead silts, washed downstream by water cutting through buried remains of slag deposits, has been responsible for the location of a significant number of sites in Derbyshire.

With the introduction of the reverberatory furnace, the cupola – in north Wales late in the seventeenth century and in the Pennines during the eighteenth century – the pattern of two-stage smelting was maintained, the slag hearth remaining in use to re-smelt slags from the cupola.

A remaining difficulty is to make a visual distinction between the slags from the ore hearth, the first stage of smelting, and those which are residues from slag hearths. Emphasis has been given to the ore-hearth slags (Murphy 1992), and there has been no systematic programme of analytical identification coupled with visual characterisation of these materials, which would enable slag-hearth waste to be more easily identified. This is important for future work on distinguishing activities at smelting sites, some of which may have had slag hearths and others not.

Glass

At the end of the Middle Ages glass production in England was on a small scale, the output being of vessel and flat glass of poor quality by comparison with continental imports. The industry was active only in the western part of the Weald of Surrey and Sussex, and in the wooded regions of Staffordshire. Examination of residues has suggested, but not fully established, the reasons for the apparently poor durability of these medieval and early sixteenth-century glasses, and for variability in composition (Crossley 1967; Welch forthcoming).

The first development in the technology of the English industry corresponded with the arrival of French makers of high-quality green glass in the quarter century after 1567, the date of the first patent of monopoly for the regulation of manufacture. The immigrants came first to the western Weald, but by the end of the 1580s could be found in many forest regions, from Hampshire and Gloucestershire to Lancashire and North Yorkshire. The extent to which an indigenous group of glass makers remained active is an important issue: the range of materials found on excavated and field-walked sites in Sussex and North Yorkshire suggests that the makers of French-style glasses were not alone. The products of the latter, however, are distinctive, and by the end of the sixteenth century it does appear that glass of fine appearance and durability, hitherto imported, was generally available from local sources, and that glass was relatively cheap among manufactured goods, its price not rising at the rate of those of products such as iron or other metals, during a period of general inflation; hence a spiral of demand and more localised production resulted from the improved quality of glass selling at stable prices.

The reasons for the superiority of immigrant methods have not received sufficient attention, and there is a need for examination of a substantial sample of glasses of late sixteenth-century English manufacture, to establish the reasons for the consistency with which quality was maintained. There is also a need for further examination of crucibles, to determine the sources of refractories, in those regions remote from the fire clays of the coal measures.

The major change of the early seventeenth century was the introduction of coal as a fuel, necessitating a change in the technology of furnaces. The change took place with a rapidity that has no parallel on continental Europe, where the shift to mineral fuel was spread over the following two centuries. Excavations of early and middle seventeenth-century furnaces, at Kimmeridge, Dorset (Crossley 1987), Denton, Lancashire, and Red Street, Staffordshire (Hurst Vose 1994), have clarified the features of furnace design. Sites of the subsequent period, 1650–1820, have shown further developments in furnaces and crucibles, and have identified the documented use of lead in glass, as well as the widening range of qualities and prices of the products (Ashurst 1970; 1987). Nevertheless, more sampling remains to be done, particularly directed towards examination of the early lead glasses. The material examined at Bolsterstone came from waster dumps, which were not firmly dated within the period of use of the glasshouse, and there is a case for the location and examination of production deposits of lead glass of the decades immediately following Ravenscroft's experiments of the 1670s.

Sampling strategies for industrial residues

The laboratory examination of samples from sites of the industries noted above has an important part to play in furthering our understanding of technological change. Some of the problems indicated in the preceding section require further work on assemblages of some size, but the current pattern of archaeological fieldwork raises questions of how this need should be approached. During the past five years rescue excavations on early industrial sites have been few, in part an effect of the procedures brought about by PPG16 (Department of the Environment 1990). Nor have there been many opportunities for archaeological research other than by surface survey and field walking. This does mean that sampling of residues either from surface or near-surface contexts, or from small-scale interventions, forms the prime means whereby our knowledge of processes can be extended. It is opportune to set out some comments about sampling of this kind, where distortion can take place owing to degradation and recycling of waste material, varying according to the industry.

The causes of physical degradation of, or distortion between, classes of process residues need to be recognised. The impact of such variations has been brought home while re-examining sites of the glass industry for the English Heritage Monuments Protection Programme. Glass furnaces normally yield a range of residues of four types. These are, firstly, the glasses: some are materials that have been shaped and then discarded, largely because of breakage during the annealing process, or glass that has become waste at the time of blowing, the 'knock-offs' from blowing or gathering irons. Lumps of glass that have never been gathered are found, broken from crucible bases when the latter have been separated from their placings in the furnace.

Secondly, glass-like materials, sometimes misleadingly named slags, result from the clearance of impurities floating on the top of the batch in the crucible, and have a bubbly appearance.

Thirdly, there are also fragments of furnace structure, of stone or clay, which may bear accumulations of spilled glass.

Finally, crucible fragments often bear traces of glass, and may be of sufficient size to establish the form of the pot.

What is clear is that the balance of the sample shifts over time. In the first place, the ability of the glassmaker to recycle glass led to the collection of glassy residues at or soon after their deposit, creating a bias towards the products of the last phase of use of a site. Even the product of this final operation may have been reduced if the site has been scavenged by a neighbouring maker. Consequently, the balance between glass and other materials was liable to be altered at an early stage, but subsequent land use, particularly with modern agricultural equipment, leads to the pulverisation of glasses and clay furnace fragments. Hence, crucible, the most durable material, is apt to be overrepresented, although even this becomes fragmented. Broken crucible does, however, often continue to bear glass residues, which, despite the effect of interaction of glass and ceramic at the interface, can provide the best glass sample on severely eroded sites.

The distortion of samples on metal-working sites is frequently a result of recycling. In the case of iron, there are two types of event. In the first place, smelting of slags is known to have occurred. Bloomery cinders could contain sufficient iron to be attractive to operators of blast furnaces, as has been shown by the recent work on material from Rockley furnace, where, as noted above, the composition of iron and slag from a late use of the blast furnace suggested that bloomery slags had been charged along with ore. A bloomery had been present nearby, in whose excavation there had been a noticeable lack of large deposits of slag on the surrounding contemporary surfaces. The deficiency is now explained by the analytical work on the blast-furnace residues. After the closure of ironworks, slags have frequently been used as hardcore; indeed the end of the charcoal iron industry came at a time when road construction by turnpike trusts made use of slag deposits as quarries. Again taking the case of Rockley, which appears to have finally gone out of use *c* 1800 after a short phase using coke, the scarcity of surrounding slag deposits is matched by the construction of a system of colliery railways nearby, along whose routes scatters of blast furnace slags can be found.

In the case of non-ferrous metals, the pattern of use of slags is rather more complex. In the lead industry there was a progression of technical improvement through the post-medieval centuries, in which the smelting of slags was essential to the economics of processing. Within each phase lead-rich slags were re-smelted in secondary hearths: the blackwork oven accompanied the medieval and sixteenth-century bole, and the slag hearth was sited with the ore hearth and its successor, the cupola. In addition, when the bole was succeeded by the ore hearth, the latter could profitably re-smelt bole or blackwork oven slags; indeed it could also use ores discarded by the bolers. Likewise, the cupola was capable of using ores unsuited to the ore hearth, as well as

slags discarded from the latter and from early slag hearths. Hence there have been successive denudations, and it is only at inaccessible sites that archaic waste deposits remain. Given these losses of material, it is important that sampling should be tightly controlled and that minimum quantities should be removed (Barker and White 1992).

In these and other industries, sampling strategies must be planned with full awareness of the risks to which residues have been exposed. These considerations are an important part of the briefing and training of those, professional and amateur, who, by providing material for examination, can make an important contribution to the enlargement of our knowledge of early industry when excavation is likely to remain a rare event.

References

Ashurst, D, 1970 Excavations at Gawber glasshouse near Barnsley, Yorkshire, *Post-Medieval Archaeol*, **4**, 92–140

—, 1987 Excavations at the 17th–18th-century glasshouse at Bolsterstone, Yorkshire, *Post-Medieval Archaeol*, **21**, 147–226

Barker, L, and White, R, 1992 Early smelting in Swaledale: a further look, in Willies and Cranstone 1992, 15–18

Crossley, D W, 1967 Glass making at Bagots Park, Staffordshire, in the 16th century, *Post-Medieval Archaeol*, **1**, 44–83

—, 1987 Sir William Clavell's glasshouse at Kimmeridge, Dorset: the excavations of 1980–81, *Archaeol J*, **144**, 340–82

—, 1990 *Post-medieval archaeology in Britain*, Leicester

—, 1995 The blast furnace at Rockley, South Yorkshire, *Archaeol J*, **152**, 381–421

Crossley, D W, and Kiernan, D T, 1992 The lead smelting mills of Derbyshire, *Derbyshire Archaeol J*, **112**, 6–47

Department of the Environment, 1990 *Planning policy guidance note 16: archaeology and planning* [PPG16], London

Greeves, T, 1996 Tin smelting in Devon in the 18th and 19th centuries, *Mining History*, **13**, 84–90

Hurst Vose, R, 1994 Excavations at the 17th-century glasshouse at Haughton Green, Denton near Manchester, *Post-Medieval Archaeol*, **28**, 1–71

Kiernan, D T, 1988 *The Derbyshire lead industry in the sixteenth century*, Derbyshire Record Ser, **14**, Chesterfield

Kiernan, D T, and Van de Noort, R, 1992 Bole smelting in Derbyshire, in Willies and Cranstone 1992, 19–21

Murphy, S, 1992 Smelting residues from boles and simple smeltmills, in Willies and Cranstone 1992, 43–7

Pickin, J, 1992 Early lead smelting in Teesdale, in Willies and Cranstone 1992, 25–7

Smith, R, 1996 An analysis of the processes for smelting tin, *Mining History*, **13**, 91–9

Welch, C M, forthcoming Excavations at Little Birches, Wolseley, Staffs, *Post-Medieval Archaeol*

Wild, M, and Eastwood, I, 1992 Soil contamination and smelting sites, in Willies and Cranstone 1992, 54–7

Willies, L M, and Cranstone, D (eds), 1992 *Boles and smeltmills*, Matlock

23 Organic artefacts and their preservation

by Jacqui Watson

Abstract

Organic materials, such as animal products, wood, and vegetable fibres were widely used in antiquity, more so than lithics, metals, or ceramics, which form the bulk of archaeological assemblages. In exposed conditions wood, leather, textile, and basketry are readily broken down by various forms of microorganisms, as well as being burnt, so their preservation in the UK is comparatively rare and they are usually only found in waterlogged conditions or as traces on corroding metalwork. Waterlogged sites can preserve large structures, including trackways, quays, and buildings as well small domestic or personal items. Material preserved in this way can be subjected to wide ranging scientific analysis, including dating, technology, and environmental studies. Many sites have produced material that has enabled the identication of carpentry practices in the Neolithic, Bronze Age, Roman, and medieval periods; but there is little evidence for the Iron Age or Anglo-Saxon periods. Organic material preserved on metalwork is mainly of interest when found in burials, as under these circumstances more and varied materials are preserved that can usually be reconstructed. Complex pagan burials provide the greatest wealth of material, and most work in this area has been on Anglo-Saxon cemeteries, with some Iron Age and Bronze Age examples also.

Introduction

Organic materials were widely used in antiquity and the skills needed to make basketry, cordage, and work leather would have developed very early on. Unfortunately the preservation of such materials on archaeological sites is rare, and mainly confined to sealed and waterlogged levels. The first waterlogged sites excavated in the last century brought to light an unprecedented range of organic objects and structures that had been the main components of everyday life. Since then peat cutting in the Somerset Levels has led to the discovery of trackways but few artefacts (Coles and Coles 1986), and the excavations at Glastonbury Lake Village by Bulleid and Gray between 1893 and 1907 are still the largest collection of prehistoric wooden artefacts ever recovered (Earwood 1993). Most of the objects from other sites have come from isolated waterlogged deposits, including graves, ditches, wells, and cesspits, and these are mainly of Roman or medieval date (Fig 23.1). Roman levels in Carlisle and London have produced large amounts of material, and large assemblages of Viking material have been found in York and London. The bulk of artefacts are made from wood but the same deposits often contain significant quantities of leather, such as shoes, cobbling waste, and even saddlery (Fig 23.2).

Fig 23.1 Roman wooden bowls from Carlisle, Cumbria

Fig 23.2 Pieces of Roman leather saddlery from Carlisle, Cumbria

Basketry and textiles tend to be used almost to the point of disintegration and are then used as fuel, which makes them rare finds. Textiles are usually only found as dumps of waste from workshops, for example at Baynards Castle, London, and the group of silks are exceptional collections (Crowfoot *et al* 1992).

There are few waterlogged Iron Age and Anglo-Saxon sites, so a picture of the carpentry, dress, and personal possessions in these periods has to be built up by studying traces of organic material preserved on metalwork. The first report on organic material preserved by contact with metal salts was written by M Faraday (1836), and the potential of studying this material was discussed by Biek (1963). Now the examination of the organic traces on metalwork is more or less routine for Anglo-Saxon cemeteries. The potential of this information is often under-estimated and it is hoped that the examples quoted below will encourage the fuller retrieval of objects with preserved organic material on them in the future.

Preservation of organic materials

All objects will have suffered a certain amount of damage and even breakage during use prior to being discarded or abandoned, unless they were specifically made for burial as in the case of grave structures. Additionally most organic materials, and especially wooden structures, would be exposed to weathering, microbial, and insect attack. In open water all materials would be readily colonised by various fungi and bacteria, and the damage they can cause is dependant upon temperature and other factors. Waterlogged environments are anaerobic, but the material still slowly dissolves owing to chemical hydrolysis and anaerobic bacteria.

In the case of wood, its own natural acidity is sufficient to cause hydrolysis, and the effect increases with temperature. Hardwoods are more susceptible to chemical hydrolysis than softwoods (Stamm 1970). Over time all materials slowly degrade, their shape and cellular structure being supported by the permeating water.

Waterlogged objects are therefore mainly water, and highly susceptible to changes in local water tables.

The degree of acidity (pH) of the deposit will give preferential preservation to some materials. Acidic environments favour the preservation of proteinaceous materials, and slightly alkaline ones favour plant materials. This can mean that parts of some composite objects are not preserved, for instance stitching on leather shoes and bags is frequently not preserved, as vegetable fibres were used. Bog bodies may have originally worn vegetable fibre clothing such as linen, but these materials would not survive in peat bogs, unlike the beautifully preserved skin or woollen cloth.

Wood, in particular, appears to take up iron salts from the surrounding environment as a result of iron-reducing bacteria (Wiltshire *et al* 1994), as well as from adjacent corroding ironwork on the more recent sites. In both cases it appears to be in the form of ferric sulphides, which on exposure to air can readily oxidise to produce various oxides, ferrous sulphates, and free sulphur, and, in the presence of hard water, gypsum crystals are also formed (MacLeod and Kenna 1990; Watson 1981). In highly degraded wood, minerals can account for up to 50% of the dry weight of the wood, or around 5–10% of the structure.

Horn and skeletal materials can be preserved in almost pristine condition in waterlogged environments. Horn is rarely preserved in dry aerobic conditions except as traces on metalwork. The preservation of bone, antler, and ivory is very pH dependant and these materials will more or less dissolve in acidic environments such as peat bogs or in sandy soils. In these conditions skeletal material will only be preserved by contact with metal salts.

In damp conditions most metals will corrode and the resulting corrosion products will stain any adjacent organic material. When buried, organic material impregnated with metal salts cannot readily be broken down by soil micro-organisms, and over long periods this material will become chemically altered by these minerals (Keepax 1975). Inhumations, particularly in sandy soils, provide an aggressive environment for the metalwork, and the resulting corrosion promotes the large scale preservation of organic material for study.

Mineral preserved organic material is more common on ironwork, as this metal corrodes more rapidly than copper, lead, or silver alloys. Iron-preserved organic material is heavily impregnated with corrosion products, and in some cases the whole structure has become replaced by iron salts while the organic component has dissolved away. On the other hand, organic material preserved by copper corrosion still resembles the original material, which is sometimes stained green; this mainly applies to bone or ivory. In only a few instances copper corrosion has replaced the structure of organic material.

Identification of organic materials and collection of associated data

A brief introduction to the range of studies that can usefully be undertaken on waterlogged wood is outlined in Brunning (1996), along with the details of necessary recording. This includes woodworking information, woodland reconstruction, radiocarbon dating, tree-ring analysis for dating, site phasing, timber provenancing, and the reconstruction of palaeoclimates. Organic materials, in particular wood, have the potential for absolute dating through ^{14}C and dendrochronology, which can be used to refine existing chronologies based on metalwork and ceramic typologies. The main problem with waterlogged materials is that once exposed they are very susceptible to biodeterioration and all forms of recording and analysis must be undertaken quickly.

Fresh and waterlogged organic materials are identified by examining their microscopic structures and this is also true for mineral preserved examples. It has been possible to distinguish between most materials such as horn, bone, wood, leather, and textile with the aid of a hand lens or low powered incident light microscope. For the most part identification of wood species has been done by observing either thin sections of lightly coated material or gold coated specimens in the Scanning Electron Microscope (SEM) (Watson 1988). It is important to know what the traces of organic material actually relate to before embarking on extensive identification work, and especially before taking samples (Edwards 1989).

It is also possible to see the remains of surface decoration on wood and leather, especially when it has been engraved. Recent work has shown that most of the Anglo-Saxon boxes were decorated with engraved patterns mostly made up of lines and chevrons, although complex designs like the Franks Casket and St Cuthbert's coffin may have also been more commonplace (Cronyn and Horie 1985).

Well preserved leather can be examined for evidence of heat treatments using the SEM. Cameron (1991) has noted the occasional use of *cuir bolli* for covering Anglo-Saxon shields, where the leather was probably applied to the wooden in a wet state then heated so that it shrank and hardened. This technique would have produced a light weight but durable shield for combat (Watson 1995a).

Evidence for organic coatings such as resins can sometimes be implied by abnormal preservation of the impregnated material. Wood or textiles that have been soaked with pitch or oil to make them water repellant will tend not to absorb iron corrosion products when buried, at least initially, but at the same time they will be protected from the normal decay processes. Over time the resin itself will eventually break down, but the organic material will continue to be preserved by locally high concentrations of metal salts. This type of preservation has been noted on clench nails from reused ship timbers, where caulking had been used between the planks. When examined microscopically the caulking, which was originally made of animal hairs impregnated with a resin, appeared in almost pristine condition, while the fragments of untreated wooden planking were full of iron salts (Fig 23.3).

Textiles preserved by just a light coating of copper salts can be tested for dye residues, for example the headdress from West Heslerton was found to have originally been dyed red (Walton-Rogers forthcoming). In the case of iron-preserved textiles, the use of different colours is usually only shown by the variation in spin direction of warp and weft threads.

Material selection

Certain materials and species of wood have been used for particular purposes over a large range of periods and cultures – quite simply they are the best material for a particular job. Horn has been used for knife, sword, and dagger hilts from the Bronze Age to the fifteenth century. There are examples of scabbard stiffeners being made from willow or poplar on sword blades of Bronze Age to Viking date. Ash has been used to haft spearheads from the Bronze Age to the Anglo-Saxon period. The scales for medieval knife handles appear to be made exclusively from bone, horn, box, and maple (Cowgill *et al* 1987, 34-9). Such uniformity suggests that medieval knives may have been produced in a few manufacturing centres, probably controlled by guilds.

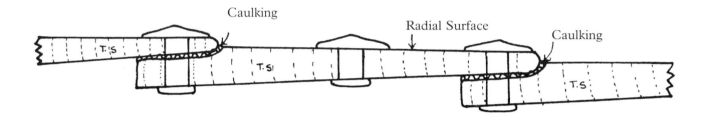

Fig 23.3 *Anglo-Scandinavian clench nails from York; Minster: above, reconstructed cross section of the original structure; left, dark and light fibres from one clench nail, representing the caulking between the planks (x8)*

Frequently organic materials are also chosen for their aesthetic qualities, such as colour and texture. Evidence for this can be seen by the choice of antler and horn components for La Tène sword hilts (Fig 23.4)

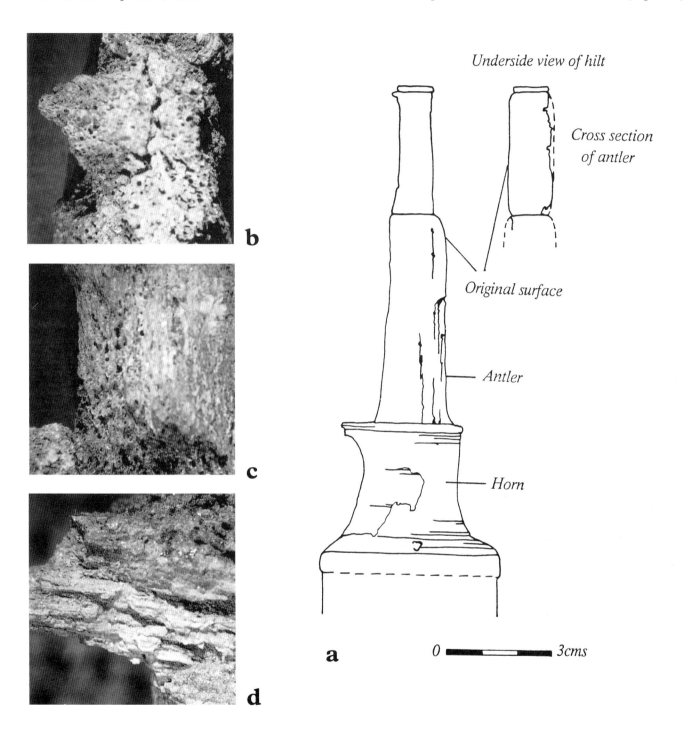

Fig 23.4 Iron Age sword hilt from Burton Fleming, Yorkshire: a = diagram illustrating the various organic components, b = 'pommel' made from cross section of antler (x4), c = central grip portion made of antler (x4), d = 'guard' section made from horn (x8)

from North Yorkshire (Stead 1991; Watson and Edwards 1992), and composite Bronze Age dagger hilts from Ashgrove, Fife (Clarke *et al* 1985, 221, 267) and Gravelly Guy, Oxfordshire (Watson 1995b) (Fig 23.5).

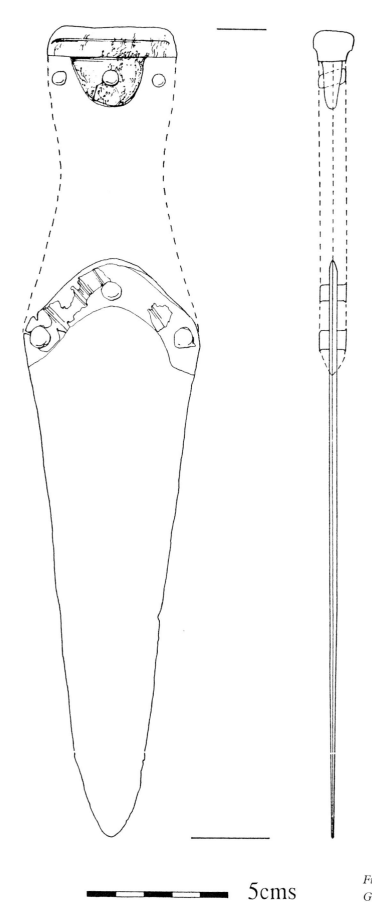

5cms

Fig 23.5 Reconstruction of Bronze Age dagger hilt from Gravelly Guy, Oxfordshire

Potential for reconstruction

It is often possible to reconstruct large organic items such as clothing, coffins, caskets, and even furniture from traces of the materials used in their manufacture, preserved in the corrosion products on the metal fittings. A great deal of work has been done on mineral preserved textiles, where in addition to recording weave details (Walton and Eastwood 1983) it has been possible to indicate the style of garments worn (Owen-Crocker 1986).

Most wooden objects can potentially be reconstructed by carefully recording the surface orientation and grain direction of either the wood fragments or traces in the corrosion of any metal additions. Lathe-turned wooden vessels and stave-built buckets have been identified in this way. Caskets and coffins can frequently be reconstructed if locks and decorative metal fittings have been mounted on them (Watson and Edwards 1990) (Fig 23.6). In the Anglo-Saxon period this pro-

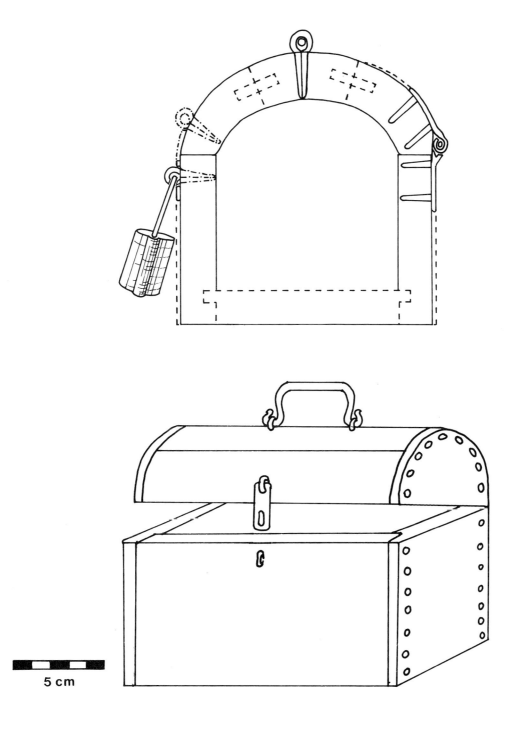

Fig 23.6 Reconstruction of an Anglo-Saxon casket from Harford Farm, Norfolk

vides rare evidence for the sophisticated carpentry that was carried out at this early date. From about the seventh century AD the quantity and quality of many wooden artefacts, particularly containers, indicates the existence of full-time woodworkers, and commercial areas dedicated to these crafts have been identified in Viking York and Dublin (Earwood 1993). Pieces of furniture were frequently placed in Merovingian graves, as can be seen at the waterlogged cemetery of Oberflacht (Paulsen 1992, 121; Schiek 1992). These items are rarely recognised in British cemeteries unless they had decorative metalwork attached to them, for example the beds from Swallowcliffe Down (Speake 1989) and Barrington (Malim forthcoming) (Fig 23.7).

In addition to recording carpentry details, it is possible to suggest how the timber was reduced into planks: by flat sawing, quarter sawing, radial splitting, or tangential splitting (Darrah 1982). If oak has been used it may be possible in some instances to count the number of annual rings over a given distance, which could indicate whether the tree had grown in a forest or in open land. It is also worth noting the type of wood used for haftings, for instance mature timber or coppiced poles, as such information will add to our knowledge of woodland management.

The growth patterns of horn, antler/bone, and ivory can be used as a basis for reconstructing the original object from residual traces. The orientation of the horn remains on several inlaid dagger plates made it possible to reconstruct the original Roman dagger scabbard from Chester (Fig 23.8).

Recognition of imported materials and trade items

It is widely assumed that the Romans introduced a number of tree species into England, particularly sweet chestnut (*Castanea* sp) and walnut (*Juglans* sp). According to Godwin (1975) sweet chestnut is a warmth-demanding tree and although it is regarded as a Roman introduction the archaeological evidence may merely indicate that the timber was imported. Walnut was introduced to the Netherlands by the Romans and the same may apply in the UK. Silver fir, larch, and cedar were frequently used for barrels and writing tablets in the Roman period, and none are native to Britain. Items thought to have been brought to Britain by the Roman army can often be confirmed if they have components made from non-indigenous wood species, for example chisels from the early phases of the forts at old Penrith and Housesteads on Hadrian's Wall were found to have sweet chestnut handles (Mould 1991).

In addition to the woods listed above, many other exotic materials were imported into Britain during the Roman occupation and it has generally been thought that with the end of Roman rule Britain returned to being self-contained, with little contact with the Continent let alone the Near East. The study of fragmentary organic objects placed in graves or cremations is now bringing to light a significant number of items for which the raw materials at the very least would have had to be imported. Elephant ivory purse rings have been discovered in many Anglo-Saxon cemeteries particularly among cremated remains (Catherine Hills personal communications). These must have originated in North Africa, and with the exception of a few groups of gaming counters, are the only objects made from elephant ivory that have been recognised in Britain at this date. It is quite likely that neither the ivory nor the rings were directly imported into Britain, but the purses themselves were, especially as a purse from West Heslerton in North Yorkshire also contained a piece of coptic-style weave textile (Walton-Rogers forthcoming).

Textiles originating from the Continent can be recognised by their weaves, for example the tapestry weave cloth found in a sixth-century leather purse at West Heslerton (see above); Germanic textiles have been found in seventh-century East Anglian graves at

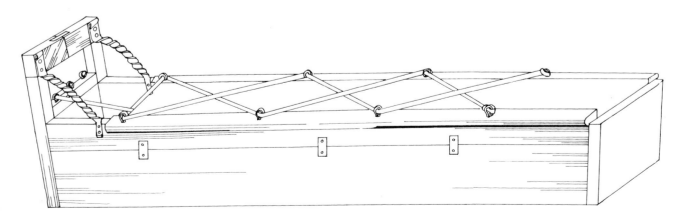

Fig 23.7 Possible reconstruction of Anglo-Saxon bed from Barrington, Cambridgeshire: original length c 1.7m

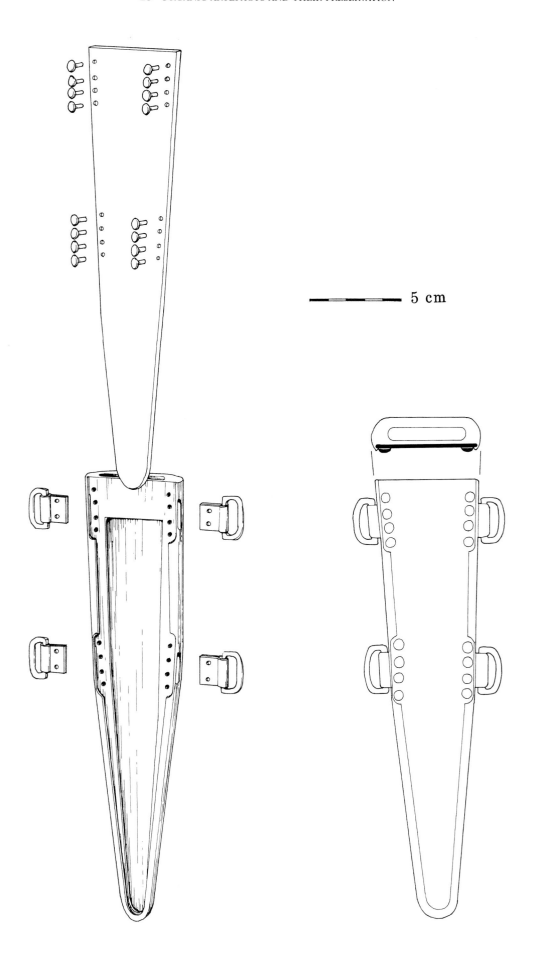

5 cm

Fig 23.8 Reconstruction illustrating how the inlaid iron plate was slotted into the horn dagger scabbard from Roman Chester

Harford Farm and Buttermarket (Crowfoot, forthcoming a and b). Textile made from camel hair has been noted from medieval Carlisle.

Areas of interest for the future

The potential wealth of information that can be extracted from organic materials, however they are preserved, continues to grow with the development of scientific techniques. The excavation of sites with the potential for good organic preservation will undoubtably add a great deal to archaeological knowledge. In order to collect more data on organic objects preserved by minerals, complex assemblages need to be routinely lifted as soil blocks for excavation in the laboratory. This will of course mean that the excavation is a more lengthy procedure, and it is only worthwhile when the excavator or conservator understands the potential needs of recording this type of material. There are still numerous instances where the well meaning have enthusiastically excavated complexes leaving a box of tiny fragments without comprehensible records as to how these fragments relate to one another.

Although many complete organic objects are items of beauty in their own right, fragments of rare and imported goods can usually only be recognised by detailed examination and identification to species level of the materials used. This means that specialists need to look at all the material from a site, not just a few chosen items. The evidence for organic objects preserved by contact with metal corrosion products is much more ephemeral than the waterlogged examples, and for this reason their potential can usually only be realised by specialists who are used to examining such material.

There is a lack of comparative organic material preserved on metalwork recorded for continental sites. This inevitably means that the data sets collected for the British material have to stand alone for the time being, with the exception of textiles. The range of textiles, garments, and textile manufacture in north Europe and Scandinavia are well documented for all periods (Bender Jorgensen 1992; Henshall 1950; Walton and Wild 1990; Wild 1970).

It is possible that the changes in burial environments may be detected in the microstructure of organic materials by the presence of microflora and corrosion products, which can only exist or be formed in very specific conditions. Initially this type of study is most likely to apply to structural timbers, not only because of the amount of material preserved, but also because the processes of wood deterioration are already very well understood.

It is hoped that it will become possible to look more closely at organic residues associated with organic materials. Decoration in the form of dyestuffs and paint has

hardly been looked into, with the exception of textiles, and is potentially an area worth investigating as it is almost certain that many of the wood and leather objects in the early medieval period were very colourful to complement the highly decorated metalwork.

Acknowledgements

I would like to thank Glynis Edwards for helping with the textile references, and Elisabeth Crowfoot and Penny Walton-Rogers for allowing me to read their unpublished reports.

References

Bender Jorgensen, L, 1992 *North European textiles*, Aarhus

Biek, L, 1963 *Archaeology and the microscope*, London

Brunning, R, 1996 *Waterlogged wood: guidelines on the recording, sampling, conservation, and curation*, London

Cameron, E, 1991 Identification of skin and leather preserved by iron corrosion products, *J Archaeol Sci*, **18**, 25–33

Clarke, D V, Cowie, T G, and Foxon, A, 1985 *Symbols of power*, London

Coles, B, and Coles, J, 1986 *Sweet Track to Glastonbury*, London

Cowgill, J, de Neergaard, M, and Griffiths, N, 1987 *Knives and scabbards*, Medieval Finds Excav London, **1**, London

Cronyn, J M, and Horie, C V, 1985 *St Cuthbert's coffin*, Durham

Crowfoot, E, forthcoming a Textiles from the Anglo-Saxon cemetery at Harford Farm, Norfolk, *East Anglian Archaeol*

—, forthcoming b Textiles from the Anglo-Saxon cemetery at Buttermarket, Ipswich, *East Anglian Archaeol*

Crowfoot, E, Pritchard, F, and Staniland, K, 1992 *Textiles and clothing c 1150–c 1450*, Medieval Finds Excav London, **4**, London

Darrah, R, 1982 Working seasoned oak, in *Woodworking techniques before AD 1500* (ed S McGrail), BAR, Int Ser, **129**, 219–29, Oxford

Earwood, C, 1993 *Domestic wooden artefacts in Britain and Ireland from Neolithic to Viking times*, Exeter

Edwards, G, 1989 Guidelines for dealing with material from sites where organic remains have been preserved by metal corrosion products, in *Evidence preserved in corrosion products* (ed R C Janaway and B Scott), UKIC Occas Pap, **8**, 3–7, London

Faraday, M, 1836 Letter on recent discovery of Roman sepulchral relics in one of the greater barrows at Bartlow, in Ashdon, Essex, *Archaeologia*, **26**, 30–31

Godwin, H, 1975 *The history of the British flora: a factual basis for phytogeography*, Cambridge

Henshall, A, 1950 Textiles and weaving appliances in prehistoric Britain, *Proc Prehist Soc*, **16**, 130–62

Keepax, C, 1975 Scanning electron microscopy of wood replaced by iron corrosion products, *J Archaeol Sci*, **2**, 145–50

MacLeod, I D, and Kenna, C, 1990 Degradation of archaeological timbers by pyrite: oxidation of iron and sulphur species, *Proceedings of the fourth ICOM-Group on Wet Organic Archaeological Materials Conference* (ed P Hoffman), 133–42, Bremerhaven

Malim, T, forthcoming *The Anglo-Saxon cemetery at Edix Hill, Barrington, Cambridgeshire*, CBA Res Rep

Mould, Q, 1991 The metalwork, in *Bewcastle and Old Penrith: a Roman outpost fort and the frontier vicus* (P S Austen), Cumberland and Westmorland Antiq Archaeol Soc Res Ser, **6**, 185–214

Owen-Crocker, G R, 1986 *Dress in Anglo-Saxon England*, Manchester

Paulsen, P, 1992 *Die Holzfunde aus dem Graberfeld bei Oberflacht*, Stuttgart

Schiek, S, 1992 *Das Graberfeld der Merowingerzeit bei Oberflacht*, Stuttgart

Speake, G, 1989 *A Saxon bed burial on Swallowcliffe Down*, English Heritage Archaeol Rep, **10**, London

Stamm, A J, 1970 Wood deterioration and its prevention, *IIC New York Conference on conservation of stone and wooden objects* (ed G Thomson), 1–12, London

Stead, I M, 1991 *Iron Age cemeteries in East Yorkshire*, English Heritage Archaeol Rep, **22**, London

Walton-Rogers, P, forthcoming Textile report, in D Powlesland *The Anglo-Saxon cemetery at West Heslerton, North Yorkshire*, English Heritage and Univ Nottingham

Walton, P, and Eastwood, G, 1983 *A brief guide to the cataloguing of archaeological textiles*, York

Walton, P, and Wild, J P, 1990 *Textiles in northern archaeology*, London

Watson, J, 1981 The application of freeze-drying on British hardwoods from archaeological excavations, *Proceedings of the first ICOM Waterlogged Wood Working Group Conference* (ed D Grattan), 237–242, Ottawa

—, 1988 The identification of organic materials preserved by metal corrosion products, in *The use of the scanning electron microscope in archaeology* (ed S Olsen), BAR, Int Ser, **452**, 65–76, Oxford

—, 1995a Wood usage in Anglo-Saxon shields, *Anglo-Saxon Stud Archaeol Hist*, 7, 35–48

—, 1995b Mineral preserved organic material associated with metalwork from Gravelly Guy, Stanton Harcourt, Oxon, *Anc Mon Lab Rep*, **64/95**, London

Watson, J, and Edwards, G, 1990 Conservation of material from Anglo-Saxon cemeteries, in *Anglo-Saxon cemeteries: a reappraisal* (ed E Southworth), 97–106, Stroud

—, 1992 The identification of organic material preserved on ironwork from Burton Fleming, Yorkshire, *Anc Mon Lab Rep*, **67/92**, London

Wild, J P, 1970 *Textile manufacture in the northern Roman provinces*, Cambridge

Wiltshire, P E J, Edwards, K J, and Bond, S, 1994 Microbially-derived metallic sulphide spherules, pollen, and the waterlogging of archaeological sites, *Aspects of archaeological palynology: methodology and applications* (ed O K Davies), Amer Assoc Stratigraphic Palynologists Contribs Ser, **29**, 207–21

24 An agenda for archaeological science: concluding remarks

by Martin Jones

Introduction

It is not easy these days to achieve a comprehensive appraisal of archaeological research within a single meeting; our subject has become too big. The major archaeological jamborees, such as the Annual Meetings of the *Society of American Archaeologists* and in the UK the *Theoretical Archaeology Group*, have become not so much 'meetings' as 'junctions', where numerous impressive convoys of intellectual traffic cross paths without actually coupling. It was therefore an unusually ambitious venture for English Heritage to hold the conference leading to these papers, which are testimony to the success of that ambition.

The programme's rather conventional 'chest-of-drawers' chronological structure has surprisingly not partitioned period studies, but had the reverse effect. It has actually made it easier to pick out the cross-period connections that so often elude us. This was undoubtedly helped by the agenda-setting papers in each section, backed up in the conference itself by discussants. The resulting quite intensive emphasis on discussion and agenda has given the intervening scientific contributions a great deal of structure and context. Very many delegates working in later periods remarked upon how interesting and accessible the Palaeolithic had become in recent years. We shared a collective memory of arid typologies of exquisitely drawn stone chippings, neatly arranged in rows across the screen, a memory now being blown away by living, breathing, thinking ancestors, interacting with each other and the plants and animals around them. The later period sessions also demonstrated how much the period caricatures were subsiding beneath a set of questions about the human past common to all periods.

Having said that, the juxtaposition of sessions within them beckons thoughts about how much more of that commonality could be sought, how interesting it would be to release a Palaeolithic archaeologist on mediaeval data and vice versa, or to similarly invert practitioners of technological and environmental studies. There is still a prevalence of tunnel vision within the various archaeological specialisms, to some extent an inevitable consequence of the growth of the subject and of the scientific methodologies within it. A major achievement of this meeting has been to signal the virtues of penetrating the walls of those various tunnels, and exploring scientific issues as they relate, not to a particular material or culture history, but to the wider study of the human past.

With this point in mind, my concluding remarks cut across the four period sessions to themes that straddle two or more of them.

Human biology

It is most fortunate that the species with the brain and inclination to pursue archaeology also has a durable skeleton, packed with details which help in that pursuit. Simon Mays' lament over the neglect of skeletal biological in historical periods makes one think perhaps a few Palaeolithic specialists should have a go at the rich body of accessible medieval skeletal data. The Palaeolithic contributions remind us how very much could be gleaned, not just from ancient skeletons, but even from some simple observations of living bodies about human prehistory.

An elegant example of this is Leslie Aiello's discussion of the brain and the gut, and the pay-off between the two in human evolution, and the connecting argument of 'external digestion', through cooking and fire, which transform raw foods that are hard to digest into easily digestible cuisine. The concept of external digestion brings to mind other features of the archaeological record, which have not always been used in physical anthropology to its full potential. Clive Gamble, during the conference itself, pointed out that the scale of the evidence for prehistoric fire was not really commensurate with the scale of the dietary need implied by this argument, a point that gained some resonance with the bioarchaeological discussions of the following session. From the Upper Palaeolithic onwards, the quality of bioarchaeological datasets improves dramatically. These superior datasets reveal not a series of narrow meat diets partially ameliorated by external digestion, but instead the most versatile and varied omnivorous dietary range of any mammal, ranging from mammoths to seeds, and limpets and fish to underground tubers. The Holocene record, however, also reveals other forms of external digestion leaving little trace. Fermentation processes may, for example, have been greatly underestimated.

The other major paper on human biology as a route to understanding prehistory was Bryan Sykes' contribution on mitochondrial DNA and early European population movements. Sykes has been at the forefront of ancient DNA analysis, and a number of the key substantive findings have come from his laboratory, funded in part by NERC's Ancient Biomolecules Initiative. He has recently crossed swords with one of the key figures in human genetics, Luca Cavalli-Sforza, on the place of early farmers in accounting for the genetic variation of modern Europeans (Ammerman and Cavalli-Sforza 1984). In his written version, Sykes has taken a conciliatory tone, but the relationship between agricultural spread and population movement is still very much open to debate.

Cavalli-Sforza's 'wave of advance' model for the spread of agriculture across Europe, at least in its simplest form, implies something sufficiently radical to be visible in a variety of ways, and not just through human genetics. It implies, for example, the collapse of natural vegetation in advance of the wave, and a sufficiently dense settlement pattern in the lea to drive the wave yet further. Neither the pollen record nor the settlement survey record supports either of these contentions. Indeed, the earlier phases of 'farming' may have been rather more distant from recent 'agriculture' than has commonly been acknowledged. The past may well comprise a far greater variety of human ecosystems than we have hitherto imagined.

Human ecosystems

The first human ecosystems to incorporate domesticated plants and animals provide an interesting example of how archaeological perspectives have shifted. Going back to Childe's Neolithic Revolution, an image of early agriculture is found with close parallels in the modern age. The dramatic spread of highly productive farming settlement in Neolithic Europe seemed in many ways to mirror the similarly dramatic spread of farmers across what was left of the global wilderness. Indeed, the agrarian transformation of the New South Wales of Childe's early years, a fast-moving frontier of pioneer farmers radiating inland from his home town of Sydney, provides a direct analogue for the radiation of prehistoric farmers: the past is organised around categories familiar in the present. Two things are changing that: first a realisation that many aspects of the archaeological data reflect some kind of difference from modern age analogues, and second, a preparedness, enthusiasm even to emphasise and explore that difference.

A number of contributors to this volume allude in one way or another to the mismatch between early human ecosystems incorporating domesticates, and modern-age analogues. Richard Bradley makes the point that the change in Neolithic settlement density through time does not match up with a linear story of agricultural intensification. His observations are made of Britain, but are germaine to many parts of Europe. He also points out that there are many queries surrounding monument building and supposed agricultural surplus, not least of which is the persistent evidence for wild resources from contemporary sites. Kevin Edwards, at the same time as being sympathetic to the exploration of Cavalli-Sforzas 'wave of advance' model, is well aware that the pollen record offers no simple ratification of the model.

Willis and Bennett (1994) emphasised the surprising palynological invisibility of the wave of advance as it supposedly swept through the Balkans. While Edwards is among those who have offered criticism of that publication, he recognises that the kinds of human ecosystem we are looking for in the Neolithic need not have close parallels in the more recent agrarian landscape. In addition to the useful phrase 'woodland-based cultivation', he adds 'precocious agriculture' to archaeology's overlong teleological lexicon alongside incipient agriculture, proto-agriculture, pre-adaptation, and so on, a series of transitional terms that in my view trivialise forms of human ecosystem that survived for centuries and sometimes millennia, bringing together woodland resources, wild plants, and domesticates in a manner that was a great deal more sustainable than modern prairie-style agriculture. It seems to me important to recognise both that such human ecosystems may not have good modern analogue, but also that that does not preclude their archaeological characterisation. Indeed it is a particular strength of archaeological science that such characterisations are possible without modern analogues.

The whole issue of getting beyond modern analogues to past human worlds that were differently organised in the past is a recurrent theme of the papers in the later period sessions. Millett and Johnson are acutely conscious of the constraints of imposing a wide range of modern categories, from town and villa to agriculture and religion, onto the past. A whole focus and excitement of archaeological research is to discover past ways of existing and being that took quite different trajectories through different landscapes in which activities and experiences were interwoven in ways unfamiliar to ourselves. Repeatedly in these later period contributions, authors express an optimism about archaeological science being put to this task, at the same time as noting that contemporary boundaries still carved up the research conducted. A key example is the boundaries around studies of past technology and contexts of production.

Contexts of production

An interesting comparison can be drawn between Grenville Astill's lament at not finding sufficient peat in East Brittany to lure a palynologist into his project, and William O'Brien's observation that fieldwork around the exciting new sites of Bronze Age copper mines is '... complicated by the environmental setting of many sites (peat cover on Cwmystwyth and Mount Gabriel)'. To be fair, O'Brien does go on to comment on changing attitudes in the study of technology in which peat deposits might be seen as an advantage rather than an impediment. There persists, however, a strange sense that not only peat, but also people are somewhat peripheral to the central study of technological progress through history and early history. The papers by Crossley, Baylie, Peacock, and Watson all reveal how much the studies they review have tended to treat technology as a property of the material rather than of society, with an implicit and unchallenged story of linear technological progress not far in the background.

O'Brien brings this point out, arguing for a more anthropological approach within technological studies. A telling contrast in this respect is between O'Brien's paper and that of van der Veen and O'Connor. Both are papers about the archaeology of production, but metal and food production get quite different treatments, and people and their relations of production are in far greater evidence in the latter. Once again we could see how approaches in one area of archaeology could productively be brought to another. In this case, it would be interesting to ask an environmental archaeologist to excavate one of the newly discovered mining sites, treating them as foci of human activity, involving living, working, eating, and exchanging, rather than as mere steps in a physico-chemical process. Indeed, this is already being initiated, as for example in the case of van der Veen's work on Peacock's site of Mons Claudianus (van der Veen 1997), and Mighall and Chambers work at Copa Hill and Mount Gabriel, reported in O'Brien's paper.

A key issue in reclaiming technology as a social and human process is the question emphasised by Johnson about the boundaries that ran through the way people lived, how activities and experiences were intertwined or separated. Without this perspective, there is little more we can do to understanding the past organisation of technology and production, beyond further decorating the same old tired story of universal linear progress. Central to a more sociological analysis is the issue of whether and when the working of raw materials was separated out from other activities of day-to-day levels and constructed as a separate sphere.

This issue, raised in various ways by Millett, Astill, and Johnson, leads us to pose the above questions about what miners and metalworkers ate and how and where they lived. We do have methods of addressing these questions, well illustrated by Millett's own survey of Roman pottery making sites in the Humber region (Millett and Halkon 1988). His integrated appraisal of settlement distribution, and of ceramic and environmental data supports the argument that there was little distinction to be drawn between agricultural production and pottery production. One involved gathering and working with mud, the other with gathering and working with grass, both products of the land and human labour, through which it may be misleading to place a modern-day boundary between agriculture and technology. Archaeology has the scientific approaches that enable us to question such

boundaries and explore new ones, so long as the branches of our archaeological endeavour are not constrained within those same boundaries.

Environment and landscape, bodies, and boundaries

To return to Johnson's contribution, looking beneath modern-day boundaries around human experience goes further than questioning whether agriculture and technology are naturally separate spheres. It relates to diversity within the entire human experience. Other divisions whose universality was queried by various speakers include those between secular and religious, between economic and aesthetic, and between natural environment and cultural landscape.

Twenty years ago in one of my first explorations of the possibility of NERC funding for archaeology, I remember being advised by an insider to exercise restraint with the word 'archaeology', but avoid at all costs using the word 'landscape'. While 'environment' was suitably scientific, 'landscape' was in the realm of the aesthetic, something for gardeners and artists rather than hard-nosed scientists. It is certainly true that the very word landscape embodies the notion of the observer moving through it and experiencing it. But I would question whether the concept of environment is any different. We have become used to palynologists talking of the difference between woodland and open ground as if it were an objective botanical distinction. In reality it is nothing of the kind. Woodland defines a human experience of enclosure and three-dimensionality. If the identical species are grazed down to our waist height it ceases to be woodland for no other reason than we are no longer enclosed by it. However technical our accounts of environments become, they only exist inasmuch as they 'environ' a particular organism.

There was a clear interest in the later period sessions in using archaeological science to probe deeper than these contemporary categorisations, to rediscover earlier constructions of landscape and human trajectories and productive activities within them. This was touched upon within Edwards' reference to 'post-processual palynology' and O'Brien's interest in a more anthropological approach to technology. Various speakers were concerned with how geophysical survey could come together with environmental archaeology to explore different manifestations of the human landscape (see Gaffney et al, this volume). An expression of this was the issue of bringing together geophysical and environmental methods to study early gardens, raised by Bell and Dark, and by Johnson. Gardens bring to mind another polarity or supposed boundary, between the functional environment as a least-cost route to the acquisition of food, and the symbolic and aesthetic landscape, reflecting and expressing a particular world view. Exploring interconnections in past human landscapes between the aesthetic, the symbolic, and the functional poses an exciting challenge to the discipline.

The modified landscape as both a framework for, and witness to, human experience and social relations within it brings us from environment to landscapes to built spaces and bodies moving within them, those bodies retaining evidence of social difference through food and health. While Simon Mays lamented the lack of emphasis upon skeletal evidence, he succeeded in assembling sufficient case studies to demonstrate how valuable that emphasis can be in highlighting social difference, a point picked up both by Johnson and by Astill. Furthermore, the divisions were not always the obvious ones, and skeletal detail is such that it is in principle feasible to untangle secular/ecclesiastical from sex, age, etc, given an appropriate sample size.

Timescales and questions

Alongside the authoritative accounts offered by Bayliss and Housley of how far we have come with scientific dating methods, the papers make repeated appeals to improve yet further, particularly in the case of peat sequences, which, in this meeting, have been the most recurrent focus of dating *angst*. We also have a clear and valuable airing in the agenda-setters' papers of what the dating issues for each period actually are, ranging from Gamble's focus on the rate of world colonisation, to Astill's emphasis on the minutiae of building traditions, via Bradley's appraisal of later prehistoric episodes of continuity and change. Inevitably, those dating issues remain rather period specific, as each period retains its own particular style of archaeology.

One observation I began with was of how much this conference had succeeded in juxtaposing different time periods and different methods, such that potential connections and interactions gained clarity as a result. I end by drawing some general comparisons between the archaeological science as applied to the different period blocks, and some thoughts about further coming together within archaeological science.

A clear strength of contemporary Palaeolithic archaeology is its eager embrace of global questions and big issues. The question of global spread around which Gamble structured the first session has a clarity that is all the more impressive for the way in which a new generation of methodologies has breathed life into some of the most spartan datasets in archaeology. In later prehistory and in the historic periods, those big issues have often tended to retreat as the mere complexity of data forces researchers into ever tinier pigeonholes. In this

conference, Grenville Astill has taken what seems to me to be a commendably Palaeolithic approach to the Historic period, demonstrating how accessible those big issues can be. A good example is in relation to demography and disease. Given the tiny timeframe for which direct census data exists, Europe in the historic period provides the only detailed record of the interplay between environment, social organisation, demography, and disease on the millennial timescale. A considerable dataset exists, drawing together contemporary documentation, landscape archaeology, dendroclimatology, funerary archaeology, and pollen analysis, with which to explore the Black Death pandemic, and could be assembled for the earlier Justinian Plague pandemic. The demographic issues arising from the collation have implications far beyond the historic period itself. This particular example shows how the later period, too, can involve the kind of big issues that attract both scientific funding, and a bevy of pollen analysts and other specialists to accompany Grenville Astill on his next trip to East Brittany!

One traditional strength of Holocene archaeology has been in the precision and detail of chronological and environmental frameworks. It is encouraging to read the cogent arguments of Housley and of van Andel and Tzedakis to bring similar precision and rigour in these fields to much earlier periods, and in a clearly goal-oriented context. A further strength of contributions in the later period sessions is their exploration of taking archaeological science beyond crude functionalism, and to exploring contextual issues of cultural construction. This relates to the kind of post-processual issues that have gained momentum among studies of later prehistory. This meeting made clear how much that agenda has moved on to influence thinking in later periods, in contrast to its impact upon Palaeolithic archaeology. However much Palaeolithic beings have been enlivened by new research, they tend to remain slaves to the same least-cost optimality that also governs their constituent organs (see Aiello, this volume).

There may be good reasons for this, not least of which is the variety of hominid species with which Palaeolithic archaeology is concerned, not necessarily sharing the unusual cognitive attributes of modern humans. If however, culture-specific perceptions of landscape have only been central to movement through them back to a certain point in time, do we know how far back and how that comes into being? Once we were happy to answer that it was the Neolithic Revolution that overturned the relation between nature and culture. Now that answer is outdated in both anthropological and archaeological terms. Richard Bradley's paper reminds us how that simple revolution has retreated behind a much more complex history of continuity and change.

This difference of approach between earlier and later periods now owes less to any external evidence for a revolution, and more to the internal pigeonholing of our conceptual approaches along the lines of traditional, chest-of-drawers chronology. Such pigeonholing, however, is exactly what this meeting confronted. It set a precedent for the kind of meeting we must continue to hold as our discipline grows larger and its separate period and scientific specialisms burrow ever deeper and in ever greater isolation. It does us good from time to time to come up for air and look around.

References

Ammerman, A J, and Cavalli-Sforza, L L, 1984 *The Neolithic transition and the genetics of populations in Europe*, Princeton

Millett, M J, and Halkon, P, 1988 Landscape and economy: recent fieldwork and excavation around Holme-on-Spalding Moor, in *Recent research in Roman Yorkshire* (eds J Price and P R Wilson), BAR, **193**, 37–48, Oxford

van der Veen, M, 1997 High living in Rome's distant quarries, *Brit Archaeol*, **28**, 6–7

Willis, K J, and Bennett K D, 1994 The Neolithic transition – fact or fiction? Palaeoecological evidence from the Balkans, *The Holocene*, **4**, 326–30